Practising Mathematics

Developing the mathematician as well as the mathematics

Tom Francome and Dave Hewitt

Contents

Introduction

*"In many maths classrooms,
a very narrow subject is taught
to children, that is nothing like
the maths of the real world or the
maths that mathematicians use.
This narrow subject involves copying
methods that teachers demonstrate
and reproducing them accurately,
over and over again"*
(Boaler, 2009, p.2)

As teachers of mathematics, we both feel that we want to develop mathematicians.

We want to support learners in asking questions, making conjectures, being organised and systematic, looking for patterns, noticing things and communicating what they have noticed and in explaining and justifying their ideas.

These are the things that we want to be important in our classrooms; these are the things we want to seek out and value.

It is necessary, therefore, that we provide as many opportunities for learners to do these things as possible.

It is important to us that learners are offered situations where they can work on open-ended tasks – the phrase 'low threshold/high ceiling' has become increasingly popular and with good reason.

We want learners to be able to ask their own questions and work on their own mathematics and not just our mathematics. Whilst this all sounds very noble, there are situations when we need learners to practise some particular skill – developing fluency with various techniques is an important part of mathematics education, as is making connections within the curriculum.

Learners need to be able to make links between different areas of mathematics and not work on isolated parts of mathematics. Caleb Gattegno (in Brown et al., 1989, p.12) described an experience common to many teachers and said "I teach them but they don't learn"; his response was that they should 'stop teaching!' Not that teachers should leave the profession but stop teaching in a way that is not reaching their learners.

Tom & Dave

Practice

Some might question why we feel the need to offer another set of practice exercises for mathematics. Many collections of exercises exist already in the form of textbooks or worksheets and although the textbooks are re-written with slight differences to reflect changes in the national curriculum, the content and types of activity remain largely the same. Mathematics learners might already feel they spend a lot of time practising the mathematics they have been taught. Teachers of mathematics may also feel that they spend a lot of time assessing pupils' practice work, assisting learners with their misconceptions and supporting them to do more. How often though, do teachers consider the nature of the practice that their learners do?

Textbooks and worksheet schemes are one of the most easily accessible and widely available sources of practice questions and tasks for teachers. However, as Prestage and Perks (2001) note, the activities tend to offer a similar learning experience for learners: questions are step-by-step in nature and exercises often begin with simpler tasks and get progressively harder. The questions are not often connected in any way other than that they are designed to practise a particular area of mathematics. Furthermore, some of the important mathematical work of figuring out what tools are required for a particular problem is removed by explicitly telling learners what they need to use.

Some detractors, such as Dan Meyer (2010), have pointed out that the style of questions, where everything is reduced to a series of one-step problems so learners just need to jump through the hoops, is preventing them from becoming patient problem-solvers as they never have to work out what is required or have any insights. Instead, they learn simply to decode the textbook by combining the information given in the question (never too much or too little!) to reach the correct answer. Meyer argues that this is 'hamstringing' learners and none of it seems to have much purpose for learners beyond answering questions correctly and as quickly as possible.

Textbooks tend to offer a certain type of practice. That is not to say that there is no place for this type of practice, but merely to question whether learners might benefit from different types of practice. The questions in textbook tasks are not often connected in any way other than that they are designed to practise a particular skill or area.

As teachers of mathematics we have both always tried to think about the work that our learners do. Practice is a familiar idea in most mathematics classrooms and something that both learners and teachers report spending a lot of time doing (Francome, 2014; Swan, 2006). However, there are different kinds of practice and the word may conjure up different meanings for people.

Practice in mathematics lessons takes different forms. There are many reasons why we might want learners to practise something they have been taught. Some aims of the national curriculum (DfE, 2013) are to develop learners' mathematical fluency, so they increase their conceptual understanding and can apply their knowledge to solve problems. Learners need opportunities to reason and conjecture, to specialise and generalise and to justify and prove. There is a danger that teachers may only hear that fluency, for example, is developed through frequent practice and rapid recall of knowledge, and this might conjure up particular types of practice.

When we think about practice we can broadly categorise this into some different types and a discussion of some of them follow before we focus on the issue of where attention is placed and what we call *practice through progress* (Hewitt, 1994).

Mindless Practice

The kind of mimicking of the method explained by a teacher where learners have not understood the mathematics behind a process but appear to be able to get correct answers as long as the questions do not deviate too much. Some examples of the downfall of this type of practice might be where learners find the hypotenuse of twenty or so right-angled triangles with a method along the lines of *'you square this, you square that, add them together and square root it'* then proceed to do the same for questions such as this:

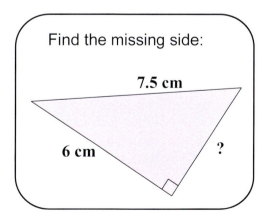

Find the missing side:

7.5 cm

6 cm

?

Or pupils may correctly solve many equations of the form: $ax + b = c$ and then answer questions like $3 + 2x = 14$ with $x = \dfrac{14 - 2}{3} = 4$.

Unconnected Practice

This involves practice of the mechanics of answering questions but where more understanding of the underlying mathematics behind the methods is required. The questions are not necessarily connected in any way other than they have been designed to practise a particular skill or idea. An example of this could be a page of questions on solving linear equations where the equations take a variety of forms so there is work to be done on both the reading of the notation and the inversing. Do not underestimate the pleasure some learners can be derive from doing this kind of work! For example, in the following, learners have to consider order of operations and inverse operations, as well as the need to 'collect like terms' when needed:

1) $2x + 7 = 13$

2) $\dfrac{3x - 7}{2} + 4 = 5$

3) $3\left(\dfrac{x + 3}{2} + 1.5\right) = 15$

4) $4(x - 1) = 5x - 7$

Open Problems

When we think about an 'open' problem we tend to imagine situations where learners ask their own questions about a particular situation. For example:

Join three points to make a triangle. What questions might a mathematician ask?

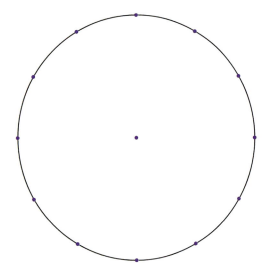

or

How long does it take to overtake?

Learners will doubtless develop their mathematical abilities as they work on these types of problems but it is difficult to guarantee quite what the learners will work on given this level of freedom and lack of constraint.

Although a very worthwhile activity for learners to undertake, this is not in the scope of this book.

Attention

Attention is a key consideration when thinking about practice. If learners answer questions of the type found in many textbooks, all the attention is on answering the question and (hopefully) getting the correct answer. It is possible to shift the focus of attention so that the mathematics you would like learners to practise and develop their fluency with is subordinated to some other purpose. We offer an example to illustrate the difference.

Suppose you want learners to work on substituting values into expressions. It is not too difficult to imagine the following as a worksheet:

Find the value of each expression by substituting in *x = 7*:

$x+2=$	$x+5=$	$2x=$	$3x=$	$-x=$
$2x+1=$	$2x+3=$	$2x-3=$	$3x+2=$	$3x+1=$
$3(x+3)=$	$3(x+1)=$	$2(x+1)=$	$2x+2=$	$x^2=$
$(2x)^2=$	$5-x=$	$10-x=$	$7-x=$	$8-x=$
$\dfrac{x}{2}=$	$x-4=$	$\dfrac{1}{x}=$	$x-1=$	$5x=$
$2x-1=$	$3x+3=$	$2x^2=$	$x-8=$	$2(x+3)=$

This task contains some practice of several areas of mathematics: reading formal algebraic notation and understanding the order of operations are both required to successfully complete the task.

However, there are some aspects of the task that are less appealing, the attention is entirely focused on the mathematics of substituting a value into the expressions, there is nothing else to do or think about and learners may view each question as unrelated to the previous one.

A further issue occurs if a student understands this work well and can answer the questions easily. There is no richness or opportunity for deeper thinking and what should the teacher offer if the student says "I'm finished!"?

Should the teacher offer more questions in the same vein? If so then more of the same may not be much of a reward for success with the activity. Alternatively, a teacher could think of and prepare an extension task on different work. This has the disadvantage of creating extra work and teachers may end up preparing extension material that is not used or on the other hand only the fastest learners ever use. This could widen the learning gap in some classrooms.

Compare this with the following task:

Write some expressions on cards.

Choose a value for the unknown.

Order the expressions for the given value.

Repeat this for different values of the unknown.

x	$x + 2$	$x + 2$	$2x$
$3x$	$-x$	$2x - 1$	$2x + 1$
$2x + 3$	$2x - 3$	$3x + 2$	$3x + 1$
$3x + 3$	$3(x + 3)$	$3(x + 1)$	$2(x + 1)$
$2x + 2$	x^2	$2x^2$	$(2x)^2$
$5 - x$	$10 - x$	$7 - x$	$8 - x$
$x - 8$	$\dfrac{x}{2}$	$\dfrac{1}{x}$	$x - 4$
$x - 1$	$5x$	$2(x + 3)$	$2(x - 1)$

This task sounds simple. From the learners' point of view, attention is with the ordering of the cards. The substitution is subordinated to this. This echoes what Tahta (1981) talked about regarding the inner and outer meanings of tasks. Learners need only be aware of the 'outer meaning' of tasks; in this case it is ordering cards. The 'inner meaning' is more like the actual mathematics the learners are working on or consolidating; in this case it is substitution and order of operations. This is where a teacher's attention might be. This can be utilised by the teacher and there are several occasions where 'what is known' to the teacher about a task can be utilised to support learners' progress.

The simplicity of this task hides some richness.

A possible way into this activity is to give out a set of expression cards and ask pupils to order them for a particular value, say $x = 7$, then change the value of x and see what happens to the order. This creates a lot of opportunity for substitution. You may choose to start with a smaller subset of the cards so they can begin conjecturing about the order sooner.

A very small set of cards like $x, x + 2, x + 5, 2x$ can provoke interesting conjectures such as '$x + 5$ is always three more than $x + 2$' but also affords an opportunity for questions about the possible position of $2x$: can you find a value of x that changes the order? Can you find values for x where $2x$ is in each of the positions numbered below?

$$\{①\ x\ ②\ x + 2\ ③\ x + 5\ ④\}$$

Some possible questions and prompts a teacher could use are:

● How do you put the expressions in order?

● Is the order always the same?

● Which expressions are always the same, never the same or sometimes the same?

● Which cards are the biggest value and when?

● When is *this* expression bigger than *that* expression? Smaller? What does that tell you about how to make them the same?

● Can you find an efficient way of finding the value that makes the two expressions the same?

- What different representations are useful? (Table of values? Graphs? ...)
- Does anyone have any conjectures about the order?
  Some cards may have the same value, is that always the case? Does the order change?
  Are there any that never change order?
- What happens if the variable is negative, fractional, decimal?
  Algebraic expressions are a really good context to practise arithmetic.
- Can you find pairs of expressions that are always the same?
  What do they have in common?
  Can you predict other pairs that might be the same?

Such a lesson offers a very different way of practising than the traditional exercise. With a traditional exercise the focus is on establishing being at a particular place in the curriculum (see Figure 1).

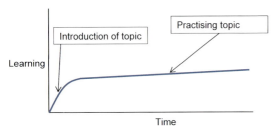

Figure 1: traditional practice

In contrast to this, we argue that there are ways of practising which not only improve the quality of practice but also have progress happening somewhere else as well (see Figure 2).

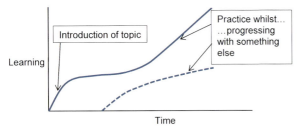

Figure 2: practice through progress

It is this *practice through progress* which we focus on for the rest of this book.

Practice through progress

When we carry out some mathematics, we will find ourselves giving particular attention to some things and less attention to other things with which we have greater fluency. For example, choose one of the following tasks:

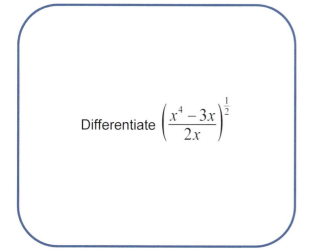

Differentiate $\left(\dfrac{x^4 - 3x}{2x} \right)^{\frac{1}{2}}$

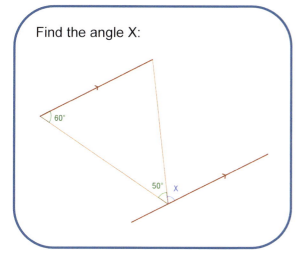

Find the angle X:

60°

50° X

For either of these examples, there will be things which were a focus of attention for you. For the differentiation question, this might have been the quotient rule or function of a function rule. For the angle question this might have been the sum of angles inside a triangle or working out that you needed to recognise alternate (or 'Z') angles.

For each of these there are other things which you used which may not have been a particular focus of your attention. For the differentiation, this might have been differentiating the x^4-3x part. For the angle question, it might have been doing the calculation to find the third angle of the triangle (already knowing that the three angles must add to 180 degrees). These required relatively little attention from you.

There are also other things which you used which you might only realise because we mention it to you now. These include knowing that for the differentiation question, one less than 4 is 3. For the angle question, it can include recognising the shape as a triangle. These are things which you are now so good at that you are not even aware you are using them when working on a problem. Yet when you were younger, you would have spent some time working on these things and they would have been the focus of your attention when learning them.

The nature of *practice through progress* is to help learners move from a learner to have to focus their attention on some mathematics in order to do or understand it, to being something which that learner can use or do so fluently that the learner is not even aware of it.

Too often practice takes place whilst learners are staying in the same place. For example, a traditional exercise can offer plenty of practice but no progress other than getting more 'practised' in carrying out a certain skill. At the end of the exercise, a learner may not have got any further in their learning of mathematics beyond what is being practised. *Practice through progress* offers a sense of not only carrying out the important practice but also progressing with a related but different aspect of mathematics.

In this book, we offer two ways in which *practice through progress* can take place. They differ in the nature of where the progression takes place.

The first is progressing in terms of the content of the mathematics curriculum; moving on to different topics within the curriculum.

The second is progressing in terms of finding out about mathematical properties and relationships when tackling interesting problems, challenges and investigations.

With both types of progression, something is being practised and the focus of attention is shifted away from what is being practised and onto other areas of mathematics.

The next two sections of this book address each of these two forms of *practice through progress* in turn.

The second of these sections is organised into topics where you can look up what you want to practise, and find problems, challenges and/or investigations which bring a purpose to the practice as there is something which a learner is trying to find out. So, the practice is not practice per se but is used as a tool to explore, notice, generalise and justify; developing the mathematician as well as the mathematics.

The first section below concerns development through the content of the mathematics curriculum and offers a way of designing exercises and schemes of work.

Practice through progress 1: progressing through the curriculum

A mathematics scheme of work will move on from one topic to a different topic. Depending upon the scheme of work, learners may not have had enough practice for something to be deeply embedded before their teacher moves on to the new topic.

This is not necessarily the fault of the teacher or the scheme of work but is sometimes due to the fact that it takes time and a lot of practice for a learner to become fluent and confident with the first topic.

The notion of practice through progress (Hewitt, 1994) is something which allows both a teacher to move on to the next topic and also have learners continuing to practise the previous topic.

The idea behind this is that learners do not have to be restricted to doing only one thing at a time. In fact, we would argue that this is never the case anyway. When working on finding areas, there are numbers which will be multiplied. So, even without any particular attention being paid to what those numbers are, the pedagogic decision not to allow calculators means that there is practice of multiplication as well as working on what area is about. If more considered thought is given to the dimensions of the areas, then practice of multiplication of fractions or decimals can also be practised whilst learning about area of shapes.

The nature of this type of practice has three key properties:

(a) a learner is learning a new topic and as such might feel a sense of 'progressing' through the curriculum;

(b) a learner is gaining further practice of a previous topic taught but in a new context;

(c) the nature of that practice is such that attention has been shifted onto something new and as such the practising begins to make a journey from being the prime focus of attention to becoming an unconsciously fluent act.

Things that we do now with very little conscious attention once required considered deliberation.

An example of this is something you are experiencing now.

It may even take you a while to become aware of what we might be talking about here; such is the depth of your learning of whatever it is we are talking about!

Currently, your eyes are glancing over a series of squiggles on the page. At one point in your life these did indeed look like squiggles, until you got to know them as letters. This, in itself, took time and a lot of practice.

Then collections of these letters were put one after the other and you had to learn that certain sounds were either associated with each letter, or associated with combinations of letters, or indeed appeared to have no sound associated at all.

This learning is complex and required much work and attention over a long period of time. Now your eyes hardly dwell on any particular letter and may indeed not dwell on a single word. There is such fluency with your reading that we suggest your attention is more on the ideas evoked by these sentences rather than in any technical detail involved in the act of reading. So, the journey to a place where something has become so well practised that it is carried out with almost effortless fluency, has two attributes: where attention is placed and the degree of effort required to be successful.

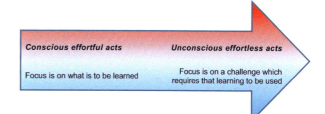

Figure 3: The Mastery Arrow - from early learning to 'mastery'

We suggest that staying with a focus on what is being learned is an attribute typical with early learning (the beginning of the 'mastery arrow' in Figure 3) and helps a learner stay with behaviours associated with the learning being at that early stage (i.e. conscious effortful acts).

However, once a certain amount of practice has been carried out, a deliberate teaching decision to shift focus onto a challenge which requires that learning to be used can help a learner shift further along the mastery arrow so that the skill involved with that learning is done with less conscious attention. Practice is still being carried out but with attention increasing being placed elsewhere.

Imagine you have spent some time working with a class on multiplying fractions together. This may have been an explicit topic which you have introduced and the learners are aware that the focus of the lesson (or series of lessons) is on multiplying fractions. There will come a point when you decide to move on to a different topic; for example, finding the area of rectangles and parallelograms. The idea of practice through progress is that you continue practising the previous topic whilst you make progress on the new topic. So, as far as the learners are concerned, they are moving onto a new topic.

However, the planning of examples used with the new topic makes sure that the previous topic is still needed to be used.

For example, Figure 4 has a parallelogram with fractional measurements which requires the multiplication of fractions in order to find its area.

The idea of practice through progress means that learners can continue to meet new areas of the curriculum whilst continuing to practise previously met areas of the curriculum. Furthermore, a learner's attention is gradually shifted from being primarily focused on learning a particular area of mathematics to using and applying that learning in new and different mathematical contexts.

A consequence of practice through progress is that you are never teaching only one thing at a time. You may have a particular focus on a new topic but you have also built into your planning the continual practice of another part of the curriculum. This helps link the mathematics curriculum together as work on one topic is seen to be used and applicable to another.

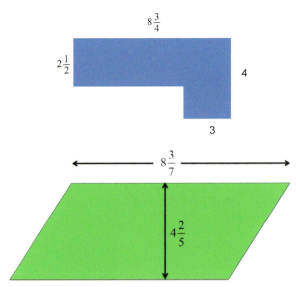

Figure 4: Two examples of finding areas whilst still practising the multiplication of fractions.

The new topic is unlikely to start with such examples as in Figure 4, instead it may be built up over a few lessons, but when practice of the new topic begins then examples using fractions can deliberately be included.

There will then become a time when moving on from areas of parallelograms is appropriate and let us assume that the next topic is equations of straight lines. Again, this might be introduced in many ways but when practice is required the challenge is to find ways to incorporate the multiplication of fractions and the area of rectangles and parallelograms as well. For example, you might ask the following questions:

1. Complete the table of values for the graph $y = \dfrac{2}{3}x + 2$:

x	-2	$-\dfrac{4}{5}$	0	$\dfrac{3}{4}$	$1\dfrac{1}{2}$	2
y						

2. The four lines below form the boundary of a parallelogram. Draw the lines and work out the area of the parallelogram:

$$y = 2x + 3\frac{2}{5}$$

$$y = 4$$

$$y = 2x - 1$$

$$y = 1\frac{4}{7}$$

3. Find the equations of four lines which bound a parallelogram with area of eleven and five-eighths.
And another... and another...

Such questions can form part of the work on equations of straight line graphs. The general principle is that of finding ways to incorporate previous topics into the new topics which are being taught. Figure 5 shows a path which starts at the left-hand side, teaching the multiplication of fractions. Progress is then made in the sense of progressing with the curriculum content, in this case addressing the new topic of area of a parallelogram.

However, the practice of multiplying fractions is maintained through careful choice of examples of parallelograms in questions to do with their area. This helps drive increased facility with multiplying fractions whilst not preventing further progress with the mathematics curriculum. With attention on the area of a parallelogram, the practising of multiplying fractions moves from being the main focus of attention to being a tool which is necessary for the completion of tasks to do with areas of parallelograms.

This gradual shift of attention is indicated in the middle part of Figure 5 where

the shading of the box for multiplying fractions has changed.

Further progress on to the new topic of straight line graphs can also maintain practice in both the area of parallelograms and multiplying fractions (again with careful choice of questions).

The multiplying of fractions becomes further embedded as it is increasingly being used whilst being more remote from the main focus of attention.

Eventually, we want learners to be able to do such things as multiplying fractions with increasing less attention being paid to doing so.

Figure 5

The power of such practice is not only in driving learning into increased fluency but also this means that different topic areas are seen to be connected.

This idea of connecting the mathematics curriculum is an important one.

If learners experience the teaching of mathematics as a collection of individual topics, then they are unlikely to be able to make such connections when they are needed. Also, the reality is that there are many connections across topics and the learning of any given topic can be enhanced and made more accessible by seeing the links with other topics.

This form of practice through progress has not only got implications for individual teachers but it also has implications for how the curriculum is managed through schemes of work. What topics might follow on from other topics so that the practising of one topic can be maintained when progressing on to the next topic? We believe that such practice can be maintained with any sequence of topics, however it is best for a department to consider these themselves so that they can see a clear way in which the practice of topics can be built into progression from one topic to the next.

Practice through progress 2: progressing as a mathematician

Here the progress shifts from progressing within the mathematical content of a curriculum to progressing with a particular challenge, problem or investigation. With traditional exercises the focus is on the practice with little of interest apart from developing a particular skill. If that practice were to be put into exploring something which can lead to a new awareness or insight into the particular situation then there is more of a sense of purpose to that practice.

For example, if your learners have recently worked on multiplication, we might suggest a task such as this:

Choose five different digits.

What combination gives the biggest product?

Is there a strategy for any five digits?

This offers plenty of practice of multiplication, only this practice is carried out as a means by which a mathematical situation is explored.

This allows progress in a number of different areas which we briefly discuss below taking the above task as an example.

Firstly, exploration of this task offers the opportunity to gain further insights in related areas of mathematics. Awareness that where the five digits are placed makes a difference to the answer offers a further appreciation of place value and its role in this activity. It also can lead to a careful examination of the process of multiplying multi-digit numbers, such as realising that 200×3 and 20×30 give the same result.

Secondly, learners have an element of choice in their work. In this case they are choosing the five numbers and then have to decide where to place those numbers within the boxes.

With a traditional exercise learners are rarely asked to make choices about the mathematics. Here the choices made are central to the challenge offered by the task. Initially choices may be relatively random but after time they are likely to become increasingly informed choices which are based upon the mathematical awareness they have gained.

The third aspect concerns the desire for learners to notice mathematical patterns and relationships. So, they may note that some arrangements of digits produce larger answers than others but it is relating that to the particular positions of these digits and beginning to notice connections between those cases where the answers are relatively large, or indeed relatively small.

Noticing such relationships can lead to making conjectures, such as 'If I put the two biggest digits in the unit boxes, then the answer will be small'.

This can be tested through considered choices of where to put the digits for the next example. This can lead to the realisation that other things need to be considered as well and gradually conjectures are tested and refined.

Conjectures often involve an element of generalisation; they apply to situations beyond the particular case being considered at the time.

Mathematics is full of generalisations. For example, the statement $3 + 2 = 5$ is a generalisation which applies to pens, chairs, people, etc. It is saying that it does not matter what things you are talking about: three of one thing plus two of the same thing will give you five of that thing.

This is not a trivial statement but a profound one as this also means that

$$\frac{3}{17} + \frac{2}{17} = \frac{5}{17} \quad \text{and} \quad 3x + 2x = 5x$$

is just as true as 3 chairs plus 2 chairs gives 5 chairs.

A learner does not have to know anything about fractions or algebra in order to know that these statements must be true as a direct result of knowing that $2 + 3 = 5$.

The ability to generalise from particular situations and also to see the general within the particular (Mason, 1987) can be developed through such tasks.

So, progress is being made in the ability to notice patterns and relationships, generalise from particular cases, and make and test conjectures.

Fourthly, as conjectures begin to appear robust through testing, the question of why a particular conjecture might be true can arise. This can lead to the desire to try to justify and prove the conjecture.

It is our opinion that justification and proof are not always given the emphasis they deserve in the school curriculum; yet they are vital for higher level mathematics.

We feel it is important to develop the ability to justify or refute conjectures and this can be done at all levels of education and all topics within the mathematics curriculum. This can be done as part of engaging tasks which also offer the desired practice as well.

Lastly, mathematical situations can be adapted and extended (Prestage and Perks, 2001) and this idea is an important one in mathematics.

For example, if a learner has difficulty with the five-box scenario above then they could start by simplifying it to a three-box situation with a two-digit number being multiplied by a single-digit number. Awareness gained from this situation can then lead to having ideas which can be applied to the original five-box situation.

It is an important skill to know when to simplify a situation in order to gain initial insights which then can be applied to the original case.

Even when someone has developed a conjecture about the five-box case and proved how to make the biggest product whatever the given five digits, this can be extended into considering the product of two numbers, one being an n-digit number and the other an m-digit number (this can, of course, also be extended again to having three numbers, etc.).

Adapting and extending situations is an important skill when working on mathematics.

To summarise, our five principles are for the exploration of tasks to offer:

1 Opportunities to gain further insights in related areas of mathematics.

2 Learners to have an element of choice.

3 Opportunities to notice mathematical patterns and relationships and make conjectures.

4 Opportunities to justify and prove.

5 Mathematical situations that can be adapted and extended.

All the above skills are important aspects of being a mathematician. We argue that as teachers we have an important role to play in developing the mathematician within our learners as well as helping them to 'do' and know what is stated in the mathematics curriculum.

The following section of the book is aimed to help learners progress as mathematicians as well as practise what is on the curriculum.

A collection of tasks

We offer a collection of ideas where practice with a particular topic goes hand-in-hand with developing the mathematician.

Except for a few of these ideas which we have developed ourselves, the vast majority are ideas which have been known for a very long time and as such the original source is unknown.

Where we do know the source from which we came to find out about the idea, we credit it.

What we have mainly done is to organise the tasks in a particular way.

They are organised so that you can look up the topic you wish to practise and under that heading will be a number of ideas which offer opportunities for learners to progress as mathematicians as well as practising that particular topic.

Many of the activities can be adapted and extended further by the teacher (or learners) using the techniques advocated by Prestage and Perks (2001) or question stems found in the ATM publication *Thinkers* (Bills, Bills, Watson, and Mason, 2004).

We hope you will find this collection a source of engaging and productive practice.

List of curriculum areas to practise

Number

Ratio, Proportion and Rates of Change

Algebra

Geometry

Probability

Statistics

Resources

Number

Place Invaders

Type a number into the calculator using the digits 1-9 exactly once.

Then press the subtract key, followed by a number with one digit and as many zeros as you like.

The aim is to turn one of the digits in the original number to a zero.

e.g. 123456789

123456789 − 700 = 123456089

123456089 − 400000 = 123056089 …

Keep going until you end up with zero.

For a greater challenge, digits could be targeted in ascending order.

Kaprekar

Choose a four-digit number.

All four digits should not be the same (e.g. not 1111, 2222, 3333, 4444, …).

Rearrange the digits to make the largest and smallest numbers possible with those digits.

Subtract the smallest from the largest.

With the result, re-arrange the digits again to make the largest and smallest numbers possible.

Subtract the smallest from the largest.

Repeat until something happens.

Write about what you notice.

e.g. 8416

8641 − 1468 = 7173
7731 − 1377 = 6354
6543 − 3456 = 3087
…

Try different starting numbers.

(Inspired by https://en.wikipedia.org/wiki/D._R._Kaprekar)

Factors, Multiples and Primes

Factors

Find a number with exactly 12 factors.

Find other numbers which have exactly 12 factors until you can describe them all and feel as if you know how to keep finding others.

What is the smallest number with 12 factors? Or 14? Or 16?

Which number(s) from 1 to 50 have the most factors?

Put the numbers 1 to 50 in order of how many factors they have.

What can you say about a number that has k factors?

If p is prime, how many factors does p^n have?

If q is also prime then how many factors does $p^n \times q^m$ have? Generalise?

Juniper Green

1	2	3	4	5	6	7	8	9	10
11	12	13	14	15	16	17	18	19	20

Two players take turns crossing out one number from the playing board above.

The first move in the game must be an even number. After that, each number must either be a factor or a multiple of the previous player's choice.

The first player who cannot cross out a number loses. Work out a winning strategy.

An individual (or group) task is to try to get the longest chain of numbers so that you have crossed out as many of the numbers as is possible.

(Adapted from Stewart, I. (2010). *Professor Stewart's hoard of mathematical treasures*. London: Profile Books.)

Factors

Go to https://nrich.maths.org/5448

Primes One Less Than a Square

Find a prime that is one less than a square number.

How many primes like this can you find?

Explain your results.

What are my Numbers?

Work in pairs.
Each of you chooses two numbers.
Find their highest common factor (HCF) and lowest common factor (LCF) and the sum of the two numbers.
Swap these with your partner – find out your partner's original two numbers.

Partitions

Choose a number (e.g. 10), partition it into 2 numbers, such as 4 and 6.
Find the LCM of those (12).
What is the partition which will give the highest LCM? Repeat for other numbers.
Repeat for partitioning into three numbers... etc.
(From a session run by Mike Ollerton)

Snooker Table

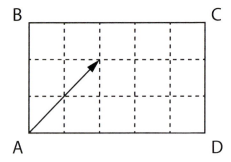

Which pocket (A, B, C or D) will the ball end up in?
Explore for snooker tables with different dimensions so that you can work out which pocket the ball will end up in without needing to draw the snooker table.

Product of 360 and HCF of 6

I'm thinking of two positive integers; their product is 360 and their HCF is 6. What is their LCM?
How many possible answers are there? Why?
(From Foster, C. (2012), Mathematics in School, 41(3), pp. 30-32.)

Calculating

Multiplication – Wittmann-Müller Multiplication

Choose two pairs of consecutive numbers.

Multiply vertically and multiply crosswise as below:

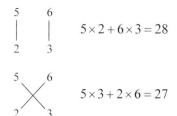

$5 \times 2 + 6 \times 3 = 28$

$5 \times 3 + 2 \times 6 = 27$

Do this for other pairs of consecutive numbers.

Explain what you notice and try to account for it.

What happens if horizontally the numbers are two apart, or three? or four?...

What happens for different differences?

Investigate what happens for triples of consecutive numbers:

$11 \times 3 + 12 \times 4 + 13 \times 5 = 146$

$11 \times 4 + 12 \times 5 + 13 \times 3 = 143$

$11 \times 5 + 12 \times 3 + 13 \times 4 = 143$

Try varying the horizontal differences…

(Adapted from: Wittmann, E.Ch. and Müller, G.N.: 1990/92, Handbuch Produktiver Rechenübungen, Vols. 1 and 2, Klett, Düsseldorf und Stuttgart.)

Multiplication $96 \times 23 = 69 \times 32$

What do you notice about this calculation?

How many other examples can you find?

Can you find them all?

Can you come up with a convincing argument that you have them all?

What happens with 3 digits? For example, 369 × 321 = 963 × 123

Four or more digits?

(Adapted from: Kordemsky, B. A. (1992). The Moscow puzzles: 359 mathematical recreations. Courier Corporation.)

Addition Array - 1111

```
  1 1 1
  3 3 3
  5 5 5
  7 7 7
+ 9 9 9
```

Replace ten of the digits in this addition with zeroes so the total is 1111

Replace nine of the digits in this addition with zeroes so the total is 1111

Replace eight of the digits in this addition with zeroes so the total is 1111

Replace seven of the digits in this addition with zeroes so the total is 1111

Replace six of the digits in this addition with zeroes so the total is 1111

Replace five of the digits in this addition with zeroes so the total is 1111

(From: Kordemsky, B. A. (1992). The Moscow puzzles: 359 mathematical recreations. Courier Corporation.)

Addition - Palindromes

Write down any 2-digit number. (e.g. 47)

Write down the number reversed. (e.g. 74)

Add the two numbers together.
(47+74=121)

121 is a palindrome (the same number read left-to-right as right-to-left), so 47 became palindromic after just one stage.

What happens for other numbers?
How many stages before they become palindromic? Can you find numbers which never become palindromic?

Kaprekar

Choose a four-digit number.

All four digits should not be the same (e.g. not 1111, 2222, 3333, 4444, ...).

Rearrange the digits to make the largest and smallest numbers possible with those digits.

Subtract the smallest from the largest.

With the result, re-arrange the digits again to make the largest and smallest numbers possible.

Subtract the smallest from the largest.

Repeat until something happens.

Write about what you notice.

e.g. 8416

8641 − 1468 = 7173
7731 − 1377 = 6354
6543 − 3456 = 3087
...

Try different starting numbers.

(Inspired by https://en.wikipedia.org/wiki/D._R._Kaprekar)

7, 11 and 13

Choose three digits e.g. 3,4 & 9.
Write them down twice to make a six-digit number (e.g. 349349).
Divide by 7. Do you get a whole number?
Repeat for other sets of three digits. Do the same again but this time divide by 11.
Repeat for other sets of three digits.
Do you always get a whole number?
What if you divide by 13 instead?
Divide your six-digit number by 7 then 11 then 13.
Make some conjectures and try to explain why they happen.

2u + t

Choose a two-digit number, multiply the units digit by 2 and add on the tens digit (e.g. 53 is $3 \times 2 + 5 = 11$).
Repeat with the new number (i.e. 11).
What happens as you keep going?
Explore other starting numbers.
Is there a number which gets back to the start? What happens if you multiply by 3, 4, etc., rather than 2?

Multiplication

Choose 5 different digits.

Put them in the boxes below so that you get the highest possible product.

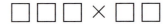

Find a strategy for placing the digits for getting the highest possible product given any 5 digits.

Which combination gives the lowest product?

Which combination gives the product closest to 50 000?

How many combinations are there for placing 5 different digits?

Negative Numbers

Negabinary Addition

What do you notice about these cards?

Which cards will add up to a total of seven?

What numbers can you make if you can choose as many of the number cards as you like and add those together?

Swap some of the numbers you have made with a partner. Can they work out which cards you used to make these numbers?

What is the smallest positive number you *cannot* make with these cards?

What is the 'most negative' number you *cannot* make with these cards?

As you move from right to left, do you notice that the following card is -2 times the previous card? What would be the next four cards, to the left of 64?

Imagine these cards are place value headings for the number 10110 (base -2):

64	-32	16	-8	4	-2	1
		1	0	1	1	0

So, 10110 (base −2) represents 18, because:

16 + 4 + -2 = 18

The following numbers are written in base −2. What are the numbers and what is the total for each pair? Write your answers in base -2.

101+11

1100+1001

100+1111

Choose other base -2 numbers to add together and try to work out how to find the answers as quickly as you can.

Negative Combinations

Use the numbers 1, −2, −3, and 5 once and only once, along with any of +, −, ×, ÷ and brackets, in order to make 24.

Find at least six ways of doing this.

Can you find a different combination of four starting integers that make 24 in more than six ways?

Choose a different number to 24 and repeat the challenge.

Consecutive Negatives

Take four consecutive negative numbers, say −4, −3, −2, −1

Do not change the order of the numbers.

How many different totals can you find using only addition and subtraction operations?

For more on this problem:
https://nrich.maths.org/5868/

Order of Operations

Four Fours

Use the numbers 4, 4, 4, and 4
(you must use all four 4s).

Use any of +, −, ×, ÷ and brackets.

Write calculations to make every number
from 1 to 20.

Now try to carry on getting all the
numbers up to 100.

You can also use the $\sqrt{}$ sign and use 4s to
form powers such as $4^4 = 4 \times 4 \times 4 \times 4$ (note
that 4^4 counts as using two of the 4s).

You can also use the '!' sign which is said
as 'factorial'. For example, $4! = 4 \times 3 \times 2 \times 1$
(note that 4! will count as just having
used one of the 4s).

One to Four

Use the numbers 1, 2, 3 and 4 (you must
use them all).

Use any of +, −, ×, ÷ and brackets.

Write calculations to make every number
from 1 to 20.

Now try to carry on getting all the
numbers up to 100.

You can also use the $\sqrt{}$ sign and use
numbers to form powers such as
$2^3 = 2 \times 2 \times 2$ (note that 2^3 counts as using
the 2 and 3).

You can also use the '!' sign which is said
as 'factorial'. For example, $4! = 4 \times 3 \times 2 \times 1$
(note that 4! will count as just having
only used the 4).

Try different numbers … 2, 3, 4, 5.

Target 24

Choose four numbers

Use +, −, ×, ÷ and brackets

Write calculations to make 24.
You must use each digit exactly once.

Use the numbers 4, 6, 6 and 8.

Write calculations to make 24.
You must use each digit exactly once.

How many ways can you find?

Make 24 using 1, 2, 3 and 4 exactly once.

Make 24 using 1, 2, 3 and 5 exactly once.

1, 2, 3 and 6 …

Bracketing

Put in brackets to make the following true.

$8 \times 5 - 4 + 12 \div 2 = 24$

$8 \times 5 - 4 + 12 \div 2 = 14$

$8 \times 5 - 4 + 12 \div 2 = 42$

$8 \times 5 - 4 + 12 \div 2 = -44$

$8 \times 5 - 4 + 12 \div 2 = 12$

$8 \times 5 - 4 + 12 \div 2 = 52$

$8 \times 5 - 4 + 12 \div 2 = 10$

$8 \times 5 - 4 + 12 \div 2 = 32$

$8 \times 5 - 4 + 12 \div 2 = -24$

Now use brackets to get different answers
to any of those you have already got:

$8 \times 5 - 4 + 12 \div 2 =$

$8 \times 5 - 4 + 12 \div 2 =$

$8 \times 5 - 4 + 12 \div 2 =$

$8 \times 5 - 4 + 12 \div 2 =$

$8 \times 5 - 4 + 12 \div 2 =$

$8 \times 5 - 4 + 12 \div 2 =$

$8 \times 5 - 4 + 12 \div 2 =$

Powers and Roots

Estimate the square root

Have a way of generating a random number from 1-100.

Get your first random number and enter it into the table below under 'Square root of…'. Write down your estimate to 1 decimal place of the square root of the random number.

Repeat the process until you have got 10 random numbers and made your estimates of their square roots.

Only then, get a calculator and find out the real square roots of each number accurate to one decimal place.

For each one find the difference between your estimate and the actual root (both to one decimal place).

Add up all the differences and that is your total 'error'.

Repeat that all again for another 10 and see whether you can get a lower total 'error'.

Try to see how low you can get your total 'error' to be.

	Square root of …	Estimate (to 1 d.p.)	Actual root (to 1 d.p.)	Difference
1				
2				
3				
4				
5				
6				
7				
8				
9				
10				
			Total of differences	

For a more demanding challenge, have your random number to be from 1-1,000 or even 1-10,000.

Lengths, Perimeters and Surds

If you draw a line from one dot to another dot on a 3 by 3 geoboard, how many different lengths are possible on a 3×3 geoboard?

Write these lengths as surds (when they are not whole numbers).

How about a 4×4 geoboard? How many on a 5×5? 6×6? …

On a 3 by 3 geoboard, create a shape where all its corners lie on dots. What is the length of its perimeter?

Can you find all possible perimeter lengths?

Without using a calculator, use estimation of surds to put your list of possible perimeters in order, from longest to shortest.

Only when you have finished doing this, use a calculator to check your list.

Draw an example of each possible perimeter length on dotty paper, from the longest to the shortest.

You might like to use the interactive geoboard by following this link - http://nrich.maths.org/2883

Perimeters, Shapes and Surds

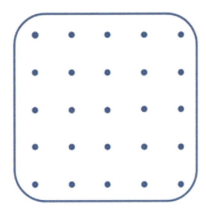

Work with a partner.

You both need to follow these instructions:

Draw five different shapes on a 5×5 geoboard. Find the perimeters of your shapes. Write the perimeters using surds and whole numbers only. Make sure your shapes all have different perimeters.

Swap your perimeter measurements with your partner. Try and draw shapes which match the perimeter lengths your partner has given you. Is there more than one answer?

Repeat – try to make it tricky for your partner!

Surd Generality

$$2\sqrt{\frac{2}{3}} = \sqrt{2\frac{2}{3}} \qquad 5\sqrt{\frac{5}{24}} = \sqrt{5\frac{5}{24}}$$

Can you find some more examples like this?

What do you notice?

Can you generalise?

Place Invaders (Powers of Ten)

Use digit cards 1–9 and a decimal point.

$$\boxed{1}\,\boxed{2}\,\boxed{3}\,\boxed{4}\,\boxed{5}\,\boxed{6}\,\boxed{7}\,\boxed{8}\,\boxed{9}\,\boxed{.}$$

Choose all of these cards in a random order and type this number into the calculator (e.g. 356891.247)

The first target digit will be '1'. Use the subtract key, the target digit once followed by $\boxed{\times 10^n}$ and any other digit (negatives are also allowed). The idea is to 'knock out' that digit (turn it into '0' or make it disappear if it is the leading digit).

The aim is to carry on doing this repeatedly to get eventually to zero.

e.g. with 356891.247:

$$356891.247 - 1 \times 10^0 = 356890.247$$
$$356890.247 - 2 \times 10^{-1} = 356890.047$$
$$356890.047 - 3 \times 10^5 = 56890.047$$

Note that digits should be targeted in ascending order.

An alternative task would be to use addition and try to target 1×10^n for some n.

Fractions, Decimals and Percentages

Two operations

Is this true?

$$\frac{1}{2} - \frac{1}{3} = \frac{1}{2} \times \frac{1}{3}$$

Find other pairs of fractions where subtracting one from the other is the same as multiplying them.

Can you find a general rule.

Is this also true?

$$\frac{1}{6} + \frac{1}{3} = \frac{1}{6} \div \frac{1}{3}$$

Find other pairs of fractions where adding them is the same as dividing one by the other.

Find a general rule for when this happens.

In-betweens

Make up two fractions and find some fractions that would be in-between them.

See if you can find at least five different fractions which would be in-between your two fractions.

Can you find the fraction that is exactly half way?

Choose three random fractions and work out the fraction which is the average (mean) of these.

Mediants

Choose two fractions where:

$$\frac{a}{b} < \frac{c}{d}$$

Work out:

$$\frac{a+c}{b+d}$$

Order your fractions.

Which of the following is true?

$$\frac{a}{b} < \frac{c}{d} < \frac{a+c}{b+d}$$

$$\frac{a}{b} < \frac{a+c}{b+d} < \frac{c}{d}$$

$$\frac{a+c}{b+d} < \frac{a}{b} < \frac{c}{d}$$

Try some other examples.

Write about what you notice.

Farey Sequences

Given the numbers 0, 1, 2, 3, 4, 5, 6, make all the possible fractions where the numerator and denominator digits in the fraction are each one of these numbers (you are allowed to have the same number as the numerator and denominator but not allowed to combine the digits to make 34, for example).

'0' is not allowed to be a denominator.

How many fractions are there?

How many *different* fractions are there (which are not equivalent to each other)?

Make a list of these different fractions (choosing the fraction with the smallest numbers to represent those equivalent to it).

Put these different fractions in order, smallest to largest.

Choose three adjacent fractions from your list. If the first and last of these are:

$\frac{a}{b}$ and $\frac{r}{s}$, then simplify the fraction $\frac{a+r}{b+s}$.

Do this with other sets of three adjacent fractions.

What do you notice?

Why does this happen?

Five Fractions 1

Draw a number line 12cm long on a plain piece of paper, marking '0' at the left-hand end and '1' at the other.

Use the digits 0-9 to make five fractions where the numerator is no bigger than the denominator. You might consider using a random number generator of some kind to choose the digit of the numerator and denominator of each fraction ('0' is not allowed as a denominator).

Order them from smallest to biggest.

Estimate where each fraction is on the number line (no ruler or calculator allowed).

Once you have marked your estimate for each fraction on the number line, use a ruler to find out where each fraction should be (calculators allowed if wanted).

Repeat for other sets of five fractions.

Draw a number line 18cm long on plain paper. Mark '0' at the left-hand end and '9' at the other end. Using a ruler also mark off where 1, 2, 3, 4, 5, 6, 7 and 8 are as well.

Now use the digits 0-9 to make five fractions where it does not matter whether the numerator is larger than the denominator. Again, perhaps use a random number generator of some kind to choose the digit of the numerator and denominator of each fraction ('0' is still not allowed as a denominator).

Mark your estimates on your number line and then use a ruler and calculator (if needed) to check how close you were.

Five Fractions – Changing Fractions to Decimals

Draw a number line of length 10cm on plain paper. Mark off and label where $0, \frac{1}{4}, \frac{1}{2}, \frac{3}{4}$ and 1 are on the line (with 0 on the left-hand end and 1 on the other end).

Use some way of generating random digits from 0 to 9. Choose randomly two digits to create a two-digit decimal number what starts '0.' (e.g. 0.72). Do this five times to produce five two-digit decimal numbers.

Estimate where they are on your number line and mark where you think each should be.

Use a ruler to check how close each one was.

Fraction Subtraction

Start with the line of fractions in the first row as in the picture below.

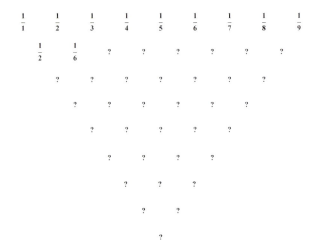

Underneath each pair of adjacent fractions, write the fraction which is the difference between them.

Write each one in its lowest form.

Continue until a triangle of fractions is formed.

What patterns can you find in this triangle?

Targets for Adding and Subtracting Fractions

Put the numbers 3, 4, 5 and 7 in the four spaces above and add the fractions to get:

1. the highest number;
2. the lowest number;
3. exactly $2\frac{7}{20}$

Using four of the numbers 3, 4, 5, 7, 11 and 13 make two fractions which you can either add or subtract to get as close as you can to $\frac{2}{3}$.

Using 3, 4, 5, 7, 11 and 13 once and only once, make three fractions. These fractions can be added or subtracted, as below:

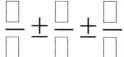

Make:

1. the largest possible answer;
2. the lowest possible answer;
3. the answer as close as possible to zero;
4. the answer exactly $2\frac{206}{429}$

Swap two numbers from 2, 3, 5, 7, 11 and 13 for two other whole numbers (keeping the final six numbers all being different), so that you can combine these six numbers in three fractions (using either adding or subtracting as above) so that you can get an answer closer to zero than you could before.

What if you had swapped two other numbers, could you have got even closer?

How close can you get when only two numbers from the above list are swapped?

Equivalent Fractions

What whole numbers can be put in for the square and triangle so that the fractions are equivalent?

How many different equivalent fractions can you find?

Change the 2 and 30 to two other whole numbers. Does this affect the number of different equivalent fractions you can make?

Choose two numbers where there are more than 20 equivalent fractions.

Decimals and Fractions

Choose four different digits from 0 – 9.

$$\frac{\square\square}{\square\square}$$

What decimals do you get if all four boxes are different digits?

What examples can you find where all the boxes are different digits and the statements are true?

$$\frac{\square\square}{\square\square} = 0.\square \qquad \frac{\square\square}{\square\square} = 0.\square\square$$

$$\frac{\square\square}{\square\square} = 0.\square\square\square \qquad \frac{\square\square}{\square\square} = \square.\square\square\square$$

Make up other arrangements of the fraction and decimals and do the same.

Fraction and Decimal Swap

$$\frac{13}{52} = 0.25 \qquad \frac{13}{25} = 0.52$$

What do you notice about this pair of calculations?

How many other examples can you find?

Can you get to a situation where you feel you can produce lots and lots of examples which work?

What about having a three-digit number on the denominator of the fraction? Can you find examples where the same thing works?

Four-digit number on the bottom, ... ?

ABCF2P - Fractions to Percentages

$$\frac{a}{b} = \frac{c}{100}$$

Find as many whole numbers as you can for a, b and c where this is true.

How many answers are there if $\frac{a}{b}$ is restricted to proper fractions?

Can you be systematic?

Find all the possibilities. How do you know you have them all?

Percentage Rectangles

Use two sets of digit cards 1 – 9 and mix them up. Draw two at random.

Write the two cards as a percentage e.g. 28% if you drew 2 then 8.

Draw a rectangle within another rectangle and shade so the shaded amount represents the percentage. Think about how you choose the dimensions of your rectangles.

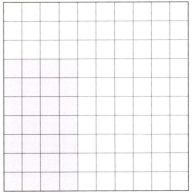

28% is shaded

Find different dimensions for the rectangles which still show the same percentage shaded in (where the larger rectangle is not mathematically similar to your previous larger rectangle).

How many options can you find?

Number Line Estimations

Draw a line 16cm long on plain or lined (but not squared or graph) paper.

Mark the left end 0 and the right end 1.

You need a list of either: all fractions; all decimals; or a mix of the two. For example:

$$0.5 \quad \frac{1}{4} \quad \frac{2}{5} \quad 0.8 \quad 0.25 \quad \frac{7}{10} \quad 0.75 \quad \frac{5}{8}$$

For each fraction/decimal, estimate where it is on the number line. For example, I might estimate $\frac{1}{4}$ to be as below. Place all the estimates with a mark on top of the line.

After all the estimates for each fraction/decimal have been marked and labelled on the top of the line, use a ruler to work out where the correct position should be for each fraction/decimal (some are easier to work out than others, depending upon what the fractions/decimals are!).

How good were you at estimating them?

Write down a set of fractions/decimals that you find 'challenging but achievable' and repeat the process with those.

For more of a challenge, instead of putting 0 and 1 on each end of the number line, put −1 and 3.

A Smaller and Smaller Collection of Fractions

Choose a number from 3 to 10. As an example, I will choose 5. Write down all the unit fractions with denominators going up to your chosen number. For me this will be:

$$\frac{1}{1} \quad \frac{1}{2} \quad \frac{1}{3} \quad \frac{1}{4} \quad \frac{1}{5}$$

Now choose any two of these (I will choose $\frac{1}{2}$ and $\frac{1}{5}$).
Do the following:

1. multiply them together
2. add them together
3. then add together the two results you got above (and simplify)

For my fractions that is:

1. $\dfrac{1}{2}+\dfrac{1}{5}=\dfrac{5}{10}+\dfrac{2}{10}=\dfrac{7}{10}$
2. $\dfrac{1}{2}\times\dfrac{1}{5}=\dfrac{1}{10}$
3. $\dfrac{7}{10}+\dfrac{1}{10}=\dfrac{8}{10}=\dfrac{4}{5}$

I end up with $\dfrac{4}{5}$.

I replace in my original list the two fractions I chose with this last fraction. So, my list is now:

$$\frac{1}{1} \quad \cancel{\frac{1}{2}} \quad \frac{1}{3} \quad \frac{1}{4} \quad \cancel{\frac{1}{5}} \quad \frac{4}{5}$$

$$\frac{1}{1} \quad \frac{1}{3} \quad \frac{1}{4} \quad \frac{4}{5}$$

Now choose two fractions from this reduced list and repeat the process to create a new list which has been reduced again to a list of only three fractions. Continue until you have a 'list' with just one fraction. What is it?

Now choose a different start number (I started with 5).
Repeat the whole process again to reduce it to just one fraction.
Generalise.
Why does this happen?

Bank Account

Suppose you have £100 in a bank account and the interest rate is 1% per year.
How long will it take to double your money?
Does it matter how much you start with?
Choose a different interest rate and find out how long it will take now to double your money.
Try other interest rates.
Draw an appropriate graph which shows what happens with different interest rates.
What happens with percentage decreases - how long does it take to halve the amount?

Percentagon

Choose an amount, say £360.
If you add on 50% you get £540.
Try to find two whole number percentages, x and y, so that you can get from £360 to £540 in two steps rather than one by adding x% on and then adding y% of the new amount on to the result.

In how many ways can you do this if the percentages are always whole numbers?

Try to find three whole number percentages, a, b and c, so that you can get from £360 to £540 in three steps rather than one by adding a% then adding b% of that to the result, then finally adding c% of the last result.

Percentage Increase/Decrease – Finding the Original Amount

Work in pairs.

Each of you secretly choose an amount and choose a percentage.

Find the percentage of the amount and add it on to the original amount.

Do this four more times with different amounts and different percentages.

Swap the results and the percentages with your partner.

You have to find your partner's original five amounts.

Repeat again only this time have a mix of some of the five involving taking off the percentage as well as some adding on the percentage.

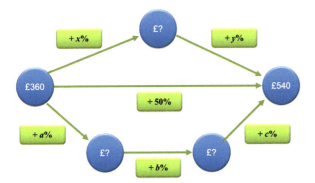

Rounding/Estimating

Number Line Estimations

Draw a line 16cm long on plain or lined (but not squared or graph) paper.

Mark the left end 0 and the right end 1.

You need a list of either: all fractions; all decimals; or a mix of the two. For example:

$$0.5 \quad \frac{1}{4} \quad \frac{2}{5} \quad 0.8 \quad 0.25 \quad \frac{7}{10} \quad 0.75 \quad \frac{5}{8}$$

For each fraction/decimal, estimate where it is on the number line. For example, I might estimate $\frac{1}{4}$ to be as below. Place all the estimates with a mark on top of the line.

After all the estimates for each fraction/ decimal have been marked and labelled on the top of the line, use a ruler to work out where the correct position should be for each fraction/decimal (some are easier to work out than others, depending upon what the fractions/decimals are!).

How good were you at estimating them?

Write down a set of fractions/decimals that you find 'challenging but achievable' and repeat the process with those.

For more of a challenge, instead of putting 0 and 1 on each end of the number line, put −1 and 3.

Get Close to 100

Use the numbers 2, 3, 5, 7 and 8, along with a decimal point and × to get as close to 100 as possible.

You can only use each digit once and once only, but you can use more than one decimal point and more than one multiplication sign if you wish.

Place Invaders

Type a number into the calculator using the digits 1-9 exactly once.

Then press the subtract key, followed by a number with one digit and as many zeros as you like.

The aim is to turn one of the digits in the original number to a zero.

e.g. 123456789

123456789 − 700 = 123456089

123456089 − 400000 = 123056089 …

Keep going until you end up with zero.

For a greater challenge, digits could be targeted in ascending order.

Five Fractions – Changing Fractions to Decimals

Draw a number line of length 10cm on plain paper. Mark off and label where $0, \frac{1}{4}, \frac{1}{2}, \frac{3}{4}$ and 1 are on the line (with 0 on the left-hand end and 1 on the other end).

Use some way of generating random digits from 0 to 9. Choose randomly two digits to create a two-digit decimal number what starts '0.' (e.g. 0.72). Do this five times to produce five two-digit decimal numbers.

Estimate where they are on your number line and mark where you think each should be.

Use a ruler to check how close each one was.

Five Fractions 1

Draw a number line 12cm long on a plain piece of paper, marking '0' at the left-hand end and '1' at the other.

Use the digits 0-9 to make five fractions where the numerator is no bigger than the denominator. You might consider using a random number generator of some kind to choose the digit of the numerator and denominator of each fraction ('0' is not allowed to be a denominator).

Order them from smallest to biggest.

Estimate where each fraction is on the number line (no ruler or calculator allowed).

Once you have marked your estimate for each fraction on the number line, use a ruler to find out where each fraction should be (calculators allowed if wanted).

Repeat for other sets of five fractions.

Draw a number line 18cm long on plain paper. Mark '0' at the left-hand end and '9' at the other end. Using a ruler also mark off where 1, 2, 3, 4, 5, 6, 7 and 8 are as well.

Now use the digits 0-9 to make five fractions where it does not matter whether the top number is larger than the bottom. Again, perhaps use a random number generator of some kind to choose the digit on the top and denominator of each fraction ('0' is still not allowed to be on the bottom).

Mark your estimates on your number line and then use a ruler and calculator (if needed) to check how close you were.

Estimating Calculations

In the table below, *(Resource – P84)*, write down your estimate of what each calculation is (no calculator allowed).

Once you have completed all your estimates, use a calculator and write down the exact answers.

Work out the difference between each of your estimates and the exact answer. Total up all the differences to produce a total 'error'.

	Calculation	Your estimate	Exact answer	Difference
1	32 × 47			
2	64 × 37			
3	23 × 672			
4	415 × 79			
5	703 × 48			
6	3078 × 18			
7	38 × 4008			
8	473 × 193			
9	206 × 953			
10	817 × 477			
			Total 'error'	

Create a new table of similar calculations and try to improve upon your total 'error' score.

Do similar tables for different types of calculations, perhaps including decimals, division or even calculations involving more than two numbers.

Ratio, Proportion and Rates of Change

Ratio

Dividing Up Money

You have £120 in £10 notes.

Write down as many ways as possible of dividing the money between two people.

Write down as many ways as possible of dividing the money between three people.

Write each as a ratio in its simplest form.

Share £240 in the same ratios.

What other amounts can be easily shared in these ratios?

Make up ten questions dividing £250 in ratios.

Make some easier and some harder … but they must give exact amounts.

Swap with a neighbour to solve.

What makes questions on dividing in a ratio easy/harder?

Difference : Sum : Product

Work in pairs.

Choose two numbers.

Work out the difference between them, their sum and their product.

Write as a ratio and simplify the ratio:

difference : sum : product.

For example, with 4 and 6, it would give the ratio 2:10:24 which is 1:5:12 in its simplest form.

Repeat this another four times so that you have five sets of ratios in all.

Swap these ratios with your partner and try to find the original numbers for each of the ratios.

Odd ratio

Which is the odd one out here and why?

Share £240 in the ratio 7:5

Share £240 in the ratio 4:7:1

Share £240 in the ratio 7:4

Share £240 in the ratio 1:5:2

Share £240 in the ratio 7:3

Make up more that are like the similar ones, and more that are like the odd one out.

Direct/Inverse Proportion

Strips

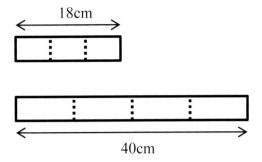

The top strip is 18cm long and is marked in thirds. The bottom strip is 40cm long and marked in quarters.

Both strips start being stretched lengthwise with the markings staying in thirds and quarters, respectively, of the total lengths.

The top strip is stretched at a steady rate of 3cm every minute (meaning that is it 3cm longer after each minute). The bottom strip is stretched at a steady rate of 2cm every minute.

Both stop stretching at the same moment when the markings are lined up as indicated below:

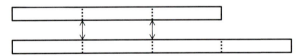

Decide how long it takes for this to happen.

Repeat except that this time the stretch rates are 9cm per minute for the top strip and 8cm per minute for the bottom strip.

What about rates of 5cm per minute and 3cm per minute?

Could you work it out for any given rates?

Growth and Decay

Bank Account

Suppose you have £100 in a bank account and the interest rate is 1% per year. How long will it take to double your money?

Does it matter how much you start with? Choose a different interest rate and find out how long it will take now to double your money.

Try other interest rates.

Draw an appropriate graph which shows what happens with different interest rates. What happens with percentage decreases - how long does it take to halve the amount?

Algebra

Notation

+5, ×5, −5, ÷5 – Expression flows

Work in pairs.

Start with the letter t.

Use each of +5, ×5, −5, ÷5 exactly once in a flow diagram and try to write your expression in formal algebraic notation e.g.:

$$t \quad \overset{+5}{\cdot} \quad t+5 \quad \overset{\times 5}{\cdot} \quad 5(t+5) \quad \overset{-5}{\cdot} \quad 5(t+5)-5 \quad \overset{\div 5}{\cdot} \quad \frac{5(t+5)-5}{5}$$

Do five different ones of these.

Swap your final expressions with your partner.

The challenge is to write the flow diagrams to match the expressions you have been given.

Now include the possibility of using
+3, ×3, −3, ÷3
as well as
+5, ×5, −5, ÷5.

Make five bigger expressions using some of these.

Swap the expressions with your partner and again draw the flow diagrams for the ones you have been given.

Substitution

Expression Cards

$x+2$	$3x+1$
$2x$	x
$x-4$	$3x$
$x+5$	$5-x$

You need the set of cards.
(Resource – P85)

Choose a value for x

Order your cards smallest to largest.

Choose a different value for x.

Do you need to re-order the cards? Which ones move, which ones stay the same?

Try some more values.

Find a pair of expressions where you know one will *always* be lower than the other no matter what the value of x.

Can you find other pairs with this property?

Now find a string of 3 cards where the order stays the same no matter what the value of x.

What is the longest string of cards you can find, where the order does not change when you choose different values for x.

How can you predict which cards will always stay in the same order?

Why is this?

(For teachers: choose your own set of cards appropriate for your class.)

Function Routes

Choose two numbers for the boxes above. For example, $3x + 5$. Call this function $f(x)$; e.g. $f(x) = 3x + 5$.

Choose a different set of two numbers for a second function, $g(x)$; e.g. $g(x) = 7x - 2$.

Choose a value for x.

Make a journey from *Start* to *Finish* in the diagram below.

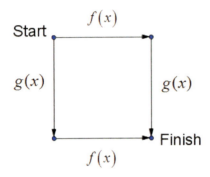

For example, you could go to the right first and then go down.

This would mean starting with your number and working out $f(x)$ for that value of x.

Your answer is the new value for x which you put in to $g(x)$, to get to the finish; e.g. if $x = 3$ then $f(x) = 3 \times 3 + 5 = 14$. So take this new value of x and substitute it in $g(x) = 7 \times 14 - 2 = 96$.

Now start with the same start number but do the other route, doing $g(x)$ first and then $f(x)$.

Do you end up with the same number as the first route? If not, can you find a start number where you do end up with the same finish number no matter which route you take?

Find two functions $f(x)$ and $g(x)$ so that you always end up with the same number no matter which route you take and no matter which start number you begin with.

$f(x)$, $g(x)$ and $h(x)$ are each a function of the form $\boxed{} x + \boxed{}$.

There are several routes to go from the start to the finish in the diagram below.

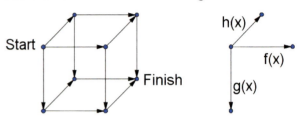

Each time you go horizontally to the right you carry out $f(x)$, each time you go down you carry out $g(x)$ and each time you go in the third direction, you carry out $h(x)$.

The arrows are one way and you are not allowed to go in the opposite direction of an arrow.

Find three different functions, each of the form $\boxed{} x + \boxed{}$, where you will get the same result at the finish no matter which route is taken and no matter which number you start with.

Can you find other sets of three functions?

What if you allow travelling in the opposite direction to an arrow (thus carrying out the inverse function)?

Can you still go by any route, including some inverse directions, from start to finish where the result will not be affected?

Can you generalise the above to n-dimensions (and thus n different functions)?

What if the functions are quadratics?

Collecting Terms

Card Collecting

Get your teacher to choose a subset of these cards *(Resource – P85)* or choose them yourself):

-6	-5	-4	-3
$-6x$	$-5x$	$-4x$	$-3x$
$-6y$	$-5y$	$-4y$	$-3y$
$-6z$	$-5z$	$-4z$	$-3z$
$-6x^2$	$-5x^2$	$-4x^2$	$-3x^2$
$-6y^2$	$-5y^2$	$-4y^2$	$-3y^2$
$-6x^3$	$-5x^3$	$-4x^3$	$-3x^3$
-2	-1	$+1$	$+2$
$-2x$	$-x$	$+x$	$+2x$
$-2y$	$-y$	$+y$	$+2y$
$-2z$	$-z$	$+z$	$+2z$
$-3x^2$	$-2x^2$	$+x^2$	$+2x^2$
$-3y^2$	$-2y^2$	$+y^2$	$+2y^2$
$-3x^3$	$-2x^3$	$+x^3$	$+2x^3$
$+3$	$+4$	$+5$	$+6$
$+3x$	$+4x$	$+5x$	$+6x$
$+3y$	$+4y$	$+5y$	$+6y$
$+3z$	$+4z$	$+5z$	$+6z$
$+3x^2$	$+4x^2$	$+5x^2$	$+6x^2$
$+3y^2$	$+4y^2$	$+5y^2$	$+6y^2$
$+3x^3$	$+4x^3$	$+5x^3$	$+6x^3$

Shuffle your cards and place them face down.

Turn over FIVE cards and write down an expression. For example, you might pick:

$-4y$	$+3x$	-3	$+x$	$-2y$

Find the total and simplify the result:

$$4x - 6y - 3$$

Continue shuffling and turning over sets of cards, each time writing down the expression and simplifying.

Shuffle and turn over a greater number of cards and repeat.

Include more cards or letters in the original set of cards. Use a different set or make one of your own. Use the 'Expression cards' (p37)

x	$x + 2$	$x + 5$	$2x$
$3x$	$-x$	$2x - 1$	$2x + 1$
$2x + 3$	$2x - 3$	$3x + 2$	$3x + 1$
$3x + 3$	$3(x + 3)$	$3(x + 1)$	$2(x + 1)$
$2x + 2$	x^2	$2x^2$	$(2x)^2$
$5 - x$	$10 - x$	$7 - x$	$8 - x$
$x - 8$	$\dfrac{x}{2}$	$\dfrac{1}{x}$	$x - 4$
$x - 1$	$5x$	$2(x + 3)$	$2(x - 1)$

Expanding/Factorising

Single and Double Brackets

Pick three different numbers and replace the squares with those three numbers – no repeats.

$$\square(\square x + \square)$$

How many possibilities are there with the same three numbers?

Write out all the possibilities.

Multiply them out and add the results together.

What do you notice?

Can you factorise the result?

Two brackets are even more interesting

$$(x + \square)\,(\square x + \square)$$

(this idea is from http://risps.co.uk)

Getting 24

Find as many expressions of the form

$$(x \pm \square)\,(\square x \pm \square)$$

which expand to make

$$x^2 + bx \pm 24.$$

How many different expressions can you find?

How do you know there are no more?

When is b negative?

When is it −24 rather than +24?

When are both b and 24 negative?

Quadratic Expression Pairs

$$x^2 + 10x + 24$$

$$x^2 + 10x + 25$$

Check that both of the above quadratic expressions factorise.

Check these do as well:

$$x^2 + 18x + 80$$

$$x^2 + 18x + 81$$

Find other pairs of quadratic expressions which factorise where the constant differs by just one.

Remember that the co-efficient of the x term can be negative as well.

Generalise so that you know all such pairs which factorise and whose constant differs by just one.

Account for why this is the case.

What other differences between quadratic pairs of expressions starting $x^2 + \ldots$ are possible when the x term remains the same in both expressions?

What about pairs of quadratic expressions which start $2x^2$?

Other coefficients of x^2 ?

Re-arranging

Choose Three Letters – forming and rearranging equations

Choose three letters, say a, b and c.

Using any operations (as many times as you like) make some equations

$a + b = c$

$c - b = a$

$b = ac$

$\dfrac{a}{b} = c$

...

How many different equations are possible where just a, b and c are used once and only once and no numbers are involved?

How do you know you have them all?

Group these equations so that any one equation within the group could be obtained from re-arranging any other equation within that group.

Choose four letters, or five, or six.

Equations

+5, ×5, −5, ÷5 – Expression flows

Work in pairs.

Start with the letter t.

Use each of $+5$, $\times 5$, -5, $\div 5$ exactly once in a flow diagram and try to write your expression in formal algebraic notation e.g.:

$$t \xrightarrow{+5} t + 5 \xrightarrow{\times 5} 5(t + 5) \xrightarrow{-5} 5(t + 5) - 5 \xrightarrow{\div 5} \frac{5(t+5)-5}{5}$$

How many expressions are possible?

How do you know you have them all?

Set each one equal to 100 – find t each time.

e.g. $\dfrac{5(t+5)-5}{5} = 100$

Which have the same solution?

Set each expression equal to f.

e.g. $\dfrac{5(t+5)-5}{5} = f$

Find the inverse, making t the subject of each one (so it starts $t = \ldots$).

Fold and cut some paper so that you have enough pieces of paper to write an equation on each piece.

Write all the equations and their inverses with just one on each piece of paper.

Mix the pieces of paper up and then match up each equation with its inverse.

Solutions to Equations

Put the numbers 1, 2, 3 and 4 into the places below:

$$\Box x + \Box = \Box x + \Box$$

How many different equations can you make?

How many different solutions are there?

Use four other numbers and repeat the process; do you get the same number of possible solutions?

Box Equations

Choose four numbers to go in the boxes below:

$$\Box x + \Box = \Box x + \Box$$

Solve the resulting equation.

Can you choose the numbers so your solution is an integer?

Can you choose the numbers so your solution is a particular integer?

Can you choose the numbers so your solution is $\frac{1}{2}$, or $\frac{2}{7}$, or ... ?

What if you put an x in one of the boxes?

What about one of $2x$, $3x$, $4x$, ... in one of the boxes?

What about an x^2 in one of the boxes?

Equivalent Equations

Choose two numbers, say 4 and 18.

Make an expression involving x so that when x is equal to your first number, the expression has a value equal to your second number (e.g. taking the two numbers 4 and 18, make an expression involving x so that when $x = 4$, the expression equals 18).

Find pairs of expressions with the same value, e.g. $3x + 6 = 18$ and $5x - 2 = 18$ (which both give 18 when $x = 4$).

Swap with your neighbour an equation using your expressions in this form:

First expression = Second expression

e.g. $3x + 6 = 5x - 2$

See if they can find your two numbers and you try to find theirs.

Choose another five sets of two numbers, finding pairs of expressions for each.

Swap with your neighbour the five equations made from each pair.

See if you can find the two numbers for each equation.

For each equation, e.g. $3x + 6 = 5x - 2$, plot two graphs, $y = 3x + 6$ and $y = 5x - 2$.

What do you notice?

A Magic Square

Make all the rows, columns and two diagonals add up to the same number.

?	19	96
1	?	?
?	?	?

Rules on Graph Paper

Make up some coordinates where the first number is the same as the second. Plot them on a graph.

Write about what you notice.

What if the second number is double the first?

What if the first is double the second?

What if you pick the first number, then multiply it by three and take four to get the second number?

Make up more rules for getting coordinates and see what happens.

Try to find general rules for what these look like on a graph so that you could sketch a graph without needing to plot points.

Squares Game

Three people are needed to play the game: a 'scribe' and two players. *(Resource – P86)*

Draw axes and restrict the game up to 0-4 on both the x- and y- axes.

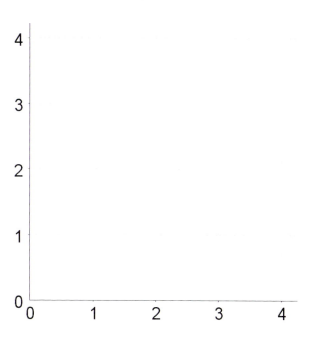

Each player in turn *says* the coordinate of a point (they are not allowed to point).

The scribe marks the position of each coordinate on the grid with a cross for player 1 and a circle for player 2.

The scribe must mark whatever co-ordinate the player says and a player is not allowed to change their mind.

If a player says a point which is already marked, then they miss that go.

The object of the game is to get four of your own points to be the corners of a square.

Remember that there can be 'squiffy' squares (with no horizontal or vertical sides).

An example of a game having just been won by circles is as follows:

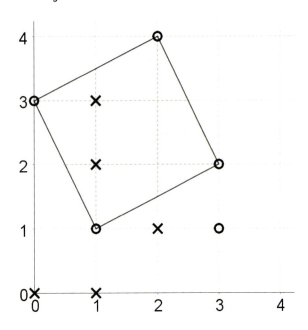

Variations can include:

Changing the size of the grid;

Having the grid to include positive and negative values on each of the axes;

Continuing to see who can be the first to get 3 squares.

Transforming Coordinates

On graph paper draw some axes with scales going from −10 to 10.

Draw a shape, noting the coordinates of each of the corners.

Investigate what happens if you do one of these things to all the coordinates of the shape:

- Add a constant to each;
- Double them;
- Make the x coordinate the negative value of what it was;
- Make the y coordinate the negative value of what it was;
- Make both coordinates the negative value of what they were;
- Swap the x coordinate with the y coordinate.
  Combinations of these ...

Describe what transformation has happened for each of the above.

What questions do you have?

How do you get a rotation about the origin?

What happens to coordinates when you rotate through 90˚, 180˚, 270˚ about the origin?

Coordinate Messages

There is a hidden message on the grid below:

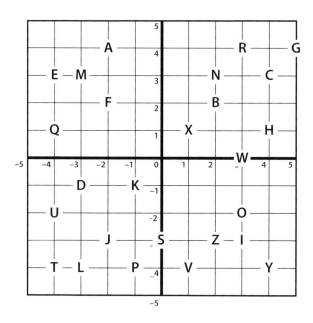

(-2, 4) describes the position of letter A

Find the letters for each coordinate below and decode the message:

(3, 0) (3, 4) (3, –3) (–4, –4) (–4, 3)

(–2, 4)

(–3, 3) (–4, 3) (0, –3) (0, –3)
(–2, 4) (5, 4) (–4, 3)

(3, –3) (2, 3)

(4, 3) (3, –2) (3, –2) (3, 4)
(–3, –1) (3, –3) (2, 3) (–2, 4)
(–4, –4) (–4, 3) (0, –3)

Write out a secret message in coordinates for your friend to read.

Swap and translate their message.

$y = 2x + 5$

Generate coordinates which fit the rule:
$y = 2x + 5$.

Plot them.

Once you find a pattern in what is happening, find more points from the graph and check them with the equation.

Find points which do not involve whole numbers and check them with the equation.

Investigate rules of the form
$y = \square x + 5$
whilst your partner investigates
$y = 2x + \square$.

Notice what happens and explain your results to each other so that your partner could draw any graph of the form
$y = \square x + 5$ after you have explained what you have noticed, and you can end up drawing any graph of the form
$y = 2x + \square$ once you have heard your partner's explanations.

Graphs

Gradients and Equations

Make up five linear equations and draw them on a graph.

For each equation, find two coordinates that fit that rule.

You will then have five sets of two co-ordinates.

Swap the five sets of two coordinates with a partner (and not the equations or the graphs).

Can you find the gradient of each other's graphs?

Can you find each other's equations?

Where Do They Cross?

Choose a number, n.

Where does $x + y = n$ cross $y = x + n$? Draw the two graphs to find out.

Where does $2x + y = n$ cross $y = 2x + n$?

Where does $3x + y = n$ cross $y = 3x + n$?

Generalise so that you know where such pairs of graphs will cross.

Choose numbers, n and m.

Where does $x + y = n$ cross $y = x + m$? Again, draw the graphs to find out.

Where does $2x + y = n$ cross $y = 2x + m$?

Where does $3x + y = n$ cross $y = 3x + m$?

Generalise so that you know where such pairs of graphs will cross.

Arithmetic Series and Graphs

Choose consecutive numbers from an arithmetic series to enter into the a, b, c, d, e and f below:

$$ax + by = c$$
$$dx + ey = f$$

The d, e and f could come from a different arithmetic series to the a, b and c.

Draw the graphs of these equations.

Where do they cross?

Choose two other arithmetic series and repeat.

(See Risp 8 activity from http://risps.co.uk/)

Square Graphs

Choose 4 points that make a square.

What are the gradients of the four sides?

What are the equations of the four sides?

Choose 4 other points which make a square (one which does not have any horizontal sides)

Find the gradients and equations of the sides.

What do you notice?

Check what you notice with a third square.

Swap with a partner the equations of just two sides of a square, can each of you find the remaining two equations?

What if the two sides were opposite sides? Adjacent sides?

Repeat the above but for a rectangle.
A parallelogram?
A rhombus?
A kite?

Swap with your partner the coordinates of two corners of a square.

Find the equations of all four sides of that square.

What if the points are adjacent corners?

What if they are opposite corners?

Minimum Point

Choose a and c and vary b in the equation $ax^2 + bx + c$.

What happens to the minimum point of the graph?

If you are told a, b and c, could you know at which value of x the minimum point will be found?

Generator

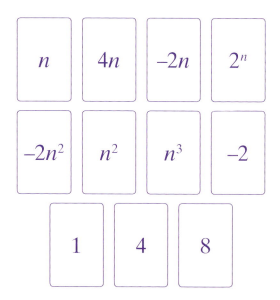

Work with a partner.

Choose one expression card and substitute in $n = 1$, $n = 2$, … into that expression to generate the first five terms of a sequence.

For example, if I choose n^2, my sequence will be 1, 4, 9, 16, 25 …

Choose any combination of the expressions above and add them to make a new expression.

Substitute in $n = 1$, $n = 2$, … and again generate the first five terms of a sequence.

Swap your sequences with your partner.

Can you find which combination of cards match the sequences?

Terms

What could the other numbers in this sequence be?

Find five different linear sequences where the third term is 7.

How many different sequences can you find where 7 is still the third term and now 15 is the fifth?

What about quadratic sequences?

How many quadratic sequences can you find?

Draw graphs for each of the quadratic sequences you have found. Draw them all on the same graph. What do you notice?

What about cubic sequences?

Two sequences 1

Find two linear sequences where the first occurrence of a common term appears at the 7th term of one sequence and the 11th of the second sequence.

Once you have found such a pair of sequences, carry on both sequences and look at which other numbers appear in both sequences.

Which terms in sequence 1 and which terms in sequence 2 do these common numbers occur?

Why is this happening?

Find other pairs of sequences which have the first common number appearing at the 7th term of one sequence and the 11th term of the other sequence.

Again, look for where other common numbers appear in these sequences.

Can you find two sequences where the regularity of common terms (after the first occurrence) is every two in one sequence and every five in the other?

Two sequences 2

Choose two sequences with different rules.

Are there any numbers that are common to both sequences?

Write these common numbers as a sequence.

Find the rule for this new sequence.

What do you notice?

Try to explain your conjectures.

$4n-1$	3	7	11	15	19	23	27	31	35
$3n+5$	8	11	14	17	20	23	26	29	32
Rule?	11	23	?	?	?	?	?	?	?

(Adapted from http://www.inquirymaths.com/ home/algebra-prompts/linear-sequences).

Quadratic Equations

Difference of Two Squares

$3^2 - 2^2 = \quad 7^2 - 6^2 = \quad 10^2 - 9^2 =$

What do you notice?

Could you come up with more like this? What conjectures can you make?

$4^2 - 2^2 = \quad 8^2 - 6^2 = \quad 11^2 - 9^2 =$

Do you need to modify your conjectures?

$7^2 - 2^2 = \quad 9^2 - 6^2 = \quad 23^2 - 22^2 =$

$12^2 - 11^2 = \quad 7^2 - 5^2 = \quad 5^2 - 0^2 =$

Try to express all the numbers from 1 to 20 as a difference of two squares.

What if the squares differ by 2, 3, 4, ... ?

When is the difference of two squares odd/even?

What numbers can you **not** make?

Can you prove your claims?

Is there ever more than one way to express a number as a difference of two squares?

Can you describe a way of working out how many ways there are to write a number as a difference of two squares?

Roots

$ax^2 + bx + c = 0$

Choose a and b, can you find c so that the equation has one root, two roots, no roots?

E.g. If $a = 4$ and $b = 12$ then find c so that $4x^2 + 12x + c = 0$

What if you choose a and c and have to find b?

What if you choose b and c and have to find a?

Getting 24

Find as many expressions of the form

$(x + \square)(\square x + \square)$

which expand to make $x^2 \pm bx \pm 24$

How many different expressions can you find?

How do you know there are no more?

When is b negative?
When is it -24 rather than $+24$?
When are both b and 24 negative?

Different Forms

$(x - p)^2 + q = x^2 + bx + c$

Choose p and q and find the values for b and c.

Swap right-hand sides with your neighbour, try to find their p and q.

Repeat with this, choosing m, p and q in:

$m(x - p)^2 + q = ax^2 + bx + c$

Repeat with this, choosing n, p and q in:

$(nx - p)^2 + q = ax^2 + bx + c$

Minimum Point

Choose a and c and vary b in the equation $ax^2 + bx + c$.

What happens to the minimum point of the graph?

If you are told a, b and c, could you know at which value of x the minimum point will be found?

Simultaneous Equations

Shared Solution

Find several equations of the form $y = ax + b$ that have $(2, -1)$ as a solution.

Find a rule which connects a and b with these equations.

Repeat, but with a different coordinate.

Generalise for the coordinate (n, m).

Squares and Rhombi

Draw a square on graph paper.

Write down the equations of the four lines which make the sides of the square.

Repeat with four other squares where none of these squares have a horizontal side.

Swap with a partner just **three** equations for each of your five squares.

You have to find the coordinates of the corners for each of the five squares.

Now go back to your squares and find the equations of both diagonals of your squares.

Swap with a partner the equations of **two** of the sides and **one** of the diagonals.

You have to find the coordinates of the corners for each of the five squares.

Does it matter which sides and diagonals were chosen?

Repeat with rhombi instead of squares.

Geometry

Area, Perimeter and Volume

12 Square perimeters

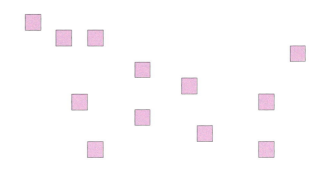

Join 12 squares edge to edge, the area will be 12, what is the perimeter?

What other ways can you find of joining the 12 squares?

Perimeter?

What is the maximum perimeter?

Minimum perimeter?

Can you make every whole number perimeter between them?

What if not 12?

Rectangles of Fixed Perimeter

Draw a rectangle with perimeter 24.

And another, and another …

What does the graph of base against height look like?

What is the equation?

What happens to the area?

When is area maximum/minimum?

What does the graph of base against area look like?

Predict what will happen for different fixed perimeters.

Rectangles of Area 12

Draw rectangles with area 12 and integer side lengths.

Write the dimensions and find the perimeters.

What if not whole numbers?

Plot the base against the height, what does the graph look like?

What is the equation for this graph?

What if not 12?

Try some other values for the area.

Area of a Triangle

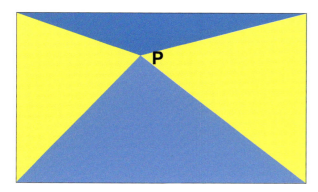

Is the total blue area bigger or smaller than the total yellow area? What if the point P was moved somewhere else?

Where can the point P lie if the yellow and blue areas are the same for different shapes such as a parallelogram?
A rhombus?
A kite?
A trapezium?
A general quadrilateral?

(Pritchard, C. (2013) *Generalizing complementary regions, Mathematics in School*, 42(2), pp. 11-13)

Stacks

You can make rectangles by stacking squares together.

Work systematically, how many rectangles can you make from n squares?

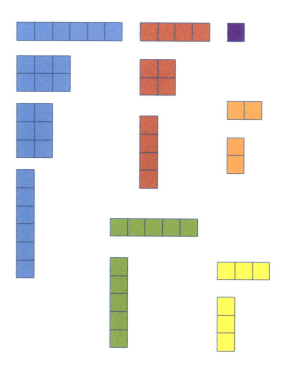

Which number (1-100) has the most possible stacks?

What can you say about a number that has k stacks?

Find a number with exactly 12 stacks.

What is the smallest number with 12 stacks? Or 14? Or 16?

Find more numbers with 12 stacks until you can describe them all.

Area and Perimeter – Equable Shapes

Two shapes are said to be *equable* if the value of their area and perimeter is the same.

What equable rectangles can you find?

What about equable right-angled triangles?

What about other equable shapes?

Area and Perimeter of rectangles

Rectangles can be changed by rules which are stated below.

The challenge is to start with a rectangle with a certain perimeter, say 10 cm, and to end up with a rectangle with a given different perimeter, say 20 cm.

The rules for changing rectangles are based around alternating between thinking about the *perimeter* of a rectangle and the *area* of a rectangle.

Start by making a table as follows:

Perimeter	Dimensions of rectangle (whole numbers only)	Area
10 cm		

The perimeter of the first rectangle is 10 cm but you can decide what the dimensions are for this rectangle as long as the perimeter of it is 10 cm (the rules are that the dimensions must be whole numbers). Suppose you choose it to be a 2 by 3 rectangle. Work out the *area* of this rectangle (6 cm²), so that your table looks like:

Perimeter	Dimensions of rectangle (whole numbers only)	Area
10 cm ———→	2 by 3 ———→	6 cm²

Copy the 6 cm² again in the cell below and now consider the dimensions of a different rectangle which still has an area of 6 cm², say 1 by 6. Now work out the *perimeter* of this rectangle (14 cm). Your table now looks like this:

Perimeter	Dimensions of rectangle (whole numbers only)	Area
10 cm ———→	2 by 3 ———→	6 cm²
14 cm ←——	1 by 6 ←——	6 cm²

Now copy down the 14 cm and consider a different rectangle which has the same perimeter, say 2 by 5. Work out the *area* of this rectangle (10 cm²).

Then copy down the 10 cm² and consider a different rectangle with this same area, say 1 by 10. Work out the *perimeter* of this rectangle. The table below shows the continuation of this until the target of 20 cm for the perimeter was obtained.

Perimeter	Dimensions of rectangle (whole numbers only)	Area
10 cm ———→	2 by 3 ———→	6 cm²
14 cm ←——	1 by 6 ←——	6 cm²
14 cm ———→	2 by 5 ———→	10 cm²
22 cm ←——	1 by 10 ←——	10 cm²
22 cm ———→	3 by 8 ———→	24 cm²
20 cm ←——	4 by 6 ←——	24 cm²

Now start with a perimeter of 20cm and try to end up with the target perimeter of 30cm. The sheet below can be used (you do not necessarily need all the rows!).

Perimeter	Dimensions of rectangle (whole numbers only)	Area
———→	———→	
←——	←——	
———→	———→	
←——	←——	
———→	———→	
←——	←——	
———→	———→	
←——	←——	
———→	———→	
←——	←——	
———→	———→	
←——	←——	
———→	———→	
←——	←——	

What is the shortest number of steps needed? *(Resource – P87)*

Choose other start and finish perimeters. Are there any which cannot be done?

h + r = 40 – Circles, Cylinders Volume and Surface Area

The height and radius of a cylinder sum to 40.

What is the biggest volume you can find?

What if not 40?

Can you make a conjecture?

Can you prove your conjectures?

When do you get maximum surface area?

V = 100 – Circles, Cylinders, Volume and Surface Area

Find some cylinders where the volume is 100cm³.

Calculate the surface area for each of these.

Find the cylinder with the minimum surface area which still has a volume of 100cm³.

Fix the surface area, can you maximise the volume?

Minimise the volume?

Can you find a cylinder where the number for the surface area is the same as the volume?

Surface Area = Volume

What shapes can you design where the number for the surface area = the number for as the volume?

Circle - Graphs

Generate some data to draw the following graphs:

- diameter against circumference
- diameter against area
- radius against circumference
- radius against area
- circumference against area

Sort the graphs. Try to say as much as you can about each graph individually and about what is the same and different about each graph compared with the others.

Semi-Circles on Triangles

Construct some semi-circles on the sides of triangles.

When is the sum of the areas of the two smallest semi-circles less than the area of the larger semi-circle?

When is the sum of the areas of the two smallest semi-circles greater than the area of the larger semi-circle?

Can the sum of the two smaller semi-circular areas ever be the same area as the largest?

Yin and Yang

These pictures are made from semi-circles. Find the area of each coloured slice.

What happens if you have five slices?
Or six?
Or any amount?

Can you prove your conjectures?

Repeat for the perimeter.

Constructions

Perimeter of Fifteen

Construct triangles with integer side lengths where the perimeter is 15 cm. How many are there?

How do you know you have them all?

Find the angles.

Order them by size of the largest angle.

Order them by area.

Circumcentre

Construct a triangle with integer side lengths.

Construct the perpendicular bisector of each side.

What do you notice?

Draw a circle through the intersection of the bisectors (circumcentre) that goes through a vertex, (the circumcircle).

Write about what happens.

When is the circumcentre inside the triangle? When is it outside? When is it on the edge?

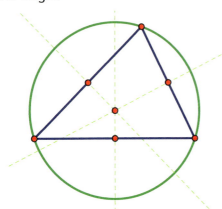

Make more triangles where the centre is on the edge of the triangle.

There is a relationship between the radius of the circle (the circumradius) and the side lengths. It is easier to test than discover!

Test this for the triangles you've drawn

$$r = \frac{abc}{\sqrt{(a+b+c)(b+c-a)(c+a-b)(a+b-c)}}.$$

Find a relationship for special triangles: equilateral triangles, right-angled triangles and isosceles triangles.

Incircle

Find some Pythagorean triples (calculate - you could use this formula $a = m^2 - n^2$, $b = 2mn$, $c = m^2 + n^2$, where $m > n$ or look up on the web).

Construct the right-angled triangle.

Bisect the angles.

From where these meet, draw a circle that just touches the sides the triangle – (drop a perpendicular from the intersection to one of the sides).

Find a relationship between the radius of the incircle and the sides of the triangle.

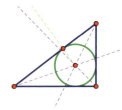

You could use any triangle with integer side lengths.

Symmetry

Triangle & Quadrilateral Properties

Add One Square

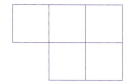

Add one square to this shape to make a shape with line symmetry.

In how many ways can you do this?

How many ways are there to make a shape with line symmetry by adding two squares?

How many ways are there to make a shape with line symmetry by adding three squares?

Adding four squares?

Five squares?

Three Shape Symmetry

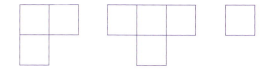

Put all three of these shapes together edge to edge to make a shape that has either reflection or rotation symmetry.

Try to invent a set of shapes that has a similar number of solutions.

Four triangle jigsaw

You will need four right-angled triangles with side lengths 1 : 2 : √5.
(*Resource – P88*)

How many different shapes can be made by joining two triangles edge to edge? What stays the same about the shapes and what changes?

What about using three triangles?

What about if you use all four triangles?

Can you make a …

- square
- non-square rectangle
- parallelogram (4 different ones)
- a larger version of the original triangle
- isosceles trapezium (2 different ones)
- rhombus
- arrowhead
- kite
- a quadrilateral with only 1 pair of equal sides and no lines of symmetry
- pentagon with 1 line of symmetry
- pentagon with no line symmetry
- octagon with rotational symmetry, order 2
- hexagon with rotational symmetry, order 2

Guess my shape
Work with a partner. Make a shape from your four triangles, do not let them see the shape.

Describe the shape to your partner so they can make it from their four triangles.

Rules:

Do not use your hands to gesture or point.

Try to use vocabulary such as 'opposite sides', 'equal sides', 'line of symmetry' etc

Only the person describing the shape can speak. Your partner cannot ask questions. (Or your partner can ask questions but you can answer only 'yes' or 'no')

(The first part of this task comes from an idea by Don Steward)

Nine Pin Quadrilaterals

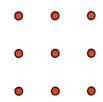

Draw as many different quadrilaterals as possible on a nine pin (3×3) geoboard.

Write down all the special names attached to each one.

How many more quadrilaterals are there on a sixteen pin (4×4) geoboard?

Investigate triangles.

How many are there for other numbers of sides or different sizes of geoboard?

Reflection on Straight Line Graphs

Investigate what happens to the coordinates a shape if you reflect it in:

$x = 0$

$y = 0$

$y = x$

$y = -x$

$x = a$

$y = a$

$y = x + c$

$y = mx$

$y = mx + c$

Reflecting in Two Lines

Draw a scalene triangle, A.
Choose a line and reflect your shape to get a new image A'.
Choose another line and reflect the image A' in this line to give A''.
Give the original object A and A'' to your partner and see if by trying different combinations of reflections they can find your mirror lines.

You might begin with two parallel mirrors. Can the process ever be described in more than one way?

Try to generalise.

Rotation - Finding your Centre

Place this shape in different positions on the grid.

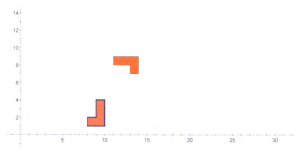

Find the centre of rotation using trial and improvement; that is by guessing where the centre of rotation might be. Then use tracing paper to make a copy of the original shape to see if you were correct.

Is there a better way?

Rotating Coordinates

What happens to the coordinates if you draw a shape and rotate it anti-clockwise:

    180° about (0,0)?
    90° about (0,0)?
    270° about (0,0)?

What if not about (0,0) but $(a, 0)$?

    ... or $(0, b)$?
    ... or (a, b)?

Coordinates and Translations

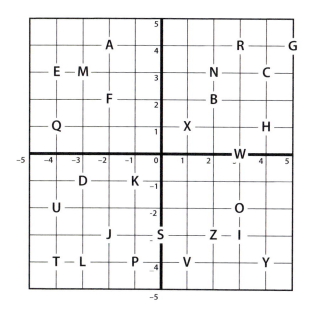

Write out a secret message as translations from one letter to another.

Give the starting letter then the movement to each subsequent letter as a vector. For example:

$$\text{F} \begin{pmatrix} 5 \\ -4 \end{pmatrix} \begin{pmatrix} 0 \\ 6 \end{pmatrix} \begin{pmatrix} -7 \\ -1 \end{pmatrix} \begin{pmatrix} 5 \\ -2 \end{pmatrix} \begin{pmatrix} -3 \\ 3 \end{pmatrix} \begin{pmatrix} -1 \\ -1 \end{pmatrix} \begin{pmatrix} 2 \\ -7 \end{pmatrix} \begin{pmatrix} -2 \\ 0 \end{pmatrix} \begin{pmatrix} -1 \\ 7 \end{pmatrix}$$

You could use this grid to write translation messages instead

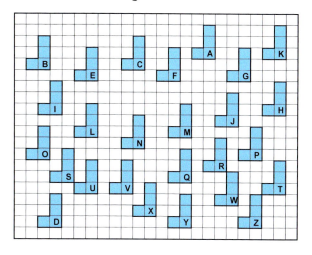

Enlargement

Choose a centre of enlargement, scale factor and a shape of your choice.
Enlarge it and give the two shapes to your partner.
Can they describe the enlargement (find scale factor and centre of enlargement)?

Alternatively, draw a shape and an enlargement of it.
Find the centre of enlargement.
Give the original shape and the centre of enlargement to your partner.
Can they find the enlargement?

Enlargement Co-ordinates

Investigate what happens to coordinates if you enlarge a shape by scale factor 2 about centre of enlargement at $(0,0)$

What if not about $(0,0)$ but $(a,0)$
   ... or $(0,b)$
   ... or (a,b)
Change the scale factor.

Replicating Tiles

Draw a shape and enlarge it by scale factor, 2, 3, 4, 5, 6, ...

What happens to the areas?

Sometimes you can fit copies of the original shape into the larger versions.

Can you find some shapes where this is possible?

These are called rep-tiles.
A Rep-tile is said to be rep-n if an enlargement can be made from n tiles. It is always possible for parallelograms and triangles.

How many shapes fit in each time?

These shapes work nicely:

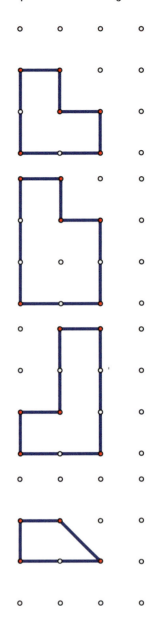

Draw a shape.

Mark a centre of enlargement.

Enlarge the shape by scale factor 2.

Fill the shape with copies of the original.

Give the transformations required to get each one from the original.

Angles

Dotty Circles - Measuring Angles

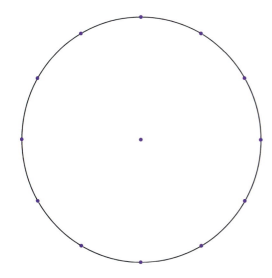

On a circular geoboard, join two points on the circumference to the centre to make a triangle.

Work out the angles – try to predict them before you measure them.

How many different triangles are there that use the centre?

Find the angles of each one.

Give a convincing reason that you have them all.

Join three points on the circumference to make a triangle.

Work out the angles – try to predict them before you measure them.

How many different triangles are there?

Give a convincing reason that you have them all.

Investigate changing the number of dots. Investigate changing the number of sides. 6 or 12 points are a good place to start. Angles can be measured initially then calculated.

(For teacher: with calculating angles a hint might be to draw triangles using the centre. They can then move on to proof.)

Two Isosceles Triangles on the Diameter

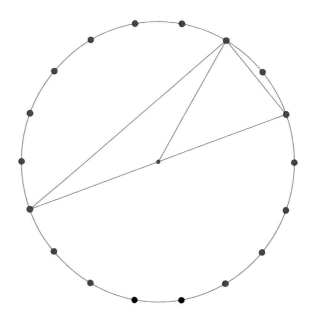

Using even-dot circular geoboards.

Draw a diameter, a radius and two chords.

Find all the angles and make some conjectures.

Try to prove these conjectures.

Change the number of dots around the geoboard.

You can measure, calculate or work algebraically.

Triangle in a Triangle

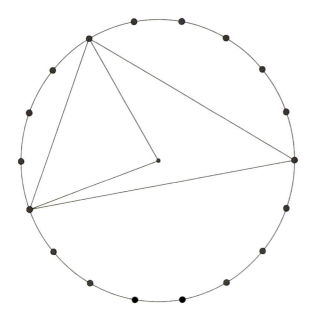

Using a geoboard.

Draw a triangle with one point as the centre.

Make a triangle to surround it that shares the base.

Find all the angles and make some conjectures.

Try to prove these conjectures.

Change the number of dots around the geoboard.

You can measure, calculate or work algebraically.

Cyclic Quadrilateral

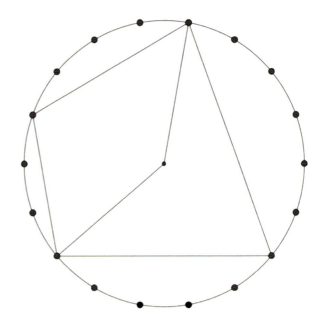

Using a geoboard.

Draw a quadrilateral with all vertices on the circumference.

Join two opposite corners to the centre.

Find all the angles and make some conjectures.

Try to prove these conjectures.

Change the number of dots around the geoboard.

You can measure, calculate or work algebraically.

Squiffy Squares and Polygons

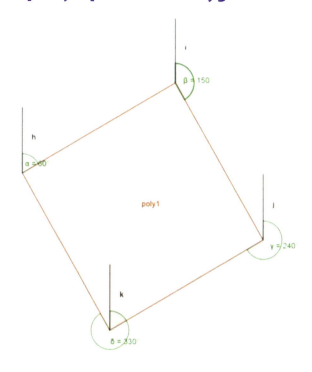

Write instructions to draw a squiffy square as bearings

E.g. 3cm on bearing 060°, 3cm on bearing 150°, 3cm on bearing 240°, 3cm on bearing 330°

Try to draw your partner's squiffy square from their instructions.

What happens to the other bearings if your first bearing is 070° and you still want a square? Or 080°?

What is the same and what is different if you draw with LOGO?

Write instructions to draw other regular polygons as bearings and try and draw your partner's polygon.

Draw some irregular polygons and work out the instructions.

Star Polygons

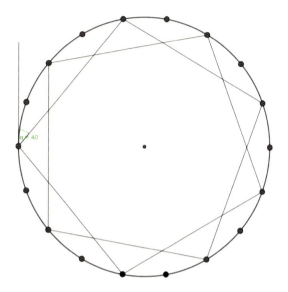

Use an n-dot circular geoboard (or mark off n points around a circle).

Choose a starting point and a value, m, less than n.

Draw a straight line to the point m dots along.

Repeat until you get back to the start.

This creates an (n,m) star polygon.

Write the instructions to draw your star polygon as bearings.

Try to draw your neighbour's star polygon from their instructions.

Repeat, changing m.

Repeat, changing n.

Back Bearings

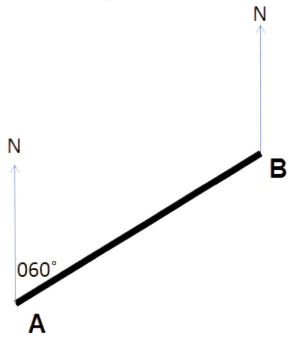

The bearing of B from A is 060 degrees.

What is the back bearing – the bearing of A from B?

If I give you any bearing (or combination of bearings) can you predict the bearing to get me back?

Angle Chasing in Circles

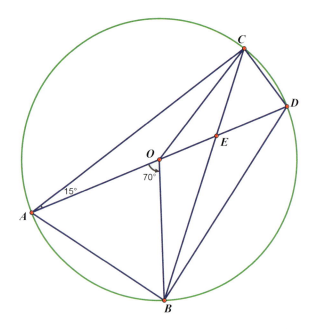

Choose 4 points on the circumference of a circle.

Join them in a diagram like this (AD is a diameter).

Measure (or estimate) two of the angles (as above) and try to deduce the rest.

What circle theorems are available in this image?

What if you measure different angles?

Angle Chasing Tangents

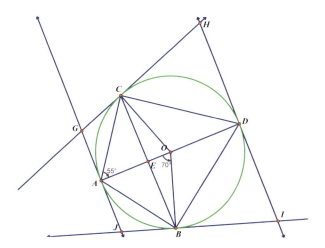

Choose 4 points on the circumference of a circle.

Join them in a diagram like this (AD is a diameter).

Measure (or estimate) two of the angles and try to deduce the rest.

What circle theorems are available in this image?

What if you measure different angles?

Minimum Measuring

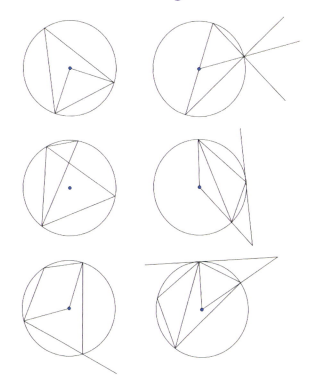

Measure the least number of angles so that you can calculate all the remaining angles. Mark the measured angles in one colour and the calculated ones in another colour.

(Resource – P89)

Pythagoras

Hypotenuse

The longest side of a right-angled triangle is 25cm.

Find possible values for the other two sides.

Plot these values on a pair of axes.

Pythagoras on Dotty Paper

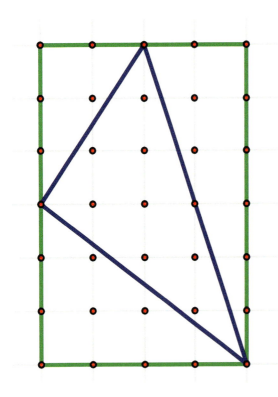

Join any three points to make a triangle, ABC.

Find some right-angled triangles which will help you work out the length of each side of ABC. Calculate the perimeter of the triangle.

Find a quadrilateral which has a perimeter as close as possible to your triangle.

Repeat for other triangles.

Four Towns

Four towns are positioned at corners of a square.

A road network is to be built made of straight lines so that it is possible to go from one town to any other town.

You are allowed to go through a third town on the way.

Find the shortest road network so that it is possible to go from any one town to any other (either directly or through a third town).

River Crossing

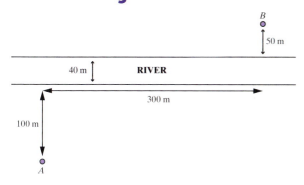

You are at A and need to get to B in the diagram below. In doing so you have to cross the river. the rules are that when you cross the river you must travel straight across, perpendicular to the bank of the river. Where should you cross the river in order to take the shortest route?

Barry and Mouldy

Barry Trotter sits in the centre of a square swimming pool whilst Mouldemort stands at one corner. Mouldemort can run round the square pool three times faster than Barry Trotter can swim.

Which direction should Barry swim in to escape Mouldemort?

(From Derek Ball at ATM conference ~2012)

Perimeters on Geoboards

How many lengths are possible on a 3×3 geoboard?

Use surds to write the lengths exactly.

Draw a shape and calculate the perimeter.

Swap perimeters with your partner.

Try to find a shape that fits their perimeter.

How many new lengths are there on a 4×4 geoboard?

How many on a 5×5? 6×6? ...

Draw a shape and calculate its perimeter.

Swap perimeters with your partner.

Try to find a shape that fits their perimeter.

Trigonometry

Four Forty Five - Trigonometry

Find all the right-angled triangles where two of the following three facts are true:

Has a side of 4cm

Has an angle of 40°

Has a side of 5cm

Put them in order from smallest perimeter to largest perimeter.

Which of these triangles has the perimeter closest to the mean perimeter of all the triangles?

Put them in order from smallest area to largest area.

Three Digit Trig

Choose three digits

Find all the right-angled triangles where one of the sides is ☐cm and an angle is ☐☐°.

Find the perimeter of each triangle.

Which of these triangles has the perimeter closest to the mean perimeter of all the triangles?

Put them in order from smallest perimeter to largest perimeter.

Put them in order from smallest area to largest area.

Try other digits or four digits so one side is ☐cm and an angle is ☐☐°.

Trigonometry – Dotty Paper

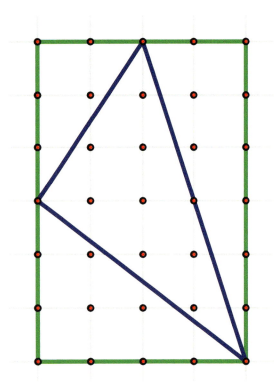

Join any three points to make a triangle, ABC.

Find some right-angled triangles which will help you work out the internal angles of ABC.

Find a triangle which has, as close as possible, one angle which is twice one of the other angles of ABC.

Repeat for other triangles.

Sine and Cosine Rule – Dotty Paper

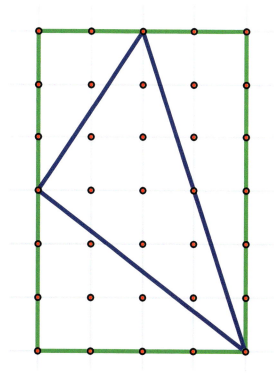

Join any three points on centimetre dotty paper to make a triangle.

Calculate the length of the sides.

Use the Cosine and Sine rules to find all the angles.

Check by measuring.

Swap the three angles and one of the side lengths (don't say which one!) with your partner.

Try to find your partner's other side lengths.

Construction Cosine Rule

On plain paper, construct some triangles with integer side lengths between 5cm and 9cm.

Use the cosine rule to calculate the angles of the triangles.

(You could use a combination of sine & cosine rule)

Check by measuring.

Swap the three angles and one of the side lengths (don't say which one!) with your partner.

Try to find your partner's other side lengths.

How many different possible triangles are there?

Trigonometry

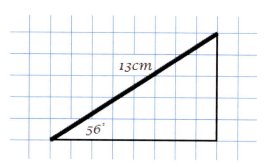

Choose an angle, choose a hypotenuse.

Draw it on squared paper. Calculate the missing sides and angle.

Check by measuring.

Give the angle and one of the shorter sides to your partner.

The challenge is to work out the other sides and angles.

Trigonometric Snooker

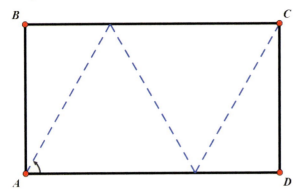

This special snooker table has pockets at corners and dimensions 2.4m by 1m.

A ball is hit from pocket **A** at an angle so that it bounces as shown in the blue path above and ends up in pocket **C**. What is the angle from side **AD** that the ball was hit at?

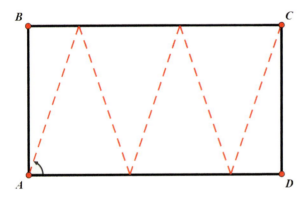

On the above red path, the ball ends up in pocket **C** after four bounces.

What is the angle now?

Find other ways of hitting the ball into pocket **C**.

What angles are needed?

The two paths below show other ways of hitting the ball into different pockets.

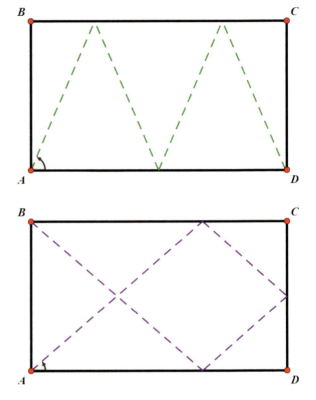

What angles are needed here?

Investigate the angles needed for other ways of hitting the ball into different pockets.

Change the side lengths of the snooker table and investigate the angles needed to pot the balls.

Finding Angles on Geoboards

How many angles are possible on a 3×3 geoboard?

What are they?

How about a 4×4 geoboard?

How many on a 5×5? 6×6? ...

Towers

There are four towers, each are 2m wide. The heights of the towers are 11m, 7m, 3m and 1m. I have five ladders, each have a fixed length of 15m. If I start at ground level, where should I place each tower so that I get the maximum horizontal distance from start to finish? What about the least horizontal distance?

Choose four different heights for the towers, keeping the ladders 15m in length. How should you arrange them now and what is the maximum and minimum horizontal distance now?

Can you generalise for any four heights for the towers?

Isometric Drawing, Plans and Elevations

Draw a cube.

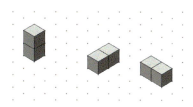

If you join two cubes together you can draw them differently though they are still the same.

If you join three cubes and draw them there are two possibilities.

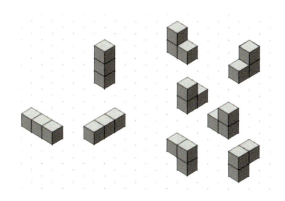

Draw at least one view of each type on isometric paper.

How many possibilities are there with 4 cubes?

Make each one and draw it on isometric paper.

When you're convinced that you have found them all, try five cubes.

Make the Solid

You will need a partner. You will each need six linking cubes and squared paper.

You both need to do the following: without showing your partner make a solid with the cubes, for example:-

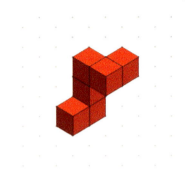

Then on squared paper draw a plan, front and side elevation of your solid and pass this to your partner, for example:-

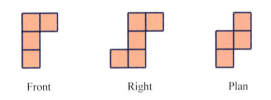

Front   Right   Plan

Your partner should try to make your solid from this information.

Nets of a Cube

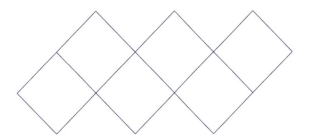

This is a net for a cube.

How many different nets can you make for a cube?

Make each one and test it by trying to fold it up into a cube.

Polyominoes

There is only one 'different' way to join two squares edge to edge.
This is the domino.

There are two triominoes, and five tetrominoes (the tetris pieces).

How many ways of joining 5 squares edge to edge (pentominoes)?
Which ones can be folded into an open cube?

How many ways hexominoes are there?
Which ones can be folded into a cube?

There is a neat way of using an ordinary dice to check.
Place the dice on a square of your net. Make a note of the value on top of the dice.

'Roll' the dice over each fold line of the cube until each face has been covered, making a note of the dice value each time.

If each digit only appears once then it is the net of cube (try to think about why).

What about the possible nets of a tetrahedron?

What about other platonic solids?

Can the Solid be Made?

Choose 3 cards from the 5 cards below.

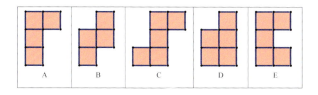

Supposing Card A is chosen as the plan, Card B as the front elevation and Card C as the (right) side elevation. Does the solid exist?

If so, make it with multi-link and draw it on isometric dotty paper.

If not, make a note in your book of which cards were the plan, front and side elevation and that it could not be made. Keeping the same three cards, swap two of them, so that, for example, the card which was the front elevation becomes the plan and vice versa. Try to make the solid now. Is it the same situation as before?

Swap another two round and repeat.

Choose a different set of three cards and repeat.

There are 10 different ways of choosing 3 cards from the 5 above. Try to make solids from all 10 possibilities. Then compare with others to see if you agree which combinations cannot make a solid.

Vectors

Vector Pictures

Draw a picture using straight lines on squared paper. You must draw your picture without taking your pen off the page and without going over any line twice.

Write each line segment as a vector in the order that you drew them.

Swap vectors with your partner and see if you can recreate each other's picture.

Vector Hexagon

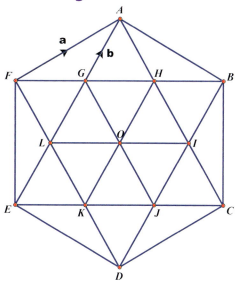

Choose two letters, say **A** and **B**. Find the vector **AB** in terms of **a** and **b**. Repeat for other pairs of points.

Swap with a partner just the vectors (not saying which points are involved).

You have to find an example of which pairs of letters each vector would represent (as a movement from one letter to the other).

Choose three letters on a straight line, e.g. **F,G** and **B**. Work out every combination of two of the three letters as vectors in terms of **a** and **b**.

i.e. $\overrightarrow{BF}, \overrightarrow{BG}, \overrightarrow{FB}, \overrightarrow{FG}, \overrightarrow{GB}, \overrightarrow{GF}$.

Swap two of the vectors with your

neighbour. Use them to prove that the three points are in a straight line.

Do we Meet?

A game for four players, two teams of two players.

Team A has two players; one writes, the other draws. No-one speaks!

Team B has two players; one writes, the other draws.

Mark two points, A and B on a square grid.

Before starting Team B secretly decide a transformation rule; such as rotate 90 degrees anti-clockwise, or reflect in a vertical mirror line, etc. For the example below, rotation of 90 degrees anti-clockwise has been chosen.

Team A will be moving from point A by a series of vectors. Team B will be following Team A's move according to their secret rule.

The challenge is for Team A to make Team B meet up with them at the same place on the grid.

Team A starts by the writer writing on the paper a vector, for example $\begin{pmatrix} 2 \\ -3 \end{pmatrix}$.

The drawer draws that vector from the point A. Neither of them are allowed to talk to one another but they have to signal that they agree that what is drawn is the same vector as what was written down.

Team B now plays by the writer writing down the vector which is the transformation of Team A's vector according to their secret rule: $\begin{pmatrix} 3 \\ 2 \end{pmatrix}$ (which is the 90-degree anti-clockwise rotation of $\begin{pmatrix} 2 \\ -3 \end{pmatrix}$). The drawer has to draw that vector from point B. Without talking, the team have to signal to each other that this is the correct vector according to their chosen secret rule.

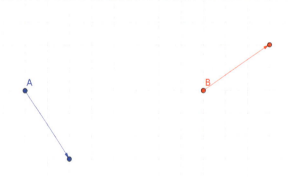

Team A now continue to move from their present position on the grid in the same way by the writer writing down the next vector, say $\begin{pmatrix} 4 \\ 2 \end{pmatrix}$; the drawer drawing that vector on the grid from their current position.

Team B must copy Team As move according to their secret rule by the writer writing down the next vector (in this case it must be $\begin{pmatrix} -2 \\ 4 \end{pmatrix}$ according

to the secret rule); the drawer drawing that vector on the grid from their current position.

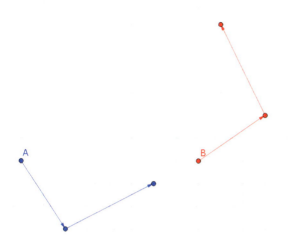

Since the two teams have not met up yet, the game continues.

The next move in this example has Team A moving $\begin{pmatrix} -4 \\ 4 \end{pmatrix}$ and Team B moving by $\begin{pmatrix} -4 \\ -4 \end{pmatrix}$ according to their secret rule.

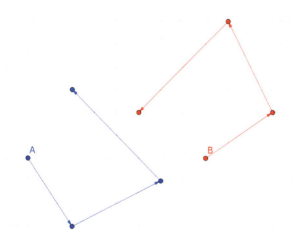

Again, they have still not met up. This time Team A decides to move $\begin{pmatrix} 2 \\ 1 \end{pmatrix}$ and Team B must move $\begin{pmatrix} -1 \\ 2 \end{pmatrix}$ according to their secret

rule and so Team A have forced Team B to meet up with them.

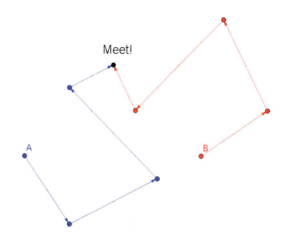

Carry out this game with team B either choosing the same or a different transformation rule.

Explore:

Is it always possible for Team A to force Team B to meet up with them?

If you play several games with the same rule, try to meet up in different places.

When you do meet up, look at the final drawings and try to describe accurately in mathematical transformation language what the picture looks like.

What are the Vectors?

Two points, P and R, are positioned on a grid as below.

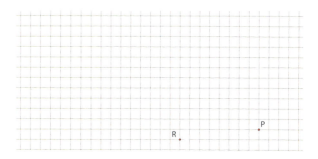

Given that OP is 5**a** + 3**b** and OR is

4**a** + **b** (where O is the origin). Where is the origin and what are the vectors **a** and **b**?

Can you find more than one solution?

Point S is added to the grid as below and OS is vector 2**a** + 3**b**. Where is the origin now and what are the vectors **a** and **b**?

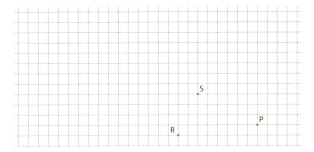

Draw P and R in two new positions on a new grid. Throw a die twice to decide the values of m and n for the vector OP (m**a** + n**b**). Do the same again to decide the vector OR. Find a place where the origin can be and draw in the vectors **a** and **b**. Can you always make the origin on a point on the grid and also make the vectors involve whole numbers of units on the grid horizontally and vertically?

Repeat and see whether you can develop some strategies.

Probability

Bag of Sweets

This is a game for two players.

There is a bag containing two types of sweets.

The first person randomly picks out one sweet and the second person then picks out another sweet.

If the two sweets selected are the same the first person wins both sweets; if they are different then the second person wins the sweets.

How many of each type of sweet should be in the bag in order to make the game fair?

What possible total numbers of sweets could be in the bag for this to work?

What if the first person was to have a 60% chance of winning?

What about other probabilities?

Odds and Evens Game

This is a game for two players.

You will need a set of numbered counters in a bag.

One person selects one at random and then a second person selects one at random.

If the sum of the numbers is even then the first person wins; if the sum is odd then the second person wins.

How many counters and what numbers are on the counters in order to make it a fair game?

Probability Fraction Cards 1

You will need two sets of counters, say red and blue.

You need a pot and these fraction cards: *(Resource – P90)*

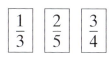

Shuffle the cards, place face down and turn over the top card.

Put some counters of each colour into a pot so that the probability of picking out one particular colour from the pot would be that fraction.

Turn over the next card and add in further counters so that the probability of picking the same colour as before changes to the new fraction.

Keep turning over the cards and adding in counters to reach the target probability.

Shuffle and repeat.

What is the minimum number of counters you would need to do this?

What is the maximum number of counters you would need to do this?

What happens if you have other fractions as the target probabilities?

Probability Fraction Cards 2

You will need a pot, counters in three different colours and these cards: *(Resource – P90)*

$\frac{1}{3}$	$\frac{2}{5}$	$\frac{3}{4}$	$\frac{1}{6}$	$\frac{5}{8}$	$\frac{3}{5}$
$\frac{7}{15}$	$\frac{3}{10}$	$\frac{1}{2}$	$\frac{4}{7}$	$\frac{5}{9}$	$\frac{3}{20}$

Shuffle the cards; place face down and turn over the top two cards.

Try to put the counters into the pot so that the probability of picking out one colour is the first fraction and the probability of picking out another colour counter is the second fraction.

Is it possible to do this?

If it is not, then try to explain why and then turn over a new pair of cards.

Repeat the process.

What do you notice?

What if you turn over three cards and use three colours?

Statistics

Averages and Spread

Averages and Spread

You can use as many threes and as many sevens as you like.

Can you find a combination of threes and sevens so that the mean is each whole number between 3 and 7?

Can you find a combination of threes and sevens so that the mean is each one decimal place number between 3 and 7? (3.1, 3.2, 3.3, …)

Choose *any* number between 3 and 7 with as many decimal places as you like and try to find a set of threes and sevens that give this target.

Change the three and the seven for different numbers

Find a way of making each whole number in between.

Give a convincing reason why you can make the mean take any value between your two numbers.

(Based upon http://nrich.maths.org/6345)

Inter-Quartile Range

Choose three digits from 1-9

Set the lowest as the lower quartile, the middle value as the median, and the highest as the upper quartile

Give 11 positive integers that fit this and draw the box plot.

How many solutions are possible?

Five Positive Integers - Averages

Give a set of 5 positive whole numbers with a mean of 5…

…and another… and another…

Give a set of 5 positive whole numbers with a mean of 4…

Give a set of 5 positive whole numbers with a mode of 3…

Give a set of 5 positive whole numbers with a mean of 4 *and* a mode of 3

Give a set of 5 positive whole numbers with a mean of 4, a mode of 3 *and* a median of 3.

Find all possible sets that satisfy these conditions. How do you know you have them all?

What happens for different means, medians and modes?

Is there a time when this is impossible?

What if mean = median = mode?

Rolling a Six

Roll a dice until you get a six.

Record how many rolls it takes,

When you have ten sixes, work out the average number of rolls it took each time.

Calculate the mean, median and mode.

Repeat ten more times so you've now rolled 20 sixes.

Calculate the mean, median and mode number of rolls it took each time.

Try to explain what will happen in the long run and anything surprising you notice.

Box Plots and Inter-Quartile Range

For each pair of boxplots create a set of data comprising 12 numbers that give boxplots similar to those given.

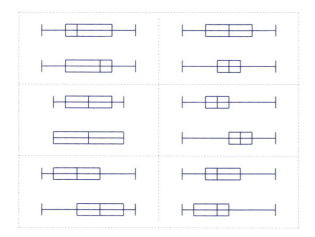

Mean Squares

Each number in the middle of a row or column is the mean of the numbers on either side of it. *(Resource – P91)*

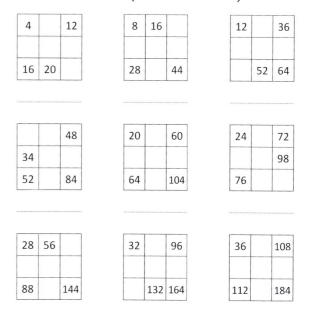

Find the average of the nine numbers in each square. Find the average of all the numbers in all the squares.

A set of five (or six) numbers

Here is a set of five values:

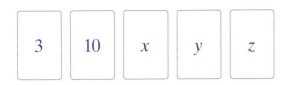

Where:
- x is the mean
- y is the mode
- z is the median

... of the set of all five numbers.

Find the values of x, y and z given that they are all whole numbers.

How many solutions can you find?

Here is a set of six numbers:

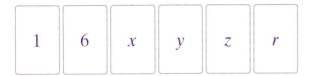

Where:
- x is the mean
- y is the mode
- z is the median
- r is the range

... of the set of all six numbers.

Find the values of x, y, z and r given that these are also all whole numbers...

How many solutions can you find?

Find whole number values for A and B so that you can find solutions for both:

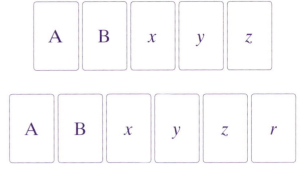

where A and B remain the same numbers across both challenges but x, y, z and r can take different values across the two challenges.

Charts and Diagrams

Making up Pie Charts

Make up a data set and construct the corresponding pie chart that would show the fraction $\frac{3}{4}$.

Construct pie charts to show every fraction with denominators from 1 to n.

6 is a good number, there are 12 fractions and you need 7 pie charts.

$$1, \frac{1}{2}, \frac{1}{3}, \frac{2}{3}, \frac{1}{4}, \frac{3}{4}, \frac{1}{5}, \frac{2}{5}, \frac{3}{5}, \frac{4}{5}, \frac{1}{6}, \frac{5}{6},$$

Pie Chart Equations

I asked the boys in a class what their favourite meal of the day was, Breakfast, Lunch or Dinner.

I drew a pie chart of the results:

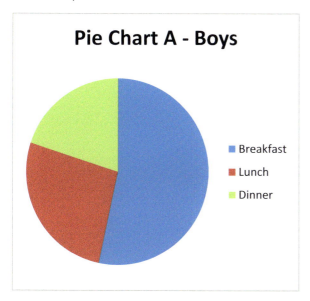

I then asked the girls in a class what their favourite meal of the day was, Breakfast, Lunch or Dinner.

I drew a pie chart of the results:

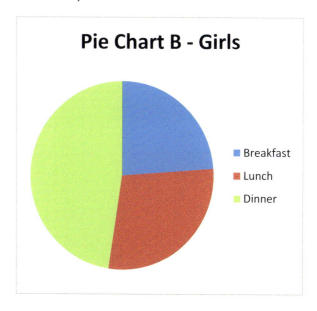

When I added all the data together I got this Pie Chart:

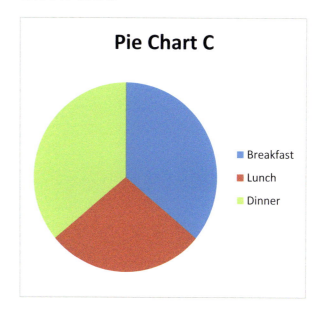

Pie Chart A + Pie Chart B = Pie Chart C

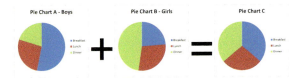

Create a set of data that would fit this Pie Chart equation.

Create a set of data to fit this Pie Chart equation where the amount of boys is different to the amount of girls.

Create a set of data to fit this Pie Chart equation where the amount of boys is the same as the amount of girls.

Create data and a pie chart equation

Swap your pie chart equation with your partner

Try to create a data set to fit their pie chart equation.

Investigate: Box Plot Equations, Cumulative Frequency Table equations or Cumulative Frequency Curve Equations

References

Bills, C., Bills, L., Watson, A. & Mason, J. (2004). *Thinkers: A collection of activities to provoke mathematical thinking.* Derby, UK: Association of Teachers of Mathematics.

Boaler, J. (2009) *The Elephant in the Classroom: helping children Learn and Love Maths.* London: Souvenir Press.

Brown, L., Hewitt, D. and Tahta, D. (Eds.) (1989). *A Gattegno anthology.* Derby: Association of Teachers of Mathematics.

Department for Education (2013) *Mathematics programmes of study: key stage 3* [online]. Available from: www.gov.uk/government/uploads/system/uploads/attachment_data/file/239058/SECONDARY_national_curriculum_-_Mathematics.pdf [Accessed 15/04/2015]

Foster, C. (2012), *Mathematics in School*, 41(3), pp. 30-32.

Francome, T. (2014) *Experiences of teaching and Learning Mathematics in Setted and Mixed Settings*, MRes Thesis. University of Birmingham. Available at: http://etheses.bham.ac.uk/5601/ [Accessed 24/11/2016]

Hewitt, D. (1994). *The Principle of Economy in the Learning and Teaching of Mathematics*. Unpublished PhD dissertation, Open University.

Kordemsky, B. A. (1992). *The Moscow puzzles: 359 mathematical recreations*. Courier Corporation.

Mason, J. (1987). What Do Symbols Represent? In C. Janvier (Ed.), *Problems of representation in the teaching and learning of mathematics*, New Jersey USA: Lawrence Erlbaum Associates, pp. 73-82.

Meyer, D. March 2010. *Math class needs a makeover* [Video file] March, Retrieved from http://www.ted.com/talks/lang/en/dan_meyer_math_curriculum_makeover.html [Accessed 9th March 2017].

Prestage, S., & Perks, P. (2001). *Adapting and extending secondary mathematics activities: New tasks for old*. Oxford: David Fulton.

Pritchard, C. (2013) Generalizing complementary regions, *Mathematics in School*, 42(2), pp. 11-13

Stewart, I. (2010). *Professor Stewart's hoard of mathematical treasures*. London: Profile Books.

Swan, M. (2006) *Collaborative Learning In Mathematics: A Challenge to our Beliefs and Practices*. London: NRDC

Tahta, D. (1981). Some thoughts arising from the new Nicolet films. *Mathematics Teaching* 94, pp. 25-29.

Wittmann, E.Ch. and Müller, G.N. (1990/92), *Handbuch produktiver Rechenübungen*, Vols. 1 and 2, Klett, Düsseldorf und Stuttgart.

1	2	3	4	5	6	7	8	9	10
11	12	13	14	15	16	17	18	19	20

1	2	3	4	5	6	7	8	9	10
11	12	13	14	15	16	17	18	19	20

1	2	3	4	5	6	7	8	9	10
11	12	13	14	15	16	17	18	19	20

6	1
7	2
8	3
9	4
.	5

	Calculation	Your estimate	Exact answer	Difference
1				
2				
3				
4				
5				
6				
7				
8				
9				
10				
			Total 'error'	

	Calculation	Your estimate	Exact answer	Difference
1	32 × 47			
2	64 × 37			
3	23 × 672			
4	415 × 79			
5	703 × 48			
6	3078 × 18			
7	38 × 4008			
8	473 × 193			
9	206 × 953			
10	817 × 477			
			Total 'error'	

$$x + 2$$

$$3x + 1$$

$$2x$$

$$x$$

$$x - 4$$

$$3x$$

$$x + 5$$

$$5 - x$$

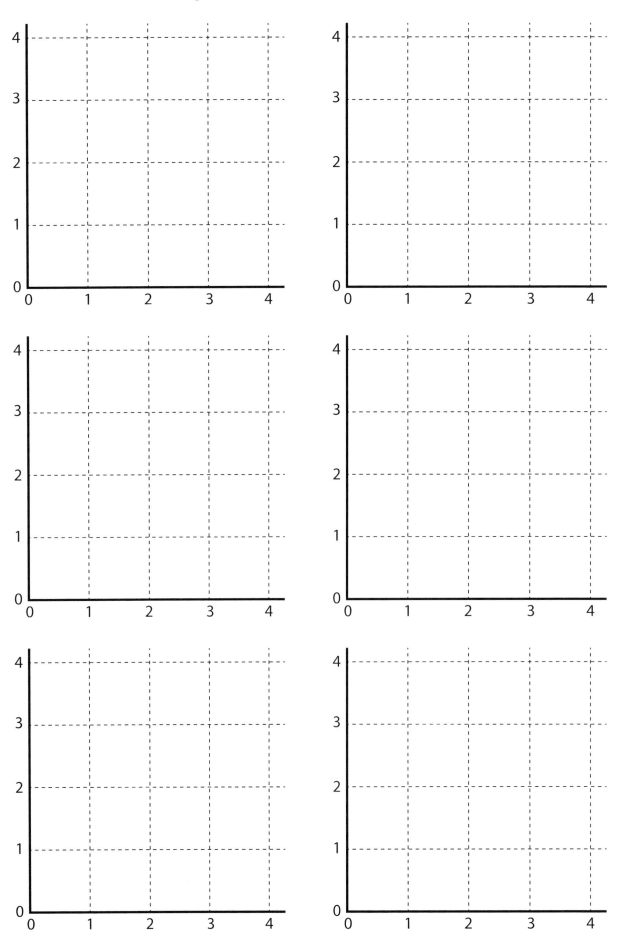

Perimeter	Dimensions of rectangle (whole numbers only)		Area

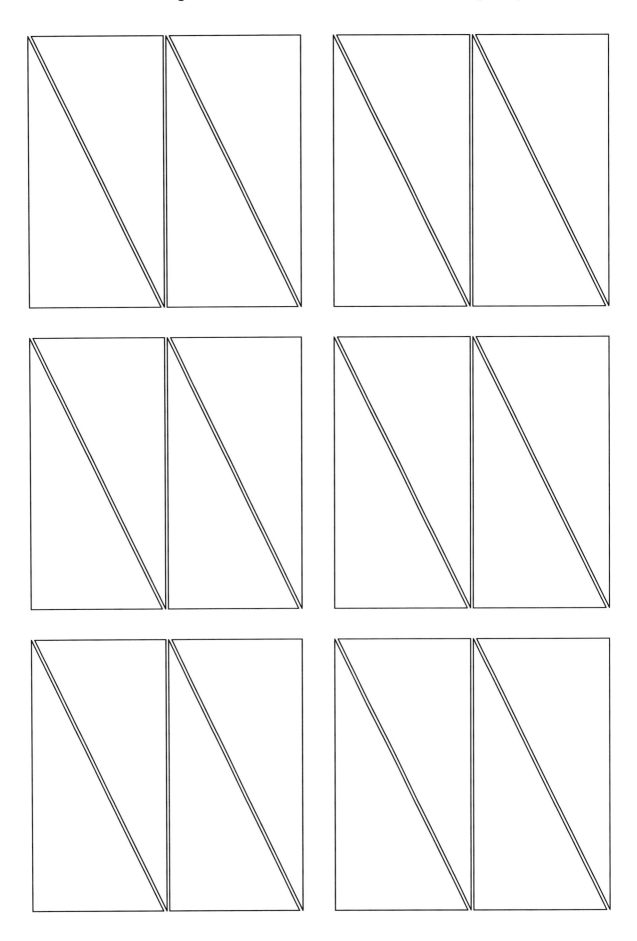

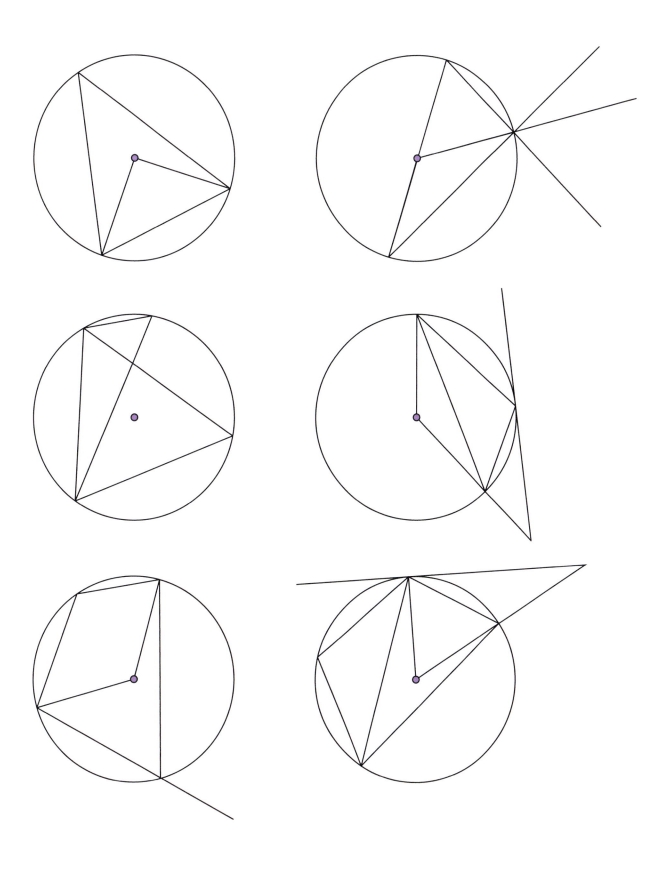

$\dfrac{1}{3}$	$\dfrac{1}{6}$
$\dfrac{2}{5}$	$\dfrac{5}{8}$
$\dfrac{3}{4}$	$\dfrac{3}{5}$
$\dfrac{1}{2}$	$\dfrac{5}{9}$
$\dfrac{4}{7}$	$\dfrac{3}{10}$
$\dfrac{7}{15}$	$\dfrac{3}{20}$

4		12
16	20	

8	16	
28		44

12		36
	52	64

		48
34		
52		84

20		60
64		104

24		74
		98
76		

28	56	
88		144

32		96
	132	164

36		108
112		184

Practising Mathematics

Tom Francome and Dave Hewitt

Published September 2017

Association of Teachers of Mathematics

2A Vernon Street Vernon House Derby DE1 1FR

©2017 Association of Teachers of Mathematics

Printed in England

ISBN 978-1-912185-00-9

Further copies of this book may be purchased from the above address

www.atm.org.uk

Woodlands

The Conservation Volunteers is the UK's leading practical conservation charity. We connect people with place, build healthy, sustainable communities, and increase people's life skills. We aim to create a better environment where people from all cultures feel valued, included and involved. The Conservation Volunteers support thousands of volunteers each year taking hands-on action to improve their urban and rural environments. Our Community Network supports local groups. We offer regular conservation tasks, UK and International Conservation Holidays, the Green Gym®, training opportunities and an on-line shop making products and services accessible to all. For information about any of these opportunities, please contact us at the address below.

Other titles in the
Practical Handbook series:

Dry Stone Walling

Fencing

Footpaths

Hedging

Sand Dunes

Tool Care

The Urban Handbook

Tree Planting & Aftercare

Waterways & Wetlands

To order any of these publications,
please contact:

The Conservation Volunteers,
Sedum House, Mallard Way,
Doncaster DN4 8DB
Tel: 01302 388883

www.tcv.org.uk

Woodlands

a practical handbook

Elizabeth Agate

ACKNOWLEDGEMENTS

From production of the first edition of *Woodlands* in 1980, to this third edition, the author would like to thank all the individuals and organisations who have contributed their advice and experience. With particular thanks to George Darwall for contributing the section on hurdle making in this edition (pages 124-130).

NOTE: In April 2012, BTCV changed its name to The Conservation Volunteers. References to BTCV in the text of this publication refer to the organisation now known as The Conservation Volunteers

DISCLAIMER: The information given in this publication on behalf of The Conservation Volunteers is believed to be correct, but accuracy is not guaranteed and the information does not obviate the need to make further enquiries as appropriate. This publication is not a comprehensive statement on all safety procedures and the reader must take all reasonable steps to ensure the health and safety of all users and to take all necessary steps to implement a health and safety policy. This publication is issued without responsibility on the part of The Conservation Volunteers for accidents or damage as a result of its use.

ISBN   0   946752   33   8

Written by Elizabeth Agate

Illustrated by Linda Francis

First published 1980

Third edition 2002

Appendices revised June 2005. Cover redesigned and current references to BTCV in the text changed to The Conservation Volunteers 2012

Typeset in Palatino and Franklin Gothic

Printed by Severnprint Ltd (ISO 14001), Gloucester, with vegetable oil inks on recycled paper by presses powered by renewable ©ecotricity

Published by The Conservation Volunteers, Sedum House, Mallard Way, Doncaster DN4 8DB Telephone: 01302 388883 Registered Charity, England 261009, Scotland SC039302

Contents

Introduction

This is a handbook of woodland management, designed for use by conservation volunteers and others interested in the management of traditional British woodlands, the creation of new woods and the management of associated habitats.

The natural woodland cover of Britain was already mainly cleared for agriculture 1,000 years ago, as recorded in the Domesday Book. From prehistoric times, management of woodland was essential to man's survival, with archaeological evidence showing that Neolithic peoples were skilled in coppicing and using woodland produce.

The wildlife and landscape value of nearly all Britain's remaining woodlands is dependent on this interaction between people and natural processes. The traditional management of ancient coppiced woodlands, wood pastures and areas such as the New Forest has been vital in creating and maintaining their special qualities.

Many of the traditional skills in coppicing, pollarding, green woodworking and charcoal burning are still relevant today for woodland management, and in recent years there has been an upsurge of interest in these skills both amongst volunteers and professional woodworkers, with new products and markets being developed.

Along with the traditional management of existing woodlands, there is great interest in the planting of new native woodlands, both in rural and urban fringe landscapes. Regeneration of former industrial and other areas through the creation of wooded landscapes are focussed in the National Forest and the Community Forests in England, with similar regeneration schemes elsewhere in the UK. The benefits of trees and woodlands on the health and well-being of local communities are widely recognised.

The Woodlands handbook was first published in 1980, revised in 1988, and has now been revised again to provide information on traditional woodland management skills that is relevant for today's use. The handbook is one of a series of ten handbooks on practical conservation published by The Conservation Volunteers.

Elizabeth Agate
Knitson, Corfe Castle, 2002

1 A brief history of woodlands in Britain

For the last million years the climate of Britain has been arctic, interrupted with brief warm periods or interglacials of thousands of years, one of which we are part way through. The history of British woodland since the last glaciation is, in geological time, extremely brief, and is inextricably linked with the development of civilization. To quote Oliver Rackham in *Trees and Woodland in the British Landscape* (1990), 'the gulf of time which separates us from the end of the last glaciation is only about six times as great as that between us and Julius Caesar'.

Table 1a on pages 8 and 9 summarises the changes in British woodland since the last glaciation.

Wildwood

At the height of the last glaciation (100,000 – 12,000 BC), most of Britain would have been bare of trees. Birch and willow scrub possibly persisted along the lower margins of the ice, with pine in places. Relicts of pre-glacial flora may have survived in sheltered bays along the western coasts of Great Britain and Ireland, but elsewhere as far as the south of England, ice swept the land clean.

The development of Britain's post-glacial flora can be deduced from studies of pollen and seed deposits in peat, and by means of radiocarbon dating. Tundra and moorland followed the retreating ice, and then waves of colonisation by different tree species spread from the south. The first were birch, aspen and sallow, and then about 8500 BC pine and hazel spread north, replacing birch which became uncommon for several thousand years. Oak and alder followed the pine, then lime, elm, holly, ash, beech, hornbeam and maple in succession spread northwards. The earliest trees were those of arctic conditions; the later trees were those of warmer climates. The earliest trees spread the furthest north, with alder reaching Ireland shortly before it was cut off as sea levels rose. The later species were slower to move north and to become abundant, as there was no vacant ground to colonise. Beech and lime did not spread beyond southern Britain.

From the time lime arrived, in about 7300, to about 4500 BC there was a period of relative climatic stability called the Atlantic Period, during which the various species settled to form a series of wildwood or wilderness types, as shown in the diagram. The tree line was much higher than now, as shown by the remains of trees found in present-day moorland. The tree line varied across the country. The far north of Scotland was treeless to sea level, but in the eastern Highlands may have been as high as 915m (3,000ft). In the North York Moors tree remains have been found at 360m (1150ft), but parts of Dartmoor at 610m (2,000ft) have apparently always been treeless. The only natural grassland was probably small areas on high mountains, or on exposed maritime cliffs.

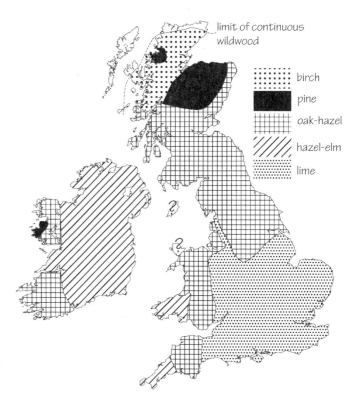

limit of continuous wildwood

birch
pine
oak-hazel
hazel-elm
lime

What did the wilderness or wildwood look like, before man starting interfering with it? A recent theory is that the wilderness in Western Europe was a mosaic of grassland, scrub, individual trees and groups or groves of trees (Vera, F.W.M, 2000). It was not a closed, impenetrable wildwood, but was a park-like landscape, maintained by the grazing and browsing of wild herbivores. This may have been true in Britain during earlier interglacials, when the great beasts of the Palaeolithic era required large areas of grassland. Pollen records show that a wide range of grassland plants persisted in the last interglacial. However, since the last glaciation, the bison, elk and other large herbivores which persisted on mainland Europe were extinct in Britain, so Vera's theory may not apply so well to Britain.

However, the persistence of oak in Britain throughout the period since its spread northwards after the last glaciation may be an indication that the wildwood was not continuous. Oak is a pioneer species, which requires open ground in which to regenerate (p.14). It requires grazing animals to maintain open areas, and regenerates in the thorny scrub which protects it from browsing. Archaeological evidence shows that red deer, which are grazers of grass as well as browsers of trees, were a mainstay of the Mesolithic economy in Britain, being used for their meat, skins, antlers and bones. Aurochs or wild cattle, which were present in Britain until the Bronze Age, were specialised grass eaters, and required grassland not closed forest.

Woodland clearance and management

At the end of the Mesolithic era there is evidence of the beginnings of agriculture. The sudden decline of elm around 4,000 BC, which occurred throughout Europe, is thought to be not due to clearance, but to elm disease. There was an increase in agricultural weeds, such as plantain and stinging nettle, together with archaeological evidence of Neolithic settlement. In some areas, such as East Anglia, the chalklands and the Somerset Levels, population increased dramatically, and virtually all the wildwood was cleared.

Clearance increased during the Bronze Age (2400-750BC) to its probable height in the early Iron Age. Oliver Rackham (1990) estimates that about half of England had ceased to be wildwood by 500BC.

Much of the remaining woods were managed by coppicing. Neolithic man had discovered that the regrowth from a stump is more useful than the original tree. During the Iron Age, the Celtic peoples developed woodworking to a fine art, as shown by remains of houses, boats, wheels and other artefacts. The management of woodland by coppicing was hugely important for about the next two millennia, producing material for buildings, roads, fences, carts, and the fuel for heating, cooking, metalworking and pottery. Coppicing is discussed further in the next section.

Since Roman times there has been a sharp distinction between wooded and non-wooded areas of Britain. The *Domesday Book* (1086) is evidence that every wood in England belonged to some person or some community, and had an economic value. Many woods were 'exclaves' owned by communities some miles away. The fact that it was worth transporting the woodland produce over some distance indicates their value, and that ownership had been established long previously.

In 1086 only about 15% of England was woodland or wood-pasture, 35% was arable, 30% pasture, 1% hay meadow and the remaining 20% was mountain, moor, heath, fen or urban land. The Domesday landscape was more like modern day France than the untamed woodland of folklore. Nearly all woods were highly managed, as coppices or wood-pastures.

The nearest natural remnants of woodlands are those on inaccessible steep slopes. These fragments can teach us about the persistence of vestigial forest under extreme conditions, but they cannot reveal widespread or characteristic features of the ancient natural woodland.

The produce of English woodlands was mainly underwood for fuel and other uses, with small oaks used for domestic building. Typical medieval timber-framed houses were built mainly of oaks less than 18" diameter. Large timbers were in short supply, and were reserved for the great ecclesiastical buildings. The builders of Ely Cathedral in the 13th century had to use smaller roof timbers than planned, and the pine poles for the scaffolding were imported from Norway. Thin oak boards or wainscot for domestic building were imported from Central Europe.

Even from its low proportion of 15% in 1086, woodland cover shrank further to 10% by 1350, due to population increase. The Black Death of 1349 brought this to a sudden stop, and any woods surviving in 1350 had a good chance of surviving the next 500 years.

Throughout history, nearly all clearance of woodland has been for agriculture. Industry tended to sustain woodland rather than destroy it. Up until the industrial revolution, industries relied on coppice woodland for fuel. To quote Rackham (1990), 'the survival of almost any large tract of woodland suggests that there has been an industry to protect it against the claims of farmers'. Such areas included The Weald, the coastal fringes of the Lake District, the Forest of Dean and the Merthyr and Ebbw Valleys. It was the agricultural areas of East Anglia, the Midlands, lowland Scotland and elsewhere where woodlands almost completely disappeared.

Coppicing

From earliest times in Britain, woodland needs were fulfilled not by the felling of new areas of wildwood, but by the periodic harvesting of managed coppice plots. Coppicing allowed the natural deciduous woodland to survive, in modified form, because of its exploitation for fuel, building wood and other purposes. The wide-held belief that woodlands were cleared for charcoal, fuelwood for brick and lime kilns and for tanbark is erroneous. In fact, these demands sustained the coppice woodlands, and it was with their demise that clearance increased.

'Coppice' comes from the French word couper, to cut. Coppices or 'copses' are woodlands cut on a fairly short rotation of five to thirty years. In most cases, one part of the wood, called a 'coupe', is harvested each year. The coppice trees and their produce are known as 'underwood'. Underwood species, which are all deciduous, respond to cutting by sending up multiple stems from the stools. Periodic cutting greatly extends the life of most trees, so that coppiced stools may be many hundreds of years old.

The practice of coppicing can be traced back to Neolithic times (4500 BC). Neolithic wattle trackways in the Somerset Levels are evidence of sophisticated coppicing systems which produced rods of exactly the same size. Archaeological evidence shows that coppice products were used for numerous rural needs throughout the Bronze, Roman and Saxon periods. It's estimated that 23,000 acres of coppice were required to provide charcoal for the Roman military ironworks in the Weald (Rackham, O, 1986). Coppicing remained the most widespread method of woodland management until the mid 1800s. The reason for its importance over such a long period was that it allowed the woodland crop to be harvested and converted with simple hand tools. Large, mature trees are difficult to cut, transport and convert, whereas coppice growth is of a size which is easy to handle.

One year regrowth of hazel coppice

The long history of coppicing is the reason why ancient coppice woodlands can be seen as the direct descendants of the original wildwood. It is perhaps a paradox that a coppiced wood, with a structure which looks least like one's idea of the ancient natural forest, is biologically closest to it. It is unlikely that trees were planted for coppicing, or that any particular selection of species was made. Even in the late 18th century, it is recorded that 'the underwood was not carefully selected and planted; the production of it, both in quantity and quality was, for the most part left to chance' (Peterken, 1981). In some places coppices were 'improved' through encouraging the valuable species by layering, planting and natural regeneration, to fill any gaps where old stools died. Unwanted shrubs and invasive species such as birch were sometimes removed to favour the desirable species. However, the general pattern of species remained very close to the natural cover. Planting only became commonplace from the late 18th to the late 19th centuries, and then again in the period after World War II.

The system of 'coppice with standards' is also ancient, with records of felling dating from the 1200s. Under this system, some trees are grown as standards over a longer rotation, with the coppice beneath cropped at more frequent intervals. The coppice or underwood suppressed the lower side branches of the standard trees, so encouraging the growth of tall, unbranched trunks. During the reign of Henry VIII, there was a legal requirement that at least 12 standards per acre (30 per hectare) be grown, but at other times numbers varied greatly, according to the demand. Periods of felling occurred during time of war, as well as after the Dissolution and during the Commonwealth.

The words 'timber' and 'wood' have historically described different woodland products. Timber referred to the large beams and planks cut from standard trees, used for large buildings and other structures. Wood referred to anything less than 2 foot in girth (7" or 18cm diameter), and included coppice poles, pollard poles or the branches of large trees felled for timber. The coppice with standards system provided both timber and wood, and in a single plot the timber and wood often belonged to different people. Historically, wood was generally the more valued crop. From both the timber and wood crop, nothing was wasted, with branches, bark, '*loppium et choppium*', twigs and even leaves having a use.

Oak was by far the most abundant standard tree, although other species such as ash were occasionally allowed free growth. Every soil type and region had characteristic combinations of coppice species. These included hazel and ash on the Midland clays, beech and sessile oak on western sandstone, and lime in central Lincolnshire. Hornbeam and sweet chestnut, a Roman introduction, grew widely in the south east, while local or minor underwood species included whitebeam, wild cherry, crab apple, maple and elm. Some underwood species were particularly suited to specialised uses, and there was some selection in favour of these, but most coppice remained mixed, to serve a variety of needs.

In the uplands, sessile oak was by far the most common species and dominated both the underwood and canopy of the coppiced woodland. Where conditions were difficult, standards grew too slowly and erratically to be worth fostering, so 'scrub oak' coppice without standards developed. Much of this was used for tanbark or charcoal.

From the late 18th century, coppicing began to decline. One reason for this was the trend towards growing more standard trees for the production of timber, and the fashion for new plantations (p6). Many landowners greatly increased the density of oak in their coppice woods through supplementary planting, although much of this was never harvested. In the Chilterns, coppice working as well as wood-pasture management declined due to the planting of beech for the furniture industry. From the mid 19th century, some of the most important traditional uses of coppice products diminished as coke and coal replaced charcoal and firewood for fuel, and artificial substitutes replaced tanbark in the leather industry. In addition, the general agricultural decline of the mid and late 19th century meant that less hazel was needed for sheep hurdles and other farm products. However, many coppiced woods continued in use, and apart from a lengthened rotation, many coppices were much the same at the beginning of the 20th century as they had been a thousand years earlier.

Active commercial coppicing survived throughout the 20th century, mainly in the sweet chestnut coppices of Kent and East Anglia, with the main outlet being the fencing industry. In the last decade or so there has been a revival of coppicing, especially of hazel, in Hampshire and other southern counties, and of oak in the North West. This is partly due to the realisation of the importance of coppicing in maintaining traditional woodlands, and partly due to coppice workers developing new markets and products. These include faggots for bank stabilisation, barbecue charcoal, greenwood furniture, yurts, garden ornaments and many other products. The demand from coppice workers for good quality coppice in many areas now exceeds the supply.

Wood-pastures

A recent theory (Vera, F.W.M, 2000) suggests that wood-pasture is the closest type of landscape to that which existed in prehistory (see p1). Pollen records show that oak and hazel, which require open conditions to regenerate, were continuous throughout prehistory. According to Rackham (1986), 'wood-pasture is well documented in England for the last 1200 years, but these written records probably only tell the last one fifth of the story that began in the Neolithic Age'.

Natural wooded, grazed, landscapes became managed wood-pastures with the domestication of stock. With limited winter fodder, numbers of stock were kept at a level which could survive through the winter. In winter, when growth stagnates, browsing and grazing is at its most damaging, but in spring and summer, when there is too much to eat, some is left ungrazed and unbrowsed. This not only allowed the survival of seedling trees, but meant that grasses, herbaceous plants and annuals would flower, as in a hay meadow. In turn this supported invertebrates, leading to the diversity of species of plants and animals which are typical of mosaic landscapes with trees, scrub and grassland.

The Domesday Book (1086) recognised *silva pastilis* or wood-pasture, as opposed to *silva minuta* or underwood/coppice. Old records list regulations about fruit, felling for timber, and cutting of foliage for fodder, but there is no regulation on regeneration, presumably because it happened naturally. Vegetative or coppice regrowth had to be protected from livestock, but protection of seedling trees was not required, as sufficient grew up protected in thorny scrub. Thorns and holly were considered so important for the regeneration of trees that a statute dating from 1768 laid down a punishment for damaging thorns and holly in the New Forest (Rackham, 1980). Palatable species such as ash, elm and hazel tended to decline under grazing, whereas species such as oak, beech and hornbeam, which are less palatable and better able to withstand browsing , tended to survive.

Domesday records that nearly all woodland which was not coppice was some type of wood-pasture. Most were communal, with rights to grazing, fuel, fencing wood, timber, and other products long since apportioned. Pannage, the right to feed swine on acorns, was less important in Britain than on the continent, as the acorn crop in Britain is less reliable. Some wood-pastures were later enclosed as parks (see below).

Trees intermixed with pasture had a number of advantages. Trees provided shade and shelter for livestock. Their branches could be pollarded at 2.3m (6-10') above ground level, out of reach of grazing animals, to provide winter fodder or to produce many of the same woodland products as coppice underwood. Sometimes the trees were left to grow up for timber, or even 'shredded' by repeatedly cutting off the side branches, leaving a tuft at the top, a practice still seen in parts of France.

Pollarding, like coppicing, reinvigorates many species of broadleaved tree and prolongs their lives. Even when pollarding ceases, these trees are likely to live on despite retrenchment, when branches die back to remain as 'stag's heads'. Many surviving pollards are 300-500 years old. These veteran trees, worthless from the point of view of timber production, are important for the habitats they provide for lichens, bryophytes, the specialised invertebrates of dead or dying wood, and for hole-nesting birds (p17).

Compared to the rest of Europe, Britain retains a large number of wood-pastures with ancient trees.

WOODED COMMONS

On the wooded commons, which were a feature of lowland Britain, the trees themselves were often owned by the lord of the manor, but commoners had the right to cut pollard poles for fuel or feed. Grazing was carefully regulated, with commoners allowed to graze a certain number of animals. Wooded commons had disappeared in many areas by the 13th century. Many had been taken over by private landowners and cleared for cultivation, and others had been enclosed as private parks. Where grazing was unregulated, either over-grazing resulted in treeless commons, or under-grazing allowed tree cover to spread. Commons have characteristic straggling outlines, because they comprise land which it was no one person's duty to fence. Houses tend to front the common, with their private land to the back.

PARKS

Parks or policies, as they are known in Scotland, are enclosures for semi-wild animals. They came into vogue under the Normans to contain herds of fallow deer, an introduced species. There were also parks for red deer, semi-wild white cattle, hares and swine. The Domesday Book (1086) records 35 parks in England, a number which Rackham (1990) estimates grew to a maximum of about 3,200 by 1300, covering nearly 2% of England, and enclosing about a quarter of the woodland of England.

Medieval parks usually had a characteristic compact outline with rounded corners to save fencing costs. Often they contained both woods and pastures, but unless they were protected the former tended to turn into the latter, from the effects of grazing and browsing. After a decline in the late middle ages, there was a revival under Henry VIII, who created at least 7 parks, the largest of which, Hampton Court Chase, enclosed 4,000 hectares (10,000 acres) of land and 4 villages. Some of those parks which remained through to the 17th and 18th centuries were remodelled by the great landscape designers. Many old trees were retained, valued for the air of antiquity which they gave to the landscape. There are about 100 parks

still in use in England, mostly for fallow deer.

WINTER-GRAZED WOODLANDS

Winter-grazed woodlands are typical of parts of the upland North and West. These are woods where domestic stock are enclosed, or where sheep and deer are allowed free access from the adjacent uplands during the winter months. In many areas the seasonal migration from the open moor to sheltered woodland was essential to the grazing economy.

Forests

Nowadays the word 'forest' is usually taken to mean a large, densely wooded area. The association of the Forestry Commission with plantations of conifers has helped equate 'forest' with dense, mainly coniferous woodland. However, the word Forest, as in the New Forest, Forest of Dean, Sherwood Forest and others described an area that was subjected by the king to special law, called Forest Law, concerned with game and hunting. Forests were not necessarily wooded, and many comprised large areas of heath and moorland. A Forest was a place of deer, not of trees (Rackham, O, 1986).

William the Conqueror introduced the system of Forest Law, which had long been operating in Europe. By Domesday (1086) there were about 25 Forests, and the number grew until by the time of King John (1199-1216) there were 143 Forests in England. Although the hunting of deer and other game was important, the operation of the Law and the revenue gathering which accompanied it was the main reason for the Forests' existence. A corrupt bureaucracy developed, and the tension caused between the king and the nobility led to the curtailment of the king's power under Magna Carta (1215), after which no more Forests were created in England.

The location of Forests was related partly to existing Crown lands and palaces, which needed provisions of deer and game for feasting and entertaining. Forests were mainly on heath and moorland soils which were not suitable for cultivation. The most wooded areas of England, such as the Weald and the Chilterns, had few Forests. The total area of Forest in England was about one million acres, or 3% of the land area, but less than half was wood-pasture. The Crown did not have a dominant interest, as Forests included commons with pre-existing common rights, and most of the grazing and woodcutting was done by the landowners and commoners.

Similar systems developed in Wales and Scotland, with over 100 Forests created in Wales and about 150 in Scotland. The Forest system slowly declined in England, with many subject to Enclosure Acts, which turned them over to commercial forestry or low-grade agriculture.

In Wales and Scotland the Forests lasted much longer than in England, with some operating in Scotland until modern times.

Many of these ancient Forests keep their names, but as an institution, only the New Forest survives, with its courts, verderers and other traditions. Many Forests retain important areas of wood-pasture, heathland, moorland and other valuable habitats. Some of the ancient trees of Windsor Forest still exist in what is now Windsor Great Park, and the New Forest contains an exceptional number of ancient trees.

The planting of woodland

There is a long history of planting orchard and garden trees, grown for their crops, for shelter and shade, and for ornament. The ancient Greeks and Romans were knowledgeable at growing, transplanting and tending trees. Trees were valued, and were not only transplanted from nearby woodland, but were collected and traded over great distances.

For their fruit, the Romans introduced to Britain the cultivated apple, the black mulberry, the fig, the sweet chestnut, the common walnut and the medlar. Laurel, cypress and myrtle were brought to Britain for garden planting, and the native box, holly and ivy were also used for hedges and topiary.

Throughout the middle ages, planting of garden and orchard trees continued. *The Domesday Book* (1086) lists many large and small gardens, and by the mid 12th century, the wealthy citizens of London had quite large gardens adjoining their houses. The greatest gardens were those attached to the monasteries, with large orchards of fruit and nut trees.

Hedges also have a long history, and archaeological and literary evidence suggests that hedges were in use in Roman Britain. It's not known though whether these were planted, whether they were relics of woodland plants managed to form hedges, or whether they grew up protected from grazing by dead hedges (*Hedging*, BTCV, 1998).

There may have been some transplanting of trees in managed coppices during the middle ages, to fill gaps and maintain the coppice crop. The high value of the coppice crop also meant that some new coppices were planted. The coppice with standards system (p3) probably included the transplanting of young trees, to give a reasonably even coverage of standard trees. As early as the 13th century, trees were being planted in parks and hedgerows. There are records of some planting of small areas of woodland in the middle ages. However, the first major planting of native trees was not so much for their wood or timber, but for their beauty. Extensive

planting of avenues, clumps and plantations by wealthy landowners was common by the 1500s.

It was not until the 1600s that the idea of planting for timber took hold. This was partly influenced by the publication in 1664 of *Sylva, A Discourse of Forest Trees*, by John Evelyn, a diarist, statesman, gardener and arboriculturist. This advocated the planting of trees for timber, and influenced many landowners, including King Charles II, to make extensive new plantations. Evelyn believed, wrongly, that the woods were in serious decline due to being cut down for the iron industry, shipbuilding and other purposes. He failed to recognise that it was the iron industry and other uses that sustained the woodlands, and that the cutting down of native broadleaved trees does not destroy them. To quote Rackham (1990) on *Sylva*, 'much of the misinformation about trees that is still current today can be traced back to it'.

The plantings made pre-1600 were coppices, following the pattern of existing woods by sowing and planting a mixture of local species, and are difficult to distinguish from other woodland. Evelyn encouraged the planting of only one or two species, often conifers or exotic species, with the intention of producing particular timber crops.

The 'plantation movement' was very active in Scotland and Ireland, where the area of plantations overtook the area of native woodland cover during the 18th century. In Ireland planting was ordered by statute.

Beech was widely planted throughout Britain during the 18th and 19th centuries. At various times there were fashions for planting wych-elm, hornbeam, larch, and in the 20th century, Scots pine, hybrid poplar and lodgepole pine. Rackham (1990) notes that often the markets for which these species were chosen had disappeared by the time the trees matured, or with the passing of time, their purpose was forgotten.

The 20th century

The plantation movement did little to offset Britain's growing reliance on overseas supplies, or the decline in management of traditional woods. By the beginning of the 20th century about 90% of all timber and forest products were imported. The bulk of this trade was softwoods from Scandinavia and North America, with tropical hardwoods also important. The strategic danger of this situation became obvious in the First World War (1914-1918), when enemy action prevented imports getting through. Over the four years, about 180,000 hectares (450,000 acres) were felled to meet the demands.

The establishment of the Forestry Commission in 1919 aimed to ensure that the near disastrous shortage of wartime timber would never occur again. By 1939 the

Commission had established 230 forests on about 265,000 hectares (655,000 acres) of land, with 145,000 hectares (359,000 acres) actually planted up. These forests were of fast-growing timber, mainly conifers, planted close together to get the maximum amount of timber per acre. Large even-aged blocks of single species or simple mixtures of straight line planting were often thrown across the landscape with little regard for variations in terrain or local features.

By the time of the Second World War (1939-1945), the Commission forests were still too young to provide much timber, and about 212,000 hectares (524,000 acres) of private woodland were felled to meet the demand.

However, felled woods, left to their own devices, regrow. Much more damaging to the remaining semi-natural woodlands of Britain were the agricultural and forestry policies which were followed after World War II. Rackham (1990) estimates that nearly half of the remaining ancient woodlands of England, Wales and Scotland were seriously damaged or destroyed in the period 1945-75. In that 30 years there was more damage and destruction than in the previous 1000 years. The biggest losses were to agriculture and to forestry, with housing, roads and industry using only small amounts. After the food shortages of World War II there was a perceived need to maximise food production by bulldozing woodlands and hedgerows, destroying them so they could not regrow. Agricultural grants were directed at the clearance of woodlands and hedgerows in order to maximise production. At the same time, improved varieties of agricultural crops were increasing yields to such an extent that these clearances were in fact unnecessary. Many semi-natural woodlands were cut down and replanted with conifers, for timber production. The damage here has turned out to be less severe than might be expected. In many woods the planted conifers failed to thrive, and the deciduous species grew back and are now once more dominating these woodlands.

During the last decade of the 20th century there was a great change in Forestry Commission policy. The UK commitment to biodiversity following the Rio Earth Summit (1992) has resulted in Biodiversity Action Plans being drawn up by government conservation and forestry agencies and other organisations, which include commitments to conserve and extend semi-natural woodland (p34). The publication by the Forestry Commission of their Practice Guides *The Management of Semi-Natural Woodlands* (1994) signalled the great change in policy and practice. The importance of using local provenance planting stock is now accepted (p49). Grants are given towards encouraging natural regeneration (p42). Ancient woodlands which were planted with conifers are now categorised as Plantations on Ancient Woodland Sites, and advice is directed at their restoration. Management and felling of the maturing plantations continues, but the way forward is by managing woodlands through continuous cover systems (p41), coppicing, and other systems which maintain traditional woodland cover. The importance of veteran trees is now recognised (p149).

Grants are directed at tree and hedgerow planting and management, creation of ponds and other habitats, in a direct reversal of the post-war policies. Those who have farmed throughout this period have been given grants to clear and destroy, and then grants to plant, create and restore.

Chapter 1 continued overleaf...

Table 1a: TIMELINE OF WOODLAND CHANGES IN BRITAIN SINCE 10,000 BC

PERIOD	YEAR	WOODLAND CHANGE
Last glaciation	c. 100,000 – 12,000 BC	
Post-glacial / present interglacial	c. 12,000 BC onwards	
Palaeolithic	to c. 10,000 BC	
Mesolithic	c. 10,000 – 4,500 BC	Trees spread north in the following order: birch, aspen, sallow, pine, hazel, alder, oak, lime, elm, holly, ash, beech, hornbeam, maple. Climate stabilises, and 'climax woodland types' develop (map p1). Grassland rare. Tree line higher than present day. Britain becomes an island c. 5,500 BC. Elk, aurochs (wild cattle) and red deer widespread
Neolithic	4,500 – 2,000 BC	Neolithic settlers arrive c. 4,000 BC, bringing crops, animals and weeds, shown by sudden reappearance of grasses, cereals and grassland herbs in pollen records. Sudden loss of elm due to elm disease. Stonehenge (2,800 BC) and other monuments suggest unobstructed horizons and large areas of open land. Hurdle-making and other evidence of extensive coppicing from c. 3,000 BC. Round-houses are evidence of sophisticated woodmanship. Formation of heaths with podzols due to woodland clearance on light, acid soils. Formation of peat and moorland in high rainfall areas, partly due to wildwood clearance, and partly due to climate change.
Bronze Age	2,400 – 750 BC	Aurochs probably became extinct. Area of heath extends. Moorland areas are abandoned as peat layers deepen.
Iron Age (in England)	750 BC – AD 40	By 500 BC, probably half of England had ceased to be wildwood.
Roman (in England)	AD 40 – 410	Extensive coppicing to supply fuel for domestic use, ironworking, corn-drying and other uses. Great demand for timber for buildings, bridges and ships. Sweet chestnut introduced.

Period	Dates	Description
Dark Ages (in England)	AD 410 – 700	Little evidence of spread of secondary woodland.
Anglo-Saxon (in England)	AD 410 – 1066	Anglo-Saxon charters (600-1080) are evidence of primarily a pastoral and arable landscape in England. Woods have names and boundaries, and were owned and managed, mostly as wood-pasture. Wild beavers become extinct.
Middle Ages	AD 1066 – 1536	*Domesday Book* 1086. Woodland and wood-pasture comprise 15% of England. Wood-pastures enclosed as parks for fallow deer (3,200 parks in England by 1300). Underwood rotations very short. Financial returns from underwood were greater per acre than from arable land. Clearance continues, to leave only 10% woodland cover by 1350. Timber for building imported from Norway, Baltic and Central Europe. Land shortage pushes cultivation back up onto the moors. Forests, for deer, mainly on heath and moor, are declared (25 at Domesday, reaching maximum of 143 in England by Magna Carta in 1215.) Black Death in 1349 causes halt in population growth. Woods present then remained until 1800s. Secondary woodland spread on unused agricultural land. Rabbits and fallow deer introduced in early 1100s. Rabbits confined in warrens until late 1700s. Wild swine rare by 1200s. Wolves extinct in England in 1396. Red deer survive in moorland.
Post-medieval	AD 1536 onwards	Importance of oak bark for tanning 1780-1850, from oak coppices. Trees spread on heathland with the decline of heathland cropping. Woodland cover in England in 1870 is below 5%. Conifers, sycamore, rhododendron and other exotics planted in existing woods. Coppicing declined sharply as other fuels became available. Many heathlands planted with conifers. Destruction of ancient woods for agriculture and conifer plantations mainly from 1945. Forestry Commission Inventory 2001 records England's woodland cover at 8.4%, of which 60% is broadleaved. Estimate of 1.3 billion trees. Oak is most common tree.

2 Woodland flora and fauna

The woodland ecosystem

STRUCTURE

The complex structure of semi-natural broadleaved woodland offers a great diversity of habitats in which plants and animals can live. Like other aspects of the woodland environment, structural features change over time. One of the main aims of woodland management for conservation is to create, maintain or restore structural diversity where it has been lost or where, without management, it would decline.

Four layers are recognised in the woodland structure: the tree canopy, shrub layer, field layer and ground layer. The importance of the underground layer should not be forgotten (see p12).

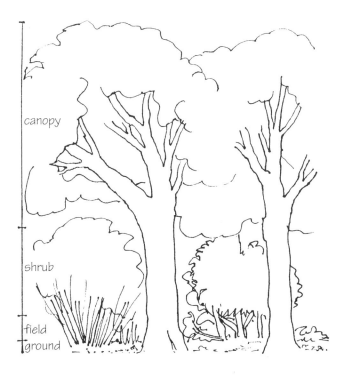

Further layering may develop where the dominant canopy trees are overtopped by occasional emergent trees, or where they grow in the company of somewhat lower understorey trees. The field layer may develop two sub-divisions: a layer of tall herbs and undershrubs, and a layer of low herbs. Trees of the canopy and shrub layer may consist of plants of a single species, but of different ages and sizes, or they may be of different species which reach varying heights when mature. In a mixed wood, typical emergent species may include elm or beech, with oak or ash as dominants and crab apple, wild cherry, holly, rowan or field maple forming the understorey. This shrub layer may include hazel, hawthorn or blackthorn. Bracken (*Pteridium aqualinum*), rose-bay willow-herb (*Epilogium angustifolium*) and bramble (*Rubus* spp) may form a tall herb layer with bluebells (*Endymion non-scripta*), dog's mercury (*Mercuralis perennis*), ramsons (*Allium ursinum*) and smaller ferns among the low herbs. The ground layer consists of mosses and liverworts, plus the seedlings of the plants of the taller layers. Where the woods are coppiced, the lower layers are likely to include coppiced shoots of the canopy species.

Not all woods have all these layers, and none would be likely to have them throughout. Some canopy species, such as ash, let in quite a lot of light so that full layering can develop. Others, such as beech, cast a heavy shade so that the shrub and field layers are largely absent except where there are breaks in the canopy. Plantations usually show little diversity within stands. A well-stocked oak plantation is unlikely to contain much besides sparse brambles and a ground layer of mosses. Conifer plantations are dense and dark and most have little other than fungi from the time the canopy closes over until the first heavy thinning. Wood pastures usually lack the shrub layer and higher field layer, due to grazing, while in scrublands the shrub layer forms a canopy in the absence of taller woodland trees.

Woodland plants are adapted to the structural conditions. For example, yew and holly are typical trees of the understorey, as being evergreen, they are able to compensate for the dense shade of summer by growing at other times of year. Dark leaves, such as holly and ivy, also contain a relatively large amount of chlorophyll, so they are able to use low light levels efficiently. Holly and yew are amongst the few trees which can regenerate in dense shade. Many of the species in the tree and shrub layers produce flowers before they come into leaf, as being wind-dispersed, the seeds need to ripen before the unfolding leaves shelter them from the wind. The plants of the field layer have to grow and flower early, before the canopy closes over them. Annual plants, that must germinate and complete their cycle within one growing season are at a disadvantage, and hence are poorly represented in woodlands. Most of the field layer plants are perennials, with bulbs, corms, tubers or rhizomes to give a rapid early start in spring.

Lateral structure is also important for diversity. Where woods are allowed to develop unhindered, some canopy trees eventually die and create gaps, where seedlings of canopy, shrub or field layer can spring up. Coppiced woods are often especially diverse because at any given time they are likely to contain some coupes which have recently been cut over, some where the coppice has created a dense shrub layer, and others where the coppice has matured into an understorey with standards as canopy dominants.

For some forms of wildlife, these relatively short-lived openings in the canopy are less important than longer-lasting glades, margins, lawns and rides. Such sheltered, humid but well-lit areas are much richer in species of epiphytes and invertebrates than either shaded woodland or open-ground habitats. It seems likely that they occurred frequently in the primaeval woodland, maintained under natural conditions by heavy grazing and browsing. In this respect, relatively open wood pastures may retain more similarity to the original forests that do dense plantations, or ungrazed, unmanaged woods.

However, the maintenance of shelter within a woodland is of great importance, providing a microclimate that is moist, sheltered and shaded, with smaller temperature fluctuations than those that occur outside the wood. Many woodland species, including flowering plants, mosses, ferns, liverworts and invertebrates have limited ability to disperse, and can be lost by changes in the woodland cover that are too drastic.

Topography may also influence lateral structure. For example, in those Scottish pinewoods which grow on irregular moraine topography, pines occur mainly on the moraine ridges with more open cover in the hollows between. Even small changes in topography and in soils can affect the distribution of tree species, with accompanying differences in layering.

Within a woodland, various associated features provide many additional habitats, especially for fungi and invertebrate animals which are often restricted to these situations. The most important of these from a management viewpoint include large and old trees, decaying wood, streams and ponds, and climbing plants. Important microhabitats include flowers and fruits, fungi, carrion, dung and nests.

One of the most important parts of the woodland structure is the part you can't see. Beneath the soil surface is a complex ecosystem of roots, fungi and soil micro-organisms. Tree roots are often surprisingly shallow, with the most important feeding roots occurring in the top 30cm (1ft) or so of soil. The roots may spread out beyond the outer edge of the canopy, so damage at some distance from a tree may have adverse effects.

Amongst the most important organisms in the soil are a type of fungi called mycorrhiza, which forms a symbiotic relationship with roots of trees, shrubs and other flowering plants. Mycorrhiza occur in nearly all plant communities, and it's estimated that 90% of the world's plant species depend on a mycorrhizal association. Mycorrhiza fungi form highly branched, interconnected networks that invade the roots of plants in order to obtain a supply of carbohydrate. In return, the mycorrhiza converts organic nitrogen to inorganic nitrogen, supplies phosphate to the host plant, and may also confer some degree of pest, disease or drought resistance. For many plants the nutrient and water uptake is mainly by way of mycorrhiza, and not directly through the roots. It's estimated that the fungal network extends the volume of soils that plant roots can exploit for water and nutrients by a factor of 12 to 15. Mycorrhizal threads are more efficient than plant roots at nutrient uptake, as they are finer and more active.

In woodlands, the ability of mycorrhiza to make nutrients available to the trees, shrubs and other woodland plants is vital for the self-renewing fertility of the wood. Mycorrhizal associations are partly the reason why natural regenerated tree seedlings in soils with mycorrhiza already present tend to thrive. A seedling transplanted into a cultivated soil or disturbed soil, where there is little mycorrhizal activity, will struggle.

Some species of mycorrhiza will only associate with particular plant species. Others will associate with various plant species, though possibly with little benefit to the host. 'Easy to grow', tolerant plant species such as ash, cherry, alder, willow and sycamore can form associations with a range of species. At the other end of the spectrum, many orchids are totally dependent on a particular mycorrhizal association, without which the seed cannot even germinate. This accounts for the rarity of orchids, their ability to thrive in particular places and not in others, and why transplanting leads to failure. With other plants, a particular mix of mycorrhiza may be needed.

Mycorrhiza are very fragile, and are easily damaged by cultivation. Being symbiotic, they need their host plants to survive, so the removal of woodland above is also the destruction of all the mycorrhizal associations below. This is why it is so difficult to create a woodland ecosystem simply by planting or seeding, and why it is so important to protect remaining areas of woodland and woodland soils.

Mycorrhiza can be artificially added to the nursery soil or at planting, or inoculated into the ground around existing trees or other plants (p51). However, with the huge range of mycorrhizal species and the complexity of their associations, inoculation with a few of the generalist species is likely to be a pale imitation of the natural situation.

COMMUNITIES

Woodlands, wood pastures and other wooded areas support a huge range of organisms. The National Vegetation Classification describes 19 major types of woodland, with their distinctive mixtures of trees and shrubs, and associated flora of flowering plants, ferns, mosses, liverworts and lichens (p39). The biodiversity of woodlands is recognised in the Biodiversity Action Plans (p34).

Semi-natural broadleaved woods may contain many of the 60 or so native species of trees and shrubs, as well as a wide variety of flowering plants and ferns, with even small woods containing 20 or more species, and large diverse woods supporting over 200 species. A diversity of plant species in turn supports a variety of insects, birds and other fauna. Some tree species, notably oak, willow, birch and hawthorn are outstanding in the fauna they support, with blackthorn, aspen, elm, hazel, beech and Scots pine also being important.

The bark of trees also provides a habitat for epiphytes, which are non-parasitic plants that grow on other plants. Epiphytes are normally only found on trees within woodland, where the shady, humid atmosphere allows sufficient moisture for them to survive. Mosses, liverworts, algae and lichens may all be found growing as epiphytes, with one higher plant, the fern (*Polypodium vulgare*) also occurring in Britain. Epiphytic growth tends to be much more lush in the moist and mild westerly areas. Lichens only survive in unpolluted air. Lichens and other ephiphytes grow slowly, with the richest communities found on the oldest trees of stable, undisturbed woodland, making an assemblage of great conservation interest.

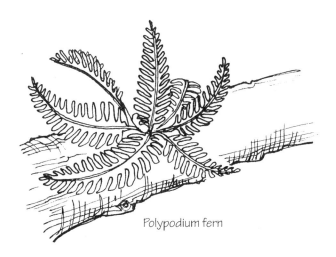
Polypodium fern

The table below lists the total number of taxa of epiphytic lichens recorded from some trees and shrubs in Britain. 'Taxa' includes species, sub-species and ecologically distinct varieties.

Table 2a: EPIPHYTIC LICHEN

Tree or shrub	Number of taxa
Oak, pedunculate and sessile	324
Ash	255
Beech	206
Elm spp	187
Sycamore	183
Hazel	160
Willow spp	160
Scots pine	132
Birch, hairy and silver	126
Rowan	125
Alder	105
Holly	96
Field maple	93
Lime spp	83
Hornbeam	44

SUCCESSION

Woodlands, like all communities of living things, are dynamic. Sometimes they change so slowly that little seems to happen in a human lifetime. At other times, as when a felled wood is left to regenerate or a grassy area is allowed to grow up to scrub, the changes are noticeable within a few years. It is important to take account of this dynamic aspect of woodland ecology when managing woodlands, since to ignore it may make management difficult, frustrating and ultimately unsuccessful. Where woodland succession is understood, it can be accounted for, and if necessary, manipulated.

'Natural succession' is the process by which one community of organisms gives way to another, in a series from coloniser to climax. To give an idealised example, bare land is first colonised by annual 'weeds', then by grasses and mixed herbaceous meadow species, followed by shrubs and finally by trees, which grow up through the shrubs and largely suppress them. The weeds are the pioneer species, while the forest trees form a 'climax' community which tends to persist indefinitely.

In reality, succession seldom takes place uninterrupted by natural or man-induced agencies such as fire, grazing, felling or drainage. It is also usually much more complex that the picture given above. Certain trees and shrubs may come in immediately, depending on the proximity of parent or 'donor' plants, and on the feeding patterns of birds, which distribute the seeds of many of these species.

Tree species vary in their tolerance of shade and other conditions, and in their ability to regenerate within the woodland. Even without interference by man, woods may change in their species composition with time. 'Tolerant' species are those that can survive and regenerate under the canopy. They tend to be species that live longer, and flower later and more irregularly. They can persist in the understorey as suppressed seedlings, and then quickly take advantage of any increase in light due to canopy loss, for example when mature trees are blown down. Tolerant species are poorly adapted to long distance dispersal, so are not found early in the woodland succession, but tend to be part of the climax community. Species include hornbeam, lime, elm and beech. 'Intolerant' species are those which cannot tolerate shade, and tend to be succeeded by tolerant species. Intolerant species are fast-growing, quick-maturing, short-lived species which produce seed regularly and in quantity. They are pioneers in two ways. Firstly they are opportunistic, and can quickly occupy sites which come available, and secondly, they can persist and reproduce in infertile or difficult sites. Species include alder, willow, pine and birch.

Some species have characteristics of both tolerance and intolerance. Oak is intolerant of shade, but is very long-lived. Holly and yew are tolerant of shade, but are widely dispersed by birds.

The climax community may itself be more dynamic than theory may suggest. Pinewoods regenerate best at their edges, where shading is reduced, and many Scottish pine and birch woods seem naturally to shift their positions over time, unless constrained by climatic and altitudinal limits. In some of these woods, pine also seems to alternate with birch in a relatively stable long-term cycle, depending on which species is better able to regenerate in a given area at a given time.

Oak is a pioneer species and is often present very early in the succession of grassland to scrub, and is not a stable climax woodland species as is often imagined. Oak cannot regenerate under its own canopy or under the canopy of other trees, as there is not sufficient light. Acorns may germinate and seedlings appear, but unless an opening appears in the canopy due to windblow or felling, the seedlings wither away, or are defoliated by tortrix moth caterpillars which fall down from the parent tree above. Oak is dependent on being spread, mainly by jays, which select ripe and fertile acorns in autumn and bury them for food stores. The jays choose sites in long grass and under thorny bushes at the edges of woodland, in bare or waste ground, and in loose soil which is easy to penetrate. The acorns are buried singly. During late winter and through the following spring and summer the jay will return and retrieve some of the acorns, in the later part of the season by tugging at the seedling tree and removing the acorn, but normally without damaging the tree.

Oak is also adapted to withstand browsing and competition from grasses, herbaceous plants and thorns. Its large seed produces a deep taproot which sustains the seedling, and if browsed it can normally regrow.

A young oak tree can remain browsed and small for many years, and then take advantage of any break in browsing to put on a spurt of growth. Oak frequently grows up in the shelter of thorny shrubs including holly, hawthorn, blackthorn and gorse, where it is protected from grazing. There is an old English proverb, that 'the thorn is mother to the oak'. Old oaks are often found growing in close association with holly, which is another long-lived tree.

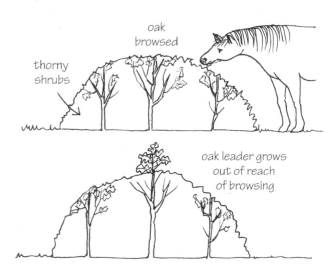

Oak, and other species which cannot regenerate in closed woodland, may therefore be dependent on grazing animals maintaining open areas in which regeneration can take place. In natural conditions, oak would have colonised grazed areas. In managed landscapes, it can colonise cleared ground, waste ground, roadsides and railway embankments. If left unmanaged, oaks eventually get overtaken and suppressed by species such as lime, hornbeam, elm, sycamore or beech, except on poor soils or exposed sites. In western coastal areas oak is the climax vegetation of rocky dells and slopes which have little soil, where other trees cannot survive.

Woodlands with fairly closely spaced oaks are nearly always plantations. Old oaks in woodland with wide spreading branches low on the trunk show by their shape that they grew originally in open ground, and the woodland by which they are now surrounded has grown up since. Oaks were also planted and promoted as the standard trees in 'coppice with standards' (p3).

Other tree species take advantage of holly and other thorny shrubs for protection from browsing. Trees have to become established in holly in the first 20 years or so after the holly starts to grow, or the shade is too dense. The next opportunity does not arise until the holly degenerates, after 2-300 years.

There are many situations where natural woodland succession needs to be managed to benefit wildlife diversity. Trees encroaching on rare and valuable habitats such as heathland, downland, wet grassland, marshes or dunes may need to be kept in check. Another situation where intervention is necessary is where succession favours one species over others which are considered more valuable. Introduced species, notably rhododendron and sycamore, are the most common culprits.

Field and ground flora

The field layer of woodlands consists of plants which are adapted to the conditions of shade, shelter and high humidity. The flowering plants have to seize the opportunity in early spring when rising temperatures allow insect pollination to take place, but before the canopy is in full leaf. Primroses, wood sorrel and wood anemones are amongst the earliest to flower. As the canopy begins to close, there is a second burst of flowering of the more shade tolerant species, with dog's mercury, bluebell, bugle and ground ivy typical of southern lowland oakwoods. In damp northern woods on limestone soils, ramsoms, bellflower and yellow archangel are found. Less common and easily overlooked are several species which are now more associated with gardens, including violets, yellow star-of-Bethlehem, lily-of-the-valley, columbine and monk's hood. Orchids and helleborines are amongst the rarest woodland flowers. Many woodland plants grow from bulbs or rhizomes, storing food during the long periods of shade, and allowing a rapid burst of growth in spring. The woodland field flora of ancient woodlands is very specialised, and cannot be replicated.

The variable conditions of woodland edges, rides and glades allow a much greater range of generally more common plants to flourish. Woodland edge habitats vary from sunny, dry banks to shady, damp ditches, and are affected by grazing, mowing and other management. Plants vary from those that are able to take advantage of recent clearance, to those that are adapted to stable, undisturbed conditions. Large grassy glades and clearings may have a flora more typical of old meadow or pasture, depending on how the clearing is managed.

Ferns are adapted to the damp, shady conditions of the deciduous woodland floor. They die back in winter, the dead fronds protecting the crown, and then in late spring the new fronds uncurl. Typical species include hart's-tongue, male, soft shield and broad buckler fern. The size and appearance of the fronds can vary considerably between different individuals of the same species, and many different varieties of most species have been identified. Some species of ferns can grow in the humus that accumulates on the spreading branches of mature trees, particularly oak, giving an almost tropical appearance to some ancient deciduous woods in the damp mild parts of Britain. Bracken is the most adaptable fern, and can grow not only in woodlands but in pastures and other open areas, where it can become an invasive weed.

Mosses are a primitive type of plant, many species of which are adapted to growing in woodland. They have no true leaves, stems or roots, but instead absorb water and nutrients over their entire surface, and so every moss cell must be within reach of the growing surface to obtain its water supply. Some of the most spectacular mosses are found in very damp places, near springs and upland streams, where the water is rich in oxygen and minerals. Mosses are sensitive to soil acidity and alkalinity, to light and shade, and to moisture conditions. They grow actively when it's cool and damp, and are at their most luxuriant in late winter. In spring they produce their spore capsules, and then gradually wither and die as summer progresses.

Mosses also grow on tree trunks, especially on the shady, lee side of leaning trunks where moisture can accumulate. The water-trapping ability of mosses enables them to grow on rocks and other exposed places, where they can play a significant role in succession, by providing a suitable substrate for seeds of other plants to germinate. Tree trunks are also host to other epiphytic plants, including lichens and liverworts, which absorb their nutrients from the air around them. Lichens are either crustose and pressed to the branch, or foliose, forming festoons of branching, trailing growth. They are particularly abundant in damp, western areas as they require moisture-laden air and are sensitive to pollution. Epiphytes grow most abundantly on fissured bark of old trees, which grows only slowly.

Where wood is decaying there is often a distinctive epiphyte flora due to the nitrogen being exuded from the tree.

Fungi that appear on living trees, decaying branches and on the woodland floor are the visible signs of the complex breakdown process which is an essential part of the woodland ecosystem. The visible toadstool, mushroom or other fruiting body is only a short-lived part of the intricate thread-like mycelium which penetrates wood, leaf litter and soil. Fungi lack the ability to make food, but instead break down living and dead plants into simple substances on which they can feed and grow. There are many hundred species of fungi in Britain that require wood for their survival, and most are host-specific, living on only one species or group of species. Standing trees can become infected by spores which settle on them and develop in damp conditions. Fallen trees and branches are infected by the mycelium that is abundant but invisible in the leaf litter on the woodland floor.

Woodland fauna

'Take care of the habitats and the animals will look after themselves'. This is the best rule where the aim is general wildlife protection. The creation and maintenance of floristic diversity is usually the key to animal conservation, since all animal food webs are based on plants, and because the greater the variety of plant life the better the chance of providing the necessary conditions for most animals.

INVERTEBRATES

Diversity of habitats is the main requirement for invertebrates, as their complex life cycles require a range of conditions. Leaf litter contains vast populations of mites, as well as spiders, ground beetles, woodlice, springtails and other organisms which help initiate the decay of leaves and plant debris.

Woodland edges, glades, rides and dead or dying trees are particularly important for many invertebrates. The management of these features is described in chapter 12. Trees and shrubs vary widely in their importance for invertebrates, with native plants much more valuable on the whole than introduced species. Many adult insects depend on trees and shrubs for food in the form of nectar and pollen. Early flowering species such as willow, and late flowering species such as ivy are especially useful at a time when other food is scarce. Some invertebrates have very restricted distributions, specialised habitat requirements or poor rates of dispersal.

Table 2b, opposite, lists the number of insect species associated with common trees and shrubs in Britain. An asterisk indicates an introduced species.

Woodland butterflies require specific food plants during their larval stage, as listed below.

Table 2b: TREES AND ASSOCIATED INSECT SPECIES

Tree or shrub	Number of insect species
Oak, pedunculate and sessile	284
Willow spp	266
Birch	229
Hawthorn	149
Blackthorn	109
Poplar spp (including aspen)	97
Crab apple	93
Scots pine	91
Alder	90
Elm	82
Hazel	73
Beech	64
Ash	41
Spruce*	37
Lime	31
Hornbeam	28
Rowan	28
Maple	26
Juniper	20
Larch*	17
Fir*	16
Sycamore•	15
Holly	7
Sweet chestnut*	5
Horse chestnut*	4
Yew	4
Walnut*	4
Holm oak*	2
Plane*	1

Table 2c: WOODLAND BUTTERFLIES

Butterfly	Larval food plant	Habitat
Speckled wood	Grasses, esp couch	Woodland
Wall	Grasses	Woodland edges
Scotch argus	Grasses, esp couch, molinia	Upland conifer woods
Ringlet	Grasses	Woodland rides
Pearl-bordered fritillary	Violets	Open woodland
High brown fritillary	Violets	Woodland clearings
Comma	Nettle, willow, elm	Woodland edge
White admiral	Honeysuckle	Woodland
Holly blue	Ivy, holly, buckthorn	Open woodland
Purple hairstreak	Oak	Woodland

Speckled wood laying egg on grass

REPTILES AND AMPHIBIANS

Of Britain's six native species of reptile, three are at home in wood margins and hedgerows, as well as heathlands and commons. These are the common lizard (*Lacerta vivipara*), the adder (*Vipera berus*) and the grass snake (*Natrix natrix*). The common lizard and adder are widespread, while the grass snake is limited to southern and central England and Wales, where it is found mainly in woods and hedgerows near water at low elevations.

Woodland management for reptiles consists mostly of habitat protection and freedom from disturbance. The most important measure is to allow hedgerows, rides, glades and other edge habitats to develop a border of coarse grasses and low shrubs. Where rides and glades are mown, it is worth leaving rough patches or sections for reptiles to bask. On sites where wood and hedge-banks are overgrown, it may be worth cutting them back in places on the south or west sides to let sun reach the ground. Hibernicula can be constructed on suitable sites.

One of the few benefits of rhododendron is that it provides hibernation cover for adders and other reptiles, especially on sandy soils and heathland sites. This should be borne in mind during winter clearance operations, and any known hibernation sites should be left untouched.

The creation of marshy areas and ponds can improve the conditions for grass snakes. Piles of leaves, log stacks or other material which provides undisturbed conditions will provide overwintering sites for reptiles. Loose piles of branches or brash are not particularly valuable for reptiles, because they do not provide the advantage of constant temperature conditions that closer piles do (chapter 12).

Undisturbed and uncleared woodland ponds, with plenty of weed growth and varying depths of water are important for amphibians, especially the great crested newt (chapter 12).

BIRDS

The management of woodland and scrub for birds concentrates on providing suitable breeding habitat, mainly through the management of the woodland edges, glades and open spaces within the woodland. At the same time, it's important to recognise that large blocks of woodland usually contain more species, though at a lower population density, than smaller woodland areas. Management work should be timed to avoid disturbance during the nesting season, which is April to July inclusive for most species. Other measures include providing nest boxes or bunches of branches tied to tree trunks, where existing nest sites for hole and shrub-nesting species are in short supply (chapter 12).

Trees such as oak, which support a large and diverse insect population, supply the most food for insect-eating birds such as tits and tree-creepers. Dense, thorny shrubs are good for nest sites, as are old or dying trees which have holes and loose bark. Ash is particularly good because although fairly short-lived, the dead tree remains standing a long time. Shelter is most important for fledglings and overwintering birds. Clumps or belts of evergreen trees and shrubs can significantly improve the value of broadleaved woods for birds in winter. Ivy, when in its mature, bushy stage, is very valuable for birds and other types of wildlife. Loose piles of brash, especially where overgrown with bramble or other scrambling plants, can provide useful roosts for birds.

Unchecked increases in deer may lead to shifts in the species composition of woodland bird communities, due to the loss of the understorey habitat. Moderate levels of grazing and browsing are thought to be associated with the highest diversities of birds in woodland. Many species of woodland birds have adapted well to the habitat of wooded suburbs, with their gardens and parks, as a replacement for the old wood-pasture habitats.

MAMMALS

In the past in Britain, there was a much more diverse range of mammals in the woodland ecosystem. Aurochs (wild cattle), elk, red deer and roe deer were the main grazers and browsers, with populations kept in check by bears and wolves. The actions of beaver and wild swine affected woodland structure and succession. Grey squirrel, rabbit, and sika, fallow and muntjac deer were not yet introduced. As well as the direct effect of man's activities on woodlands, the losses and gains in the mammalian fauna have had, and still have, a very significant effect on woodlands and trees in Britain.

Deer are probably now more numerous than at any time in history, due to the lack of predators, the recent growth in woodland cover and the lack of culling. Winter cereals, an important food source, and recent mild winters have reduced losses. In Scotland, red deer are a major influence in preventing the regeneration and spread of native woodland. In many parts of England and Wales, natural regeneration of woodland is impossible without protection against deer. Parts of Wales and the Midlands, the extremities of Kent and Cornwall, and the Isle of Man and the Isle of Wight are the only areas to remain relatively free. In some areas deer numbers are as high as 40 per sq km. Muntjac have spread rapidly in recent years, and have an effect on the woodland field layer plants as well as young trees. For details of fencing and tree protection, see chapter 7.

Foxes have adapted well to woodland loss, and are now numerous in suburban and urban areas. Badgers, now protected against killing, injury or disturbance (chapter 3), have maintained active populations in most areas. Favoured places for setts are sloping copses and woods adjoining pasture, where the badgers can forage for earthworms. Well-established setts may be hundreds of years old, and are easy to recognise, with mounds of earth near the many entrance holes, which are at least 25cm (10") wide. Signs of use are usually obvious in spring, with discarded bedding of hay or bracken outside the entrances, fresh soil and evidence of footprints. All setts are protected by law where they show signs of current use.

Among the smaller woodland mammals, a number of bat species are of management interest because they roost in hollow trees during at least part of the year. The best way to maintain roost sites is to preserve these trees, and where appropriate, to pollard new trees to provide habitats in the future. Provision of bat boxes can provide suitable roosting and nesting sites (p160).

Dormice favour middle-aged to mature coppice or coppice with standards. Young or senescent coppice are not suitable habitats, as they lack the variety of food sources and nesting sites. A 15-20 year cycle is most favourable, with adjacent coupes cut at different times so there is always some suitable habitat. Some mature growth should be left to provide 'bridges' across rides and tracks.

Dormice occur in the south of England and in parts of Cumbria. They thrive in warm summers, but numbers can be reduced during mild winters interrupted by cold spells. Botanical diversity is important to provide a succession of food sources through the seasons. In May, oak flowers and various types of pollen may be eaten, followed by caterpillars and aphids in June, ash keys in July, and nuts and berries through the late summer and autumn.

Dormice nest in tree holes up to 10m high in the canopy, and amongst honeysuckle and bramble, with individuals often having more than one nest. They normally breed early in July and again in August. In suitable habitats, nest boxes can be very successful, with perhaps 60-70% of boxes being used. Boxes similar to tit boxes can be used, but with the hole facing the trunk. The only predators are human, so boxes should be put out of easy reach. Dormice may still be present on the margins of otherwise unsuitable woods, so it may be worth putting up nest boxes along woodland edges. For further details see the *Dormouse Conservation Handbook* (English Nature, 1996). The dormouse is the subject of a Species Action Plan (p34).

Wood mice are one of the most widespread mammals in Britain, but highest densities are found in mixed woodland. The mice prefer areas with low vegetation, fallen branches and logs through which they will make their runways. Wood mice are seed-eaters, gathering the seeds of oak, beech, ash, hawthorn and sycamore for storage over winter. Seeds of other woodland plants, small invertebrates and fungi are also eaten. Wood mice are prey to various species, notably tawny owl and weasel. Numbers fluctuate in an annual cycle, being highest in autumn and winter, during which survival is determined by the size of the autumn seed crop. The rarer yellow-necked mouse is larger than the wood mouse, and spends part of its time in the woodland canopy. Although not aggressive to the wood mouse, the two species are rarely found together.

Woodland adjacent to river margins are important habitats for otters, and where they are thought to be present, disturbance should be avoided.

3 Woodlands, trees and the law

This chapter outlines some aspects of the law relating to trees and woodlands. Laws and regulations may differ in England, Wales, Scotland and Northern Ireland, and are subject to change. Further advice should be sought from the nature conservation agency, forestry agency, local planning authority or solicitor, as appropriate.

The internet is the best resource for comprehensive and current information on legislation regarding conservation, wildlife and other matters. Some useful websites are listed on page 184.

Conservation

The most important law regarding conservation in England and Wales is the Wildlife and Countryside Act (WCA) 1981, which includes protection of birds, other animals and plants, as well as other legislation regarding the countryside. Some of the WCA legislation and other laws which affect woodland plants and animals are outlined below.

PLANTS

General protection

Under the Wildlife and Countryside Act 1981, it is an offence for any person to uproot any wild plant without permission from the landowner or occupier. Uproot is defined as to 'dig up or otherwise remove the plant from the land on which it is growing', and includes plants without roots. Lichens, fungi, mosses, liverworts and vascular plants are thus covered under the Act. Similar protection is given in Scotland and Northern Ireland.

Under the Theft Act 1968, it is an offence to dig up and take for commercial purposes any plant, tree, shrub, soil, peat, gravel etc without permission from the landowner or occupier.

Under common law it is not normally an offence to pick fruit, foliage, fungi or flowers, which are growing wild, if they are for personal use and not for resale, and providing that none are specifically protected. Thus seasonal gathering of blackberries, mushrooms or holly is normally permissible, provided this is from a right of way or other public place, and that there are no bylaws prohibiting it.

Endangered plants

The Wildlife and Countryside Act contains a list of endangered plants (Schedule 8), which are protected against intentional picking, uprooting, destruction and sale. Schedule 8 is revised every five years. In addition, bluebells (Britain) and primroses (Northern Ireland) are listed for protection only against sale.

There are exceptions to the General and Schedule 8 protection if the person has a specific or general licence issued by a relevant authority, or if it can be shown that the action was an incidental result of a lawful activity and could not reasonably be avoided.

Protected areas

In SSSIs or ASSIs (Northern Ireland), owners and occupiers may be prosecuted if they destroy plants growing in these sites or remove plant material, unless they have first consulted the statutory nature conservation agency. In other areas bylaws may forbid the picking, uprooting or removal of plants.

Mosses

As noted above, it is illegal to gather moss without the landowner's permission. There are 28 moss species listed under Schedule 8 for which collection is illegal, whether or not the landowner's permission has been obtained. In some areas Forest Enterprise issues licences for the collection of moss from forestry plantations, from where collection is not damaging, for use in floristry.

International protection

Under the Conservation (Natural Habitats) Regulation 1994, certain internationally rare plants are listed as European Protected Species. This makes it an offence to deliberately pick, collect, uproot or destroy one of these plants, and includes similar protection for their seeds and spores.

For further details see the Code of Conduct for the conservation and enjoyment of wild plants (BSBI and JNCC, 1999).

ANIMALS

The Wildlife and Countryside Act applies to wild animals, which are defined as those that are living wild or were living wild before being captured or killed. All wild birds, excluding game birds, are protected, and those animals listed under Schedule 5. This includes bats, many reptiles and amphibians, wild cat, pine marten, dormouse, some moths, butterflies and other invertebrates.

Badgers

Badgers are protected under the Protection of Badgers Act 1992. Under the Act, it is an offence to wilfully kill, injure or take a badger; to interfere with a sett by damaging or obstructing it or by disturbing a badger when it is occupying a badger sett, with intent or recklessly. The Act also contains provisions to permit, under licence, certain activities which would otherwise be prohibited by the Act. These activities may include construction of forest roads, quarrying, protection works for ancient monuments near badger setts and some types of recreational activities. The licensing authorities are the agriculture departments or nature conservation agencies, depending on the type of activity.

The law protects all setts which show signs of current use, including seasonal or occasional use. Badgers live in groups of about 5-12 animals, and usually have more than one sett in their territory. The main breeding sett is normally used continuously, and signs of use are fairly easy to find. Outlying setts up to 150m away from the main sett may only be used occasionally. Tunnels are often only 600mm (2') or so below the surface, and can be disturbed by heavy machinery. Where management work is taking place, a protection zone should be established so that no work takes place within 20m of any entrance to a sett believed to be in current use.

The nature conservation agencies (EN, SNH, CCW) or agriculture departments should be consulted for further advice on woodland management work near badger setts. For further details see *Forest Operations and Badger Setts* (Forestry Commission, 1995).

Bats

All bats are protected under the Wildlife and Countryside Act (Schedule 5). They are also included in Schedule 2 of the Conservation Regulations 1994. These make it illegal to:

- Intentionally or deliberately kill, injure or capture bats.

- Deliberately disturb bats, whether in a roost or not.

- Damage, destroy or obstruct access to bat roosts.

A bat roost is any structure or place which is used for shelter or protection, whether or not the bats are present at the time. For details on recognising bat roosts in trees, see chapter 12. For further details contact The Bat Conservation Trust (p182).

European Protected Species

Under the Conservation (Natural Habitats) Regulations 1994 it is an offence deliberately to kill, capture or disturb a European Protected Species, or to damage or destroy the breeding site or resting place of such an animal. Anyone wanting to undertake an operation that would breach these regulations must apply for a licence from the nature conservation agency.

European Protected Species of animals include horseshoe bats (all species), wild cat, dormouse, sand lizard, great crested newt, otter and smooth snake.

Shooting and hunting

The law regarding shooting, hunting and angling is complex. Most animals which are hunted have a close season when they are protected. This varies with different species and places. Control of deer and rabbits may be required as part of woodland management. For detailed information consult *Law of the Countryside* (Countryside Management Association, 1994) or other publications on countryside law. Detailed information is given in *A Guide to Wildlife Law Enforcement in the UK* (online at www.defra.gov.uk/paw).

Felling

FELLING LICENCES

A licence is needed from the Forestry Authority to fell growing trees (though not for lopping and topping), but in any calendar quarter up to 5 cubic metres may be felled by an occupier, provided that not more than 2 cubic metres are sold.

A licence is not needed if any of the following conditions apply:

- The felling is in accordance with an approved plan under a Forestry Commission grant scheme.

- The trees are growing in a garden, orchard, churchyard or public open space.

- The trees are all below 8cm in diameter measured 1.3m above the ground; or in the case of thinnings, below 10cm in diameter; or in the case of coppice or underwood, below 15cm in diameter.

- The trees are interfering with permitted development, or statutory works by public service providers.

- The trees are dead, dangerous, causing a nuisance or are badly affected by Dutch elm disease.

- The felling is in compliance with an Act of Parliament.

There is a public register of applications for felling licences. All applications have to rest there for 4 weeks and any person or body can comment on them. The public register is available on the Forestry Commission website at www.forestry.gov.uk

Application

The application for a felling licence should be made by the landowner, tenant, or by an agent acting on their behalf. Applications should be submitted at least 3 months before the proposed date of felling. No felling should be carried out until a licence has been issued. A licence may only be issued on condition that replanting is carried out. Planting grants will normally be available where a replanting condition has been imposed.

For further information see the leaflet *Tree felling: getting permission* (Forestry Commission).

Other permissions

In certain circumstances, whether or not a felling licence is needed, permission may be needed for any proposed felling. This may include trees in SSSIs, Conservation Areas or where a Tree Preservation Order applies.

Planning control

TREE PRESERVATION ORDERS

Tree Preservation Orders (TPOs) are the principal means of planning control over the felling or maltreatment of amenity trees.

TPOs may be made by a local planning authority to cover individual trees of exceptional amenity value, groups of trees, woodlands or trees within a specified area, whether urban or rural. TPOs do not normally include protection over large areas. Orders are designed to protect amenity trees which might be at risk, but not to hinder careful silvicultural management.

A TPO may:

- Prohibit the damage or destruction, felling, lopping, topping or uprooting of trees, except with the consent of the local planning authority.

- Ensure the replanting according to specified conditions of any part of a woodland area which is felled as part of permitted forestry operations.

- Require the replacement as soon as reasonably possible of any tree (other than one which is part of a woodland) which is removed or destroyed in contravention of that order, or which dies.

There are four types of TPO, although any one Order can contain any number of items which can be of one or more types. The types are as follows:

1 **Individual**: can be applied to an individual tree.

2 **Group**: can be applied to a group of individual trees which together make up a feature of amenity value but which separately might not.

3 **Area**: covers all trees in a defined area at the time the Order was made.

4 **Woodland**: covers all trees within a woodland area regardless of how old they are.

A landowner whose trees are made subject to a TPO must be informed by the Council making the order, and the trees identified on a map. A seller of land is bound to inform a buyer about any TPOs that apply to the property. Anyone can check whether TPOs are in force on any trees, by contacting the relevant planning authority.

CONSERVATION AREAS

Conservation Areas are areas designated by local authorities for building and landscape conservation. Anyone proposing to cut down, top, lop or uproot a tree in a Conservation Area is required to give six weeks notice of their intention to the local authority concerned. A felling licence is also required, unless any of the exceptions listed above under felling licences apply. The trees may also be subject to a TPO, in which case the details given above apply.

Miscellaneous

RIGHTS OF WAY AND PUBLIC SERVICES

Local authorities can cut back or fell trees and shrubs which obscure public rights of way, including footpaths, which obstruct light from street lamps or the sightlines of car drivers. Railway, land drainage, electricity and telephone authorities can require removal of trees or parts of trees which may cause an obstruction. Electricity authorities pay a continual annual compensation for loss of the use of ground. BT does it own lopping, and pays no rent for land occupied by its poles or for wayleaves. Similar powers are available to other public service providers.

Any woodland management work or tree planting in the vicinity of overhead power lines and underground services may require the prior permission of the appropriate authority.

UNSAFE TREES

The owner of a tree will not be held responsible in law for damage caused by it falling or losing branches if the failure of the tree could not reasonably have been foreseen or prevented. However, if the tree had obvious signs of disease or weakness, the owner might be sued for any damage caused. It is therefore very important that trees under which the public have access are regularly inspected to check on their condition.

BOUNDARIES

Trees on boundaries are often the cause of dispute. In the case of trees which overhang from another property, it's advisable to contact the owner and if possible come to an agreement about any work needed. An owner may claim compensation if a neighbour damages or kills a tree by cutting overhanging branches. If the branches or roots of an overhanging tree are interfering with the fabric of a building, the insurers of the building should be contacted for advice before any action is taken.

Before taking any action about overhanging trees, you should check that the tree is not protected by a Tree Preservation Order, planning conditions, or is in a Conservation Area. It is the responsibility of the person intending to do the work to check with the local planning authority, regardless of who owns the tree or if ownership is not known.

- Property deeds may or may not contain details of ownership of trees along a boundary. Where trees are in hedgerows with a bank and ditch, the boundary normally follows the edge of the ditch away from the bank.

- The owner or tenant of any land is entitled to cut off branches which overhang or roots which penetrate from adjoining property, as long as he does it on his side of the boundary. The boundary is presumed to run vertically up and down from the line at ground level. Expenses cannot be claimed from the owner.

- All cut material remains the property of the tree owner, and the neighbour who cuts off branches cannot utilise them in any way. He can place them on the owner's land. If the owner throws them back, the neighbour can claim for any financial loss incurred.

- The neighbour must exercise every care to do no injury to the overhanging trees when cutting overhanging branches or penetrating roots.

- A neighbour has no legal right to any fruit on overhanging branches. If he can show that he has enjoyed the privilege of picking overhanging fruit, based on the present or previous owner's consent, the owner cannot withdraw the privilege.

- The owner of the fruit may, with his neighbour's permission, enter the neighbour's land to pick any fruit from overhanging branches, or pick up fruit which has fallen from these branches. If he is refused permission, and his neighbour refuses to deliver to him any fallen fruit, then the owner is justified in entering without permission. But he must not use force, nor must he do any damage, even to the extent of trampling on dug soil, or he can be sued for trespass.

FLY-TIPPING

Fly-tipping or the unauthorised dumping of waste is a problem in many woods, especially near urban areas. Fly-tipping includes the dumping of fridges, furniture and other material, normally from a vehicle at a pull-in or car park, and the regular tipping of garden waste and other material, normally at boundaries with gardens. In both cases the law is difficult to enforce because the person has to be caught in the action of tipping the waste. Where fly-tipping involves the use of a vehicle, the driver can be prosecuted and police have powers to seize the vehicle. Some waste may be hazardous, and should not be handled. For further advice contact the Environment Agency. If you witness a fly-tipping incident, contact the Environment Agency hotline on 0800 807060.

4 Safety, equipment and organisation

The following information on safety and equipment is basic to most aspects of tree planting, tree nursery and aftercare operations. Tools suitable for coppicing and felling small trees are described, but felling of large trees is not covered by this handbook.

Safety precautions

GENERAL

- A suitable first aid kit (see below) must be on hand at the work site. There should be at least one Basic Trained First Aider on all practical volunteering projects, training courses or other events.

- All workers should be advised to be immunized against tetanus.

- Postpone the work if it is raining heavily. Once gloves, tools and the ground become sodden and slippery, there is an increased risk of injuring yourself or others.

- Wear suitable tough clothing (see below).

- Safety helmets should be worn when using post drivers (p25).

- Only trained operators should use powered equipment, including strimmers, brush cutters and chain saws. Training is available through The Conservation Volunteers, Lantra (p187) or local agricultural or land-based colleges.

- Attend to splinters promptly, taking particular care with the thorns of blackthorn, which are liable to cause infection.

- Take great care when lifting and handling heavy or awkward objects (see below).

- Clear up as you work, and don't leave cut material or debris littering the area.

- If you need to attract the attention of someone using an edged tool, do not approach closely but call out from a safe distance.

TOOL USE

The following points are basic to all tool use. Further details are given where appropriate in later chapters. All tools must be properly maintained (p27). Any tools with loose heads, cracked or splintered handles or other defects should be put aside for repair. See *Toolcare* (BTCV, 1995) for full details.

- Edged tools are safest when sharp. See page 27 for details on sharpening in the field.

- Carry edged tools at their point of balance, just below the heads, and positioned at your side with the edges pointing down and slightly away from you. Bowsaws should be carried with the blade protected by a plastic sleeve, or one made from sacking. Don't carry more tools than you can safely grip.

- If unfamiliar with a tool, don't use it until you have been shown the safest technique.

- Take great care with billhooks, slashers, axes and saws.

- Keep a safe distance from other workers, equivalent to at least twice the length of an arm and tool.

- When using a billhook, slasher or axe, always make sure there is a clear path to swing the tool. Even a small twig can deflect the tool and cause injury.

- Never cut towards yourself with an edged tool.

- When using a short-handled tool, keep your free hand away from the line of cutting.

- Don't leave tools lying around, as they are likely to cause injury, or get mislaid. Prop tools against a nearby tree or stump, or keep them together in a hessian sack or tool box. Store the tools centrally on the site so that all users know where to find and return them.

LIFTING AND HANDLING

- Before lifting and carrying, plan the route carefully, and clear it of any hazards which may trip people up.

- When moving heavy objects, particularly when working in a pair or team, think through the ergonomics of the situation, and plan your moves carefully.

- When lifting, bend your knees, not your back, and lift using your leg muscles.

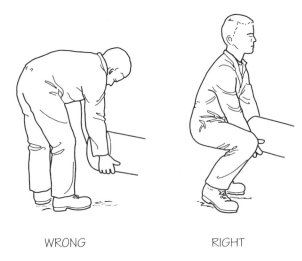

WRONG   RIGHT

- Be aware of your own and other people's physical limitations, and never try to lift more than you or others are capable of.

- Ensure you have a good grip on heavy or awkward objects, using the whole hand, not just the fingertips.

- Avoid manual handling where possible, by using wheelbarrows or machines.

Clothing

For work clothes, the aims are always safety and comfort. For general work you will need the following:

- **Overalls, boilersuits or close-fitting work clothes**. The wearing of loose clothes and scarves is dangerous when working with edged tools and among branches and brambles.

- **Boots**. Heavy leather work boots with deep moulded soles and safety toe caps, either external or internal, are best. In wet conditions, wellingtons with safety toe caps are recommended. Trainers, light shoes and normal wellingtons do not give adequate protection.

- **Gloves**. These are essential when dealing with brambles and thorns. Hedging gloves with gauntlets give extra protection against thorny scrub. For general work, suede palmed 'rigger' gloves are suitable. Gloves should not normally be worn when using edged tools, as the tool can easily slip. Criss cross 'gripper' gloves give improved grip. Gloves may be necessary to prevent allergic reaction to bracken, nettles or other plants.

- **Safety helmet**. This should comply to EN 397 and should be worn when using a post driver (see below). Working with chainsaws, brush cutters, near heavy machinery or working aloft, none of which are covered by this handbook, will require the wearing of helmets and other protective items.

Tools and accessories

Items are listed by category according to their most important type of use.

FOR ALL PROJECTS

A First Aid Kit, complying with current Health and Safety requirements, should be available at all times. For projects involving up to 10 people, the contents should be as follows:

1	guidance card
20	waterproof plasters
2	No. 16 sterile eye pads
6	triangular bandages
6	safety pins
6	medium sterile dressings 12 x 12cm
4	large sterile dressings 18 x 18cm
10	alcohol free cleansing wipes
2	pairs latex gloves
1	pair scissors, blunt-ended

The following welfare kit is also useful:

- Pair of tweezers

- Pair of scissors

- Safety pins

- Needle and thread

- Pencil

- Sanitary towels

- Whistle

- Toilet roll

- Cotton wool

- 30 plasters

- 3 finger pouches

- rubber gloves

- insect repellent

- 2 x 10p pieces

- sun cream

- barrier cream

A list of local hospitals with casualty departments should also be to hand.

PLANTING AND EARLY CARE

Planting equipment

- Heavy duty treaded garden spade

- Heavy duty garden fork

- Junior garden spade, for use by children

Specialist tree planting spades are available as follows:

- The Schlich spade and the Mansfield planting spade both have a ridge down the face of the spade which makes a hole to take the main tree roots.

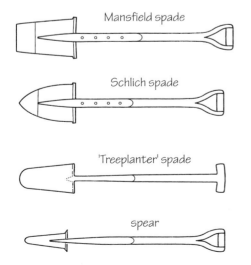

Treeplanter spades have slightly dished, treaded blades to make deep notches for planting transplants.

- The treeplanter bar is a solid all-steel tool for planting in difficult conditions.

- The spear is a special tool designed for planting cell grown plants.

- Marker canes or similar, to mark planting positions or lines.

- Planting bags for carrying planting stock from the supply point to the planting position. Clean, heavy-duty plastic sacks are suitable, or specialist planting bags can be used for large-scale projects. Some growers of cell-grown plants can supply special carriers for use during planting operations.

- Lump or sledgehammer, for treeshelter stakes.

Fencing tools

Fencing may be needed around tree nurseries or tree planting areas.

- Crowbar, for making pilot holes for stakes.

- Post driver (Drivall), mell or maul for driving posts.

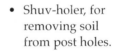

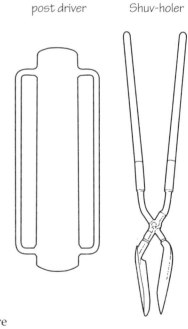

- Shuv-holer, for removing soil from post holes.

- Wrecking bar (swan neck).

- Claw hammer

- Fencing pliers

- Mallet and chisel

- Wire strainers

- Heavy-duty wire cutters

- Tinsnips, for cutting netting.

Pruning tools

- Secateurs. Bypass action type are recommended.

- Loppers. Various grades are available for cutting branches up to 3 or 5cm (1 or 2") diameter.

- Treetop pruner. Extension poles give 3m cutting reach, for high pruning or seed collection.

- Pruning saw. Extension poles available for high pruning.

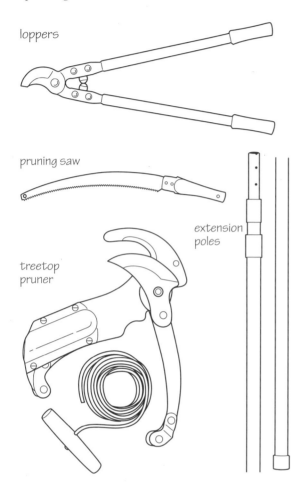

loppers

pruning saw

extension poles

treetop pruner

Easy reach tools

Several manufacturers produce tools to which optional longer handles can be attached to extend their use. These are ideal for weeding and other tree nursery work, especially for those people who find it hard to bend or who work from a wheelchair. Tools are available from Wolf, Spear and Jackson and other manufacturers.

Thrive offer a comprehensive information service on all aspects of gardening and horticulture for those with special needs (address on page 184).

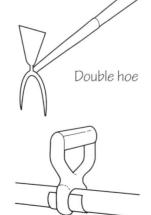

Double hoe

Auxiliary grip

CLEARANCE AND COPPICING

Clearing tools

- Long handled scythe (Turk scythe) for cutting grassy rides and glades.

- Grass hook, for cutting herbaceous material.

- Brushing hook (slasher) for bramble and other light woody material.

- Heavy-duty slasher for scrub clearance.

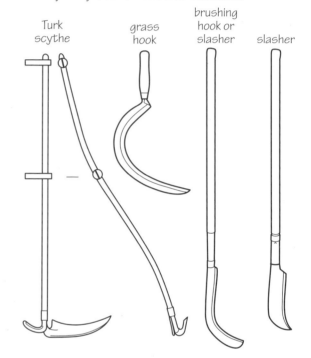

Turk scythe

grass hook

brushing hook or slasher

slasher

Coppicing

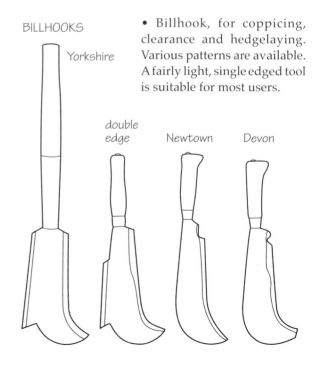

BILLHOOKS

Yorkshire

double edge

Newtown

Devon

- Billhook, for coppicing, clearance and hedgelaying. Various patterns are available. A fairly light, single edged tool is suitable for most users.

- Bowsaw. The 53cm (21") bowsaw is suitable for most coppicing work, as its triangular shape makes it possible to use in confined spaces. Suitable for cutting wood up to 12.5cm (5") diameter. The 60cm (24") bowsaw is suitable for felling large coppice stems, small trees, and for cross-cutting felled timber.

- Clearing or snedding axe, for snedding, trimming and coppicing.

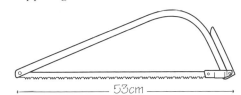
53cm

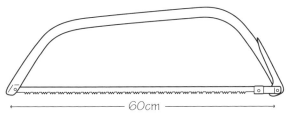
60cm

←15cm→ ←45cm→

- Sharpening stones

Tool and equipment maintenance

Proper maintenance of tools and equipment is essential for safe and efficient working. This section includes general points on storage, transport and care of tools, and techniques for sharpening tools in the field. Workshop tasks are described in *Toolcare* (BTCV, 2000).

STORAGE AND GENERAL CARE

- Keep all tools clean and dry. Carry a rag with you to wipe off the handles in wet weather. Keep edges free from mud, or they will dull very quickly. Clean tools immediately after use. If mud is left to harden, tools will be more difficult to clean and sharpen.

- Oil all metal parts before storing to prevent rust. Ordinary vegetable oil is suitable. Wipe unvarnished wooden handles with linseed oil when new and occasionally thereafter, as this helps keep them supple.

- If handles are rough or splintery, sand them smooth. Nicks in metal handles should be removed by filing.

- Store tools in a dry, well aired building, preferably in racks or on wall brackets. Keep similar tools together.

- Hang bowsaws with the blade tension released.

- Tools and equipment carried inside a passenger vehicle must be in secure containers fixed to the floor. Tools that will not fit into appropriate containers should be carried in a separate vehicle, or stowed securely in a trailer or on a roof rack. Edged tools should be protected with plastic guards, or with sacking or similar. In cars, tools should be transported in a boot, or covered hatchback area, preferably in a strong container.

SHARPENING EDGED TOOLS IN THE FIELD

Edged tools should go into the field sharp. Major sharpening is a workshop task, and should not be attempted in the field.

- Sharpen tools at least twice a day when in use, or more often as necessary. Sickles and scythes need frequent honing to remain effective. Axes and billhooks should be checked whenever you stop to rest.

- Use the correct whetstone for sharpening each tool. Fine cylindrical (cigar-shaped) stones are used for sickles and scythes. Cylindrical or flat (canoe-shaped) stones can be used for billhooks and slashers. Axes are best sharpened with flat rectangular stones or round stones, fine one side, coarse on the other.

- Stones are fragile, and should be carefully stored and transported in a box or 'frog'. Broken stones are dangerous and should not be used.

- Always wear a glove on the hand holding the sharpening stone. Place the tool on a firm surface such as a stump, with the edge projecting, or sit down and steady the tool on your knees.

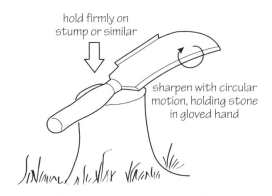
hold firmly on stump or similar

sharpen with circular motion, holding stone in gloved hand

- Moisten the stone with water, then hold it at the same angle as the existing taper of the blade. Avoid the temptation to use a wider angle to get an edge on the blade more quickly. With a combination stone, use the coarse side first to eliminate any flaws and bring to an edge, and then the fine side after to give an even taper and good polish. Sharpen with small circular motions, as this is safer than sweeping the stone along the edge, and is easier for the inexperienced worker.

- Take care to sharpen the hooked part of billhook and slasher blades, as this part of the blade does much of the cutting work.

- On single bevel tools, sharpen the bevelled side only. To finish, remove the burr on the flat side with a few light strokes.

- To check for sharpness, sight along the edge. You should see a uniform taper with no light reflected from the edge itself. Reflected light indicates a dull spot, so keep sharpening until this disappears. Don't touch the edge to check for sharpness.

SAW MAINTENANCE

- Oil blades frequently. When sawing through resinous trees, keep blades clean and free-cutting by dousing them with an oiling mixture of 7 parts paraffin, 2 parts white spirit and 1 part lubricating oil. Wear gloves to protect your hands.

- Change bowsaw blades when they are blunt or have lost their 'set'. Blunt blades take more effort to use than normal, and produce fine dust rather than crumbs or small chips of wood. Blunt blades are not worth resharpening, and should be removed from the saw and broken in half to avoid re-use. Take the pieces away for safe disposal.

- Blades can lose their set by being trapped in the felling cuts of trees, which gives the impression they are blunt. Reverse the blade in the saw (points into the bow), to make it easy to identify later. The set can be replaced in the workshop by gripping the blade in a vice, and then tweaking each tooth in turn to the correct side using a pair of fencing pliers.

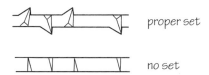

proper set

no set

Top view

- To change the saw blade, first release the tension. If this is hard to do by hand, put the saw on the ground with the frame upright and the blade pointing away from you, and pull back on the lever, using a metal bar if necessary. Then put your foot on the lever to hold it, and push the saw frame away from you.

- Remove the rivets, position the new blade and then replace the rivets. Retension the blade by pressing the lever against the ground until it closes.

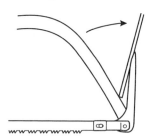

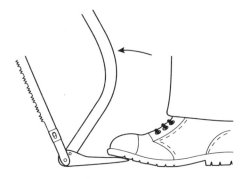

- If a bowsaw blade tends to 'run' (cut in a curve), reverse it in the frame. If this is ineffective, adjust

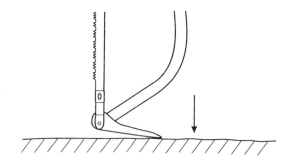

the set on the 'gaining' side by running a whetstone once lightly along the blade, with the stone held flat against the blade.

- A bowsaw blade must be under high tension to cut straight. Increase the tension by fixing the blade using the inner holes of the pair at each end of the blade. The frame can be 'opened' when held in a vice, to increase the blade tension.

Organising group work

These points are basic to organising group work. Further details are given where appropriate in the following chapters.

- The site manager or project leader should explain the purpose of the work, general site safety, demonstrate safe tool use and set the objectives for the day.

- Where possible, verbal explanations can be backed up with work plans, demonstrations or samples of work. For example, clear labelling of trees for planting and copies of planting plans will help avoid mistakes, and allow workers to get on without constantly asking for instructions. A tree 'library', consisting of marked twigs will help volunteers identify trees as they prune or thin.

- Small groups should work methodically on one goal at a time, rather than piecemeal on several things, none of which may get finished by the end of the day.

- Large groups should be divided up and work on several tasks or different parts of the site.

- Whatever the division of labour, don't leave anyone out, but find a place for people of all strengths and abilities. New volunteers can work alongside more experienced workers.

- Keep a close watch on tool use, and repeat earlier instructions as necessary. Don't hesitate to offer advice even to experienced volunteers, as otherwise new workers may follow poor practice. If a volunteer doesn't have enough skill for a job, tactfully suggest a change of tool or activity.

- Count out and count in the tools at the start and finish of work, and note any which need repair.

- In organising the group, aim for a balance between high work standards, and conditions which are not only safe but also rewarding for the volunteer.

Risk assessment

Employers are required to assess the risks to their employees and volunteers arising from the work being planned. The purpose of the assessment is to enable the employer to decide what measures are necessary to comply with all applicable health and safety legislation. This may include safe systems of work, personal protective equipment or guarding of dangerous parts of machinery. A risk assessment first involves identifying the hazards which could arise from the work, the machinery or equipment used, or the workplace. If hazards cannot be eliminated, the extent of risk must be evaluated. Risk is the likelihood that a particular hazard will cause harm, together with an estimation of the severity of the consequences.

For further details see *Risk assessment – a learning resource pack* (BTCV 1998) and *Generic Risk Assessments* (2002), or contact your nearest office of The Conservation Volunteers.

5   Woodland management

This chapter outlines some of the issues which need consideration when planning the management of a wood. Most woodlands are managed in consultation with other agencies, and any woodland planting or management for which grant aid is being sought will require consultation with the Forestry Commission or other grant aiding body.

Woodlands are an important part of the UK Biodiversity Action Plan, and management should be in accordance with the Action Plans drawn up for woodland habitats and species. For further details visit www.ukbap.org.uk, or contact your local biodiversity officer through the local authority or nature conservancy agency.

General principles

These apply primarily to woodlands managed for wildlife and amenity, but also to those managed for production of wood and timber. Historically these aims were not conflicting, and now after a century or so of divergence, they are again coming together.

- Take time to get to know a woodland before making decisions about changes. Visit the woodland frequently over a year and make notes of plant and animal species, gaps in the canopy and any signs of regeneration. The form of individual trees, the woodland structure and landforms in the woodland are easiest to see in the winter, but conditions of light and shade are easiest to see in summer, along with the herbaceous flora of the wood.

- Take advice. There is information available on the history of individual woodlands, through old maps and other archives. Consult property deeds, local libraries, local historical societies or county archives. Most ancient woodlands have been recorded (p35). Many woodlands have been studied for their flora and fauna. Records may be held by the county Biological Records Centre, Wildlife Trust or local office of the nature conservation agency. Local naturalists, local historians and other local specialists may have knowledge of the wood. Local residents and landowners may have knowledge of past management or uses of the woodland, or have old photos which reveal changes in the extent or structure of the woodland.

- The natural distribution of native woodland species

has been extensively studied through the National Vegetation Classification (NVC). With knowledge of the location, soil type, soil wetness and aspect of any site, a clear picture can be given of the type of woodland which the site would naturally have supported. This information includes species of trees, shrubs, flowering plants and mosses, and can be used in restoring woodlands which have been altered by planting, and in creating new native woodlands (p38).

- There should be no replanting in ancient semi-natural woodlands, which should only be managed using systems which allow natural regeneration. Other semi-natural woodlands and long-established planted woods should also be managed primarily by encouraging natural regeneration of the native species which they contain.

- Allow nature time to recover before intervening. The elm disease and drought of the 1970s, and the storms in southern England in 1987 and 1990 were not the disasters for woodlands and trees that they were thought at the time. Replanting has not always been successful. Elm is recovering in many areas and the regrowth from suckers has long overtaken many trees which were planted to replace them. In many cases clearance and replanting of storm damaged woodland has been detrimental, whereas those left mainly untouched are regrowing and recovering. Working with the natural growth is likely to be far more successful than replanting. Even semi-natural woods damaged by replanting with conifers are recovering in many places, as the native growth returns and suppresses the conifers.

- Exotic species and cultivars of native species have no place in semi-natural woodlands, and should only be planted in arboreta, gardens and urban parks. Some exotic species may be needed to establish woodland cover on polluted or otherwise damaged sites.

- Don't make changes which can't be sustained. Lapsed coppicing regimes should only be restarted if they can be sustained, and if damage by deer can be controlled. Glades should only be created if they can be maintained by mowing or grazing.

- Not all woodlands or all areas of woodlands need management. Non-intervention may be appropriate.

- Woodland ecosystems are kept in balance by a degree of browsing and grazing by wild animals. Total and permanent exclusion by fencing can sometimes lead to excessive natural regeneration of woody species.

- Successful methods of establishing new native woodland are well proven. The NVC gives clear guidance on the appropriate species for any particular area. All planted trees need weeding for at least three years, and those planted on disused agricultural land need particular attention. With correct choice of species, close spacing, rigorous weeding and early thinning, it is quite possible to establish self-sustaining woodland cover within about 10 years. If weeding and other early maintenance cannot be given, it's better not to plant at all.

Advice on the principles and practices of woodland management is given in a series of eight Forestry Practice Guides: *The Management of Semi-Natural Woodlands*, available from the Forestry Commission (p198).

Management plans

GENERAL PROCEDURES

The diagram below shows the outline approach to the preparation and development of a management plan for a woodland site. The same approach can be followed whatever the scale of the scheme under consideration.

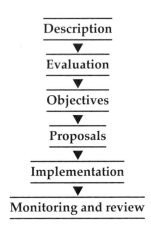

Description
▼
Evaluation
▼
Objectives
▼
Proposals
▼
Implementation
▼
Monitoring and review

A list of the details which may be relevant under each stage are given below.

DESCRIPTION

- Name and location, with the OS map grid reference for the entrance to the wood. The 1:2500 scale map is suitable for small woodlands, and the 1:10000 for large woodlands. Standard methods of marking maps are used by the Forestry Commission, with details given in grant applications.

- Statutory designations.

- Areas, with sub-divisions if these clarify management proposals.

- Aspect, soils, drainage.

- Historical aspects, including past management.

- Trees and shrub species, dominant trees and abundant underwood shrubs.

- Age class distribution of trees: stocking; composition and condition of any natural regeneration.

- Ground flora; dominant species and any unusual species.

- Fauna, especially any rare or notable species.

- Conspicuousness in the landscape.

- Archaeological features.

- Existing public access and planned future access.

- Surrounding land use and other nearby woodland.

EVALUATION

Any special values such as rare species, veteran trees, natural features, timber potential or prominence in the landscape should be noted. The site's importance in contributing to a local Biodiversity Action Plan, Habitat Action Plan or Species Action Plan should be noted.

MANAGEMENT OBJECTIVES

These may include any of the following:

- Maintaining and creating new wildlife habitats

- Producing wood and marketable timber

- Regenerating woodland

- Enhancing the landscape

- Restoring or improving industrial or derelict land

- Providing public recreation

- Providing employment

- Providing sporting use

- Providing shelter for crops, animals or buildings

- Involving the local community

- Screening unattractive views, reducing traffic noise

Some of these are discussed further below.

MANAGEMENT PROPOSALS

This should include the long term strategy and a five year summary work plan. The long term strategy may include any of the following operations. The five year summary plan will specify the areas to be worked and the main operations to be done in the next five years:

New planting or replanting
Site preparation
Species to be planted
Mixtures and planting patterns
Spacing
Protection against deer, rabbits, domestic stock, people
Weed control
Beating up (replacement of losses)

Natural regeneration
Species
Site preparation
Felling of parent trees, stand opening
Respacing, protection and weeding

Felling and thinning
Reasons for felling and thinning
Type and pattern of felling and thinning
Route for removal of timber

Clearance
Removal of invasive species such as rhododendron
Clearance of undergrowth to diversify habitat or improve access

Coppice
Maintenance of existing coppice regime
Restarting coppice regime
Converting coppice to high forest by singling

Pollards and veteran trees
Management work to perpetuate pollards and ancient trees

Access
Access improvements for management and recreation purposes

Glades
Management of glades and other open spaces

Other habitats
Ponds, streams and wet ground. Hedges, woodbanks and other boundaries. Planting or sowing of woodland ground flora.

MONITORING

Monitoring must be included, so that the results of any management work are measured and evaluated. Lessons from monitoring can then be included in a review of the management plan, which should normally be made every five years. Monitoring involves recording the state of the woodland at the start of the period, the work done and how the wood responded. There are many aspects of management which may be monitored, including the following:

- Response of the woodland to coppicing, thinning, felling, fencing or other operations.

- Changes in woodland structure or species composition.

- Amount and type of natural regeneration.

- Success rates of tree planting.

- Success rates of woodland flora planting or sowing.

- Control of woody weeds such as rhododendron.

Fixed point photography is a simple and useful method of recording changes in the woodland. Further advice on monitoring vegetation changes is available in Forestry Commission Bulletin 108 (1992).

Management objectives

When considering management of existing woodlands, or creation of new woods, the following objectives may be considered. Many of these objectives are complementary, and can be fulfilled within a single area of woodland. Most woodlands are now managed with multi-purpose objectives, partly as a way of making woodland management economically viable. In large woodlands, zoning can be used to fulfil different objectives which may otherwise conflict, for example by providing recreation facilities well away from areas of high conservation value. Small woods are more difficult to manage for multi-purpose objectives, as the different uses may conflict.

CONSERVATION

Woodlands are complex and valuable ecosystems which support a huge variety of organisms, and are genetic reservoirs from past times. The most valuable woodlands for nature conservation are recognised and protected as nature reserves, Sites of Special Scientific Interest or other designations. The local authority, Forestry Commission, English Nature or other authority will hold details of these designations.

The importance of woodland ecosystems is recognised under the UK Biodiversity Action Plan (BAP). There are eight Habitat Action Plans (HAPs) covering most types of semi-natural woodland, and including lowland wood-pasture and parkland.

TABLE 5a: HABITAT BIODIVERSITY ACTION PLANS FOR WOODLAND HABITATS

Habitat Biodiversity Action Plan
Broadleaved, mixed and yew woodland
Coniferous woodland
Lowland beech and yew woodland
Lowland wood-pasture and parkland
Native pine woodlands
Upland mixed ashwoods
Upland mixed oakwood
Wet woodland

Species Action Plans (SAPs) have been drawn up for many species of animals and plants which are associated with woodland habitats, including the dormouse, greater and lesser horseshoe bat, red squirrel, pearl-bordered fritillary, and many species of moss and lichen. Various organisations are championing different Action Plans. For full details see www.ukbap.org.uk

COPPICE OR UNDERWOOD

Coppice or underwood has been of great importance historically, and remains a significant objective for some lowland mixed woods. The market for hazel coppice products has improved to the extent that good quality coppice is in great demand by coppice workers. Coppice management combines well with management for wildlife, and although fairly regular rotations are needed, is sufficiently flexible to adapt to changing markets. New methods of using roundwood for building and other purposes are being developed by the Greenwood Trust and other organisations.

TIMBER

Historically, the growing of trees for timber has been far less important than the growing of trees for underwood. This changed with the widespread planting of conifers by the Forestry Commission through the 20th century, but the vast majority of timber requirements in Britain are met by imports. Planting for timber has historically not been very successful in financial terms, because the market has usually changed by the time the crop has matured. Timber remains a relatively unimportant objective in broadleaved woodland management in Britain.

RECREATION

Recreation is now an important objective for all woodlands managed by the Forestry Commission, and most owned by other organisations and local authorities. Woods for recreation are particularly valued near urban areas, and even small woods can be important locally. Low intensity recreation conflicts little with other objectives.

LANDSCAPE

Woods, hedgerow trees and individual trees are very important landscape features, both in rural and urban areas. Planting or management of woods for their value in the landscape probably started with the 18th century 'landscape movement', and has been continued by estate owners, local authorities and others to the present day.

SHELTER

Many small woodlands in rural areas have been planted or managed for shelter. These include shelterbelts around isolated farmsteads, shelterbelts for crops and livestock, small woods for pheasants and coverts for foxes. Where the timber or underwood value has been low, the value for shelter and game has been sufficiently important that many small woods have been preserved that might otherwise have been cleared for agriculture.

LAND RESTORATION

Large numbers of trees have been planted in recent decades with the objective of restoring abandoned industrial land. Such areas typically have highly disturbed and compacted soils, artificial land forms such as tips and quarries, exposed conditions and extremes of soil moisture from waterlogged to very dry. Some have buried toxic materials and are not suitable for cultivation or building. Conversion to woodland, for landscape and recreation value, is normally the cheapest form of land restoration, as it avoids the need for site levelling, topsoil importation or underdrainage. Poor soils and the need to establish woodlands quickly may require the use of some exotic species, such as fast-growing nitrogen-fixing alders, to act as a nurse for slower growing, less tolerant native species.

URBAN REGENERATION

Wooded landscapes, both urban and rural, are generally considered more attractive than those with few trees. The leafy suburbs describe the more prosperous urban and residential areas, where there are gardens, parks and street trees which green the urban landscape. Trees improve the urban microclimate, help reduce traffic noise, bring wildlife into urban areas, engender feelings of well-being and raise property values. Urban regeneration schemes include woodland creation and tree planting to improve the quality of the local environment, create jobs and attract investment.

Woodland classification

Woodlands and wooded areas can be classified by various criteria, as outlined below.

AGE

Ancient woodlands

Ancient woodland is land that has had continuous woodland cover since at least 1600 AD, and is categorised into two types. Ancient Semi-Natural Woodlands are sites that have retained their native tree and shrub cover, and have not been altered by planting. The woodland may have been managed by coppicing or felling, and allowed to regenerate naturally. Ancient Replanted Woodland is woodland where the original native tree cover has been felled and replaced by planting, usually with conifers, and usually during the 20th century.

The year 1600 was chosen because there was little planting of woodlands before that date, and maps are available from about that time which can be linked to evidence on the ground. In Scotland, ancient woods are those which were present before 1750, when the first national survey was made. Woods can still be ancient even if they have been felled many times, as the trees grow up again from the same genetic stock. Ancient replanted woodlands can be partly restored by removing the introduced species, and allowing the native cover to re-establish. Continuity of ancient woodland is broken by alternative land use such as agriculture or urban development.

Some ancient woodlands are remnants of the primary or prehistoric woods, while others are secondary woodlands which have grown up on ground cleared at some time in the centuries before 1600.

The Ancient Woodland Inventory for England lists over 22,000 ancient woodland sites. The Inventory is being constantly updated as new details become available. Ancient woodland is identified using presence or absence of woods from old maps, information about the wood's name, shape, internal boundaries, location relative to other features, ground survey, and aerial photography. The Inventory is managed by English Nature. For further details see *Guidelines for Identifying Ancient Woodland* (English Nature, 1999), or visit the English Nature website. Similar information is being compiled for Wales and Scotland by their respective nature conservation agencies, who should be contacted for further details. In Scotland, the Caledonian Pinewood Inventory of native Scots pine woodland has been compiled.

Recent

Recent woodlands are those that have grown up since 1600, on previously unwooded sites. They may be planted, or naturally regenerated trees.

Primary

These are woodlands which have existed continuously since the original wildwoods developed. It is difficult to prove that a woodland is primary. All primary woods are ancient.

Secondary

These are woodlands which have grown up on land which was cleared at some time in the past for agriculture or some other purpose. All recent woodlands are secondary.

Apart from the difficulty of identifying the age and origin of woodlands, the classification blurs at the edges of woodlands. The expanding margins of ancient woodland onto unaltered soils can be classified as ancient. Woodland which has grown up or been planted on altered soils next to ancient woodland is classified as secondary.

Why ancient semi-natural woodlands are valuable

- They include all primary woods, which are the lineal descendents of the wildwood, with wildlife communities and soils unaltered by clearance or cultivation.

- Their wildlife communities are usually richer than those of recent woods, which tend to be dominated by fast growing species, or have elements of the habitat which they replaced.

- They contain a high proportion of the populations of rare and valuable woodland species.

- They may contain natural features such as springs and streams, and microtopographical features formed under periglacial conditions.

- Rides and glades within ancient woodlands may

contain rare communities of plants, invertebrates and other organisms.

- Most ancient woodlands have been managed, and some have detailed historical records associated with them.

- Some ancient woodlands contain earthworks which predate them, and which are of archaeological value.

In the uplands, the difference between ancient and recent woodlands is less marked.

- Upland woods are typified by pine, birch and oak which regenerate in open areas, so woodland cover tends to be mobile over time, and is less strongly associated with particular sites.

- Upland woods are more open, and there is less microclimatic difference between the interior of the wood and the land around, so a specialised woodland flora and fauna does not usually develop.

- Most upland woods are severely modified by grazing, and tend to merge into moorlands.

- There are few historical records.

SPECIES

The National Vegetation Classification (NVC) describes 19 major types of woodland plant communities. Each has a distinctive mixture of trees and shrubs, with a characteristic associated flora of flowering plants, and for most types, ferns, mosses, liverworts and lichens. Each type is limited to a particular climatic zone and soil type, and represents the kind of climax vegetation which could develop wherever such conditions occur, if succession was allowed to occur. Succession has been highly modified by man in most woodlands in Britain, but they still preserve much natural diversity.

The 19 woodland types are listed on page 39, with further details on pages 190-194.

The full details of the 19 woodland types and their distribution are given in *British Plant Communities Volume 1: Woodlands and Scrub* (CUP, 1998) and summarised in *Summary of National Vegetation Classification woodland descriptions* (JNCC, 1994). For details on using the NVC for designing new native woodlands, see *Creating New Native Woodlands* (Forestry Commission, 1994).

SYSTEM OF MANAGEMENT

Woodlands can also be classified by how they have been managed. The effect of management is most obvious in the structure of the woodland and the form of growth of the trees within it, but past management may also have affected the species mix, either by intentionally or unintentionally favouring particular species over others, or by planting.

All woodlands in Britain have been affected by man's activities. It's essential to understand how a woodland was managed in the past before making decisions for future management. Most new native woodlands will also need to be managed in order to become attractive habitats for amenity and wildlife.

Few woodlands have been managed continuously under the same system. Those coppices and wood pastures that have had continuity of management over centuries are amongst the most ecologically and historically valuable woodlands in Britain. The management of most woodlands has lapsed at various times, or the management system has changed from one type to another.

Coppice

This describes the regular cropping of deciduous trees by cutting growth down to the stump or stool. Rotations of 5-30 years are used, depending on the species and the end use. The cut material is used for fuel, fencing, greenwood crafts and many other uses. Hazel, a multi-stemmed shrub, is the most common coppice species, and declines as it becomes shaded by other trees. Alder, oak, lime, hornbeam and sweet chestnut were widely coppiced in the past for various purposes. Where coppicing is abandoned, these species tend to grow up into a form of high forest. Coppice (except hazel) can be converted to high forest by singling, which involves cutting all the stems but one, which is left to grow on to form a single-stemmed tree. For further details see chapter 9.

Coppice with standards

This two-storey system developed to provide a coppice crop and a timber crop from the same piece of woodland. The coppice or underwood was cut at frequent intervals, and the timber trees, normally oak, were allowed to grow into standards and were felled at intervals of 80-100 years. The number of standards was regulated so that they did not outshade the coppice growth. Coppice and coppice with standards were the most widespread method of woodland management in lowland mixed woods from at least the early Middle Ages until the 20th century. For further details see page 97.

Wood-pasture

Wood-pastures probably developed as a consequence of domestic animals being grazed in woodlands, which over time favoured grasses rather than trees. The Domesday

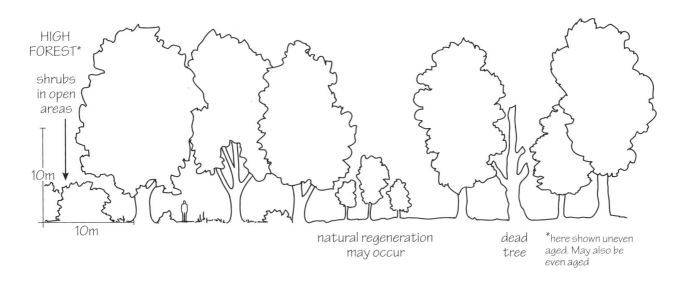

HIGH FOREST*

shrubs in open areas

10m

10m

natural regeneration may occur

dead tree

*here shown uneven aged. May also be even aged

COPPICE

10m

10m

newly cut, showing first year growth

mature

COPPICE WITH STANDARDS

10m

10m

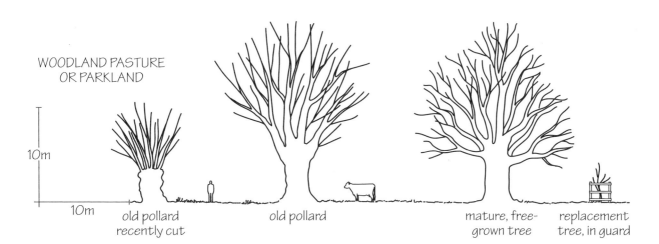

WOODLAND PASTURE OR PARKLAND

10m

10m

old pollard recently cut

old pollard

mature, free-grown tree

replacement tree, in guard

Book (1086) recognised wood-pastures as a different category from coppice woodlands, and the rights to graze animals, cut timber, cut pollards, collect fruit and other rights of the system were strictly regulated. Some regeneration of trees took place naturally in thorny scrub, and other trees were pollarded, so that new growth occurred out of reach of grazing animals. Many wood-pastures were enclosed as deer parks or landscape parks, of which some still survive. Where grazing in wood-pastures lapses, seedling trees and shrubs survive and develop, and open grassy areas decline, until the area is mainly wooded. Amongst the more recent trees, the presence of wide-spreading mature or veteran trees, whose form indicates that they developed in the open conditions of wood-pasture, are a clue to the previous management system.

High forest

In a high forest system, the trees are allowed to grow to their mature height, creating a closed canopy. The trees may be of even age, as in a plantation, or of mixed ages. Historically, this system was little used in Britain. Many oak plantations of the 19th century were left unmanaged and have grown up into densely-stocked high forest. Conifer plantations are managed as high forest. Selection of species, brashing or pruning, removal of underwood species and other management may take place.

New woodlands

Most new woodlands are created by planting, rather than by natural regeneration. There is a strong commitment through the grant system of the Forestry Commission, the UKBAP and through other agencies and initiatives to new woodland planting of native, local provenance species in mixtures which imitate natural vegetation communities, to create multi-purpose woodlands.

Although new woodlands cannot replace the ancient woodlands, with the right management they can quickly become important features for wildlife, amenity, landscape and other values. Many of the woodlands planted from the 1960s onwards around new towns, reservoirs, in reclaimed industrial areas and elsewhere have become mature, attractive landscape features and valuable habitats. Mobile species, such as mammals and birds, and including some rare species have taken advantage of the new woodland habitats.

When planning new planting schemes of over a hectare, it should be borne in mind that grants for planting new native woodlands give higher priority to those woodlands which:

- Are in priority areas such as Rural Priority Areas or Community Forests.

- Contribute to a national or local BAP, HAP or SAP target (p34).

- Extend an Ancient Semi-Natural Woodland.

- Include proposals for public access.

- Include proposals for community involvement in design or management.

See page 185 for further details on grants.

CHOOSING SPECIES

The species chosen should be native to the local area. The species and mixture chosen should mimic local semi-natural woods on similar soils, and with aspect and other conditions to the site you want to plant. Advice may be needed on which local woodlands are thought to match the local type most closely, and whether the planting site has any limitations of soil, drainage or other factors which may make it unsuitable.

The National Vegetation Classification (NVC) describes 19 different woodland types, which are listed in Table 5b. Further details on the species, distribution and soils of 15 of these woodland types are included on pages 190-194 For full details see *Creating New Native Woodlands* (Rodwell, John and Patterson, Gordon, 1994).

The National Vegetation Classification table (Table 5b) can be used to:

- Predict the type of woodland vegetation which would naturally develop on a site.

- Provide lists of ecologically appropriate trees and shrubs to plant, with an indication of the proportions and patterns that could be used.

- Identify optimal plant precursors that may already occupy the site, to give a head start in the development of appropriate ground cover.

- Indicate other desirable plants characteristic of the woodland type, which could be planted or otherwise encouraged.

- Suggest forms of woodland management which could aid development of the full community of woodland and herbaceous plants.

For small amenity woods, planting schemes in urban areas, shelterbelts and other 'non-woodland' planting, species and communities of the local woodland type may not be the most appropriate. Native trees, notably beech and Scots pine, have been widely planted over many centuries out of their natural range, where they

Table 5b: WOODLAND TYPES: CLASSIFICATION AND NOMENCLATURE

This table lists the National Vegetation Classification semi-natural woodland types, together with the equivalent new native woodland type. Adapted from *Creating New Native Woodlands* (Forestry Commission, 1994)

Zone		NVC woodland type	New native woodland type
Lowland South and east	W8	Ash – field maple – dog's mercury	Lowland mixed broadleaved with dog's mercury
	W10	Pedunculate oak – bracken – bramble	Lowland mixed broadleaved with bluebell
	W16	Oak – Birch – wavy hair grass	Lowland oak – birch with bilberry
	W15	Beech – wavy hair grass	Beech – oak with wavy hair-grass
	W12	Beech – dog's mercury	Beech – ash with dog's mercury
	W13	Yew	*Yew
	W14	Beech – bramble	Beech – oak with bramble
Upland North and west	W9	Ash – rowan – dog's mercury	Upland mixed broadleaved with dog's mercury
	W11	Sessile oak – downy birch	Upland oak – birch with bluebell
	W17	Sessile oak – downy birch – *Dicranum majus*	Upland oak – birch with bilberry
	W18	Scots pine – *Hylocomium splendens*	Scots pine with heather
	W19	Juniper – wood sorrel	Juniper with wood sorrel
Wet soils			
Mainly south	W1	Sallow – marsh bedstraw	*Sallow with marsh bedstraw
Mainly south	W2	Sallow – downy birch – common reed	Alder with common reed
North	W3	Bay willow – bottle sedge	*Sallow with bottle sedge
Mainly north and west	W4	Downy birch – purple moor grass	Birch with purple moor grass
Mainly south	W5	Alder – tussock sedge	*Alder with tussock sedge
Mainly south	W6	Alder – stinging nettle	Alder with stinging nettle
Mainly upland, north and west	W7	Alder – ash – yellow pimpernel	Alder - ash with yellow pimpernel
* Planting these types not recommended			

are valued. Shelterbelts may need to include non-native species which are able to survive in exposed conditions, and act as a nurse for native and locally native species. Planting on reclaimed sites, which normally have soils which are compacted, prone to waterlogging or otherwise disturbed, may need to include pioneer species which are not of the local type. These may include alder, rowan, birch and goat willow. For further details see *Reclaiming Disturbed Land for Forestry* (Forestry Commission, 1994).

Local provenance

The use of planting stock which has been propagated from trees native to the locality is important for the maintenance of local genetic variety. Its importance is recognised in the Forestry Commission's UK Forestry Standard, BAPs, the UK Woodland Assurance Scheme, grant schemes, and through the advice of forestry and nature conservation agencies.

One approach is to grow your own planting stock from seed collected locally. Comprehensive details on collection and propagation are given in *Tree Planting and Aftercare* (BTCV, 2000).

Many nurseries supply native provenance trees and shrubs, and supplies of local provenance trees and shrubs are increasing. The voluntary scheme of local seed zones is described in *Using Local Stock for Planting Native Trees and Shrubs* (Forestry Commission, 1999). Under this scheme 24 different seed zones are identified in England, Scotland and Wales, to help growers source and supply, and buyers identify, stock of local provenance. Some nurseries are able to collect seed and propagate trees 'to order', to replicate local genetic stock for particular planting schemes.

Species mix

The woodland types recommended for creating new native woodlands (p39) include details of the recommended major and minor tree species, and major and minor shrub species for each woodland type (see pages 190-194).

From the lists of recommended tree and shrub species, a mixture should be chosen which suits the particular soil type and other physical aspect of the site, and which suits the purpose of the planting. For upland types, the choice is limited to only a few tree and shrub species. For lowland mixed broadleaved woodland on neutral and alkaline soils, there is a much larger range of trees and shrubs which can be used.

The species mixture must ensure that vigorous species do not suppress the slower growing species, and that the mixture has the potential to create the desired woodland structure. Recommended percentages of each species should be chosen after consideration of all factors affecting the individual site.

There are some rare species which it is recommended should not be planted, because their remaining distribution pattern is of intrinsic importance, and could be altered by planting. They are listed below. Any planting of these species should be recorded with the nature conservation agency, and only local provenance stock should be used.

SILVICULTURAL SYSTEM

This describes the system which is going to be used to manage the woodland, and may vary between different areas or compartments of the woodland. Systems include coppice, coppice with standards and high forest (p37). Management of high forest will require thinning and selection. Systems of shelterwood, group felling or continuous cover (p41) may be used for maintaining and regenerating the woodland.

OPEN SPACE

Glades, rides and other open grassy spaces within woodlands are valuable for wildlife and amenity. The recreational use of most woodlands is concentrated in these open spaces, and given the choice, many people prefer to walk along the woodland edge, or in the grassy spaces between wooded clumps, rather than actually under the canopy of trees.

When planning the open spaces in a woodland, their future management must be considered. In most locations, unplanted areas will rapidly grow over with rough grasses, brambles and scrub. This may create a useful wildlife habitat, but supporting different species to an open grassy space. Eventually, scrub will succeed to woodland. Grassy spaces have to be regularly maintained by mowing or grazing, and grazing whilst preventing damage to young trees is difficult to manage. Small glades are awkward to mow, and will 'shrink' as the trees mature, so open spaces should be designed in simple,

Table 5c: RARE TREE SPECIES NOT RECOMMENDED FOR PLANTING

SPECIES	CHARACTERISTIC WOODLAND TYPE
Small-leaved lime *(Tilia cordata)*	W8, W10
Large-leaved lime *(Tilia platyphyllos)*	W8
Wild service tree *(Sorbus torminalis)*	W8
Midland hawthorn *(Crataegus laevigata)*	W8, W10
Rare whitebeams *(Sorbus rupicola, Sorbus lancastrienis, Sorbus devoniensis)*	W9
Box *(Buxus sempervirens)*	W12
Wild pear *(Pyrus communis)*	W8

generous shapes. Clumps of trees in grassland, parkland and wood-pasture type landscapes are normally much more expensive to maintain than closely-spaced and fairly uniform tree planting. The Woodland Grant Scheme (p185) allows 20% of the area to be unplanted.

PLANTING PATTERNS AND SPACING

The standard plant spacing for large scale planting, as required under Forestry Commission grant schemes for broadleaved and conifer planting, is 2,250 trees per hectare (910 per acre), which is equivalent to 2.1m x 2.1m (6'10" x 6'10") spacing. This is the quickest way to establish woodland cover, as the canopy closes rapidly, reducing the competition from weeds. Strong upright growth for maximum timber value is encouraged. A mixture of canopy and underwood species can be used, and thinning will be needed.

The plant spacing for new native woodlands, amenity woodlands and small broadleaved woodlands less than 3 hectares (7.4 acres), under current grant schemes, is 1,100 per hectare (445 trees per acre), which is equivalent to 3m x 3m (9'10" x 9'10").

Wider spacing results in slower canopy closure and a bushier form of tree or shrub. There must be equal attention to effective weed control (pp64-67) whatever the spacing, but with the wider spacing there will be more need to manage the 'inter-row' vegetation. In the years before the canopy closes, the gaps between 3m spaced trees will normally need be mown, in order to prevent brambles and scrub overtaking the planted species. If cut once a year in late summer, the inter-row vegetation may provide a useful short term habitat for ground nesting birds, small mammals and invertebrates, before it closes over to a shaded habitat. The wider spacing means there will be less requirement for thinning.

The subject of planting patterns is complex. Different species of trees do not grow at the same rate, and slower growing species will be at a disadvantage. Groups of at least 9 of the same species are recommended for 2m x 2m spacing, from which one or more trees will be selected during thinning. At 3m x 3m, groups of 5 or 7 may be appropriate. Repetitive formula-driven patterns of groups of species at regular spacing are easy to plan and plant, but may not introduce sufficient variety for a natural effect. Clumps of unevenly spaced trees of varying species mixes, with varying gaps between clumps can be used to introduce a more natural pattern. However, this is more difficult to plan and plant, and complicates the management of 'inter-row' vegetation in the early years. Even gaps of about 10m, which appear so large at planting, will eventually disappear as the canopy closes, and management in the interval may be a problem. It may be easier and cheaper to plant fairly uniformly, and then use thinning to introduce variation. Natural variation will develop as trees grow at different rates due to site conditions and other factors. For further information on planting patterns see the Forestry Commission publications *Creating New Native Woodlands* (Rodwell, John and Patterson, Gordon, 1994) and *Creating and Managing Woodlands around Towns* (Hodge, Simon J, 1995).

Where grants are not being used, the plant spacing and pattern is open to choice. Wider spacing is cheaper to supply and plant, but maintenance in the establishment years may be a problem. Close spacing is more expensive to supply and plant, but is the quickest and cheapest way to establish woodland cover. The establishment of a woodland flora is likely to be more successful and can be started earlier under a closely-planted canopy. Open grassy spaces, to remain open as the trees mature, need to be at least 25m diameter.

Woodland regeneration

Intervention may be needed in mature, understocked or heavily grazed woodlands to ensure that they survive as woodlands. This will require the encouragement of natural regeneration, or planting. Fencing or individual tree protection is likely to be needed.

Natural regeneration may be needed in ancient replanted woodlands, from which exotic or non-local species have been removed, or in other woodlands which have been cleared of rhododendron or other invasive species.

In the past, 'high forest' or plantations in Britain were managed by being clear felled and then replanted. Increasingly, continuous cover systems are being used, under which some woodland cover is retained throughout, and regeneration or replanting takes place amongst it. Continuous cover systems include:

Single tree selection

This is the method of regeneration, used in woods managed for timber production, which most closely matches natural woodland succession. Single trees are selected for felling as they reach the optimum age, and are replaced by natural regeneration or planting. This is only suitable for beech and other shade-tolerant species which are able to grow up in the shade of other trees.

Single tree selection

Felling is difficult because of limited space and access, and this system is more expensive than the other systems described below. Its advantage is that it allows the creation of uneven-aged woodlands with a mixture of ages spread through the woodland. It's most suitable for smaller areas or strips of woodland, where there is light from the side which encourages regeneration and growth.

Group selection

Group selection allows some woodland cover to be retained continuously, whilst giving potential to regenerate light-demanding species. The smallest group felling possible should create a gap with a diameter at least twice the height of adjacent trees. The largest group felled should cover about half a hectare.

Regeneration is normally by planting, but natural regeneration may be possible. Growth should be good, because the site is sheltered but with adequate light.

Group selection

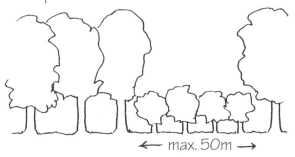

← max. 50m →

Shelterwood

A stand of trees is partially felled, leaving a scattered overstorey of mature, seed-bearing trees, spaced with a 6-10 metre (19-33') gap between the remaining crowns. The overstorey trees supply the seed for regeneration, provide shelter and frost protection to the young trees, and help shade out weed growth. With ash, alder, birch, cherry and sycamore, the overstorey trees are felled three or four years after regeneration. Oak is removed five to seven years after regeneration, and beech can be removed in stages over 15 years after regeneration. Shelterwood systems are common on the continent but not in Britain, apart from in some oak plantations in the New Forest, where planting is used instead of natural regeneration.

Shelterwood

NATURAL REGENERATION

Natural regeneration as a method of perpetuating woodland is suitable where:

- The desired parent species are present.

- There is already some regeneration taking place, which indicates that regeneration could be successful as a management technique.

- There is no particular need to fell and replant in any one year, and there can be flexibility in the timing of felling to make use of regeneration when it occurs.

- Conservation of local genetic stock is important.

Where regeneration of the desired species is occurring, this can be favoured by weeding and protection. Where regeneration of less desirable species is occurring, this can be used as shelter, and the desired species planted within them.

Regeneration requires:

- Plentiful seed. Apart from rapid colonisers such as birch and sycamore, most British tree species do not produce seed every year, with intervals of 3-5 years being typical. Beech only produces seed every 5-15 years. For further details on seed production see *Tree Planting and Aftercare* (BTCV, 2000). Seed production tends to be more prolific following warm, dry conditions in late summer of the seed year and the previous year. Late spring frosts, high winds or seed predation can cause loss of a seed crop. Successful natural regeneration therefore requires being prepared to use a good seed year when it occurs. An assessment of the developing seed crop can be made with binoculars in late June.

- Sparse ground vegetation. Most species require weed-free ground, although oak regenerates through a grass sward (p14). Bramble, bracken, scrub and rough grasses must be controlled for successful regeneration. This is best cleared by hand or by herbicide application in the August of the seed year. The activity of clearance also roughens or scarifies the ground, which aids regeneration. Beech leaf litter is slow to break down, and if the seeds fall onto deep litter they find it difficult to root through to the mineral layer below. In a beech mast year, you can encourage germination by raking the seed-covered ground, to mix the litter and seed into the soil, and discourage predation by squirrels.

- Protection from animals. Seed may be eaten by mice, squirrels and other animals during the autumn and winter. Some predation is unavoidable, but where this is excessive, for example in some beech woodlands, regeneration will be prevented. Baiting is the only method of control. For protection of seedlings and young trees from browsing animals, see page 62.

- Low levels of weed competition during the regeneration period. After successful regeneration, the young trees must be kept clear of weed growth, in the same way as planted trees (p64-67). To give a more even coverage, natural regeneration can be 'respaced', by transplanting seedlings into any gaps.

The seed trees

A correctly thinned plantation at rotation age, or a mature managed woodland should have trees appropriately spaced and of suitable growth to allow successful natural regeneration. Normally felling takes place in the winter after a seed year, with timber extracted before April to prevent damage to the regeneration. There are two options for felling.

One option is to fell between 50-75% of the trees, leaving a scattered overstorey, similar to shelterwood, to provide some shade to restrict weed growth, and reduce soil rewetting. When an area is clear felled, the ground tends to become very wet because of the sudden loss of transpiration, which before felling extracted large volumes of water from the soil. Damage by machinery also damages and compacts the ground. This can result in waterlogged ground, the growth of rushes and sedges, and adverse effects on young trees. The retained trees are removed in one or two operations over the next 10 years, taking care to cause as little damage as possible to the young trees. If the expected regeneration is not successful, these trees can be retained until there is another seed year, so giving a second chance. Although more expensive in felling costs, this option is preferable.

Alternatively, all the trees in the area to be regenerated are felled. This is cheaper than phased felling, and avoids potential damage to the regenerating trees. However, there will be strong weed growth which will have to be controlled, and rewetting may be a problem. Also, if the expected regeneration fails, there is no second chance for natural regeneration, and the area will have to be replanted. Replanting a failed regeneration plot, with strong weed growth and patches of waterlogged ground, is likely to be difficult.

Stand opening

Where only a small group of trees are felled, as in group selection (see above), or where shelterwood is used, the amount of light reaching the young trees is limited. Germination does not require light, but growth in the early years does. Different species have different requirements for light, with oak being notable as a light-demanding species. Oak regeneration is more successful at woodland edges or outside the woodland. Ash and beech can tolerate fairly heavy shade for the first few years, but after that full overhead light is required. In shelterwood, the remaining trees must be removed for successful establishment of the new trees. With group selection, further felling or thinning may be necessary to increase light to the new group.

Management of the new stand is needed for at least 10 years, to ensure that shrubby and climbing weed growth is kept under control, and that invasive tree species are removed. Respacing or new planting should be used to fill any gaps larger than 6m between the regenerating trees.

Timber measurement

AGE

The age of a tree can be roughly estimated from measuring the diameter of the trunk, and observing the conditions in which it is growing. In its early life, a tree tends to grow fast, increasing in height, spread and circumference of the trunk. As the tree ages, growth slows, and height and spread increase may stop, but the trunk continues to grow slowly in girth. The mean growth in girth of most native broadleaved trees, grown in open ground and with a full crown, is 2.5cm (1") per year (Mitchell, Alan, 1974). Therefore an open-grown tree 2.4m (8') in girth is usually about 100 years old. Yew tends to conform to the 2.5cm rule for the first 100 years, but then slows to less than half this rate over the next 4-500 years.

Table 5d: ESTIMATE OF GIRTH IN RELATION TO AGE FOR OPEN-GROWN BROADLEAVED TREES (2.5CM PER YEAR INCREASE)

Girth	31	62	94	126	157	188
dbh (cm)	10	20	30	40	50	60
Age	12	25	37	50	63	75

Trees put on girth more slowly when in competition with other trees, so that a tree growing in a woodland will show a mean growth in girth of 1.5cm (1/2") per year or less. Species also vary in their speed of growth. The table on page 44 is based on Forestry Commission estimates for trees grown in closed woodland.

Table 5e: APPROXIMATE RELATIONSHIP OF TREE DIAMETER TO AGE (TREES IN WOODLAND)

dbh (cm)	10	20	30	40	50	60+
Species	Age in years					
Beech	35	55	75	95	115	140+
Oak	30	50	70	90	120	150
Ash, sycamore, cherry	20	30	40	60		
Alder, birch	15	25	35			
Pine	20	40	60	80		
Spruce	25	40	55	80		
Larch	15	30	45	70		

An accurate age can be obtained from counting the annual rings of a felled tree. An increment borer, available from forestry suppliers, can be used to take a core of wood from a living tree, from which the annual rings can be counted. For notes on estimating age of veteran trees, see page 1490.

LENGTH AND HEIGHT

All lengths should be measured in metres, rounded down to the nearest tenth of a metre for lengths up to 10m, and to the nearest whole metre for lengths greater than 10m. The length of a piece of timber should be measured with a tape following the curvature of the log.

The total height of a standing tree is the vertical distance from the base to the uppermost point (tip). The total height of a felled tree is the straight line distance from the base to the tip.

The timber height (or timber length) of a tree is the distance from the base of the tree to the lowest point on the main stem where the diameter is 7cm overbark. In hardwoods, and occasionally in conifers, this may be the lowest point at which no main stem is distinguishable.

There are several types of instrument which can be used to measure the height of a standing tree, and which are available from suppliers of forestry equipment. Two alternative methods of estimating height, using simple equipment, are as follows.

- Cut a cane or suitable piece of wood to the exact distance measured from your eyeball to the farthest stretch of your grasping finger and thumb. Stand at a distance from the tree to be measured, holding the cane vertically at this same outstretched reach. Then walk back or forth until the tip and base of the tree

are exactly in line with the upper and lower end of the cane. Mark the ground directly below the cane. The height of the tree is equivalent to the distance from this mark to the base of the tree.

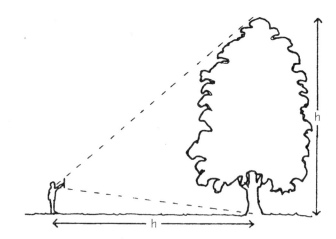

- This method requires two people, and a 30cm ruler, clearly marked at the 3cm point. One person holds the ruler vertically at arm's length, and moves back or forth until the tree is aligned vertically with the ruler. The second person holds an easily visible marker against the tree, and moves it up or down, guided by the calls of the first person, until the marker aligns with the 3cm mark on the ruler. This point is marked on the tree and is then measured from the ground, and this measurement is one tenth of the total height of the tree.

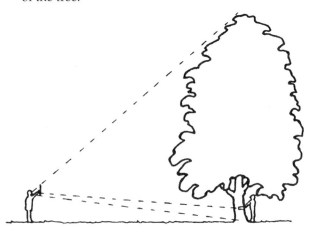

Note that it is only in spire-topped trees that the apparent top shoot is the true tip of the tree. On wide-spreading trees, the shoots on the nearest branches will appear higher than the actual tip. Where possible, walk around the tree and study it from several angles before choosing the point which appears to be the top centre.

DIAMETER

Tree diameter should be measured in centimetres, rounded down to the nearest centimetre for individual trees. Mean diameters are recorded to the nearest whole centimetre. Diameters are usually measured with a special girth tape, available from forestry equipment suppliers, which is placed around the trunk 1.3m above the ground, and from which the diameter can be read. This measurement is called the diameter at breast height (dbh). Alternatively, use a standard tape measure, and divide the measured circumference by 3.142 to obtain the diameter.

VOLUME

Volume should be recorded in cubic metres, to two or three significant figures as required. Volume measurement may be required for estimating the volume of a standing tree, the volume of a stand, or the volume of felled timber.

There are several different methods of measuring volume, with varying degrees of accuracy. The method chosen should relate to:

- The reason for carrying out timber measurement. If the stand is being measured for sale, a more accurate method should be used than if the stand is being measured for drawing up a management plan.

- The value of the stand. Very high-value stands should be sold only on the basis of measurement of the felled timber. High- to average-value stands should be measured by a method called tariffing, which requires the use of tables. Low-value stands can be estimated by a method using basal area. These methods are described in the Forestry Commission publications *Forest Mensuration* and *Timber Measurement*.

The methods noted above require not only the estimate of the volume of a selected tree, but an estimate of the number of trees within the stand to give the total volume. For small projects, tree volume can be estimated from the table given below, by measuring the dbh of individual or selected trees.

Table 5f: ESTIMATE OF TIMBER VOLUME (CUBIC METRES)

		dbh (diameter at breast height, cm)							
		10	20	25	30	35	40	45	50
Timber height (metres)	3	0.024	0.094	0.147	0.212	0.289	0.377	0.477	0.589
	4	0.031	0.126	0.196	0.283	0.385	0.503	0.636	0.785
	5	0.039	0.157	0.245	0.353	0.481	0.628	0.795	0.982
	6	0.047	0.188	0.295	0.424	0.577	0.754	0.954	1.178
	7	0.055	0.220	0.344	0.495	0.673	0.880	1.113	1.374
	10	0.079	0.314	0.491	0.707	**0.962**	1.257	1.590	1.963

0.962 = approximately 1 tonne of timber

6   Planting and early care

Planting a small tree is not a difficult or time consuming job, but ensuring that the young tree thrives requires care and attention to detail. The young tree must be kept free of weeds for at least three years, and protected against browsing and other damage. Trees and shrubs of local provenance should be used where these are obtainable (p49).

Trees should not be planted in ancient semi-natural woodlands or other woodlands of ecological value, where natural regeneration should be used as a way of perpetuating the woodland. In general, trees should only be planted within existing woodlands where there is a need to change the species composition, for example from introduced species to a more natural mix of native species, or where commercial objectives require replanting.

Trees should not be planted on unwooded areas of high conservation value, including wet grasslands, chalk downland or heathland.

The use of natural regeneration should be considered on all sites where the aim is woodland cover. (pp42-43).

For information on planning new woodlands, see pages 38-41.

Planting stock

HOW TREES GROW

There are a few points relating to tree growth which are useful to remember when planting and caring for trees.

- The major roots of trees last for the lifetime of the tree, and become thicker, in the same way that branches do. They spread out in a shallow network that is mainly within the top metre of soil, with occasional deeper roots called sinkers. Often, though not always, there is a tap root below the tree's trunk.

- The main roots bear masses of smaller roots, which, like the leaves in the tree's crown, have only a short life. Each separate root hair explores a patch of soil, extracts water and nutrients from it, and then withers away. Only those just behind the root-tip are active, and so continued growth of the tree depends on the constant growth of the fine, white new roots.

- When you plant a tree in autumn, its roots will start growth at once, using nutrients stored in the stem, though its shoots remain stationary until spring. Root growth stops about mid December. There is a burst of new feeding roots early in March, as the soil warms to 5°C, and before the aerial parts show any growth. Root growth then slows during the main period of leaf and shoot growth. This is why autumn planted trees have such an advantage over spring planted trees, as they have made some root extension in autumn, and are able to maximise the important early spring growth of root hairs.

- Root hairs extract water from the soil by osmosis. The hairs contain sap with dissolved nutrients at greater concentration than the salts in normal soil-moisture. The root hairs are semi-permeable membranes through which the soil moisture can pass, and be drawn up into the plant. If the soil moisture has a high proportion of dissolved fertiliser or salt, water will pass the other way, and the root hairs will be 'scorched'. Water cannot be absorbed through main roots, but only through root hairs.

- Roots of most species require free oxygen in the soil. However, common alder, grey sallow and some other species can survive in wet conditions by making use of oxygenated fresh water.

SIZE OF PLANTING STOCK

Trees transplant best when they are small and young. Younger trees have the following advantages:

- Because they have a better root to shoot ratio than larger stock, they more easily overcome the shock of transplanting and quickly put on new root growth.

- They are easier and cheaper to transport and handle, and less prone to physical damage or drying out when in transit.

- They can be notch planted rather than pit planted (see below), which is much quicker and just as effective.

- There is less requirement for staking.

- Being grown for only a short time in the nursery, they are cheaper to buy or less time-consuming to grow yourself.

Tree shelters or guards are commonly used with small transplanted trees. Shelters or guards add to the expense of planting, but have a multiple use in enhancing growth, protecting the tree from browsing animals, acting as a marker so that small trees can easily be located, functioning as a stake to keep the tree upright, and allowing the efficient use of herbicide spray (see below).

There are two types of stock generally used for woodland creation and other native tree planting schemes. These are bare-root stock and cell-grown stock.

BARE-ROOT STOCK

Bare-root stock for woodland planting is normally 1-3 years old. These plants are grown in open ground in a nursery, and lifted in late autumn when growth is dormant, for final planting out. They can be described by their height, and / or by the age and method of growing. A tree described as 1 + 1 has been grown for one year and then transplanted in the nursery and grown for another year. 1 u 1 describes stock which has been grown for one year, undercut, and then grown for another year. The reason for moving or undercutting in the nursery is to promote the growth of a fibrous, branching root system, which will sustain the tree when it is planted out. Plants which are grown for two or three years without this disturbance tend to produce fewer, deeper roots, which are awkward to dig up and transport, and which are slow to produce new growth after final planting.

The quality of bare-root stock should be judged by the volume of fibrous roots, and by the root collar diameter, rather than by the height of the plant. The root collar diameter is a good measure of the sturdiness of the plant, and its ability to thrive after transplanting.

Table 6a: MINIMUM ROOT COLLAR DIAMETERS (mm) FOR BROADLEAVES (from BS 3936: Part 4)

SPECIES	HEIGHT (cm)				
	20	30	40	50	60
Birch	3	4	4.5	5.5	6.5
Beech	4	5	6	7.5	9
Oak, ash, cherry, lime	5	6.5	8	9.5	11

Table 6b: STOCK TYPES SUITABLE FOR WOODLAND PLANTING

STOCK TYPE	HEIGHT (cm)
Bare-root	
Seedling (1 + 0)	15-30
Transplant ($\frac{1}{2}$ +$\frac{1}{2}$, 1 + 1)	20 -120
Undercut ($\frac{1}{2}$ u $\frac{1}{2}$, 1 u 1)	30-60
Cell-grown seedling	15-30

CELL-GROWN STOCK

Cell-grown or rootrainer trees are one-year-old seedlings, grown in special tall, narrow pots designed for tree seedlings, which promote good downward root growth without spiralling. Once roots start to grow spirally inside a pot, they tend to continue growing spirally even when planted out. The plants are normally grown for one season only in the cell or rootrainer, before being planted out in the autumn.

The diagrams show the development of root systems in a rootrainer.

ROOT DEVELOPMENT

  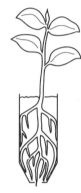

first root grows straight through drainage hole and dries off

lateral roots quickly grow out and down grooves, which prevent spiralling

the lateral roots grow through drainage hole and dry off, which promotes further root development

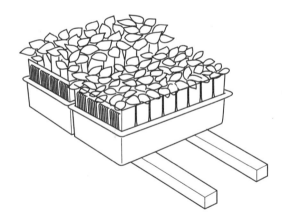

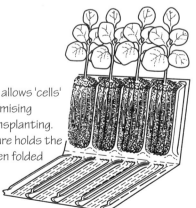

OPEN BOOK
The hinged design allows 'cells' to be opened, minimising damage when transplanting. The 'Clip Top' feature holds the cells together when folded

48

Cell-grown plants are more expensive than equivalent age bare root seedling trees, and are more bulky to transport. However, cell-grown stock has the advantage that the roots are not disturbed when planting out. Water-retaining granules, fertiliser or mycorrhiza (p12) can be included in the growing medium. Because the roots are protected, cell-grown plants can be planted before they become fully dormant, while they are still in leaf. They should put on some root growth in the autumn after planting, and then grow away quickly in the spring, putting on more height growth than similar age bare-root plants. The ability to plant in early autumn reduces the pressure to get all planting done in the late autumn/early winter period. Cell-grown plants can be planted between July and December, with September/October normally the best time, depending on season and location. Planting in July and August should only be done where the plants can be regularly watered.

Cell-grown plants are grown in polytunnels or glasshouses, and must be moved outside in the nursery for hardening off several weeks before they are due to be planted. If there is a delay between delivery and planting out, store the plants in a shady, sheltered place, and keep watered while in leaf. If storage is required during the dormant season, keep the plants in a frost-free place, or cover at night with horticultural fleece or similar to prevent the containers freezing. Planting should not be delayed until the spring, as the plants will deteriorate, and the advantage of using cell-grown stock will be lost.

All transplanted trees benefit from weeding (see below), but for cell-grown stock thorough weeding is absolutely essential. The plants are very small and easily swamped by weed growth, and although they have a good root to shoot ratio, their small size means that roots are also small. Cell-grown stock must be nurtured during the year after planting, by being regularly checked for weed growth and watered in dry spells. Because of their small size, cell-grown plants have the most to gain from the use of tree shelters.

PROVENANCE

The provenance of a plant is the place from where the seed or cutting it was grown from was originally collected.

Plants of the same species vary in their adaptations to local conditions, shown by differences in flowering time, flower or leaf size, form of growth and other characteristics. They also vary in the range of other organisms which they are able to support.

In the past, trees grown in British tree nurseries tended to be from seed of trees selected for their form and timber quality, often collected originally from trees on the continent. These may lack the special adaptations for local conditions, and the ability to support a wide range of organisms. By not perpetuating plants of local provenance, particular genetic strains may also be lost for ever.

Identifying trees of local provenance can be difficult, as trees have been widely planted for over 400 years. However, reproductive material is considered to be of local provenance if it is from stands of trees which appear well adapted to the location in which they are growing. Many nurseries in Britain now stock trees and other plants of native and local provenance.

How to plant

Note the following general points:

- The roots of bare-root plants must be kept covered at all times, to prevent them drying out. Even a few minutes' exposure to air can dry the delicate root hairs, reducing the plant's ability to establish quickly. Keep small bare-root plants completely within a polythene sack until the moment of planting, and keep the roots of larger plants similarly covered.

- Don't soak or dip bare-root plants in water before you plant. Roots are not able to absorb water this way, and the water may damage the delicate root hairs by washing off the protective soil covering. If plants are delivered with dry roots they should be returned to the supplier. An exception to this rule is when using a root dip (p51), which coats the root hairs with a fine gel that aids establishment.

- Preferably plant on mild, damp days. Avoid days with frost or strong, drying winds.

- Don't dig planting pits or notches until the day of planting, as they are liable to fill with water. The easiest and most efficient method is to make the pit or notch and plant the tree in one operation.

- On variable ground choose each planting position with care. Keeping to rigid spacing patterns is less important than maximising tree survival. Avoid hollows or dips which may become waterlogged, or patches of ground which are prone to drying out. Don't plant too close to existing stumps or rocks. On exposed sites, plant in the lee of any mounds or ridges.

- The planting notches or pits must be big enough to take the roots, without having to bend or break any to fit. The main roots stay in the position in which they are put at planting, so take time to ensure they are spread evenly.

- A bare-root tree should be planted to the same depth or slightly deeper as it was growing previously, as shown by the soil mark on the stem. Cell-grown plants are planted slightly lower than previously grown (p53).

- After planting, tread carefully around the stem, taking care not to scrape the bark with your boot. Don't stamp hard, as this may displace the tree and spoil the soil structure. In clay soils, don't make a depression around the stem, as this may gather water and result in stem rot.

- Check for firmness by pulling gently on the stem, which should not move. Check again at least once during the four weeks after planting, and firm back in any plants that have worked loose from wind or frost action.

- If at all possible, water the tree immediately after planting, using a bucketful of water per tree, tipped slowly around the stem of the tree so it trickles down into the rooting zone. Such watering aids establishment, and it is worth putting effort into providing a supply of water on the planting day.

- Pit planting should not be used as an alternative to whole-site preparation on heavy clays or other difficult soils (see below).

- Stakes should not be necessary when planting small transplants within woodlands or on other fairly sheltered sites. Some movement in the wind helps develop a strong base to the stem and a good root system. However transplants in very exposed situations may need staking for a year or two, until their root systems are established. Tree shelters and most other tree guards include stakes, which are needed to hold the shelter in position (p56), and so help protect the tree from wind damage. Transplanted standard trees will require staking.

GROUND PREPARATION

Tree species should be chosen to suit the location, site and soil, rather than trying to alter site conditions to suit particular species. Planting within or near existing woodlands should follow the local woodland type, which will be adapted to local soil conditions.

Areas available for new woodland planting may be on highly disturbed soils within urban areas, old industrial workings or derelict land, which tend to have poor soil structure and moisture holding capacity. Amenity grassland areas often have soils which are badly compacted from frequent trampling. These sites are often dry in summer, but waterlogged in winter, creating anaerobic conditions which kill tree roots. Pre-planting site preparation to provide at least 500mm of

uncompacted, freely draining soil greatly improves tree establishment and long-term stability. On the large scale, this will require ripping or subsoiling using specialist machinery, which can break up the ground beneath grassland without disturbing the turf. For further details see Hodge, Simon J (1985) or Kerr, Gary and Williams, Hugh V (1999). On the small scale, double digging may be needed, as for garden cultivation.

Clay soils

Trees can be difficult to establish on clay soils, which become waterlogged in winter and dry out in summer. Tree roots of most species require air in the soil, and die in waterlogged, anaerobic conditions. Clay soils, although containing plenty of moisture, hold it by strong suction in the minute gaps between the clay particles, making it unavailable to tree roots. Loamy soils, with bigger gaps between the particles, make water more easily available to plants. Where trees establish in a free draining layer over clay soils, they can be very unstable because of the shallow roots. In summer, when the top layer of soil dries out, the tree may suffer from drought because it has no roots into the waterlogged area below. Small cell-grown or notch planted trees tend to dry out in summer as the topsoil dries and cracks. Pit planting is not the answer, as the pit will normally become waterlogged. The only exception are soils which have a ploughpan or impermeable zone in the subsoil, which can be broken up to allow water to drain through. Addition of organic matter may improve the appearance of a clay soil at planting time, but is not necessarily helpful to tree growth (see below).

For large-scale tree planting schemes on clay soils, mechanical cultivation of the whole site will be necessary. For small schemes the following approaches should be considered:

- Reconsider. It may be better not to try planting trees on the site. If the site is damp grassland, it may have ecological value as it is.

- Fence the site against grazing animals, and then natural regeneration of shrubs and trees that are tolerant of the site conditions may eventually appear.

If planting is still required, consider the following options:

- Plant only trees or shrubs that are tolerant of wet sites.

- To increase the range of species which can be grown, improve drainage by digging drainage ditches. The ditches should be aligned to take water slowly off the site. Dig approximately to the dimensions shown, and mound the material in a flattened ridge, starting about 100mm back from the edge of the ditch, so material doesn't slide back in. The tree should be planted at least one metre from the centre of the ditch.

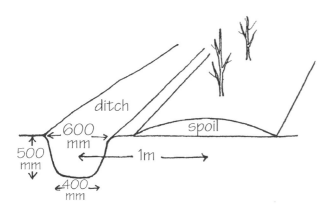

Soil ameliorants

Research has found that the incorporation of organic amendments into planting pits is rarely beneficial and can be harmful (Hodge, Simon J, 1995). Compost and other organic matter can make the planting pit soil more coarsely textured than the surrounding soil, which can result in waterlogging in the winter and increased drought stress in the summer. Soil ameliorants with high levels of nutrients can damage or 'scorch' the roots, when water moves out of the roots under osmotic pressure.

Water retentive gels can be added at planting time. These can absorb many times their own weight in water, which is then available to the plant as needed during dry periods. However if there is a prolonged drought, irrigation will be needed to 'recharge' the gel.

Mycorrhiza

Mycorrhiza provide a beneficial association between certain soil fungi and the roots of trees and other plants, through which the fungus supplies dissolved nutrients and water to the tree. Mycorrhizal associations are vital to woodland ecosystems (p12). Mycorrhizal activity can be encouraged at planting by the use of root dips or powders which contain mycorrhizal spores. For suppliers see page 189.

Alternatively, the introduction of rotted leaf mould from around an existing nearby tree of the same species is thought to help initiate mycorrhizal associations. Rake away the top 25cm (1") layer of leaf litter from an area of about two square metres, and then carefully scrape away the top centimetre or so of organic material, taking care not to damage any surface roots. Add about half a spade of this material into the planting notch or hole.

Planting in grass

When planting in a grass sward, for example planting a new woodland on a former pasture, it's best to leave the grass sward undisturbed, and then use mulches or herbicide after planting to create a grass-free zone around each tree. If the whole sward is ploughed or treated with herbicide before planting, there is likely to be strong growth of weeds. These are much more difficult to manage than the grass they replaced.

Planting notches or pits are relatively easy to make in short turf thathas been regularly grazed or mown, but more difficult through a thick thatch of long grass. Consider mowing the planting area a few times in the months prior to planting, as this will make it easier to dig notches or pits, and herbicides or plastic sheet mulches are also more effective on newly-grown short grass.

If making a notch through grass is too difficult, you may need to remove a few turves first and then plant into the bare ground. Removing a few turves will also be necessary if you want to make a planting pit. The turves can either be broken up and discarded, or turned over around the planted tree.

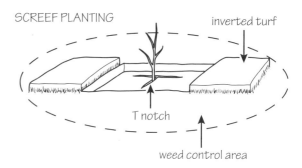

In damp ground, cut a thick turf, preferably about 230mm (9") thick, and turn it over to create a better drained planting position. Make a slit through the turf and plant the tree. Inverted turves are not effective in controlling weeds, and herbicides or mulches will be needed.

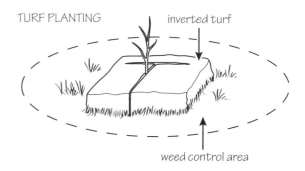

If you don't plan to use either a herbicide or a plastic mulch to control weeds, you will need to start with a generous weed-free area, and maintain it by hand weeding or hoeing. An area with sides equivalent to four spades' width is not too big, though it will seem so when you plant. You must weed regularly, or by mid-summer the planting square will be grown over with weeds, adversely affecting tree growth. This method of weed control is labour intensive, and it is easy to damage the tree stem or roots with a hoe or fork.

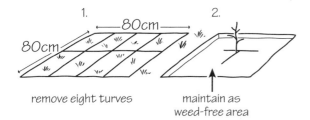

remove eight turves   maintain as weed-free area

Ploughed or ripped ground

Where soils have been ploughed to reduce compaction, ridges will be formed. Planting along the ridges will be beneficial in providing a better drained planting position, as shown above. On exposed sites, plant on the leeward side of the ridge, to give some shelter.

Where compacted ground has been loosened by ripping or subsoiling, it's not advisable to plant along the rip line, as this will tend to open up in dry weather, exposing the tree roots. Plant between the lines instead, using either notch or pit planting.

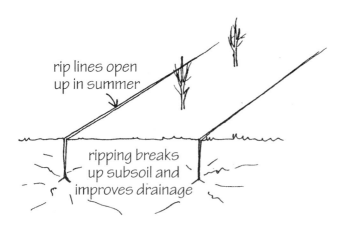

rip lines open up in summer

ripping breaks up subsoil and improves drainage

Planting in existing woodlands

Ground preparation will not normally be needed for planting within existing woodlands, as soils will be suitable for tree growth. Planting may be needed because of lack of natural regeneration, or to improve age or species diversity. However note the following:

- Following tree felling, either for clearance or harvesting purposes, soils tend to become wet because of damage to the soil structure during extraction, and because of the sudden loss of transpiration due to tree loss. Temporary drainage ditches may be needed to take water off the site. Plant on mounds or any dry patches within the cleared area.

- The absence of trees at a particular place within a woodland may indicate that the soils are unsuitable, and it may be best to leave the site unplanted.

- When replanting a recently cleared area, plant in the gaps between the stumps, rather than close to them. If the stumps are being left to regrow, they will soon outgrow any tree planted nearby. Planting close to rotting conifer stumps or treated broadleaved stumps may increase the risk of fungal damage.

NOTCH PLANTING

Notch planting is generally the best method of planting young bare-root trees, which are in turn the best size of plant for rapid establishment (p48). Roots of vigorous young trees are very strong and will have no difficulty penetrating normal soils, provided they are not competing with grass for water and nutrients. Notch planting reduces the effects of windblow because the transplant is held firmly in the notch, which is made with minimal ground disturbance. This lessens the requirement for staking. However if notch planting is badly done, with roots crammed into too small a space, or notches not properly closed, losses will result. Young trees with spreading roots will need to be pit planted (p53), and trees should not be notch planted direct into clay soils without previous soil preparation (p50). Trees notch planted into recently cultivated ground should be planted so that the soil mark on the root collar is about 2-3 cm below ground level, to allow for soil settlement. Similarly plants on newly made mounds should be planted a little deeper than normal. This is to avoid the possibility of plant roots becoming exposed through soil settlement or erosion.

Use a heavy, straight-bladed spade or specialist planting spade (p52) to make the notch, which should be just deep enough to take the roots. Push the blade into the ground, and then move it backwards and forwards to open up a notch. With a sideways, wiping motion, slide the plant into the notch and pull it upwards to spread the roots. Tread carefully but firmly around the stem to close the notch and prevent any movement in the wind.

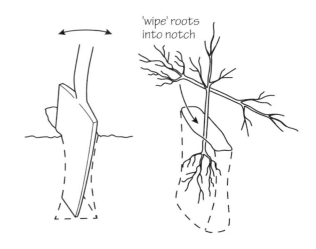

'wipe' roots into notch

For plants with larger root systems, make two cuts in a 'T' shape as shown, to open up a larger notch to take the roots.

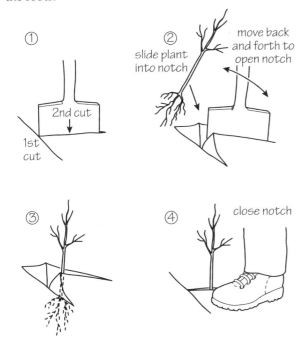

CELL-GROWN STOCK

Note the following:

- Cell-grown plants can be planted with an ordinary spade or trowel, but a special tool called a 'spear' makes planting easier and quicker.

- The top of the cell or plug must be at least 12mm (half an inch) below the soil surface, and covered with soil. It left exposed, the compost in the cell dries out and does not easily re-wet.

- In heavy clays, cell-grown plants should not be planted without earlier ground preparation (p50).

- Plant boxes and carriers are available from suppliers of cell-grown plants, for use during planting operations.

PIT PLANTING

Pit planting involves digging out a pit, large enough to take the roots, and piling up the soil temporarily at the edge of the pit. The tree is then planted and the hole backfilled. Pit planting is required in the following cases.

- For transplants or other young trees which have roots that are too bushy and spreading to fit in a notch.

- For container-grown plants other than cell-grown plants. These might include holly or other evergreens which do not survive bare-root transplanting, and are grown for two years or more in containers.

- On sites with disturbed soils that have not been prepared by machine cultivation. On steep slopes, stony ground or other difficult sites young trees will normally benefit from pit planting. However pit planting should not be used instead of whole site preparation on clay soils or those prone to waterlogging (see below).

- For standard trees which have large root-balls or are grown in large containers. Standard trees have a poor success rate, and are not recommended for planting, other than for orchards or gardens.

Pit planting has the advantage over notch planting in that it makes it easier to plant the tree without damaging the roots, and breaks up the soil to allow the roots to spread. The main disadvantage is that it takes longer. For small transplants planted into cultivated ground, there is no evidence that pit planting improves establishment, and notch planting is the standard method used for large-scale woodland planting.

Some people find that a 'hybrid' method works well, combining the advantages of digging a pit with the speed of notch planting. This is also a good system for pair working. One person cuts through the turf and digs out a sod of earth which is kept on the spade, resting on the ground by the hole. The other person places the tree in position and spreads the roots, and then the first crumbles the soil back into the hole. With experience, one person can do this on their own, by tipping the soil gently off the spade whilst holding the tree with the other hand.

When pit planting bare-root stock it is not necessary to add compost or other organic matter (see p51). Additional organic matter can be helpful in establishing container-grown stock (see below).

Procedure

To pit plant a tree:

1. When planting in grass, first remove some turves. If herbicide or mulch is going to be used for weed-control, you need only remove sufficient turves to dig the hole. To create a clear metre square for hand-weeding, remove eight turves. The turves can be inverted around the pit, chopped up in the bottom of the pit, or inverted around the tree.

2. Dig a pit large enough to take the roots or root-ball, and put the soil to one side. If there is a difference in the top and lower layer of soil, pile up separately. Dig the hole square rather than round, as round holes encourage roots to spiral.

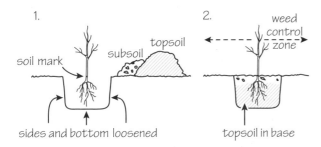

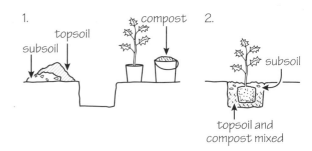

3. In cohesive soils, loosen the soil in the sides and bottom of the pit with a spade or fork.

4. Place the tree centrally in the pit, checking that the soil collar is at the correct height, and spread the roots. If working as a pair, one person can hold the tree while the other backfills carefully around the roots, using the friable top soil first. Shake the tree gently so that soil trickles down between the roots. Backfill with the rest of the soil, finishing with the subsoil.

5. Tread gently around the tree to firm the soil, taking care not to scrape the bark of the tree with your foot.

6. Water the tree if possible.

Container-grown stock

Nearly all native trees for woodland planting are supplied bare-root or cell-grown, but holly and a few introduced species such as holm oak are supplied container-grown, in peat, coir or other light, friable composts. This is because they are slow-growing evergreens, and are too small to plant out as one-year-old cell-grown seedlings, and do not transplant well bare-root. After planting, the roots may not easily make the transition into the surrounding soil, especially if there is any spiralling of roots within the rootball. Adding compost, leaf mould or other organic material when backfilling the planting pit should encourage the roots to grow out of the rootball and into the surrounding soil.

Before planting, make sure that the compost in the container is moist throughout, as if planted dry, it will tend to stay dry. If a rootball of peat compost has been allowed to dry out before planting, re-wet it with a solution of about 5ml of washing-up liquid in 5 litres of water.

Follow the general procedure given above for pit planting, but mixing in the compost and soil when backfilling. Plant so that the surface of the compost can be covered with a thin layer of soil. If the compost is exposed at the surface, the water tends to evaporate more quickly from the compost, leaving the rootball drier than the surrounding soil.

STAKING

Small transplants (eg 40-60cm) do not require staking to prevent displacement by the wind, as correct notch-planting techniques should hold them firmly in the ground. Tree shelters and other tree protection products are widely used with transplants, and protect against wind damage as well as browsing (p58). More details on tree protection are given below.

Stakes may be needed for taller transplants (90-120cm) in exposed positions, or where it is considered that stakes may help prevent accidental damage or vandalism. The Conservation Volunteers can supply square stakes in a range of sizes from 75 cm to 1.5m height, and 50-75mm diameter round stakes 1.65m height.

Procedure

It is easier and safer to knock in the stake after you have planted the tree, to avoid the chance of the stake causing injury to the face when you bend down to plant. The stake should normally be put in on the south-west side of the tree, so that the prevailing wind blows the tree away from the stake. When planting, avoid placing any spreading roots at this point, or they will be damaged when the stake is knocked in.

Plant the tree by notch planting or using the 'hybrid' method described above. Place the stake on the south-west side of the tree, and knock it in until it is completely firm in the ground, and no higher than one-third of the tree height. As explained below, it is important that the upper part of the tree sways in the wind, to encourage strong roots and lower stem diameter. Any excess height should be sawn off, as the stem may chafe against it. Attach a tree tie at the one-third height.

Where stakes are functioning mainly as markers to make trees easy to locate in nettles, bracken or other tall vegetation, it is much cheaper to use bamboo canes. Proper weed control measures should ensure that trees are not lost in vegetation.

Sturdy round diameter tree stakes have the useful incidental function of protecting tree trunks from mower damage, which is a frequent cause of damage to young trees near mown grass. It's worth 'staking' any vulnerable young trees alongside mown paths or on the outer edge of any tree planting area surrounded by mown grass. In this case ignore advice about prevailing wind, and instead put the stake where it will protect against prevailing mower damage! Retain stakes in this position for as long as mower damage remains a possibility.

Pit planted trees

Larger, pit planted trees, for which tree shelters are not appropriate, will normally require staking. This will include pit-planted young trees over about 1.5m (5') tall, or 1.2m (4') tall if planted in exposed positions. The function of the stake is to hold the base of the stem firmly and allow the roots to establish, but not to prevent wind sway. Research has shown that it is the swaying of the tree in the wind which stimulates the growth of the stem diameter. If the tree is staked and tied just below the crown, the stem cannot sway, and little increase in stem diameter occurs from base to crown. In extreme cases the stem may become thicker above the tie than below it. Wind sway also stimulates the growth of roots at the root collar.

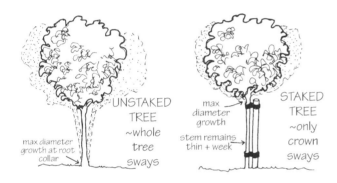

Stakes and ties cost money and need maintenance to check they are not rubbing or restricting stem diameter growth. It is much better to avoid the need for them altogether by planting younger, smaller trees.

Remedial staking

Sometimes young trees become displaced by exceptionally strong winds, or where temporary flooding has caused root damage. A short stake or stakes should be used to secure the tree until root growth has recovered. Knock the stake in on the windward side of the tree, and attach the tie at a point no higher than one-third the height of the tree. Use a proprietary tree tie, which has a spacer between the tree and stake or is tied in a figure of eight, to prevent chafing. Most ties will need nailing to the stake to stop them slipping. On buckle ties, the buckle should be at the stake, not the tree stem. Double stakes can be used as shown.

A stake should only be required for two growing seasons, by which time the tree should have put on sufficient root growth to hold it firmly. If it hasn't, improved weed

control measures should be used to encourage the tree into growth.

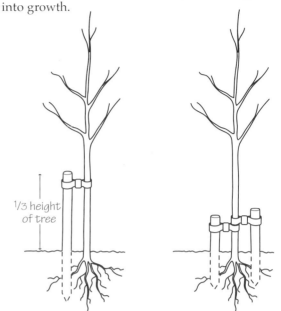

Tree protection

In most areas of Britain, newly planted trees and natural regeneration will require protection against damage by wild animals, domestic stock or people. Tree protection can be provided by fitting individual shelters or guards around each tree, or by fencing the entire area, or by a combination of the two methods.

DAMAGING AGENTS

Wild animals

Obtain advice locally about the likely incidence of damage to young trees by deer, rabbits and voles. Deer are now present in nearly all rural areas, and increasingly in urban fringe areas. The likelihood of rabbit damage can be found out by looking for burrows nearby. Rabbits rarely move more than 200m from their burrows to graze. Voles are present in most areas, and populations will increase rapidly in some years where grass is left to grow long. Weed control measures using herbicide reduce vole damage, because voles are reluctant to cross bare ground.

Domestic stock

In pastures or on grazed commons, newly planted trees must be thoroughly protected against all domestic grazing animals likely to have access to the land. Grazing animals are usually curious and hungry, and will browse on any foliage they can reach. They can also physically damage young trees by rubbing against them, or by damaging the bark. Horses may strip the bark of trees if they get bored or hungry.

People

In areas of public access, local consultation should ensure that new planting is done in accordance with the wishes of the local community. Planting that blocks access, restricts the use of open spaces for informal games, or restricts views may attract adverse attention.

Accidental damage can be avoided by careful design, so that local users are not tempted to take short-cuts through planted areas, or operators of mowing machinery are less likely to damage young trees accidentally .

Targeted vandalism is more difficult to prevent. Measures may include:

- Unobtrusive planting in long grass or scrubby vegetation.

- Planting young, small trees amongst thorny shrubs such as gorse, hawthorn, bramble or berberis.

- Fencing. Most fencing can be vandalised by cutting with wire cutters, but fencing which is difficult to climb will deter casual vandalism. Chestnut paling, strained wire fencing or barbed wire fencing may be suitable.

INDIVIDUAL PROTECTION

The cost of perimeter fencing needs to be compared with the cost of individual protection. The following factors should be considered:

- The cost of individual protection (expressed as £/tree), and the cost of fencing (expressed as £/metre).

- The size of the area to be planted.

- The shape of the area to be planted.

- The planting density.

- The public use of the area and the likelihood of vandalism.

- The effect of fencing on movement of non-damaging wildlife such as badgers and game birds.

An example, for roe deer, is shown in the graph below.

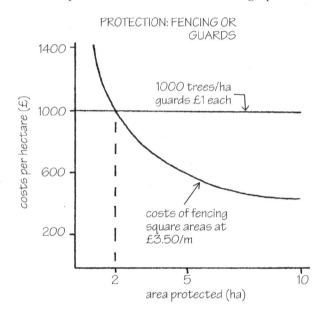

Both the graph and table are from the Forestry Commission Practice Note 3 *The Prevention of Mammal Damage to Trees in Woodland* (Forestry Commission, 1998) which should be consulted for further details.

TABLE 6c: COMPARISON OF PROTECTION BY TREESHELTERS AND FENCING

PESTS	Site 1 – roe deer and rabbits	Site 2 – rabbits
The planting site:		
Shape	Rectangular	Triangular
Dimension	100 x 60m	200 x 400 x 450m
Area	0.6 ha	4 ha
Number of plants	1200 (2000/ha)	12000 (3000/ha)
Fencing:		
Fence length	320m	1050m
Fence cost (£/m)	£4.10 (deer fencing)	£3.30 (rabbit fencing)
Total fencing cost	**£1312**	**£3465**
Individual tree protection:		
Cost of treeshelter (£/tree)	£1.00 (1.2m shelter)	£0.70 (0.6m shelter)
Total treeshelter cost	**£1200**	**£8400**
Most economical method	**Treeshelters**	**Fencing**

There may be other factors to consider for small planting schemes. It may be possible to re-use fencing or individual protection products. The role of fencing to prevent mower damage may be important. The method of weed control is also significant, as weeds growing up within shelters and guards can be difficult to deal with. For small planting schemes, a perimeter fence to protect against damage by animals or people, combined with total weed control within, can lead to very rapid establishment.

There is a large and potentially confusing range of tree protection products on the market, with new products coming available each year. For a list of suppliers see page 189. The Conservation Volunteers supply a range of well tried and tested Tubex products, which are pvc free and suitable for most tree planting applications.

Shelters or guards must be carefully chosen to suit the size, species and form of planting stock, the damaging animals present, and to combine efficiently with the chosen method of weed control. Nearly all shelters, guards or spirals for small transplants will need a stake or bamboo for support. For mixed species planting, different types of shelters or guards will normally be necessary.

A 'shelter' normally refers to a solid, twin-walled, transparent tube. A 'guard' normally refers to a mesh product. Hybrid products are also available. Some guards have solid walls for the lower 300mm or so, to protect against herbicide damage, or for extra rabbit protection. Shelterguards are of mesh with a transparent film that disintegrates before the mesh.

Spirals are mainly used for rabbit protection in areas fenced against other animals. The vole/strimmer guard can be useful for fitting to newly established trees as necessary when shelters, guards or spirals are outgrown.

Consult suppliers' current catalogues or websites (p189) for detailed advice on products.

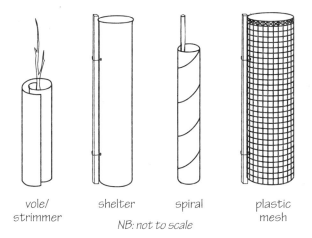

vole/strimmer   shelter   spiral   plastic mesh

NB: not to scale

Advantages

- Properly used, shelters or guards provide reliable protection against target species of animals.

- Shelters with solid walls can provide protection against damage from herbicides used for weed control.

- For most tree species, treeshelters enhance growth by raising humidity. Mesh guards can enhance growth by protecting against wind damage.

- Treeshelters or guards act as markers, to reduce the chance of trees getting trampled, and aid relocation during weeding operations. They can help protect against damage by mowers or strimmers.

Disadvantages

- Shelters and guards may be seen as an alternative to weed control, which they are not. Shelters and guards are expensive, and are a waste of money if effective weed control is lacking.

- Shelters and guards must be checked periodically to make sure they are secure in the ground, and that weeds have not taken hold inside. Solid-walled shelters should have releasable ties or a sliding attachment, so they can be lifted up for hand weeding or application of herbicide. With careful hand spraying, it is possible to spray through the mesh of some guards, but this must only be done before the trees come into leaf. It is not a suitable method for multi-stemmed shrubs in shrub shelters.

- Shelters and guards can draw unwelcome attention to trees in areas where vandalism may be a problem.

- Shelters may result in tall, spindly growth which cannot support itself (see below).

- Although most types are designed to degrade after use, this may not occur, so removal and clearing up may be necessary.

- Beech is not suitable for growing in solid walled or fine mesh shelters, as woolly aphids are a problem. Beech greater than 40cm in height at planting should be resistant if planted in fine mesh guards.

Height

Table 6d gives a guide to the height of treeshelter or guard required against the wild animals listed. Treeshelters or guards are not sufficiently robust to protect against domestic stock including cattle, horses and sheep, which will rub against or trample the shelter.

Table 6d: HEIGHTS OF TREESHELTERS AND GUARDS

ANIMAL	HEIGHT OF GUARD
Vole	20cm
Rabbit	60cm
Hare	75cm
Roe and muntjac deer	1.2m
Sheep (small breeds)	1.5m
Sheep (large breeds)	1.8m
Red, sika and fallow deer	1.8m

Treeshelters

Treeshelters were originally designed as mini-greenhouses, to increase survival and growth rates on young, newly planted trees. Growth can be from two to five times the normal rate in the first few years. Treeshelters should only be used with small bare-root transplants or cell-grown stock, which should be considerably shorter than the height of the shelter at the time of planting. There is no point in using a shelter on a tall whip which is as tall or taller than the shelter at the time of planting. For taller whips, use an open mesh tree protector as necessary to give protection against browsing wild animals.

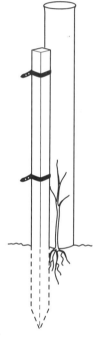

Although treeshelters are a proven aid to tree planting, there are problems associated with their use:

- On windy, exposed sites, the leading shoots may get damaged as they emerge from the top of the shelter. Roadside plantings can suffer similar damage from the slipstream of passing lorries.

- Treeshelters accelerate early height growth, but stem diameter and root growth do not increase proportionally because of the lack of wind movement, which in open conditions stimulates root and basal stem growth (p54). If shelters are removed too early, the young tree will not be able to support itself.

- Treeshelters are not recommended for protecting beech, as this can be badly damaged by the beech woolly aphid, which thrives in the humid conditions inside the shelter. Some shelter designs have holes in the lower portion, to increase air movement whilst retaining some microclimatic advantages.

- As the base of the tree stem thickens it can fill the shelter, trapping rainwater which then kills a strip of bark, so killing the tree.

- Weed growth inside the shelter will also be enhanced, and can swamp the tree.

- Treeshelters are not an alternative to weeding, but must only be used with thorough weed control measures.

- Small birds can get trapped inside shelters, and cannot clamber up the smooth walls.

To fit a treeshelter:

1. When planting in grass, it's normally easier to remove a turf first. This acts as an initial weeding, so that grass does not grow up inside the shelter, and makes it possible to push the shelter down into the soil to deter voles. Plant the tree, using the notch-planting technique. If the roots are too big to be planted this way, the tree is probably too big to require a shelter.

2. Position the shelter temporarily over the tree, to give the exact position of the stake, which should be placed on the windward side of the tree. A flat face of the stake should be flush against the shelter.

3. Remove the shelter (or a second person can lean it to one side) and knock the stake at least 300mm into the ground, finishing with the top of the stake 50-100mm above the height of the upper tie. A pre-emergent herbicide can be applied at this point, to prevent weed growth within the shelter.

4. Push the base of the shelter down into the ground to deter access by voles. Attach the ties.

5. Use weed control techniques to prevent weed growth for a 1m diameter spot or band around the tree.

The shelter must be checked at least twice a year. These checks can be combined with weed control measures, and should include at least one visit during the growing season.

- Make sure that the shelter is still upright, firmly attached and with no gap at the bottom. Remove and replace any shelters badly damaged by wind or vandalism.

- Remove any weeds that have become established inside the shelter. This will require loosening the ties, sliding the shelter up and pulling away the weeds or using a herbicide.

• During the summer, check all shelters for trees which have failed to come into leaf. Leave the shelters in position, marked with coloured tape or similar so that they can be relocated and replanted. Any replanting must be done in the following winter, so the new plants have a chance to catch up the original planting.

• Shelters are designed to split down a 'laserline' or down the fold as the tree stem swells, but shelters need checking to make sure this happens. Most shelters are also designed to biodegrade, but again this may not occur due to low light levels or other reasons, and the shelters may need removing.

Tree protectors and guards

There is a large range of products made from plastic mesh of various gauges, available as pre-formed tubes, in rolls or pre-cut in various heights and diameters. All give protection against rabbits, and those over 1.2m height protect against deer (see Table 6d, above). Unlike shelters they do not increase temperature or humidity, but give protection from wind damage, whilst allowing more natural 'unforced' growth. Fine mesh guards are claimed to give some microclimatic benefits, without the problems of high humidity and moisture build-up associated with solid wall shelters. As guards offer less wind resistance, they are also less likely than shelters to get blown over. Mesh guards do not give protection for foliage against herbicide spray drift, but conversely can be useful for hand-applied herbicide which can be used through the mesh to kill grass within the guard. Guards are less of a danger to small birds than are shelters, as any birds that fall in can clamber up by gripping on the mesh. Birds play a useful role in eating aphids, caterpillars and other damaging insects within the guard.

Pre-formed tree protectors and guards are fitted in a similar way to treeshelters. Rolls or pre-cut lengths, supplied flat, must be formed into a roll, attached with ratchet or similar ties and then stapled to the stake. Further details are available from suppliers (p189).

Spirals

Transparent spiral guards, supported by a cane, are a cheap method of protecting small hedging plants or other small transplants against rabbits, hares and voles. The outer end of the spiral should always be at the base, as shown, so that it is free to expand as the stem expands. If fitted the wrong way up, the bottom end gets trapped, and constricts the growth of the stem. To fit to small transplants, plant first, slip the spiral over without unwinding, and then insert the cane through the spiral.

Spirals can also be wrapped around the stems of larger, clear stemmed stock. To fit, hold the spiral the correct way up, and then wrap it around the stem starting at the bottom. Then hold the bottom and the top, give the top a sharp tug, and the spiral should spring into its correct form with the bottom end to the outside.

Other methods of tree protection

Standard fencing materials can be used to construct tree guards. These may be useful for protecting individual trees against damage from grazing domestic stock or deer, for which tree shelters and plastic mesh guards are not sufficiently robust. Applications include individual trees in fields, pastures, grazed commons and wood-pastures, and individual trees in woodlands with a high deer population. Such guards are mostly expensive in materials and time-consuming to build.

Against domestic stock, four posts and rails will be needed for each tree. To be proof against deer and rabbits, the 1.8m height guard, with 8 rails, will be necessary. Leave one end of the upper netting detachable, to give access to the tree for aftercare.

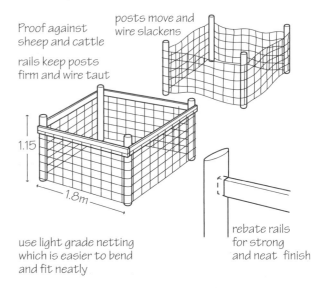

Proof against sheep and cattle

posts move and wire slackens

rails keep posts firm and wire taut

1.15

1.8m

use light grade netting which is easier to bend and fit neatly

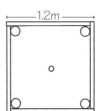

rebate rails for strong and neat finish

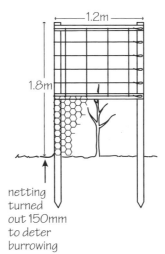

1.2m

1.8m

netting turned out 150mm to deter burrowing

1.2m

posts:
4 of 2.4mx100mm diam
rails:
8 of 1.2m half-round or 100x38mm
'sheep' netting:
c. 6-90-30 5m length
rabbit netting:
31mm mesh, 1050mm, 5m length

A less robust guard is sufficient to protect plantings or natural regeneration in woodlands, where cattle and sheep are excluded. Use a 3.6m (12') length of wire deer netting, joined back on itself to form a ring, and secured to the ground with 1.8m (6') stakes. Where rabbit protection is necessary, use a plastic mesh or spiral guard around the stem of the tree.

Various products are available to protect individual trees in parklands and orchards:

- Plastic mesh tree guards (Netlon) for sheep protection in orchards.

- Heavy grade fine plastic mesh for protection against deer and other animals.

- Weldmesh guards in a variety of height and diameters.

For suppliers see page 189.

FENCING

Fencing will be needed to protect new planting or natural regeneration in the following circumstances:

- To keep out cattle, horses, sheep or other domestic stock.

- To prevent people from accidentally or purposely damaging young trees. Damage may be caused by trampling, vandalism or by mowing machinery.

- As an alternative to individual protection, to protect against damage by rabbits and deer. No fences are proof against voles, for which vole guards are necessary.

Careful costings will be needed to choose the most cost-effective solution for each planting site. Sometimes a combination of fencing and individual protection may be used, for example a stock fence against cattle, and spiral guards around each tree against rabbits. For details see *Fencing* (BTCV, 2001).

There are disadvantages to fencing new woodlands, blocks within existing woodlands or to encourage natural regeneration:

- Fencing can hinder the natural movements of non-target species, including badgers, foxes and game birds. In coniferous woodlands in Scotland, fencing can have damaging effects on capercaillie and black grouse populations.

- Browsing and grazing has value in keeping woodland glades and rides open, and in controlling undergrowth. If all deer and rabbits are fenced out, it may be necessary to increase mowing and hand clearance to keep areas open, and to control undergrowth. A balanced woodland ecosystem requires some grazing, and is an argument for the need to bring deer populations into a sustainable balance with the woodland habitat.

- Unwanted species can be fenced in, as well as fenced out. It is essential that rabbits are eliminated before any area is fenced. Fenced areas must include a gate to give access for woodland management, as well as to allow out any deer or stock which get into the area. Alternatively site the fence near a bank or rocky outcrop, or build a ramp, so that deer or sheep which get in can leap out. Once the woodland is established, the fence can be used to enclose a sustainable population of grazing animals.

- Fences require regular maintenance, and if breached repair is essential, or the protection for the whole area is lost. Redundant fences are an eyesore and a danger, and can take as long to remove as they did to erect.

Deer fencing

This is the highest specification fence for protecting tree planting, and is also proof against domestic stock and people. Against rabbits, hexagonal mesh should be fitted to the lower section, and turned out at the base in the direction of rabbit attack. Badgers are strong enough to push their way through which then gives access to rabbits, hares and small deer. Fit badger gates on established runs, to allow badgers but no other animals through.

Rabbit fencing

This is proof against rabbits and sheep. For cattle and horses, extra line wires should be fitted mid way and at the top. Where there is heavy pressure from domestic stock, an electric line wire to keep stock away from the fence may also be advisable. This fence is not proof against deer, although muntjac and roe may be discouraged from jumping it. Where areas of tree planting are below about one hectare, most species of deer will tend to go around the fence rather than jump it, unless the fence crosses a path which the deer have traditionally used.

Temporary fencing

Temporary fencing may be appropriate to give protection for a minimum of three years, which is long enough for fast-growing newly planted species to grow beyond the reach of deer. Physical damage by cattle, sheep and horses is likely to be a problem for up to 10 years or more after planting, so temporary fencing is not normally suitable against stock. Light grazing by sheep may be possible.

DEER FENCING – spring steel line wires with netting
(based on Forestry Commission specification)

Stakes (round)
2.5m x 100mm diam

Straining posts (round)
2.8m x 150mm diam

Struts (round)
2.5m x 125mm diam

Wire: 2.65mm spring steel

HEAVY (fallow, red, sika)
Netting - upper
C6/90/30
Netting - lower
a) deer only or
deer and sheep: C8/80/15
b) deer and rabbit: 1050mm wide
hex. mesh, Mesh-31mm, 18 gauge

LIGHT (roe)
Netting - upper L8/80/15
Netting - lower
a) deer only L8/80/15
b) deer & rabbit - hex. mesh

Fence connectors

Lashing rods

Staples

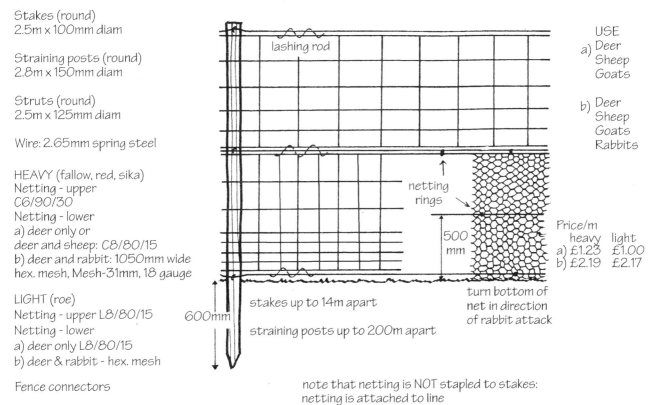

lashing rod

netting
rings

500
mm

600mm

stakes up to 14m apart

straining posts up to 200m apart

turn bottom of
net in direction
of rabbit attack

USE
a) Deer
Sheep
Goats

b) Deer
Sheep
Goats
Rabbits

Price/m
heavy   light
a) £1.23   £1.00
b) £2.19   £2.17

note that netting is NOT stapled to stakes:
netting is attached to line
wires with lashing rods at approx 2m intervals;
hexagonal mesh is attached with netting rings
at approx 500mm intervals

RABBIT FENCING – spring steel lines with hexagonal mesh
(based on Forestry Commission specification)

Stakes (round)
1.8m x 75mm diam

Straining posts (round)
2.3m x 125mm diam

Struts (round)
2.3m x 100mm diam

Wire: 2.65mm spring steel

Netting (hexagonal mesh)
1050mm height
Mesh-31mm, 18 gauge

Staples: 40mm

Fence connectors

Netting rings (e.g. Gerrard)

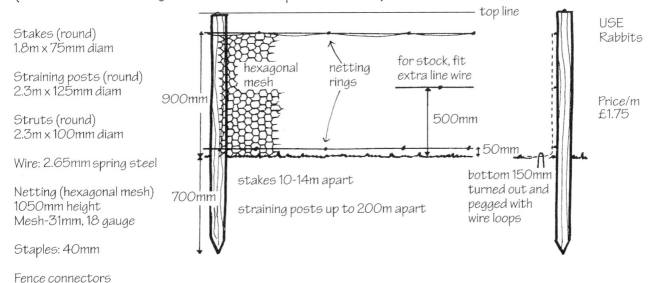

top line

hexagonal
mesh

netting
rings

for stock, fit
extra line wire

900mm

500mm

700mm

50mm

stakes 10-14m apart

straining posts up to 200m apart

bottom 150mm
turned out and
pegged with
wire loops

USE
Rabbits

Price/m
£1.75

Temporary fencing is appropriate for protecting newly-cut coppice coupes from deer. Lightweight plastic netting, dead hedging or electric fencing may be suitable. For details see page 107.

PROTECTING NATURAL REGENERATION

Areas within or on the edges of woodland can be fenced against deer and rabbits, to protect any natural regeneration of trees from being browsed.

In many woodlands there is ample regeneration, but all apart from the unpalatable species are browsed away within a few months of the seedlings emerging. However, in spite of its name, natural regeneration may not happen without intervention in managed woodlands, as there may be insufficient seed trees, not enough light or other reasons. Woodland succession may mean that the species mix changes as the woodland ages (p13).

Natural regeneration ensures the survival of local genotypes of tree, and saves the cost of purchase and planting. Natural seedlings usually establish more quickly than transplants due to the lack of root disturbance, and because they are adapted to local conditions.

Some species such as ash, sycamore, birch, rowan and aspen produce seed virtually every year. Others, notably beech and oak, only produce seed in 'mast' years, which may occur at intervals from 3-5 years for oak, and 5-15 years for beech. Most species of trees will require ground that is free of other growth, although oak germinates through a grass sward. Oak, hazel and other species (p14) do not regenerate under a closed canopy, because it is too shady. The seedlings germinate, but wither away after a few years unless the canopy is opened up. Oak is spread by jays to woodland edge and grassy habitats, where it's thought that seedlings which grow up in the protection of thorny bushes are the main method of spread in grazed semi-natural habitats. Germination and survival is normally best on soil which is well-drained at the surface, with plenty of leaf mould to suppress other growth and provide the mycorrhizal associations (p12) which most species of tree require.

For further details on natural regeneration, see page 42.

There are two approaches to protecting natural regeneration. You can either fence an area and wait for regeneration to occur, or you can protect regeneration after it has occurred. Because protection has to be put in place quickly after a successful season for regeneration, it's not normally feasible to fence a large area. One method is to use portable 'cages' (for example Gengards) or build tree guards from standard fencing materials to protect small patches of regeneration. Cages can be erected very quickly in response to regeneration, and have few of the disadvantages of large fenced areas listed above. Costs of later thinning are greatly reduced, as it's only necessary to thin the protected regeneration. Gengards are 2.4m x 2.4m x 1.2m. For suppliers, see page 189.

The progress of regeneration should be checked at intervals during the first year, as later-germinating tree species may appear through the season. A typical pattern of emergence in a mixed broadleaved woodland is firstly sycamore, followed by beech, ash, oak and lastly sweet chestnut. Weed out any unwanted species. Seedlings can also be removed and relocated as desired.

It is estimated that 5 Gengards or similar per hectare are sufficient to ensure establishment of regeneration for a single tree selection system. The Gengards can be repositioned after about five years. For group felling, 16 are needed per 0.25 hectare. Provided the guards are not damaged, making re-use possible, they represent the best-value method of ensuring natural regeneration. See *Enact* Vol. 8 No. 4 for full details.

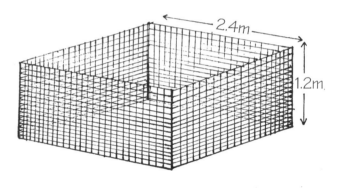

Allternatively, a ring of deer netting as described on page 60 can be used. Rabbit netting (1050mm height, 31mm mesh, 18 gauge) can be fitted around the lower half, and lapped outwards 150mm. Secure with two stakes. Re-use is possible with careful handling.

Another method is to use coppice poles or other untreated wood of suitable size, and build a guard of the type shown on page 59. Leave one top section of fence temporarily fastened, so it can be rolled back to give access for weeding and thinning. It should be possible to detach and re-use the netting if done with care, and attach to fresh poles in a new position.

Individual seedlings can also be protected with shelters or guards (pp56-58).

As can be seen on abandoned railway lines, undisturbed gravel heaps and other barren areas, tree seedlings can thrive on apparently inhospitable ground where they are free of competition from grasses and other plants. In places where there is a seed source nearby, the simple procedure of applying herbicide to an area of grass, and then protecting it against trampling, grazing and mowing as necessary, can result in a crop of tree seedlings. These are most likely to be pioneer species such as birch, sycamore, ash or oak, or suckers of nearby trees such as elm, aspen, cherry or blackthorn. Similar regeneration can occur along fencelines, in 'dead hedges' or piles of brash, or other places where weeds, browsing, grazing or mowing are absent.

Oak regeneration, through dispersal by jays (p14), tends to occur in rough grass at woodland edges, roadsides, along hedgerows and in grassy areas. Where such regeneration is desirable, protect the seedlings in early summer from browsing or mowing, and use mulch or herbicide to reduce competition from weeds. Seedlings can be transplanted in the late autumn as required.

Weeds

Weed control is the key to successful tree planting, and without it even the best planting stock in the most expensive shelters will either fail or be very slow to establish.

The importance of weeding for tree establishment was shown many years ago in trials by the Forestry Commission (Davies, R J, 1987), and the evidence from tree planting schemes over the years since have backed up the findings. Young trees surrounded by long grass or mown grass will struggle to survive. At best, they will put on very slow growth, leaving them vulnerable to trampling, browsing and disease. Trees which are weeded establish fast, and quickly grow out of the reach of animals, grow too big to be easily vandalised, and are not so prone to wind damage and disease.

Effect of weeds on trees

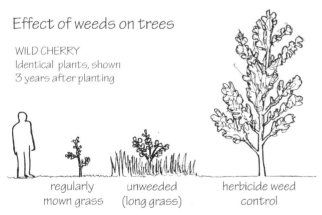

WILD CHERRY
Identical plants, shown 3 years after planting

regularly mown grass

unweeded (long grass)

herbicide weed control

based on Forestry Commission trials (in Hodge, Simon J, 1995)

The use of larger planting stock is not a substitute for weed control. Stock over 120cm high, including whips, feathered stock and standards need similar or better weed control as small transplants, as they have a poor root/shoot ratio. Just because a transplanted tree is tall enough to be visible above long grass doesn't mean that it is thriving. Bare-root, cell-grown and container grown stock all have the same requirement for regular weeding.

HOW WEEDS COMPETE

Moisture and nutrients

Weeds interfere with tree growth in several ways. Weeds use up moisture in the soil through transpiration, and also intercept rainfall before it reaches the soil. This lessens the amount of water available to the tree. The tree responds by growing fewer and smaller leaves, which reduces photosynthesis and in turn reduces root growth. Nutrient uptake is also reduced. The young tree is starved of food and water, and either fails to put on growth or dies back. The weak growth is subject to disease. Heavy rainfall or frequent watering does not help, as there is insufficient root growth to take advantage of it, and the water merely washes away nutrients and encourages the growth of weeds.

Grass is the most damaging of the weeds which affect young trees, partly because grass grows almost year round, starting before trees come into leaf and continuing after leaf fall. Mown grass is even worse than long grass. Mowing stimulates the grass to regrow, using up more soil and nutrients, and produces a thick mat of turf which reduces the amount of water percolating through. A side effect is that the mower or strimmer often damages the bark of the tree. Young trees should never be surrounded by mown grass. Mown grass also similarly interferes with the growth and health of mature trees, which is the reason why commercial fruit trees are always grown in grass-free ground. Established trees which are not flourishing can be helped into growth by killing off the grass surround. Care also needs to be taken when a thicket of newly-established trees is thinned. If the increased light allows grass to grow, the growth of the trees will be checked.

The suckers of trees and shrubs such as elm, cherry, aspen and blackthorn can compete with grass, because their moisture and nutrients are being provided from the roots of the nearby mature tree.

Light and shelter

Tall grass, bracken, nettles and other weeds may reduce the light reaching young trees, but this is much less important than the effect on roots. Most species of tree are adapted to regenerating in the shade of other trees, and reduced light levels are not usually a problem. There may be a benefit in tall weeds providing shelter from the wind, creating a humid microclimate, but again, this benefit is normally outweighed by the damage weeds do to root growth. Tall weeds which shelter young trees can also encourage height growth at the expense of stem diameter and root growth, in a similar way to staking (55). However, tall growth between rows of trees, at least 500mm away from the stem, and short enough that when it collapses it will not smother the trees, may be beneficial in providing shelter.

Physical damage

Any climbing or scrambling weeds including goose grass, wild hop, bindweed, honeysuckle and bramble can severely damage young trees by smothering and distorting tree growth. These weeds need controlling until the trees are physically large and strong enough to support them, or until shade prevents their growth. Herbaceous weeds such as bracken, nettles, thistles and docks, which die down in winter, can smother young trees as they collapse. Tall weeds also give shelter to voles, slugs and snails which can damage young trees. Voles are reluctant to cross bare ground due to fear of predators. Beneficial side effects of tall weeds may include the habitat provided for ground nesting birds, reptiles and other animals, and the fact that the weeds hide the trees and make the ground uninviting to walk through, so reducing accidental and intentional damage by people.

Mycorrhiza

Trees, shrubs, grasses and other plants have an association with soil fungi, called mycorrhiza, which have a beneficial effect on plant growth by helping the plant absorb water and nutrients. Different types of plants have different mycorrhiza, and it is thought that mycorrhiza associated with grass and some herbaceous plants have adverse effects on those associated with trees.

MINIMUM STANDARD FOR WEED CONTROL

On most large planting schemes the minimum which can be achieved is to keep weed-free a one metre diameter circle around each tree, or a one metre width strip along the line of trees. This is sufficient to allow quick and healthy establishment. For very small planting schemes, the gardening approach of keeping the whole planting area free of unwanted growth will result in very rapid growth of trees and shrubs. A combination of herbicide to kill weeds, and a loose mulch to retain soil moisture, soil warmth and to increase organic matter in the soil will give the best results. If this level of maintenance is kept up for three years, the site will normally have been 'captured', with the trees shading out other growth, and producing their own mulch of leaves. Only minimal weeding will be needed in future years, with thinning the next operation to consider.

Trees planted within woodland normally suffer less competition from grasses, but are easily overwhelmed by brambles, nettles, bracken, old man's beard or other plants which can thrive in woodland clearings. Planted trees should be clearly marked by their tree shelters or guards, or if not individually protected, by tall canes. A clearing in winter is normally overgrown by early summer, hiding the young trees. Check the trees at least twice during the growing season, and either trample or cut back any encroaching growth (see below).

Trees planted on exposed sites, poor soils or in upland areas may appear to suffer less weed competition. However, Forestry Commission trials (Davies, R J, 1987) indicated that because poor soils have fewer reserves of nutrients and water, the presence of even sparse weed growth can be detrimental to the trees.

Weed control

HERBICIDES

Herbicides are the cheapest and most effective method of weed control. The combination of a winter application of pre-emergent/residual herbicide, and a spring and summer application of a translocated/foliar acting herbicide in spring and summer is widely used in commercial tree planting schemes. The foliar acting herbicide can be used as the residual product wears off, and also on any weeds which are resistant to the residual product. This leaves bare ground, to which the residual herbicide can be applied again to delay reinvasion. Using a translocated herbicide does have the disadvantage that it can only be applied to growing weeds, so by the time it takes effect, there has already been some interference with tree growth. The dead growth, particularly of grass, can form a useful mulch around the tree which reduces evaporation from the soil, and helps delay reinvasion, but may provide unwanted cover for voles.

The Control of Pesticides Regulations 1986 covers all aspects of the development, sale, supply, storage and use of herbicides. The regulations cover proprietary products rather than active ingredients, and classify these products according to approved use. 'Professional' products are formulated for use in agriculture, horticulture and forestry, and 'amateur' products are formulated for use in the garden. Amateur products may contain the same active ingredients as those in the professional category, but at lower strength, so there is less dilution required before application.

From the range permitted for amateur use, there are two products which are widely available from garden centres and tree growers, and which are suitable for use on small-scale tree planting schemes. For large schemes, or for groups undertaking regular tree planting, training in the use of professional products is advisable, as these are much more cost-effective than the equivalent amateur products.

When using herbicides, whether professional or amateur, follow the instructions on the label. Note the recommended dosage and the required weather conditions for effective use. Clothing and equipment should be correct and appropriate, as identified by the assessment of the chemical's use.

Propyzamide (Kerb Granules) is a residual and foliar acting herbicide, although it is more effective as the former. It can be applied to bare ground to prevent weeds germinating, or it can be applied to weeds in growth and is translocated to kill the roots. It remains active for at least 12 weeks. As a residual herbicide, results are best if it is applied to soil with a firm, fine tilth. If applied to very lumpy soil, as the lumps crumble untreated soil will be exposed and weed growth will result. Rain is needed after application to move residual herbicide into the soil. Kerb Granules are available in a 120 tree shaker pack (£10.50 at 2002 prices), or in larger quantities.

Glyphosate (eg Roundup Biactive) is a widely used garden herbicide, which is applied by spray to the leaves. It is translocated through the plant, killing all of it above and below ground, and is effective on all grasses and herbaceous growth. It is inactivated and biodegrades on contact with the ground. Contact with tree foliage, shoots and bark must be avoided, or tree growth will be damaged. Glyphosate can be used at any time when vegetation is actively growing. The addition of a dye makes it easier to apply the spray evenly and effectively. Depending on weed growth, glyphosate should be applied in March / April, and again in August to benefit late summer tree growth. It costs about 5p per tree per application (2002 prices), and can be applied using a garden sprayer of one litre capacity or greater.

The sale and use of professional herbicides is strictly regulated. Products can only be sold to and used by holders of the National Proficiency Training Council (NPTC) Certificate of Competence. Professional products are only available from specialist suppliers, whose staff must also be certificate holders in order to advise on herbicide use.

Training leading to the NPTC Certificate of Competence is provided at agricultural colleges and other centres throughout the United Kingdom. Enquire through the NPTC or Lantra. For further information on training see page 187.

Information on herbicides for professional use in forestry and farm woodlands is given in *The Use of Herbicides in the Forest* (Forestry Commission, 1995) and *Herbicides for Farm Woodlands and Short Rotation Coppice* (Forestry Commission, 1996).

MULCHES

Mulches are materials which are put down on the ground to suppress weeds and retain soil moisture by reducing evaporation. Mulches can be either sheet material, such as polythene, bitumen or various textiles, or loose materials such as bark, chipped wood or gravel. Most sheet mulch materials also increase soil temperature, which encourages early root growth in spring. Mulches,

either sheet or loose, are not recommended for use on damp ground, as by preventing evaporation they increase the tendency of the ground to become waterlogged and anaerobic, which kills tree roots.

Proprietary sheet mulches

Sheet mulches are available either in a roll, for hedge or shelter-belt planting, or in pre-cut squares or mats to fit around individual trees. Sheet mulches need to be substantial enough to last at least two years, thick enough to resist wind or animal damage, and large enough to be effective. The sheet mulch tends to invigorate the growth of grasses around its edge, so a mat smaller than 500mm square will be ineffective. The larger size mats, usually 840mm, 900mm or 1m square, are recommended.

The cheapest mats are made of black, single-sheet polythene, but are not sufficiently durable. The 'Thermat' is a multi-layered anti-tear polyethylene mat which is durable for at least two years, and is effective in raising soil temperature. It degrades after about three years, so no clearing up is necessary. Other mats are available made of mixtures of wool, jute and hair, or flax and hemp. Some mats are supplied with a cross-shaped slit in the centre, and others have a slit from the edge to the centre, making them easier to fit to multi-stemmed shrubs. Depending on type and quantity ordered, expect to pay between £1 and £2 per mat.

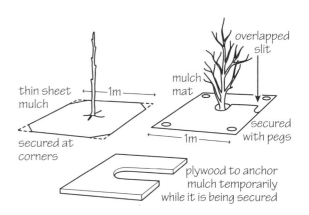

Mulch mats can be fitted directly over short mown grass, into which trees have been notch planted. Otherwise, fit the mat onto bare soil. Do not try and fit the mat over long, tufty grass. The mats are normally fitted after planting, by carefully threading the growing tip of the plant through the slit, and then anchoring the mat. The mats should be fastened at the corners by pushing down into a slit in the soil, or by pegs available from the supplier. Suppliers will recommend the best method for particular products. Non-biodegradable mats can be further anchored by stones, gravel, upturned turves or a small amount of soil, to weight down the mulch and discourage animals from disturbing it. Don't use too thick a layer of soil, or weeds will establish in it. Biodegradable mats should be anchored by pegs or stones, and not by covering with soil, as this makes the material degrade more quickly.

Mulch mats need checking at least once during the growing season. Weeds can grow up through the gap around the stem. Mats may be disturbed by vandals, or torn by the wind, and may need replacing during the initial three year establishment period. Voles may use the shelter provided by the mulch and then damage the tree stem, and foxes may tear the mulch to get at the voles! Some fibrous mats may be damaged by large birds seeking nesting material.

Loose mulch materials

Loose mulch materials such as composted woodchips or bark can be used for mulching, although they are not as effective as herbicides or sheet mulches in controlling weeds. As the material breaks down it is incorporated into the soil, which has the benefit of adding to the organic matter content and improving soil structure, and may introduce beneficial mycorrhiza. However, a layer at least 100mm (4") thick is needed, and the mulch will need replacing every year, as it becomes incorporated into the soil. Addditional hand weeding will be needed at least once during the growing season. Mulches can be used in combination with herbicides, for example in early spring after a winter application of residual herbicide. This reduces herbicide use during the summer, and gives the soil benefits of mulching. The mulch also looks more attractive than bare, 'weedkilled' ground. If the whole tree planting area can be mulched, this will speed tree establishment and the formation of a woodland-type ecosystem.

The mulch should cover an area at least 1m diameter. Keep it away from the stem, or rot may result. Mulch can be laid at the time of planting, or in very early spring, before growth starts again. Replace annually in winter. Continue until the canopy starts to close over and the trees produce their own mulch of fallen leaves.

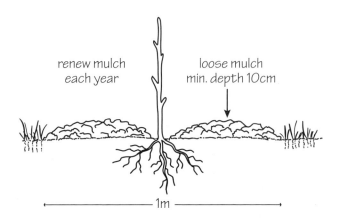

renew mulch each year

loose mulch min. depth 10cm

1m

Loose mulch materials are only worth using for tree planting schemes if they can be acquired cheaply in bulk, or home-produced from woodchipping. Woodchips, bark, leaves and other organic material should be composted for about six months before use, or the young trees may be deprived of available nitrogen as the material decomposes. See page 88 for information on woodchippings. Leaf mould is a useful and beneficial material. Leaves swept from roads and parks may be available for free from local councils.

HAND WEEDING

Hand weeding is labour intensive, and only suitable for small planting schemes. As in a garden situation, weeding will be needed regularly throughout the growing season. Avoid using any tools near the stem of a tree, but hand-pull weeds instead. Where grasses have taken hold, it's generally best to use a contact herbicide to destroy the sward, and then try to keep the area weed free by mulching or hoeing.

Weak herbaceous growth such as nettles, creeping thistles and many tall annuals and biennials can be hand pulled, but make sure this doesn't then allow the growth of grasses, which will be much more damaging. Pulled material that hasn't gone to seed can be spread around the trees to act as a mulch. Larger areas of nettles, thistles or bracken can be trampled, which suppresses rather than stimulates growth, but may need to be repeated a few times through the season. Cutting with a grass hook must only be done with extreme care, because it is so easy to damage the young trees. Bracken can be 'whipped' with a stick as the fronds open, to weaken the growth, but beware of damaging the trees.

Bracken can be a problem in old pasture woodlands and parks. One of the best control methods is to trample or roll the growth in July, which flattens and bruises the stems, but does not sever them. This encourages water loss from the plant, and prevents re-supply of nutrients to next year's dormant buds. Various commercial rollers are available which can be towed by small tractors and four-wheel drive vehicles (*Enact* Vol 5 No 3). A deep accumulation of bracken litter can be a serious fire risk on tree planting sites, and should be raked away before planting is carried out.

INTER-ROW VEGETATION

The 1m radius circle around each tree must be kept free of weeds. At 2m tree spacing, this weed-free area amounts to about one sixth of the total area. The remaining area between the trees can be left to grow up, or can be mown.

Leaving the inter-row vegetation to grow up unmanaged

is useful for hiding the trees from vandals, and for discouraging unofficial access across the site. On exposed sites, it may help shelter the young trees from wind. However, you need to check that growth does not get so tall that when it collapses in late summer, it crushes the young trees. This can be a problem if there is a wet spell in late summer. Voles are more likely to be a problem in long grass, so vole guards may be needed. Tall vegetation can provide useful habitat for ground nesting birds, and may include plants which add to the wildlife value of the site.

Where neatness is important and vandalism unlikely, mowing is an option. This prevents brambles, thistles or other troublesome weeds establishing, and discourages voles. Take great care when mowing, brush cutting or strimming, and never be tempted to cut near the tree stems, even if there is weed growth there, as damage to the stem in inevitable.

Long-handled scythes are not recommended for use near trees, and short-handled grass hooks should only be used with extreme care. Shelters and guards make it easier to see the trees, but are not robust enough to protect trees from a sharp tool.

Techniques to encourage the development of a woodland flora are discussed in the next chapter.

7 The young woodland

Pruning, thinning, the establishment of woodland field layer plants and the management of glades are described in this chapter.

Maintenance

Weed control should be continued for at least three years after planting, when for closely planted trees, the canopy should be closing over. Widely spaced trees or trees in wood-pastures or parks will benefit from a weed free area around the base for five to ten years after planting, depending on speed of establishment. See chapter 6 for details on weed control of grasses and herbaceous growth. See chapter 8 for details on controlling unwanted shrubs and other woody weeds.

Treeshelters and guards should be removed once they are no longer needed. Treeshelters are designed to break down with time, but may not do so due to increased shade. Spiral guards become useless once the spiral has opened, and if left can become tangled in the base of the stem.

Fencing against domestic stock will normally need to be kept in good condition permanently. However, limited grazing by domestic stock enclosed within the woodland, or allowed access at certain times, can help encourage diversity. The need for permanent fencing against deer and rabbits needs assessment, as limited grazing may improve the woodland habitat by keeping glades open and undergrowth under control.

The likelihood of squirrel damage must be assessed, and action taken in time to prevent damage occurring. Grey squirrels can severely damage or kill trees between 5 and 40 years old, by stripping the bark anywhere on the main stem from the base to the crown. Beech, oak, sycamore and sweet chestnut are most vulnerable. Damage occurs between the middle of March and the middle of July, with the worst damage usually occurring about the third week in June. By the time it's noticed it's too late to do anything. Traps baited with Warfarin are the normal method of control, which must start before damage occurs. There are strict regulations regarding the use of Warfarin, and a National Proficiency Test Certificate is required for its use. Advice should be sought from the local office of the Forestry Commission.

The woodland is established when the trees are growing vigorously without the need for regular weeding.

However, periodic work is still needed, and in particular thinning must be done at the appropriate time. If thinning is neglected, the trees will become overcrowded and spindly. Late thinning will be much more difficult, expensive and less effective.

The management aim in newly established woodland should be to manipulate species composition and woodland structure to lead to the development of diverse and attractive woodland. This may include pruning and thinning, the removal of unwanted invasive species, the clearance of undergrowth and the favouring of any desirable natural colonisation. Small areas can be coppiced to add structural diversity, or understorey shrubs can be planted.

Once conditions of shade are suitable, woodland bulbs and flowering plants can be introduced to the woodland (pp73-75).

Pruning

The section covers the pruning of young trees during the establishment phase, from about 7 to 15 years after planting. Pruning and surgery of large, mature trees should only be carried out by fully trained and competent persons.

FORMATIVE PRUNING

Pruning is not necessary for native trees, and in many situations trees can be left to develop naturally. Formative pruning involves removing some of the side branches to encourage strong upright growth in the leading stem. When making a decision on pruning, the following points should be considered:

- The value of a timber tree can be considerably increased by formative pruning, to produce a tall, straight trunk without side branches. Branching reduces the straight length of timber, and any side branches which die leave a knot in the timber. Where part of the management objective is timber production, potentially valuable species such as oak, beech, ash and cherry should normally be pruned.

- Pruning of side branches speeds the upward growth of the tree, which can be useful in getting the leading shoot out of the reach of browsing animals or vandals.

Young trees are very vulnerable for the first few years, and pruning may be worth doing if it shortens this period.

- In urban and amenity woodlands, the preference for most users is for fairly open woodlands, with views through the trees to encourage feelings of safety. Pruning of lower branches opens up views and access through the trees.

- Pruning as an activity can be useful because it involves close inspection of the trees, and combines well with other aspects of aftercare. The labour intensive nature of pruning work is not a problem for most voluntary groups.

Pruning of broadleaves should commence from when they are 6-8cm (2½-3″) diameter at breast height (dbh).

Time of year

The best time for pruning oak, ash and cherry is from mid June to mid August, as this reduces the chance of bacterial or fungal infection. In the dormant season wounds are slow to heal and susceptible to damage by frost. Other species can be pruned at the same time, or between September and December. Never prune during the early growing season of February to May, when the sap is rising fast.

There's no need to prune every tree, but choose the strongest growing, most upright ones of each species, leaving others to branch more freely and create structural diversity. Leading shoots which have forked due to damage or browsing should be pruned to leave a single leader. Trees which have been heavily browsed by deer and have formed a bushy top should be cut back to the main stem to encourage a single leader to emerge. Protect the tree with a sufficiently high tree protector (p58).

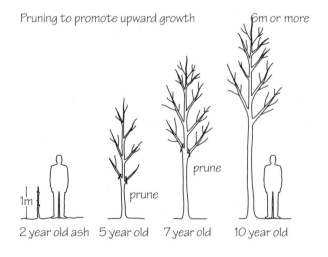

Pruning to promote upward growth

6m or more

prune

prune

1m

2 year old ash   5 year old   7 year old   10 year old

Pruning of side branches from the stem can be repeated every other year until the tree is about 10 years old, aiming for a crown of branches about half the height of the tree. Long-handled pruning saws or treetop pruners (p26) will be necessary to reach the side branches. New shoots from the trunk, called epicormics, can be rubbed off or cut away with a sharp knife. Through this type of pruning it's quite possible for an ash or cherry to grow to at least 6m (20′) height within 10 years. Pruning should stop when the trunk has a diameter at breast height (dbh) of about 12cm (5″).

How to prune

Side branches should be removed before they reach 25mm (1″) in diameter, using a cut as shown below. Don't cut too close, or you will damage the main stem. Always make the pruning cut to the outside of the branch collar position, although note that the branch collar only becomes obvious on older or mature branches (see below). On the other hand, don't leave a 'coat peg', where rot can start. It's best to prune at a stage when branches can still be cut through with secateurs or pruners, either long-handled or treetop type for high reach. Pruning saws, both pocket size and long handled can also be used. If the branches are too big to be cut this way, you have left it too late.

branch collar →

High pruning

This involves progressively pruning above 2m (6′) to produce knot-free timber, and is normally only done to selected trees of potentially high value. Pruning up to 4m (13′) can be done using a long-handled pruning saw.

REMEDIAL PRUNING

In established woodlands it may be necessary to cut larger branches which are overhanging paths or tracks, or to remove branches that are unsafe. Branches over about 150mm (6″) diameter should only be cut by trained and competent persons.

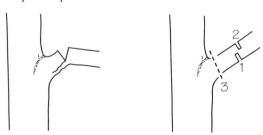

incorrect cut   correct sequence of cuts

Cut branches over about 25mm (1") in three stages, as shown. If you try to saw through them with one cut, they are likely to break and pull off a strip of bark, which damages the tree.

Make the first cut about one third of the way through the branch from the bottom, but not so far that the saw binds. Make the second cut as shown, to sever the branch, leaving a projecting stub. Finally, trim the stub with a third cut, starting at the top. Don't leave a snag or stub. At best, this will only produce unwanted regrowth. More often, stubs die back, providing a foothold for infection and rot which can then be more easily transmitted to the rest of the tree.

healthy callus formation

Decaying trees are very valuable habitats, and should not necessarily be viewed as a problem, unless they cause a danger to the public. See chapter 3 for notes on the legal situation regarding unsafe branches.

Wound treatment

There is normally no need to treat cuts and wounds in trees with a wound paint, which in the past was recommended for sealing wounds against fungal attack. If the pruning cuts have been made cleanly and correctly, no further treatment should be necessary. The branch collar forms a barrier to prevent the inward spread of pathogens.

Thinning

There is a direct relationship between the size of the crown and the diameter of the tree stem or trunk. Without sufficient crown to generate food, the stem will remain thin, and growth of the tree will stagnate, resulting in weak, spindly trees. The timing of thinning will depend on the species and rate of growth, and also on available markets for the thinnings. However, thinning should not be delayed, or the trees may be so weakened that they

are unable to respond when thinning eventually takes place. Thinning operations should be included in the management plan for a new woodland.

GENERAL PRINCIPLES

Closely spaced planting is the best and quickest way to establish trees (p41), but thinning must be carried out to allow sufficient space for the remaining trees to thrive. In woodlands planted at 2m spacing for wildlife and amenity, thinning should start about 10 years after planting, when the trees should be 6-8m high. Early thinning will encourage diversity of form and add variety to the woodland structure. Trees planted at 3m spacings may not need thinning until about 20 years after planting. In commercial broadleaved woodland, thinning is usually started between 15 and 25 years after planting, when the trees are about 10m high.

As a general rule, for trees planted at 2m spacing, about 25% of the total number of trees are removed during each of the early thinning operations, reducing to about 15% after five or more thinning operations.

Visual assessment

Within the guidelines given above, each situation will need individual assessment. A visual check will show where crowns are overlapping and thinning is needed. Any trees, apart from understorey species, which have failed to reach the canopy and have been suppressed, will need removal. The aim should be to create a 'ring of sky' around each tree that is retained, into which it will spread. The woodland edge should normally be left unthinned, to create dense, branching growth which shelters the woodland from the wind.

In amenity woods, trees can be selected to give a variety of form and structure, and to break up planting lines. In commercial woodlands, selection should be for commercial value (see below).

The old forestry rule is that the stem thickness in inches (dbh or diameter at breast height) should equal the radius of the crown in feet. For example, a tree with a dbh of 8 inches should have a crown of radius 8 feet, or diameter 16 feet. Another rule-of-thumb is that at early

Table 7a: THINNING

Stage	Age	Thinning operations
Establishment	0-10 yrs	
Thicket	5-20 yrs	1st thinning. Remove 25%
Early pole stage	15-50 yrs	Thin at 5-7 year intervals. Remove 25%
Late pole stage	30-100+ yrs	Thin at 8-10 year intervals. Remove 15%
Mature	40-150+ yrs	

pole stage, spacing between trees should be about one fifth of average tree height, and at late pole stage, should be about one quarter of average height.

Thinning operations in established woodlands and those managed for commercial production will require careful assessment, including the total volume of standing timber, and the size class distribution, which gives a measure of the percentage of trees of different ages. For further details see the Forestry Commission publications, *Thinning Control* and *Timber Measurement – A Field Guide* (p199).

Selective thinning

This involves individually selecting trees for thinning, normally removing those that are weak, diseased, forked or dead, and retaining the strongest, straightest and most healthy trees. Where growth is good throughout, the removal of viable trees will be necessary. Selective thinning in amenity woodlands should also aim to partially break up planting lines, so that the woodland develops with a more varied and natural spacing of trees.

It's important that thinning operations are planned in advance, and marked by a competent person. Selection of trees should be made in winter, when the crown and upper stem can easily be seen. Normally trees to be retained are marked with spots of aerosol paint (available from forestry suppliers), and trees to be cut are marked with a billhook. Marks are made on both sides of the trunk so that mistakes are avoided. Alternatively, tape can be tied around the trees to be felled.

Evans (1985) gives the following criteria, in order of priority, for the selection of broadleaved trees to favour in thinning, to maximise commercial value.

1. Good stem form and freedom from defect on the lower 7m (23') of stem.

2. Absence of deep forking in the crown.

3. Good vigour.

4. Freedom from defect in upper stem and crown.

5. Low incidence of epicormic branching.

6. Proximity of other selected trees. Even spacing should only be considered after other criteria are satisfied.

Line thinning

Where growth is fairly uniform and timber production is the main aim, complete rows of young trees can be removed. This is very much quicker than selective thinning. Depending on the species and growth, every third, fourth or fifth row may be removed, or in mixtures, any faster growing nurse species may be removed. In very dense plantations, especially if left too long, occasional lines or 'racks' will have to be removed to gain access to the wood for inspection purposes.

Extraction and use

The first thinnings are usually too small to be of commercial use, and are left where they fall. Sned the side branches and leave the trunks and brash on the woodland floor, where they will provide some deadwood habitat. Depending on access and other factors, the wood can be extracted from the woodland for firewood, green woodworking or other uses.

Later thinnings will be of value for green woodworking, fencing or other purposes, and should be extracted from the woodland as part of the thinning operation. There is a range of vehicles designed for the extraction of timber. Horse extraction may also be a possibility in woodlands with poor access or on sloping ground. See *Practical Solutions Handbook* (English Nature, 2001).

THINNING NEGLECTED WOODLAND

Where thinning has been neglected, the woodland will be characterised by closely spaced, spindly trees with small crowns. Access into the wood for assessment, felling and extraction, will be difficult and time consuming. The newly thinned woodland is likely to suffer from windblow and other problems (see below), and some of the trees may be so weak that they are unable to respond. Ash has a very poor response to late thinning, and may fail to develop. Beech is intermediate in response, whereas oak normally grows away well even if thinning has been neglected.

Where thinning has been neglected, the first action may need to be to cut access tracks or tracks into the woodland, so that it can be assessed and further practical action planned. A single heavy thinning is risky. Several light thinnings, at perhaps three year intervals for 9-10 years, should restore the woodland to a better stocking rate.

Effects of heavy thinning

Infrequent, heavy thinning produces a greater volume on each occasion, which may make marketing more viable, as well as being efficient in terms of labour, access and ground disturbance. However, heavy thinning can cause windblow, epicormic branching and variation in ring width. It is usually more damaging to wildlife that frequent, light thinning.

Windblow is caused when the removal of the shelter of surrounding growth exposes the remaining trees to the wind. They are particularly vulnerable immediately after thinning, as the root systems are not adapted to cope with the amount of movement, and the trees can easily be blown over. Gradually, in the increased light and space, the root systems expand to keep the tree wind-firm. Root growth is also stimulated by the swaying action of the tree in wind. Trees on the edges of woods or at ride sides are most vulnerable, and a smaller percentage should be removed for the first 10 metres or so, than in the rest of the wood. Retain shrubs and small trees at wood edges, as this helps deflect the wind up and over the woodland, and retains shelter for wildlife within the wood.

Epicormic branches are those that arise directly from the trunk of the tree. They particularly occur on English oak, and where they persist for more than one year, form a knot in the timber which will lessen its commercial value. Epicormic branching usually occurs when increased light after heavy thinning stimulates dormant buds on the trunk. It can also arise from pruning scars. The result is a thicket of horizontal branches up the trunk, with weak epicormic branches also developing on main side branches. Where they occur on potential high-value trunks the shoots should be pruned or rubbed off each year in mid-season.

Variation in ring width is caused where heavy thinning results in a sudden rapid burst of growth. This affects the commercial value of the timber.

Woodland flora

Most new woodlands are planted in former agricultural land, urban fringe areas and reclaimed industrial land, which tend to have few, if any, areas of existing woodland. Those woods or hedgerows that do remain often have an impoverished field-layer flora. This lack of seed sources, together with the poor dispersal mechanisms of woodland plants means that it is nearly impossible for the traditional woodland flora to become established without help.

The field-layer of newly planted woods, especially on former agricultural land which is high in phosphates, typically becomes dominated by aggressive, shade-tolerant species such as nettle, cow parsley, bramble and ivy. These persist for many years and create a further barrier to colonisation by more desirable species.

Introduction of woodland field-layer plants must not be started until the woodland canopy has closed sufficiently that grass and other light-demanding plants have been excluded. Weed control measures which are essential for tree growth in the early years will preclude any introduction of other plants. With close planting of trees, effective weed control and thinning, a 10-year-old plantation should be in a suitable condition for starting introduction of field-layer plants. Light levels beneath the tree canopy should be between 10% and 40% of daylight in summer. Nettles, docks, thistles and other weeds of agricultural land may persist even when light levels are low. If necessary use herbicide or hand clearance to control them before starting the introduction of woodland plants.

Sowing or planting should be targeted in patches which have suitable conditions of shade, lack of competition from other plants and no disturbance from trampling. Suitable areas may only comprise 10% or less of the plantation, but if these can be successfully established, plants will spread into other areas as the conditions become suitable. The aim should be to initiate a self-supporting population of the desired plants, which do not require weeding to survive, and which form part of a balanced, appropriate woodland flora.

Species

Species chosen should be typical of the local area and the type of woodland. Advice should be sought as necessary from local ecologists, the Wildlife Trust or office of English Nature or other nature conservation agency. A similar semi-natural wood within 5km may provide a suitable blueprint, and no plants should be introduced which have not been recorded in the 10 km grid square in which the new wood is situated. It's best to start with species that are common, and are tolerant of a fairly wide range of light, moisture and pH conditions to ensure reasonable rates of establishment. No attempt should be made to introduce species that are rare in the locality. For lists of 'desired invaders' to the new native woodland types, see *Creating New Native Woodlands* (Rodwell, John and Patterson, Gordon, 1994).

The best way of obtaining plants of local genetic variety is to grow plants from seed collected locally, with permission from the landowner. Only small quantities should be gathered from any one site, and gathering should be done over several years. Some species can be sown direct, while others establish better if propagated and grown on in nursery conditions before planting out. Generally those in the left hand column of Table 7b can be sown, while those in the right hand column should be introduced as plants. Those in the middle column are slow to mature, so planting will speed the establishment of self-sustaining populations. Primroses are best established as plants, at 6-9 plants per square metre. Experience of growing plants from seed is needed for successful nursery production, as wild plants are generally more difficult to propagate than garden plants.

Otherwise, plants or seed should be obtained from nurseries able to supply seeds or plants of local provenance where available. Where not possible, use seeds or plants of British provenance. Advice and lists of nurseries are available at the Flora locale website.

Experience with establishment of woodland flora has

shown that it is best to group the species according to whether they are woodland edge plants, or those tolerant of deeper shade, and according to how they spread.

Seed

Seeds should normally be sown in autumn, to ensure cold treatment (vernalisation) which some woodland species require in order to germinate. Sow at the rate recommended by the supplier. Prepare the ground by raking away any recently fallen leaves and lightly rake the soil surface. The seed can be mixed with silver sand or fine sawdust to make it easier to spread evenly. Lightly rake the seed into the soil. Record on a map the areas which have been seeded, so they can be relocated and the success of seeding checked. Where disturbance from the public is unlikely, the seeded areas can be marked with canes or similar.

Plants

Plant in early spring as the soil is warming up but while it is still moist. Plant in single species groups of five or more plants, which should spread to form a stable clump, which can then seed or spread into new areas. Plant at the distances recommended by the supplier. If possible, water the planting holes before planting. Record the location for future reference.

Bulbs and rhizomes

The typical plants of woodland shade are those which grow from bulbs or rhizomes. These allow an early burst of growth, so that flowering and seed production can occur before the canopy closes in late spring. Plants are easy to establish from bulbs or rhizomes, and the establishment time to flowering is shorter than when grown from seed. Bulbs and rhizomes are more expensive than seed.

Bulbs and rhizomes are best planted during the autumn, as soon as they are available from the supplier. Ensure that stock is from British provenance plants, and is produced in a nursery.

Bluebells (*Hyacinthoides non-scripta*)
  Plant 2-3 bulbs in holes 100mm (4") deep, 600mm (2") apart

Lesser celandine (*Ranunculus ficaria*)
  Plant 2-3 bulbs in holes 50mm (2") deep, 150mm (6") apart

Snowdrops (*Galanthus nivalis*)
  Plant 6 bulbs in holes 50mm (2") deep, 300mm (1') apart

Table 7b: SPECIES GROUPS FOR INTRODUCTION OF FIELD-LAYER PLANTS

	Light-demanding, wood-margin and hedgerow species	Species tolerant of deep shade	
Characteristics	High germination rates; quick to flower; produce plenty of seed.	Low germination rates; long seedling phase; slow to reach flowering maturity; produce fair amount of seed	Mainly spread by runners and stolons
Introduction method	Seed at low/medium rates; 3kg/ha or 0.3g/m²	Seed at high rate; 10kg/ha or 1g/m²	Plant at 4-9 plants per m²
Suitable species	Garlic mustard Lords and ladies False brome Foxglove Giant fescue Hedge bedstraw Wood avens Hairy St John's wort Red campion Betony Hedge woundwort Greater stitchwort Upright hedge parsley	Ramsoms Pignut Wild strawberry Woodruff Bluebell Primrose Sweet violet	Bugle Wood anemone Wood sedge Enchanter's nightshade Wood spurge Ground ivy Yellow archangel Wood sorrel Wood sage Wood speedwell Common dog violet Ferns

Ramsoms (*Allium ursinum*)
   Plant 3-4 bulbs in holes 50mm (2") deep,
   300mm (1') apart

Wood anemone (*Anemone nemorosa*)
   Plant 2-3 rhizomes, horizontally, 50mm (2") deep,
   300mm (1') apart

Aftercare

The aim is to establish populations of plants which will spread by seeding or vegetative growth. Nurturing the original plants by weeding in the first season will help the plants to establish, and by reducing competition from other plants, flowering and seeding rates should be improved. The preparation of a suitable seed bed close to established plants may help encourage further regeneration. Wood chips from thinning operations, raked out to leave a layer no thicker than 100mm (4"), rot down to make a good substrate for the germination of woodland plants. In contrast, wood chips have been found not to enhance the spread of woodland edge plants, which are better adapted to seeding into bare soil. Where seed production is prolific, some seed can be gathered by hand and spread in other areas in the woodland.

Glades and rides

Glades, rides or other open spaces in woodland which are light enough to support the growth of grasses and flowering plants are valuable for wildlife and amenity. Wood-pastures and park-like landscapes have a long history in Britain, and are some of our most valuable sites ecologically, as well as being very popular for recreation. However, open spaces do not look after themselves, but must be mown or grazed if they are going to retain their unwooded character. Grazing by wild animals does not fulfil this need, as sufficient numbers to maintain grassy areas will have a damaging effect on the wooded areas. Domestic livestock can be used, once the trees have reached sufficient size to withstand damage, and provided that protection is given to regeneration or further planting.

In a young woodland, open spaces should be maintained by mowing. Mowings should be removed, to avoid enriching the site, and to encourage the growth of the less aggressive species of flowering plants, which are generally of higher wildlife value.

Areas can be sown with particular mixes of grasses and wildflowers to suit the soil and site, and to flower during different periods of the spring and summer. A floristically interesting sward is easier to establish on poor soils rather than fertile soils, so sites and mixtures can be chosen accordingly. Seed mixes are available from several suppliers (p188), who can advise on suitable mixtures, sowing rates and other details. Ensure that local or British provenance seed is used. Thought must be given to the way that the conditions of light and shade will change as the trees grow. Any existing sward should be destroyed by cultivation or herbicide. Seed mixes can be sown from August to mid-September, or from early March to early May.

The mowing regime must suit the type of mixture sown. There are three regimes which may be suitable for different open areas in the woodland:

- **Flowery lawns**. These can survive with close frequent mowing and trampling, and include rosette plants which are adapted to withstand trampling. Typical plants include daisy, plantain, cat's ear, speedwell, self-heal, white clover and bird's foot trefoil. Mow regularly through the growing season, except for a few weeks from early May to mid June. This will allow the plants to flower and set seed.

- **Early flowering mixtures**. These are left to grow in spring and early summer, and then cut as for a hay crop, so are suitable for glades which are not regularly trampled, or for broad sunny strips alongside paths or tracks. Typical plants include cowslip, bugle, meadow buttercup, lady's bedstraw, wild carrot, ox-eye daisy and ragged robin. In the first year after sowing, the sward must be cut about every six weeks, to prevent the grass from overgrowing the other species. Remove the cuttings. In following years, make the first cut in late May, and another cut in September.

- **Late-flowering mixtures**. These flower from mid summer, and may include scabious, knapweed, harebell, vetch and sorrel. The new sward should be mown regularly in the first year. In the following year, mow regularly in early summer, but then leave it to grow and flower from June until mid-September. Mow once in the autumn. Remove all the cuttings.

8 Felling, clearing and extraction

This chapter describes basic practical techniques for felling small trees, clearing undergrowth and other woodland operations suitable for groups of volunteers using hand tools. Coppicing is described in detail in chapter 9.

Risk assessments (p29) must be carried out for all projects involving volunteers or work involving paid employees.

Before commencing work, you may need to apply for a felling licence from the Forestry Commission. This is required for felling more than 5 cubic metres (about 2 large trees) per calendar quarter (p20). For further information contact your local office of the Forestry Commission.

Felling and clearing may be carried out in woodland for a variety of reasons:

- To thin young woodlands or overstocked plantations.

- To initiate or maintain coppice cycles.

- To diversify woodlands by creating glades and rides.

- To create paths for access, or to clear growth to make woodlands more open and inviting for public enjoyment.

- To suppress exotic species such as rhododendron and sycamore, where they are smothering native woodland plants.

- To supply fuel, material for fencing, building, greenwood crafts and other uses.

All deciduous native species, if felled, have the ability to regrow from the stump. This is the basis of coppicing and pollarding, and was the main method of producing and harvesting wood from Neolithic times until the age of modern commercial forestry. If it is the intention that the trees should not regrow, then the stumps must be removed (p91). This will be necessary for:

- Clearance of tracks, paths and other access routes.

- Clearance of permanent glades.

- Removal of unwanted or invasive species.

When thinning, stumps can normally be left, as the shade cast by the remaining trees will mean that stumps will only produce weak regrowth.

Coniferous trees do not regrow from the stump, although stumps may need to be removed when clearing tracks or paths.

Assessing the commercial timber potential of a woodland and making decisions about thinning requires specialist knowledge, including measurement of standing timber, crop densities, growth rates, market knowledge and other matters. Advice should normally be taken from a specialist, and the practical work is likely to beyond the scope of most volunteer groups. For further information see Broad (1998), NSWA (undated) and Rollinson, TJD (1999).

The selection of trees and the timing for thinning in woodlands managed primarily for conservation and amenity is less critical, and is largely a matter of local knowledge, observation and common sense. Guidelines are given on page 71. The practical work may be suitable for skilled and experienced volunteers and other individuals.

In this chapter, felling generally refers to cutting the stem but leaving the stump to regrow, whereas clearing involves also removing the stump, or treating it so it will not regrow.

Planning the work

GENERAL INFORMATION

- Felling and clearance work is dangerous. Follow the safety procedures on pages 78-79.

- Felling is only part of the work. Preliminary clearance prior to felling, removal of cut material and stump removal, if necessary, must also be considered.

- Felling and clearing should be done in late autumn and winter, from October to March. At this time the trees are less sappy and are easier to cut and handle than in spring or summer. Herbaceous growth has died back, and disturbance to wildlife is minimised.

- Sort and stack material as you go. Material for green

woodworking (chapter 10) needs to be used as soon as possible after cutting, and is not stored. Other material can be stacked in the wood and removed at a later date. Take advantage of any dry or frosty weather to remove material from the wood, to ease the work and minimise damage to the ground. Avoid extraction when the ground is waterlogged.

• Where felling may be impeded by the growth of brambles and other woody weeds, cut these out from around the base of trees and along routes used for access and dragging. Pile them up into windrows where they can be collected for burning if necessary.

Thinning

Before starting work, the trees must be assessed (p 71) and marked for thinning. Either the trees to be retained, or the trees to be thinned can be marked, depending on the relative proportion of each, but ensure that the system is understood! Trees to be retained are generally marked with a blob of tree marking aerosol paint (available from forestry equipment suppliers). Trees to be cut are generally marked by cutting two blazes, on opposite sides of the stem, using a billhook or slasher. Alternatively, use a band of plumber's tape or similar tied around the trees to be felled.

Where particular species, or all trees below a certain stem diameter are being thinned, workers can proceed without individual trees being marked first. If there are no obvious boundaries to the area to be thinned, use tape, stakes or some other markers to avoid work straying outside the boundary.

Clearance

See the general information on glades (chapter 12) and access (chapter 13). Care must be taken that clearance does not create instability in surrounding trees, which will be opened up to the wind. Mark the areas to be cleared with tape or stakes as necessary.

Procedure

Most felling or clearance tasks consist of the following:

1. Felling

2. Snedding

3. Cross-cutting to manageable lengths for dragging or carrying.

4. Cutting to length according to use.

5. Stacking or burning.

6. Stump removal or treatment may also be necessary for clearance work.

• A typical division of labour is to have three-person teams for the main felling work: for example one person with a saw, one with a billhook and one dragging. In addition one or two people will need to stack or burn. For clearance work, one or two people will be needed to remove or treat stumps. Allow people to change tasks, within their capabilities and training, so that they do a variety of work.

• Where material to be felled is of a wide range of sizes, it is best to fell and remove the lighter growth first, before returning to fell larger material.

SAFETY PRECAUTIONS

• Choose the right tool for the job, depending on the size, form and position of the tree to be felled (p27).

• Chainsaw use is not described in this book, as a training course is essential for learning the safe use of power chainsaws. Use of chainsaws on projects covered by The Conservation Volunteers insurance requires operators to have a Chainsaw Card and to comply with the The Conservation Volunteers' Code of Practice on the use of the chainsaw. Other organisations and employers will have similar training requirements. Private individuals planning to use a chainsaw on their own property are strongly advised to obtain proper training (p187).

• Wear a helmet when felling all but the smallest trees. Don't wear gloves when using edged tools, but have a pair available for handling thorny shrubs and heavy timber after felling.

• Before felling, plan your escape route, which must be free of obstacles. Despite care, the tree may fall the wrong way. If this happens, get clear, but never turn your back and run.

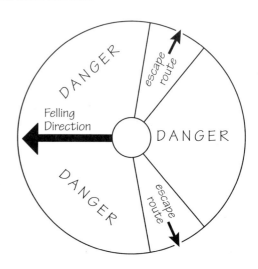

• Clear the danger zone of volunteers, other than your assistant if you are working as a two-person team. The danger zone is a minimum of two tree lengths in any direction. Make sure there are no hung-up trees within one tree length. Extra care must be taken on sites with public access, or any site where members of the public may unofficially gain access. Station people as necessary to prevent anyone entering the danger zone.

• Never approach a feller once he or she has commenced cutting.

• Take great care with hung-up trees, as they are unsafe until fully felled.

• Inspect the tree for any deadwood in the canopy which may become dislodged during felling. If deadwood is assessed as a hazard, don't fell the tree.

• Try to choose a felling direction that lets the tree fall freely without getting hung up in the branches of neighbouring trees. Never fell a tree over an adjacent stump, boulder or another felled tree, as the tree can kick back dangerously and the stem may break.

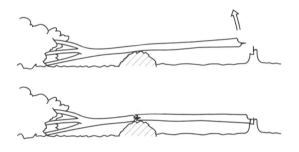

• Take great care when felling in the vicinity of power cables, buildings or other obstacles. Don't fell within 15m (50') of power cables.

• Prepare the cutting area. Remove debris, brambles and branches which might snag a saw or deflect an axe or billhook. Check the trees around you as well as the one you are working on. Clear dead wood to ensure a sound footing. Inspect the stem for embedded wires, especially if the tree is anywhere near an old fence line or boundary. Check out multiple or hollow boles for bottles, tins, stones and so on. If touched while cutting, these may damage the saw and cause injury.

• Take a firm stance before starting to cut. Be especially wary on slopes.

• Wind directions can affect felling safety. Assess the wind direction and force, and estimate how much it may deflect the tree as it falls. You can counteract this, if necessary, by cutting an uneven hinge (p82). Never fell in a strong wind, as you cannot predict the effects of sudden gusts.

• Unless otherwise directed, cut as low to the ground as possible, consistent with safety and efficiency. Sometimes it may be quickest and safest to cut high first and then trim the stump as required. You should do this before moving on to another tree. High cutting is necessary to give adequate leverage if you plan to winch out stumps.

• Beware of dead wood, both in the tree being felled and in nearby trees.

Throughout the felling procedures described below, the 'front' of the tree refers to the side on which it is to fall. 'Front', 'back', 'left side' and 'right side' remain the same no matter which way the feller approaches the tree for a particular procedure.

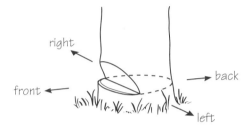

The information below (pp79-81) deals with straightforward situations. Conifers tend to be easier to fell than broadleaves, as they have a single straight trunk and a relatively small crown. Special considerations for felling broadleaves are given on page 81.

Felling small trees with hand tools

FELLING WITH A BILLHOOK

As a felling tool, the billhook is best restricted to use on light coppice material and multi-stemmed shrubs where a bowsaw is awkward. When using a billhook:

1. Stand or kneel to the side of the stem, far enough back to achieve a full swing without endangering yourself. Standing is best for a powerful stroke, but kneeling may be more comfortable or necessary to avoid obstructions. Unless the stem is heavily leaning, you will be cutting into the front of the stem as shown. Use the billhook one-handed, controlling the descent of the stem with the other hand, placed well up the stem for safety.

2. Do not try to cut directly across the grain, as the tool is not designed for this. For small stems, which can be severed with one blow, use a slightly upward sweeping stroke to sever the stem. Avoid cutting downward, as you will drive the hook into the ground and dull or chip the edge.

right　　　wrong　　　wrong

3. Cut thicker stems by notching, as shown. Progressively enlarge the notch with downward and upward strokes until you can finish off with an upward stroke. Keep out of the way of the stem as it falls.

FELLING WITH A BOWSAW

The bowsaw is an efficient and versatile felling tool, and is the best choice for most small trees. As a rough guide, you can fell trees under about 75mm (3") in diameter at the base by cutting straight through, without having to undercut on the front. Use your judgement, as you do not want the wood to split when the tree drops. A 530mm (21") bowsaw is the best saw for single-handed use on small trees.

1. Crouch or kneel to one side of the tree, to saw through from the back.

2. Make the cut level or angled slightly downward in the direction of fall. Saw with easy relaxed strokes, using the full length of the blade.

3. If the tree starts to settle back or twist, use one hand to push it in the direction of fall. Saw faster as the tree falls to minimise the risk of the stem splitting. Keep sawing to sever the stem.

Trees over about 75mm (3") stem diameter are difficult to fell accurately by cutting straight through, and the stems tend to split and fall awkwardly unless you make an undercut first. An undercut is suitable for stems up to about 130mm (5") diameter, when a 'sink' cut becomes necessary.

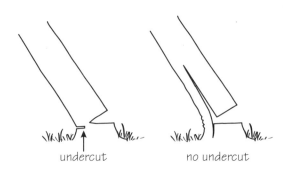

undercut　　　no undercut

FELLING LARGER TREES WITH A BOWSAW

The procedure described below is suitable for trunks up to about 200mm (8") diameter at the base. Anything larger than this should only be felled by a trained and competent person.

Basic procedure

The basic procedure is as follows.

1. Cut a sink by making a notch at the base of the front of the tree. The sink directs the tree's fall away from you as you make the felling cut. Take great care with the position and depth of the sink, as this is critical in its effect on the way that the tree will fall. Cutting sinks are described further below.

2. Sever the tree with a 'felling cut' or 'back cut' made from the back of the tree towards the sink. An uncut piece of wood, called a 'hinge' or 'hold', is left to control the rate and direction of fall.

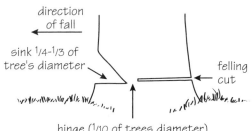

direction of fall

sink ¼-⅓ of tree's diameter

felling cut

hinge (¹⁄₁₀ of trees diameter)

Cutting the sink

The sink should extend one quarter to one third of the trunk's diameter.

Using a bowsaw, make the top cut first, and then make a horizontal cut along to it. Cut accurately, taking care not to cut into the hinge.

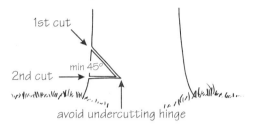

The felling cut

The felling cut should be at or slightly above the level of the bottom sink cut. Normally the felling cut should be level, but if there is any danger of the tree settling back on you, start the felling cut a little higher and angle it down slightly towards the hinge.

1. Line up the felling cut very carefully and cut accurately. If you sever the hinge you lose control of the tree, which is dangerous. The hinge should be about one tenth of the tree's diameter in width. It helps to mark the point on the tree which you plan to make the felling cut, in order to leave the hinge uncut.

2. Except in special circumstances, finish off the felling cut parallel to the sink to leave a parallel-sided hinge not less than 25mm thick, and at right angles to the direction of fall.

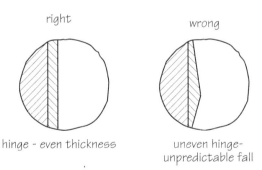

3. Keep sawing until the tree starts to move. You can use a breaking bar or wedges, driven in behind the saw blade, to keep the kerf (saw cut) open, and to allow you to control the timing of the fall.

4. Stand well clear as it falls. The tree may rear upwards or kick backwards after felling, even in a straightforward situation.

5. Saw off the 'sloven', which is the thin strip of wood torn out of the stump or stem when the hinge breaks.

Problems

The following section details some of the problems that can occur when felling trees, and is included here as a warning not to attempt anything for which you have not received the correct training, or for which you are not sufficiently experienced. Felling is rarely straightforward, and the problems listed below will regularly be encountered when felling trees.

BROADLEAVED TREES

- The weighting and lean of the tree must be assessed carefully. In comparison to conifers, most broadleaved trees have large crowns, which are often unevenly balanced, and in felling they are likely to get caught or deflected by neighbouring trees. When the tree hits the ground the butt end is likely to kick back more than conifers due to the large crown.

- Ash, elm, sweet chestnut and willow are particularly likely to twist or break off the stump, or to break up and shed limbs when being felled. Ash and sycamore may split during felling, causing a slab of trunk to spring back towards the feller. A chain or strong rope should be fixed around the trunk about 1.2m (4') from the ground prior to felling.

- Extra equipment, and the training to use it, is needed when felling broadleaved trees. In addition to the saw, an axe, a sledge hammer and wedge, a breaking bar, rope, hand winch and cable may be required. Saws are more likely to jam in broadleaved trees and especially in coppiced trees, due to the uneven weight distribution and twisted grain.

- Broadleaved trees tend to have buttresses at the base, which should be removed before felling. This requires skilled use of the axe or chain saw.

- Directional felling may be difficult due to the size of the tree and its crown. The sink should be one third of the stem diameter to aid control.

- If directional felling is required, you may have to lop unbalanced or awkward limbs. This should only be done by properly trained and equipped personnel.

LEANING AND WEIGHTED TREES

Few trees are in perfect balance. Most have at least a slight lean or imbalance in the weight of the crown, all too often in a different direction from the one in which you want the tree to fall.

Ropes or winches will be needed to control the fall. These

may also be necessary for easier trees if it is essential to fell them with great accuracy or where, because of the terrain or obstacles, you cannot make the sink and felling cuts in line with the required direction of fall.

- Where the tree is leaning or heavily weighted in the direction of felling, a chain or rope will need to be fixed around it to limit splitting. Despite the chain, the tree is likely to split suddenly and fall.

- Where the tree is leaning or heavily weighted against the direction of felling, progs, ropes or winches will be needed to counteract the lean and keep the tree from pinching the saw. Such work should only be undertaken by trained and competent persons.

- Where felling is at an angle to the lean, the sink is cut as usual, but the felling cut is made so as to leave an uneven hinge. As the tree falls, it pivots on the thicker part of the hinge and swings around at an angle to the lean. It takes considerable skill and judgement to make the felling cut in this situation. A winch or rope may be needed to give added control.

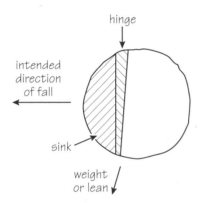

TREES ON SLOPES

Trees on slopes require extra care.

- Finding a safe stance for felling is more difficult, because of the slope and slippery ground.

- Felling downhill has increased risks because of the momentum gained by the falling tree.

- Where there is no appreciable lean or weighting, or where the tree leans into the slope, felling uphill is less risky. Although this leaves quite a high stump, and the tree may get hung up, this method is safer. The butt end of the tree may have to be shifted downhill to free it.

- The tree may 'jump' badly or break downslope when it hits the ground.

- Where it is not possible to fell uphill, felling across the slope is safer than felling downhill.

DEAD OR DISEASED TREES

Dead trees are dangerous to fell because they may give way unexpectedly or shed limbs while you are cutting. Dead trees of some species, such as elm and beech, can be hard work to fell because the standing deadwood may become much tougher, making it necessary to rest and sharpen tools more often. Ropes and winches may be necessary to guide the fall.

Diseased trees may look normal on the outside, yet may have rotted a considerable distance up the stem or down from rotten limbs. This weakens the tree and makes it hazardous to fell.

HANGING TREES

Hung-up or lodged trees can occur where the tree gets caught up in other trees while it is being felled or due to windblow. Note the following:

- Hung-up trees are dangerous and need dealing with as soon as possible by a suitably qualified person. If this is not possible, an exclusion zone of radius at least twice the length of the tree should be clearly marked with warning tape to keep people away.

- Don't work immediately under a hung-up tree.

- Don't climb under a hung-up tree to try and shake it free, or to attach a rope.

- Don't try to fell the tree which is supporting the hung-up tree. The stresses and imbalances make this highly dangerous.

- Don't fell another tree across the hung-up tree in an attempt to dislodge it.

- Beware of dead wood in both the hung-up tree and in surrounding trees, which might be dislodged as the tree falls.

WINDBLOWN TREES

Hand tools are awkward, slow and dangerous to use on windblown trees, especially where you have to cut upwards from the bottom side of the stem. A chainsaw in the hands of a qualified operator is the tool for the job. A few general points are given below.

- Windblown trees are very hazardous because they may be under considerable tension and are frequently in an unstable position. It is vital to assess the stresses on the tree before beginning to cut.

- Trees may be partially or completely uprooted, or the

trunks may be broken but still hung up. The precise cutting sequence will depend on the situation.

- In general, one side of the stem will be under tension and the opposite side will be under compression. Wood under tension may, however, be present on more than one surface of the stem at different points along it. Wherever the surface of the stem is under tension, that is the dangerous side. Cutting sequences must be designed to reduce tension progressively and gradually.

- Workers must always prepare an escape route and be ready for the unexpected.

- Large branches add to the weight of the wood under stress. See information under 'Snedding'(below).

- Cutting close to the butt is least risky, as this is the area of least stress. The root plate should never be stood on while the trunk is cut, as it may suddenly give way as the trunk is severed.

- The first severing cut should be made in the wood under compression. The final cut should be made in the wood under tension. The final cut should be staggered at least 25mm (1") closer to the root plate to minimise splitting of the stem.

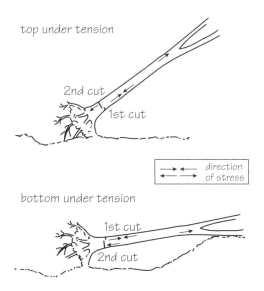

- If there is side tension, the final cut should be made on the safe (compression) side.

Snedding

Snedding is the removal of branches from a felled tree. Snedding of conifers, which have many small radial branches, is most safely done by hand rather than with a chainsaw. On large broadleaves it may be best to clear away the small branches by hand, and then get a chainsaw operator to sned the larger limbs.

Trees should be snedded and the brushwood disposed of at the time of felling, and usually cross-cutting is best done at this time as well. This avoids a hazardous pile-up of stems and tangled branches.

Note the following safety points:

- Always work in a clear area. Do not climb through brushwood to get to the main branches.

- Make sure you have an escape route, as a heavy branch could cause injury as it falls.

- Clear the ground of brushwood as you go along.

- If on a slope, always work on the uphill side so that if the tree rolls it will not trap you.

- Do not climb up onto the trunk to cut off vertical branches or those that are hard to reach.

- Aim to clear the upward projecting branches as soon as you can safely reach them, to reduce the weight which might otherwise cause the trunk to roll over. Leave the underneath branches until last.

- Do not cut any branches which the fallen tree is resting on, as they are under great pressure. If you cut one, it may either spring back and injure you, or cause the trunk to move suddenly.

BASIC SNEDDING

The following points apply to small hardwood trees and most conifers. A light axe or billhook can be used on branches under about 25mm (1") diameter, although some workers may prefer to use loppers. A 530mm (21") bowsaw is suitable for branches over 25mm (1"), and is easier for less skilled workers to use than an axe or billhook. However the saw is slower and can be more awkward, and tends to snag on thin, whippy branches and twigs.

To use a light axe or billhook:

- When possible, stand on the opposite side of the stem to the branches which you are cutting, so that the stem protects your legs and feet. This means you have to cross frequently from one side of the stem to the other to cut branches in different positions. Take great care if you have to stand on the same side as cutting.

- Never stand astride the tree to sned it. Always stand so the impact of the axe or billhook is made well away from your legs, so that you won't be hurt if the tool bounces from the cut. Always make sure there is a clear path for your swing, as even a small twig can deflect the tool and cause injury.

- Sned from the base of the tree towards the tip.

- Leave until last the underneath branches, or any that are supporting the tree or stopping it from rolling.

- A full swing is seldom necessary when snedding small branches. Hold an axe as shown below. With your hands part-way up the haft. You don't need to move your hands for the return stroke.

- For greatest control over the cut, swing the tool in a very shallow arc so that the side of the blade, near its back edge, glances against the stem just before the blade cuts into the branch. This prevents the cutting edge from digging in. This swing is easy to exaggerate and requires some practice to master, but gives the best results.

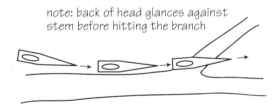

note: back of head glances against stem before hitting the branch

- Sned flush to the main stem. Snags make the log difficult and dangerous to handle, and tear up the ground if the log is dragged away.

- When all the branches except those underneath or supporting the tree are cut, place the tool out of the way. Roll the tree over from the tip, using the remaining branches as handles. If the tree is too heavy for this, lever it over with a pole. Sned the remaining branches.

LARGER TREES

Large broadleaves, trees with branches under stress or trees on slopes require particular care.

- Ensure the tree is stable before you start, and that there are no bystanders.

- Sned from the outer branches into the main limbs, and from the lower limbs towards the limbs at the top. The aim is to lessen the weight of the limbs by removing the smaller branches first. Cut to suitable lengths as you work along the branch, while it is still held firmly. Use a bowsaw for larger limbs.

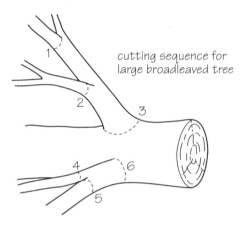

cutting sequence for large broadleaved tree

- Estimate the stresses in large limbs. You may have to treat them as windblown trees (p82). Remember to make a small cut on the compression side first, before making the main cut on the tension side. Take care, as the tree may move or the branch may spring back as you cut it.

- Remove the upward projecting branches as soon as you have safe access to them, to reduce the risk of the trunk rolling over.

- Large limbs projecting upward from the trunk should be treated as if they are standing trees. Fell each in one piece as you would a standing tree, and then sned it on the ground. Do not climb onto the trunk to fell upright branches, in case the trunk moves.

- When the trunk is supported off the ground by two or more branches, roll the trunk over by pushing it away from you, then cut off the remaining branches.

- If the supporting branches make it impossible to roll the trunk over, decide whether the limbs are safe to sned in place. Make sure your escape route is clear. Cut the limbs with an axe, and never work under the tree. Watch it carefully, and when it starts to shift, get out of the way. Then winch or roll the trunk over to expose the remaining limbs.

- Do not attempt to deal with trees which are held up too high by supporting branches to be snedded safely. Such trees should be dealt with by specialists.

Pollarding

Pollarding of wood-pasture, farm, waterside and woodbank trees should be started when the trees are fairly young, before major branches have grown thick and heavy. It is repeated at five- to twenty-year intervals, in the same way as coppicing, depending on the size of poles required. Such trees can reach immense age and girth, and pollard management should be maintained even when the poles are no longer needed, to keep the crowns from collapsing under their own weight, and to prolong the life of the tree.

Pollarding involves working from a height, and should only be done by trained and competent persons.

- New pollards are best started by the time the stem is 100-150mm (4-6") in diameter. Pollarding can be successfully initiated with trees up to 300mm (1') diameter.

- The height at which a new pollard is cut should be determined by the height to which livestock can reach. Allow an extra 300mm (1') above their reach, as regrowth may not be right from the top of the cut stem. Allow 1.8m (6') for fallow deer, 2.1m (7') for cattle, and 2.7-3m (9-10') for horses.

- A pollarding cycle can be restarted even after an extended interval, although some species, notably beech, respond poorly. Each tree should be assessed by an experienced person before work is undertaken. Specialist advice should be sought on lapsed veteran pollards. See *Veteran Trees* (Read, H, 2000) for further information.

Cross-cutting

Cross-cutting felled timber into shorter lengths is usually necessary. As a rough guide, timber over 300mm (12") dbh (p45) should only be felled and handled by trained and competent operators. Apart from the dangers of felling and handling, good quality hardwood timber of this size can be valuable and can be spoiled if not cut properly. Timber of 150-300mm (6-12") diameter has a variety of possible end uses and should be cut to length accordingly. Branches, 'lop and top' and other material smaller than about 150mm (6") diameter should be cut into 1.2m (4') lengths and stacked in a cord (p90). This can later be used for firewood, charcoal, pulp, woodchips or other uses. For greenwood crafts (chapter 10), select pieces for particular uses and stack separately for early removal from the woodland.

Cross-cutting is normally done at the time of felling, after the branches have been snedded. If the timber is to be peeled (p116), this should be done before cross-cutting. Whether you choose to cross-cut at the stump or at the disposal point depends on the size and weight of the material. Try to minimise the amount of handling. For example, material which can be dragged or carried should be taken to the stacking area before cross-cutting. Otherwise, cut at the stump into manageable lengths with final cutting at the stacking point. Do not cross-cut on very steep slopes, as short lengths are dangerous and hard to extract in this situation.

GENERAL POINTS

- Get the log off the ground, if possible, by supporting it near the point where it is to be cut. Ideally, it should be between knee and waist height.

- Where you are cross-cutting a quantity of fairly small poles, it is worth making up a saw horse to hold the wood firmly at a convenient height. A design is shown on page 115.

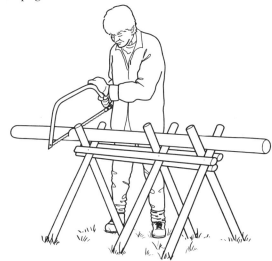

- Material which is too large for a saw horse is best supported on the stack, rather than across a single log.

- When cutting large logs on the ground, start from the lighter top end first. This makes it easier to lift the log onto a support. When cutting poles on a saw horse, cut from the butt end so that the pole does not overbalance.

- Make as many cuts as possible with the wood under tension, so that the cut opens away from the saw.

- Usually the final cut must be made with the log supported at both ends. In this situation the log is under compression, so the saw is likely to bind in the cut. Avoid this by inserting a small wedge in the cut, or support the log with one hand, lifting it just enough to keep the cut open while you finish it. Logs too heavy for this should be rotated as soon as the saw starts to bind, so that you cut through from two or three places, each turned upwards in succession.

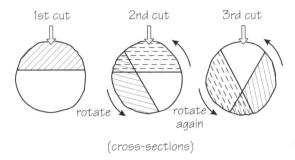

(cross-sections)

- You may not be quite able to sever the log by cutting around it. Finish the job by giving the log a knock with a lump or sledge hammer, or by pushing it off the support onto the ground, where the impact usually breaks it.

Bowsaw

- The bowsaw is the best tool for cross-cutting small logs. Use a saw of adequate size for the diameter of the logs (p27).

- Stand with your feet apart, both feet in line with the cut. Hold the saw with both hands. Don't use your thumb to guide the blade, as you would in carpentry.

- Use a more pronounced rocking motion than when felling, using your body as well as your arms to power the stroke. Saw with fairly slow strokes. To speed up the work, increase pressure on the saw rather than the speed of the stroke. Cut easily on the push stroke, and use more pressure and rocking motion on the pull stroke.

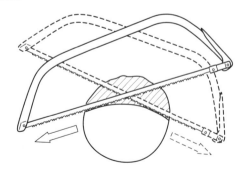

- When cross-cutting a log which is near the ground, use a half-kneeling position. You won't be able to rock the saw, so increase pressure instead. Don't push so hard that the blade starts to turn in the cut, this being a problem mainly with dull or damaged blades.

Clearing up brash

Felling of trees and shrubs produces a large amount of woody material of all sizes. In the past, when wood was the mainstay of the rural economy, nothing was wasted. All material cut in a wood was removed for use, including the tops, which were bundled as faggots for fuel. The flora and fauna of ancient woodlands are adapted to this practice, with losses of deadwood habitats, but gains in the form of a rich herbaceous ground flora, when compared to natural conditions. Trees in wood-pasture and hedgerows were also managed to produce useful woody material.

Many coppice workers today follow this tradition, needing to maximise their income from an area of coppice, and both new and traditional markets are being developed to support the coppice economy (p109). However, markets take time and energy to develop, and for voluntary projects in particular, it may not always be possible to link the need for management with an end-use for the cut material.

In the recent past, burning was the main method of getting rid of surplus woody material. This has several practical advantages. Cuttings are completely removed so that they do not interfere with plant growth by shading, obstructing the ground or altering the general soil conditions. Burning is quicker than cutting and stacking to size. Last but not least, a fire keeps volunteers warm and happy!

However, burning also has disadvantages. Any vegetation on the fire site is destroyed, and the soil becomes enriched with mineral ash so that the fire site usually gets colonised by rank invasive vegetation such as nettles, with only very slow if any recovery to more natural conditions. Burning is wasteful, in that the material can have other uses before it gets returned through the carbon cycle. Burning removes a source of deadwood habitat and returns minerals to the soil in 'raw' form which are easily leached by rainfall. Bonfires are increasingly seen as antisocial.

Within the aim of a particular woodland management project, the re-use of woody material should be increased as much as possible, and the amount of burning minimised. However, where the main aim of a project is clearance for access, glade creation or maintenance of open habitats, burning may be the only feasible method of disposal.

Note the following:

- Operations such as thinning and coppicing should be linked to re-using material if possible. The need for thinning or coppicing should be planned some years ahead, giving time to find a market for the material. However, it's important that thinning should be done at the correct time, even if the economic return from the crop is poor. Coppice cycles may also need to be maintained for conservation reasons, and for some coppices, the need for cutting and restoration is urgent, and should not be delayed until markets are found.

- Many projects involve the clearance of growth such as blackthorn, elder, bramble and other species which have little re-use value. Spiny, branched material including blackthorn and hawthorn is difficult to compact, and takes a long time to rot down, and is normally best burnt.

- Rhododendrons and other invasive exotic species are usually not possible to re-use, and the volume of material involved means that burning is normally essential. Where machines are being used for clearance and very large volumes are produced, conversion to woodchips or brash-bundling (p93) is possible, provided there is a market for the material.

METHODS OF RE-USE

The following section gives some ideas about re-using the cut material from woodland management. There are many factors to consider:

- **Access**. Vehicle access makes an enormous difference to the viability of woodland management. Where there is no vehicle access, the effort involved in carrying material, and the possible ground damage caused, may make re-use not worth considering.

- **Ground conditions for extraction**. Linked to access is the importance of ground conditions. Many woodlands are on damp ground, and most woodland management takes place in winter. Wet ground will make extraction more difficult, and damage to the ground will be much greater, both by vehicles and feet. Take advantage of dry spells of weather to extract material.

- **The time available**. Most projects have a time limit, and a decision needs to be made on the balance between cutting and clearing up/extraction. Some voluntary projects in woodlands are long-term, allowing time to store material for later re-use, and to build up local uses for the material.

- **The labour available**. Cutting up material for re-use and extraction normally takes longer than burning, but where plenty of hands are available, re-use can provide useful work for everyone. Qualified operators of machines, including chainsaws, log splitters and woodchippers will make a difference to the viability of re-use.

Within the wood

Re-using some material for projects within the woodland itself is a good option, as it reduces the need for transport, and avoids the purchase and import of other materials. Possibilities include:

- **Fencing**. Hardwoods, especially oak and chestnut are excellent fencing materials. Sections of post and rail fencing can be constructed for car parks, alongside paths, or for tree surrounds. See *Fencing* (BTCV, 2001) for further details.

- **Revetments**. Various types of wood can be used to build revetments to prevent erosion of woodland paths or banks. See *Footpaths* (BTCV, 1996) for further details.

- **Path construction**. Bundles of roundwood or faggots can be used to make path foundations through wet ground. These can be edged with larger roundwood, and topped with woodchips (p171).

- **Woodchips**. Useful for car-park surfacing, play areas, and for mulching around newly planted trees and shrubs (see below).

- **Dead hedging**. To protect newly coppiced areas, natural regeneration or new planting from damage by deer. See page 108.

- **Piles of brash.** These may be useful for discouraging access at certain points, particularly if they are left long enough to get grown over with bramble. They can also make useful bird nesting habitat. However too many 'habitat piles' are a nuisance rather than a benefit, and it's better to plant understorey shrubs or improve the woodland edge habitat if more cover is needed for birds.

In suitable habitats woodcock can be encouraged to nest by constructing 'doughnuts' of brash. Choose a dry spot with plenty of leaf litter. The brash should be piled into a ring, about 1.5m (5') high, leaving the centre free, where the woodcock can make a simple scrape in the leaf litter. The brash should be dense enough to deter foxes, but allow the woodcock through.

There are a large number of possible uses for cut material outside the wood, which are described further in chapters 9, 10 and 11. For local voluntary groups, start with re-using as much material as you can within the group. You should find you can dispose of quantities of material for pea and bean sticks, rustic poles for garden use, kindling and firewood. Try and make sure that anyone with transport goes home with a few bundles or sacks of material for themselves or their neighbours. Seek out homeowners with wood fires or wood-burning stoves, as they may be keen to cut and transport firewood for their own use. Contact local scout groups, gardening groups and others who may have use for woody material.

Further information on stacking and extracting is given in the next section.

Woodchipping

Woodchipping is routinely used by many authorities and private businesses for converting woody material from roadside trees, parks, gardens and woodland management into woodchips. These can be used for mulch and compost, surfacing for playgrounds, paths and riding arenas, or used as fuel in domestic or commercial heating systems, or for power generation.

The viability of the operation depends on the costs and quantities involved and on the market. For voluntary groups managing a small woodland it can be an efficient way of recycling brash, and a useful contribution to income. Woodchipping machines must only be used by trained operators. Two examples of voluntary schemes are given below.

At Lodge Copse, West Sussex, volunteers coppice 1.5 acres each year, on an 8 year rotation. The brash is laid butt ends to the track. A chipping machine is hired at £50.00 per day, and is towed along the track, followed by another driver with a trailer. This produces 4-6m^3 of chips per day, which is stored in bins made of stakes and sleepers. The chips are left for 2 years, with 4m^3 of chips producing about 2m^3 of compost. Charcoal at a proportion of 10% is added when bagging to keep the compost sweet. The compost is sold through garden centres, and at West Dean College. Other waste is stacked up to make dead hedges around the coupe, to keep people out and discourage deer. The group only have a bonfire on the last Tuesday before Christmas, with mince pies!

At Rocks East Woodland, Wiltshire, volunteers convert all material smaller than 75mm (3") diameter to woodchips. The composted woodchips sell at £3.50 per bag (2000), which is a better return than from firewood. Woodchips are also sold by the trailer load, at £35 per load within a three mile radius of the woodland.

BONFIRES

Where re-use is not possible, burning may be the only option.

Location

- Site the fire where the vegetation is least valuable, such as on previous fire sites, heavily used tracks or where undergrowth has shaded out the ground vegetation. If unsure about the location of any valuable flora, which may not be visible at the time of burning, take advice from the site manager.

- If working at the edge of the wood, you may be able to get permission to burn in the adjacent field.

- Site the fire downhill of the worksite, if feasible, to make it easier to drag the cuttings.

- Site the fire downwind of the worksite, to keep the site less smoky.

- Site the fire well away from the boles and crowns of standing trees. The heat from a big fire reaches far beyond the visible flames. Overhanging branches may be killed even if they are high above the fire itself. Trees exposed to intense heat may appear unharmed at the time, but can lose their bark and die in a year or so. Smooth-barked trees such as beech, sycamore and ash are particularly susceptible to scorching.

- On wet sites, build the fire in the driest place possible. Unless it is very windy, choose a raised site to maximise the draught. Avoid hollows. Avoid burning on peat. Damp peat will get damaged, and dry peat may smoulder underground for weeks and then flare up unexpectedly.

- Take extra care on sites with a high fire risk, such as heathland, pinewoods or woods on sandy soils. Clear a firebreak, and have water available if possible.

Starting and tending

- If you are clearing scrub or other difficult to burn material, it's essential to get the fire going quickly and efficiently, to keep up with disposing of the cut material. It's probably best to have one person in charge of the fire, until it is going well.

- Use newspaper, dry kindling or dead wood to get a small fire going. If the weather is bad, come prepared with a sack of dry material to start the fire. Never use petrol to start the fire.

- Once it has caught, add thin, dry wood in fairly short, straight lengths so that they pack close together to form a bed of embers. Don't put on awkwardly branched wood or green wood at this stage.

- Sned branches sufficiently so that they pack down neatly and keep the fire small.

- Lay branches on the fire with their butt ends to the wind. The twigs will thus be in the downwind and hottest part of the fire, where they will catch quickly. The pile will also pack down quickly as the smaller branches burn. Push the butts into the fire as necessary.

- Keep the fire tight, to minimise ground damage and for efficient burning.

- Some people should drag branches to the fire for the fire-tenders to cut up for putting on the fire. Use a sharp billhook, light axe, or loppers and small bowsaw. Use the axe or billhook on a chopping block, to avoid damage to tools. Avoid the situation where everyone throws on their own material, as this usually results in the fire spreading and losing efficiency.

- Keep the area immediately around the fire free of material, to avoid the danger of people tripping.

- Use a long-handled pitch fork or 1.8m (6') prog to push cuttings well down into the fire. This keeps the fire compact and burning strongly. Turn in the fire to stop it getting too big by pushing branches and embers in from the side. If the fire gets hollow, knock it down with a pole to keep it burning.

- Never overload the fire in an effort to keep pace with the cutting, as the fire may be damped down, or worse, get out of control.

- Don't leave the fire until it has burnt down to embers. If there is any doubt, turn it in and cover it with mineral soil (not peat) before leaving.

- If possible, gather up the ashes the next day to stop them enriching the fire site. Wood ash is a useful fertiliser for vegetables and soft fruit.

Extracting, stacking and seasoning

This section considers the extraction, stacking and conversion of small size timbers, produced from neglected coppices, early thinnings or clearance operations. The harvesting of large timbers is a specialist job for contractors with the necessary equipment.

EXTRACTION

- Timber should be handled as few times as possible, to save labour.

- Some woodlands have rides suitable for access by four-wheel drive vehicles and trailers, although often only at drier times of year. Many woodlands though, and especially those where voluntary groups are likely to work, have poor access. Inspect the access carefully before agreeing to any extraction work.

- Generally it is easier and safer to drag a pole along

the ground, or to lift one end and drag it along using tongs or a similar aid, than it is to pick it up and carry it. Take great care when lifting (p24). Short lengths and small-diameter cordwood can be shifted with a wheelbarrow on suitable terrain.

- Always wear gloves (p24) and steel toe-capped boots or wellingtons when handling timber.

- One of the simplest and most versatile tools for hand extraction is a 4.5m (12-16') length of 10mm (1/2") rope, spliced into a loop. A loop joined with a knot can also be used, although this is less secure than a splice. This can be used as shown for dragging poles and round timbers up to about 200mm (8") diameter.

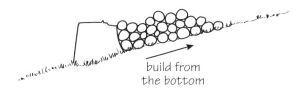

STACKING

General points

- Clear the stacking site of all obstructions, choosing a level site if possible. When stacking across sloping ground, build the stack from the bottom upwards, supported to prevent rolling. Do not support stacks against live trees.

build from the bottom

- Stack large logs parallel to each other for stability. Stack smaller logs, which are to be cross-cut, as for cordwood, but don't bother stacking to standard cord dimensions.

- Shade the ends of newly stacked material from direct summer sun, to prevent them splitting. This precaution is unnecessary once the material is partly seasoned.

- Never walk or climb over stacked wood unless absolutely essential, as you may collapse the stack. Grit from boots also collects on the timber and can damage tools which are later used on it.

- Always leave stacks in a safe, stable condition, especially where there is public access.

Cordwood

Poor-quality material and irregular branches, suitable for pulp, firewood or charcoal burning, should be cross-cut and stacked for storage and sale in cords. A cord is made up of material not more than 1.2m (4') long. There is no universal standard, but the normal cord has dimensions of 2.4 x 1.2 x 1.2m (8' x 4' x 4') to give a nominal volume of 3.46 m³ (128 ft³). A cord of dimensions 1.8 x 1.2 x 1.6m (6' x 4' x 5'4") gives the same volume.

The solid volume is actually much less than the nominal volume, since even a tightly stacked cord contains about 50% air space. A loosely stacked cord, containing much more air space, has far less sales value.

To make a cord:

1. Lay two base poles, 50-75mm (2-3") diameter and slightly longer than the cord on the ground, about 750mm (2'6") apart. If the ground is very uneven or the poles irregular, lay them on 'sleeper' poles to make a level base.

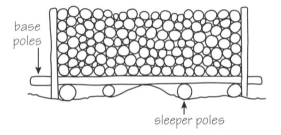

2. Provide end-stop stakes to keep the corded wood from rolling off the poles. Drive them well into the ground so that their tops are at least 1.2m (4') above ground level. Place the stakes outside the poles to prevent the poles rolling apart.

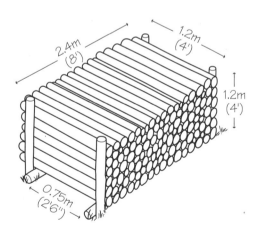

3. If more than one cord is to be stacked in a line using the same base poles, drive in stakes every 2.4m (8') along the poles to help distribute the weight, and to make it easier to count the number of cords in the stack.

4. Stack the timber as shown, being careful to centre the timber on the poles and to stack as tightly as possible.

Poles, fencing material and small produce

Stack poles and fencing materials as for cordwood, but stack each layer at right angles to the one below to aid drying. Normally no end-stops are needed, and the stack should be stable on its own.

Stack small produce, such as bean poles, pea sticks, packing rods and tree stakes, in alternating groups of layers, each group about 150mm (6") thick. Alternatively, bundle the produce ready for transport and sale. See page 112 for further details.

SEASONING

On-site seasoning of roundwood is seldom necessary, apart from that which occurs naturally if the material is left in stacks until conversion. In some cases, where material is sold by weight (eg pulpwood), seasoning should be avoided. Such material should be sold as soon as possible after felling to minimise the loss of value due to drying. Material which is to be converted into products with the bark off, including all material which is going to be treated with preservative, should be peeled at the time of felling (p116).

The time it takes for material to season depends on the type of timber and the weather. As an example, round softwood poles, 150mm (6") in diameter, stacked in spring, should fully season in about six months.

Clearing scrub, undergrowth and woody weeds

Clearing scrub and undergrowth is frequently necessary in woodlands for the reasons given above (p77). Clearance of scrub which is encroaching on grassland, heathland and wetland habitats is also often necessary.

For voluntary groups, the most effective way of clearance is to have one or more trained chainsaw or brushcutter operators, together with others working with hand tools. The cut material can be disposed of by burning or chipping. Some material can be re-used for dead hedging, firewood or other uses, although depending on the species involved, the material may be too spiny or branching to be of value. Where chainsaws or chipping machines are being used (by trained and competent operators only), they must be used at a safe distance from, or at a different time from, the rest of the voluntary work.

In amenity woods or those where public access is being encouraged, the balance between retaining undergrowth and shrubby woodland edges for wildlife value, and the public preference for more open woods may need to swing in favour of clearance. Many potential users have a fear of woodlands and of unsocial behaviour that dense undergrowth may harbour, especially in urban fringe areas. Retain undergrowth in the more inaccessible areas, or use it as a means of blocking access to particular features you want to protect. Clear undergrowth around car-parks, along main tracks and paths or wherever you want to encourage people into the wood. Children love to play and make dens in dense growth, particularly rhododendron and laurel, so retaining some bushes near picnic sites and play areas may prove popular. For further information on public use of woodlands see chapter 13.

Any clearance work should be done in winter. Working in late winter and spring will disturb nesting birds, and working in late summer and autumn may destroy useful food supplies of fruits and seeds. Make the most of any dry spells in winter, to avoid damage to the ground.

PROCEDURES

Cutting by hand

Use the basic felling techniques described on pages 79-81. Cut as low as possible to the ground, unless you plan to winch the stumps out (see below), in which case leave a stump at least 1m (3') high.

The nature of undergrowth and scrub means that there is a lot of branching growth to get rid of. The main requirement is to organise the group effectively so that work progresses efficiently, with the minimum handling of material. Re-use as much material as possible, and consider the use of a chipper, with trained operator, to chip the smaller branches and twigs. Otherwise, fires will be necessary.

Most species will regrow from the stump, and it will be necessary to either remove the stump, treat it with herbicide, or treat the regrowth.

Stump removal by hand

- The basic technique is to cut around the stump and loosen the side roots which anchor it. Destroying the stump itself by hand is not feasible.

- Use a grubbing mattock on large shrubs and saplings. The grubbing mattock has a short axe blade to sever the roots, and a longer mattock blade to lever them up. Cut all around the base with the mattock and lever the stump out with a crowbar. Don't use the mattock for levering, as the handle may break. Difficult stumps may require several people working together.

Using a winch

- To winch out stumps, use a winch with a cable that hooks to chain about 2m (7') long. The chain should have small links for flexibility, and have a large eye at each end, of unequal size so that one fits through the other. Loop the chain around the stump, and then pull it tight and hook it to the winch cable. Both cable and chain must have safe working loads as great as the winch's hauling capacity.

- The hand winch must be securely mounted to a fixed standfast, such as the base of a stout tree. Place pickets around the tree to protect it from damage. A tractor-mounted winch, necessary for really big stumps, usually has its own holdfast in the form of a metal bar that is lowered until it digs into the ground.

- It is often best to winch one way and then the opposite to break the anchor roots. Don't work around the stump while the winch cable is under tension, as it may give suddenly.

- One problem with removing stumps is that you still have to get rid of them. Stumps are heavy and awkward to lift, and damage the ground if you drag them. They also take a long time to burn. Piling them up is not usually an option as they will take years to rot down, and look extremely unsightly. Smaller stumps, which can be moved fairly easily, are best burnt. Large stumps may have to be left where they are pulled out, or moved far enough to be out of the way of access or other use. Stump grinding or herbicide treatment may need to be considered as alternatives.

- The holes from which stumps are removed can also be a problem. In peaty soil the craters gradually fill with soft peat and become masked by a mat of vegetation, presenting a hazard to man and animal. Where holes are likely to be a hazard, they should be refilled with soil or other material from nearby. Where clearance is for grassland re-creation, harrowing will help smooth out the ground and prepare it for restoration.

Herbicide treatment

Cut stumps can be killed in situ using herbicide. This is labour intensive, and leaves the stump where it may present a hazard. On the other hand, it avoids the ground disturbance caused by stump removal, and the problem of disposing of the stump.

Ammonium sulphamate (Amcide) can be applied as crystals. Drill 25mm (1") diameter holes, 50mm (2") deep, making 4 holes in a 150mm (6") diameter stump. Fill the holes with crystals and then cover with stones to keep the rain out, or the crystals will become diluted and ineffective.

Clearance by machine

Various machines can be used to clear scrub, undergrowth and stumps, from tracked excavators to smaller hand-held machines. Machines which destroy stumps in situ have the advantage of avoiding the need for disposal of the stump, or for filling in the hole. A portable stump grinder adapted from a chainsaw is available, as is a specially adapted chainsaw which allows the cutting of roots below ground level. These portable machines are useful on sites with difficult access. Stony ground may prevent their use. A stump-lifting machine, as used in tree nurseries for lifting stock can be used in some situations.

Regrowth can be destroyed with an agricultural flail machine, which if repeated for a couple of years, will prevent regrowth of most species.

Large forestry mulching machines which mulch all top growth and grind the stumps are available. Although machines have the disadvantage that they may damage the ground, this is mitigated by the fact that they also have the ability to backfill holes, level the ground and prepare it for future use. 'Creative disturbance' can also provide good conditions for regeneration of natural vegetation. See also details below for rhododendron clearance. Machines must only be used by trained and competent operators. For further details see *Practical Solutions Handbook* (English Nature, 2001).

RHODODENDRON

Rhododendron is an introduced species which can spread rapidly on acid soils, particularly in the wetter western areas of England. It spreads mainly by seed, though also by stems which root where they touch the ground, and coppices vigorously. Its thick, dense, evergreen foliage shades out virtually all other species, and fallen leaves rot slowly, leaving a thick, acid layer over the soil. Rhododendron itself can grow in dense shade. Seedlings grow slowly for the first few years, but can then spread very rapidly. The mature leaves have a thick waxy cuticle which makes the foliage resistant to herbicide treatments. The young foliage can be treated successfully.

Merely cutting and removing the cut material is not effective, as the stumps regrow and many seedlings will appear. A combination of cutting, stump removal and spraying of herbicide on foliage is normally needed, and action must continue for some years at each site, to deal with seedlings and regrowth.

Voluntary groups can tackle limited areas of rhododendron, but large areas will need clearance by machine as hand clearance will make little impact. A phased operation to which voluntary groups can contribute is suggested below. Qualified staff will be needed for the application of herbicide.

Clearance by hand

First as much rhododendron as possible is cut down. Rhododendron is fairly easy to cut with a bowsaw, and although care must be taken, this is a relatively risk-free operation. The multi-stemmed nature of the plant means that there is plenty of work for everyone! The work can be done at any time of year, although during the winter there may be disturbance to hibernating reptiles on heathland sites, especially in smaller rhododendron clumps or along the edges of large blocks. Rhododendron also provides shelter and winter roosts for many species of birds, although the amount of growth on most sites means there is usually plenty of alternative cover.

Stumps should be removed using mattocks. Large stumps which cannot easily be removed by hand are left, and the regrowth is treated the following year. Treating the cut stumps with herbicide is not usually practical, because of the number of stumps, and spraying regrowth is more effective. The cut material can be burnt immediately, or stacked to dry for later burning. Rhododendron makes good firewood and very good charcoal, although the time taken to prepare the material for the kiln compared to other species may mean it's not economic for commercial charcoal burning.

One year after the initial clearance, in early summer, a return visit is made to hand-pull seedlings and minor regrowth from roots. The regrowth on the stumps is sprayed with a herbicide, as are any small bushes which are too big to hand pull. Glyphosate mixed with a wetting agent is effective. Follow the manufacturer's instructions on dilution and application, and only spray in very calm conditions. For further details see *The Use of Herbicides in the Forest* (Forestry Commission, 1995).

Any remaining cut material from the previous year is burnt.

Each year another check is made for seedlings, which are removed by hand. Any regrowth which has been missed or not responded to treatment is resprayed. Bushes larger than about 2m (6') diameter by 1.5m (5') high will have to be cut down, and either the stumps removed or the regrowth sprayed the following year.

On large areas, a Geographic Information System (GIS) programme should be used to record and map all rhododendron clumps and scattered bushes, so that treatment can be planned effectively and progress monitored. For further details see *Enact* (Vol 7 No 4, 1999).

Clearance by machine

Large areas of rhododendron can only be effectively tackled by machine. A 13-tonne tracked excavator can clear dense growth by uprooting the entire bush with most of the roots. A wheeled machine, such as a JCB, is not normally powerful enough, and causes significant ground damage. A chainsaw operator is also needed for the clear-up operation, along with workers to burn the debris. Seedlings and regrowth from broken roots are sprayed with herbicide the following year.

To avoid the time required for burning, as well as its environmental disadvantages, a chipper can be used to process all the cut material into chippings, which can be used for surfacing, mulch and other uses. For large areas, there are the options to use more complex machinery. A forestry mulching machine can chop up standing bushes, leaving the material to rot down. See *Enact* (Vol 7 No 4, 1999) for further details. A brash-baling machine can gather and bale brushwood into bundles, each weighing up to 0.75 tonne, for use as fuel in wood-burning power-generation plants. See *Enact* (Vol 9 No 1, 2001) for further details. For heathland restoration, the ground disturbance caused by such machines is an advantage, allowing more rapid colonisation by heathland plants.

JAPANESE KNOTWEED

Although mainly a weed of stream sides, railway embankments and other 'corridors' along which it can spread, Japanese knotweed can cause problems in woodlands, especially along boundaries with corridor habitats. Japanese knotweed spreads vegetatively by its stems and rhizomes, which can extend for up to 7m (23') underground from the clump. A tiny piece of rhizome can generate a new plant. Japanese knotweed grows 2-3m (6-10') high in a thick stand of bamboo-like stems and large leaves, excluding most other plants. It occurs in nearly all parts of Britain, being most invasive in the south and west. A less common species, giant knotweed, grows 4-5m (13-16') tall.

Under the Wildlife and Countryside Act (1981) it is an offence to plant or otherwise cause the species to grow in the wild. Under the Environmental Protection Act 1990, Japanese knotweed is classified as 'controlled waste', and stems, foliage, rhizomes or contaminated soil must be disposed of only at a licensed landfill site. Contact the Environment Agency for advice.

Cutting is laborious and must be continued for several seasons, and may not be successful in controlling the plant. Never use a flail or mower, as small pieces of the plant can regrow. Instead use a sharp grass hook or slasher. Do not put the cut material through a woodchipping machine, or try to compost it. Burning on site is normally the best method of disposal. Digging out is not usually feasible, because of the spread of the rhizomes. Any soil within 7m (23') of the clump may be contaminated.

Chemical control is the recommended control method, normally using glyphosate at a rate of 5 litres/ha, with the addition of a wetting agent, applied from May to September. Two or three applications per season may be necessary over several years for effective control. New techniques of injecting the stems are being tested, to increase effectiveness of the herbicide application and avoid damage to other plants. Herbicide must only be applied by trained and competent persons.

For further details see *The Japanese Knotweed Manual* (Child, L E and Wade, P M, 2000), *Enact* (Vol 9 No 2, 2001) and visit www.ex.ac.uk/knotweed.

9   Coppicing

Coppicing, or cutting down a tree to produce new growth, has been a way of harvesting wood for thousands of years. Far from being destructive, coppicing has been the reason why many woodlands have survived, because the woodland had an economic value. Coppicing rejuvenates the tree, so some coppice stumps or 'stools' are hundreds of years old, and are an important genetic link back to the ancient woodlands. For further details on the history of coppicing see pages 2-4.

In the past, the rural economy was based on coppicing, and coppice products were used for building, fencing, fuel, furniture and many other uses. Nothing was wasted. Many of these traditional products are still needed, and new products and markets have been developed (p109).

Coppicing requires only simple hand tools and produces material which can be manually handled, the reason for its importance in the past and its relevance today. Felling and extraction is much less hazardous than with other methods of harvesting wood.

General information

SPECIES AND GROWTH

When the tree is cut down, new shoots arise from dormant buds on the side of the stump, or from adventitious shoots around the edge of the cut surface. Root buds which are close to the stump can also produce coppice shoots, especially in hazel and birch. The buds are stimulated into growth by changes in plant hormone levels produced when the previous top growth is removed.

Most native broadleaved species coppice, but some are stronger than others. The species which produce the strongest growth over the longest time are ash, hazel, oak, sweet chestnut, field maple and small-leaved lime. Birch and black poplar only produce regrowth if cut young when the stump is fairly small. The native wild cherry, aspen and elm, and the introduced white poplar and grey alder produce suckers from the roots, rather than growing from the stump. Conifers die if cut to the stump.

The number of shoots produced depends on the species, and the age and size of the stool. In the first season a large number of shoots, between 50 and 150, are produced,

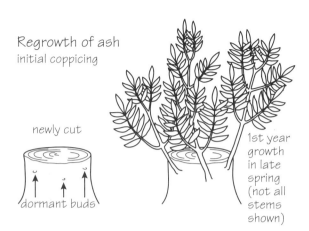

Regrowth of ash
initial coppicing

newly cut

dormant buds

1st year growth in late spring (not all stems shown)

Coppice stool after several coppice cycles

but self-thinning occurs and most die off. By the middle of the rotation, between 5 and 15 may be left. Artificial thinning is not often done, although this can be used to maximise growth per stem, where demand is for larger size poles.

Regrowth varies according to the site, the condition of the stools and the species. Where unchecked by browsing, regrowth may be as much as 3m (10') in the first season for willows, 1.5-1.8m (5-6') for ash, hazel, sycamore and sweet chestnut, 1m (3') for aspen and field maple, and 600mm (2') for hornbeam. There is an even greater increment in the second year, and then growth slows in following years. The canopy may close in the second or third year for the more vigorous species.

Short rotation coppice is grown for less than 10 years before being cut. Long rotation coppice is grown for more than 20 years.

The following table shows the main coppice species, together with their uses, rotation, spacing and number of stools per hectare (and acre). This information relates to good quality, single-species coppices which are regularly managed ('in-cycle'). Neglected coppices, grown beyond their optimum rotation, are likely to have fewer stools per hectare, with gaps where stools have died, and fewer, larger poles from each stool. The main use will be for firewood. Depending on the mix of species, mixed species coppice should be grown on about a 15 year rotation at 1000 stools/hectare (400/acre), with main uses for fencing, furniture and firewood.

Table 9a: SHORT ROTATION COPPICE

SPECIES	MAIN USE	ROTATION	SPACING	No/hectare (acre)
Willow	Baskets, willow sculptures	2-3 years	c. 2m	2250 (900)
Sweet chestnut	Walking sticks	3 years	c. 2m	2250 (900)
Hazel	Hurdles, bean poles, thatching spars	7-10 years	c. 2.5m	1500-2000 (600-800)

Table 9b: LONG ROTATION COPPICE

SPECIES	MAIN USE	ROTATION	SPACING	No/hectare (acre)
Alder	Turnery	10-20 years	c. 3m	1100 (450)
Sycamore	Turnery	10-20 years	c. 3m	1100 (450)
Ash	Turnery, tool handles, rails	10-25 years	c. 3m	1100 (450)
Sweet chestnut	Fencing	15-20 years	c. 3.5m	800-1000 (320-400)
Birch	Turnery	15-25 years	c. 3.5m	800-1000 (320-400)
Hornbeam	Firewood	15-35 years	c. 3.5m	800-1000 (320-400)
Lime	Turnery	20-25 years	c. 3.5m	800-1000 (320-400)
Oak	Fencing	18-35 years	c. 4.5m	200-500 (80-200)
Mixed species	Fencing and firewood	15-20 years	c. 3.5m	800-1000 (320-400)

YIELD

The yield will depend on the spacing of the coppice stools, the rotation and the quality of management. Site factors, such as soil fertility, moisture and shelter are also important. The following figures are for commercial coppices, where the aim is to maximise yield.

The mean annual increment over a coppice rotation (dry wood per hectare per year measured down to 5cm diameter) is about 2.5 tonnes for sycamore, birch, ash, lime, oak, alder and sweet chestnut. For poplar and willow it is about 6 tonnes/ha/yr. If twigs are included, sweet chestnut yields about 4 tonnes/ha/yr. Hazel, including all material down to 2cm diameter, yields about 2.5 tonnes/ha/yr (Evans, 1984). The total yield for example for hazel cut at year 10 of a rotation should be about 25 tonnes/ha.

Short rotation coppice willow grown on a three year rotation for energy production can produce very high yields, of 8-20 tonnes of dry wood/ha/yr. This includes all woody material, which is machine harvested and converted to woodchips before being burnt for heating or to generate electricity (Macpherson, George, 1995).

Sweet chestnut

A 15-year-old commercial sweet chestnut coppice should yield products as shown below.

Table 9c: YIELD PER HECTARE OF COMMERCIAL SWEET CHESTNUT COPPICE

Posts (1.4-1.6m)	2500-5000
Poles (1m, in bundles of 25)	900-2500
Pea sticks (bundles of 25)	50-100
Firewood	45-60 m^3

Hazel

A hectare of eight- or nine-year-old, well-stocked hazel coppice will produce 25,000 to 30,000 rods 3-4.5m in length. These could be converted into 740 hurdles or about 185,000 thatching spars. (Equivalent of 10,000 to 12,000 rods per acre, 10-15' in length, which could produce 300 of 6' x 6' hurdles or 75,000 thatching spars). In addition pea and bean sticks could be produced.

Coppice craftspeople require an average of 1.62 hectares (4 acres) a year to make a living, meaning that each person requires at least 12.96 hectares (32 acres) over an 8 year rotation.

The 70 craftspeople in Hampshire (1995) required 907 hectares (2,240 acres). Grants provided by Hampshire County Council funded 50% of the cost of restoring over 506 hectares (1,250 acres) of derelict hazel coppice between 1982-95, but the area of good quality in-cycle hazel coppice in the county was still not enough to meet the demand from coppice workers. In 1995 there was a requirement of 1,250 hectares (3,087 acres) of in-cycle coppice from the existing workforce, but only 750 hectares (1,852 acres) of in-cycle coppice were available, which included the areas which had been restored. (Hampshire County Council, 1995).

Coppice becomes a viable proposition for a landowner when the coppice is in good condition, properly in-cycle, with good access. Prices per hectare/acre, as paid by the coppice worker, should compare favourably with most broadleaved crops. There is the additional income from occasional felling of standards, and the value for wildlife, shooting, amenity and other uses.

COUPE SIZE

The coupe, cant or panel is the block of coppice which is cut at any one season. A coppice woodland should be divided up into several coupes, which are cut in rotation over a period of years. The size of each coupe will depend on the labour available to cut it, the market for the products and other factors. As far as possible one should try to keep to the planned cycle, although this may be difficult with changing markets or other factors.

The size of coupe may be anything from a minimum of 0.1 hectare (0.25 acre), 0.5 hectare (1.2 acres) in larger woods, to a maximum of 1.2 hectares (3 acres). Small plots are more vulnerable to damage by deer, and to shading by surrounding trees. Coupes should not be larger than 25% of the total area of the wood, in order to maintain continuity of the coppice habitat.

Coupes should be square or rectangular in shape, to maximise the sunshine reaching the plot, and to minimise fencing costs. Avoid long narrow shapes and convoluted edges which will be more expensive to fence, and which will produce less vigorous growth. All coupes should have at least one edge which abuts a ride, so that the cut wood can be removed from the coupe without dragging it through another coupe. If necessary create more rides (p147), as these are essential for efficient management of the wood, as well as themselves being valuable wildlife habitats. Take account of the need for deer management when planning the coupes and rides, with high seats sited for safe effective culling as necessary.

Plan the coupes so that cutting progresses sequentially around the wood, if possible with adjacent coupes cut in sequential order. To benefit wildlife, especially relatively static invertebrates, it's important that species can easily move from one coupe to another as conditions change through the coppice cycle. Some examples of coupe layout and cutting sequence are given below.

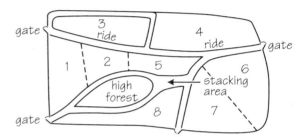

A 6.5 hectare (16 acre) hazel coppice divided into 8 coupes, one cut each year (8 year cycle)

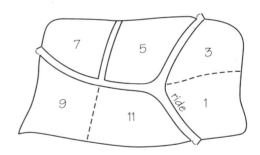

A wood divided into 6 coupes, with one cut every other year (12 year cycle)

At the end of each coppicing season, mark carefully on a map the areas which have been cut and date them, for future reference. Other details such as the volume of produce, man/days and so on can also usefully be recorded.

COPPICE WITH STANDARDS

This traditional system combined the production of timber from standard trees grown on a long rotation, with coppice species beneath grown on a short rotation. For hazel, the general guide is that there should be one-third canopy closure by the standards at the start of the coppice cycle, increasing to two-thirds canopy closure at the end of the coppice cycle. The number of standards will vary according to their age and spread, from about 30 large mature standards per hectare, up to 150 young standards per hectare. To ensure continuity of canopy, a mix of ages is needed. The following gives an ideal age range at which to aim for standard oak or ash with hazel coppice.

Table 9d: STANDARD OAK OR ASH WITH HAZEL COPPICE

50 standards per hectare total, comprising:

NUMBER	AGE
20 saplings	0-25 years
12 young trees	25-50 years
8 semi-mature trees	50-80 years
6 mature trees	80-125 years
4 ready for felling	110 years +

From *Hazel Coppice* (Hampshire County Council, 1995).

New trees can be recruited from protecting natural regeneration, or from 'singling' coppice stools of suitable species, to leave one stem to grow up to form a standard. As well as oak and ash, other species can be grown as standards where they form a natural component of the wood, with the exception of beech and hornbeam, which cast too dense a shade. Small-leaved lime, hornbeam, wild-service, crab-apple or wild cherry may be suitable where they occur naturally. Sycamore and birch should be avoided as standards, as they spread too quickly by seed. Avoid bringing new species and new genotypes into the wood, but use natural regeneration wherever possible.

In-cycle coppicing

This describes the work involved in managing a coppice which has been regularly cut over the preceding rotation. Coppice growth should be good quality, on evenly spaced stools with few gaps and little undergrowth.

With in-cycle coppicing there should be no waste, as nearly all the cut growth can be marketed (p108). Alternatively, the top growth can be re-used within the woodland for dead hedging to discourage deer. Only burn if absolutely necessary (p88).

WORK SEASON

Traditionally coppice was cut from the beginning of October to the end of February. These days, some coppice workers cut all year round for economic reasons, although this does have disadvantages.

- The cutting of the plant when in full leaf reduces the strength of the regrowth.

- The new sappy shoots are also very vulnerable to browsing by rabbits, hares and deer in the autumn when other forage is scarce. Hazel and some other species, if cut in winter, will have reached 1.2-1.5m (4-5') high by the following autumn, out of the reach of rabbits and muntjac deer. Spring browsing, when the shoots are small, is normally not so serious as there is plenty of other forage available.

- Cutting in spring causes disturbance to nesting birds, and results in trampling and damage to spring flowers.

- Summer-cut material is thought not to be as durable as material cut in winter.

For commercial coppicing, the advice is to avoid cutting from mid-April until the end of July, and only work with stored material during this time. Non-commercial coppicing should keep to the traditional season between October and the end of February.

ORGANISING THE WORK

This covers the general organisation of coppicing work, using hand tools. Detailed procedures are on page 105.

Group working

Decide how you are going to organise the site. This includes stacking of newly-cut material, stacking of trimmed poles, tool storage area, fire sites and access routes through the site. For safe and efficient group work, make sure everyone understands the system.

Start cutting the coupe in a strip or 'lane' about 4m (13') wide, preferably alongside the access road or ride, felling the poles into the clear space of the ride. When this is completed and the cut material trimmed and stacked, start on the next strip, parallel to the first. This method of working means that the danger area is clearly defined for the working party, and carrying of cut materials is made easier and safer. It gives space for people to go back and forth to the access track without crossing where others are felling. Keep the working area defined, so that if work is held up by bad weather and less is completed by the end of the season than was planned, a block will be completed, rather than a haphazard area. Avoid though leaving any inaccessible blocks of uncut coppice, which can only be reached through newly cut areas, as extraction in following years through partly grown coppice will be difficult.

Lay the fallen material tidily, with the butts all pointing the same way, to make trimming and topping easier.

GROUP WORKING

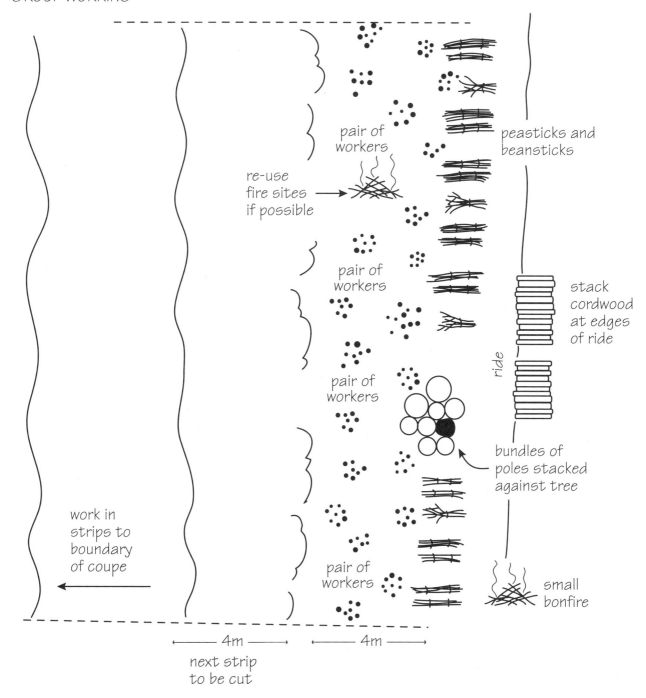

peasticks and beansticks

pair of workers

re-use fire sites if possible

pair of workers

stack cordwood at edges of ride

ride

pair of workers

bundles of poles stacked against tree

work in strips to boundary of coupe

pair of workers

small bonfire

—— 4m ——   —— 4m ——

next strip to be cut

Trim, cut, sort, bundle or stack the material according to the end-use (p109-114).

Individuals or pairs of workers

Individuals or small teams working a coppice can work in wide strips at right angles to the access track. This means that any unfinished strips are still accessible to the track in following years, without going through partly grown coppice. There are various ways of working, depending on the size of the coppice poles, the spacing of the stools and personal preference.

• Work up the strip cutting, and lay the cut material in

drifts to either side as shown.

• Once the strip is cut, work back down it cutting and sorting the cut material, and burn any waste.

• Stack the cut material at the start of the strip.

• Work each adjacent strip in the same way.

An alternative method suitable for hazel or other light coppice growth, where the stools are in lines, is shown on page 101. Under this system, the cut material is laid in a swathe over the line of cut stools, butt ends towards the ride. Laying the material over the cut stools makes

INDIVIDUAL OR PAIR WORKING

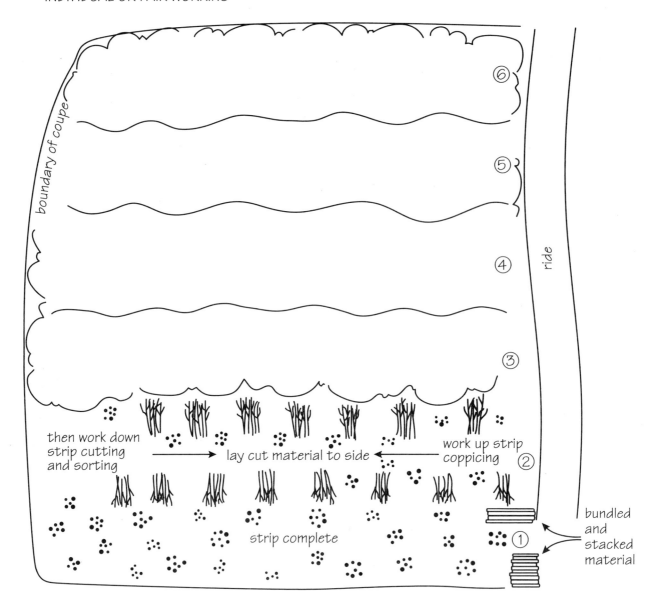

the best of the available working space, leaving clear pathways between the stools. Laying it all butt ends to the ride makes extraction easy, as you can start extracting from the ride and work back up the swathe, with all the butt ends exposed progressively as you work. You must start cutting from the far end of the line, in order to lay the material in the correct direction.

The exact procedure for cutting each stool will depend on whether you are right or left handed, and on personal preference for tools and methods of cutting. A possible procedure for right-handed cutting is as follows.

- Start at point 1a, at the far end of the first line of stools. Standing facing along the line to be cut, start cutting with your right hand into the right side of the first stool, and with your left hand, lay the cut material back to your left. Starting from the right side of the stool leaves room to use the saw or billhook, and laying material to the left gets it clear of the uncut

stems. Depending on the size of the stool, you may need to work around it in a clockwise direction, but always lay the material in a neat pile with butt ends towards the ride end of the line, as shown.

- Work back along the row to 1b, laying the cut material in a swathe along the cut stools, with all the butt ends towards the ride.

- Working in reverse to the cutting order, start from point 1b and work back up the line, extracting, trimming, bundling and stacking the cut material.

- Repeat on the next line, cutting from 2a, and extracting from 2b, and so on up the coupe.

- A pair of workers can cut two lines simultaneously, or, as shown in the diagram, one can work ahead cutting a line, while the second worker extracts and trims from the previous line.

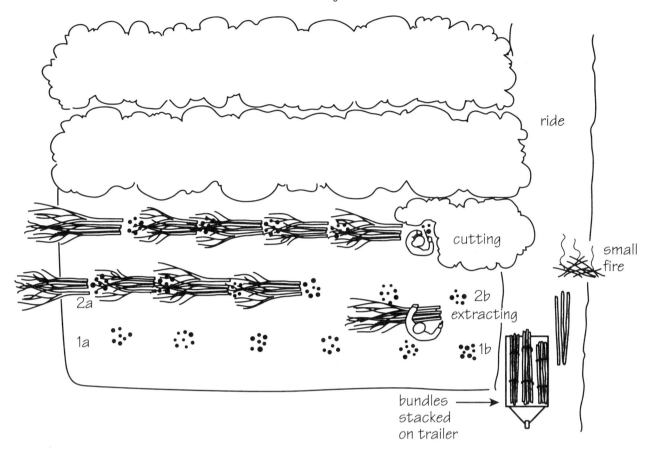

INDIVIDUAL OR PAIR WORKING - alternative system

ride

cutting

small fire

2a

1a

2b extracting

1b

bundles stacked on trailer

ROUTINE MANAGEMENT

The coppice requires little or no attention between the cycles of cutting, but checking it periodically will help keep it in good condition.

- The presence of people in the wood in the year after cutting, preferably working up cut material, or regularly walking the wood, will help keep deer away so reducing damage to the coppice regrowth. Dogs are also a good deterrent.

- Where temporary fencing is used to keep deer or rabbits away, this must be checked frequently.

- Note any stools which have failed to regrow, and replant the following autumn. Weed to clear thistles, nettles or brambles from any gaps where stools are failing to thrive.

- Clear fire sites of nettles, thistles and other weeds.

- Make sure any ditches are kept clear and free-flowing so that no long-term waterlogging occurs which could cause stool death.

- Keep tracks and rides in good condition, by keeping them clear of bramble and other growth. Surfacing or drainage work which permanently improves access

may be a worthwhile investment.

- Manage public access as necessary. Some access is useful to keep paths open, and for people to enjoy the flora and fauna of the coppice cycle. Too much access can be destructive, and action will need to be taken if the coppice is getting damaged or cut for children's dens or other purposes.

Reviving derelict coppice

Coppices which have not been cut for 50 years can be brought back into the coppice cycle, and should produce strong new growth. However, because of the large size and density of the coppice poles, cutting can be a slow and difficult job. Until a full rotation is re-established the material produced is often low grade and suitable only for firewood, charcoal or pulp, though sale of this will help offset labour and other costs.

Hazel, with its naturally multi-stemmed growth does not cope so well with dereliction, and hazel over 40 years may not all regenerate when cut. It's important that any other competing trees are cut at the same time, to provide maximum sunlight and space for the hazel. Many hazel coppices have become invaded with birch, and suffer from the shade of too many oak standards, as well as the depredations of deer.

Extraction may be difficult, especially on steep hillsides, wet sites and where ride systems have fallen into disrepair. Re-open rides in advance of coppicing by clearing away all undergrowth. It may be possible to improve access by drainage and surfacing work, which will pay off in the long term by making extraction and other management very much easier (p167).

When planning how big an area to coppice each year, consider the available labour, as well as the woodland size, type and other factors. It may be best to restore no more than 0.4 hectare (1 acre) each year, until the rotation is in order. Initial cutting is much more laborious than re-cutting on rotation, and it is easy to take on too much and do a poor job. Link the size of the coupe to the planned rotation and the available markets. See Tables 9a and b on page 96.

POTENTIAL PROBLEMS

Coppicing operations should only be revived where operations can be continued in the long term. Where this is dependent on markets for coppice products there will always be some uncertainty, but where possible ensure that long term plans are in place before coppicing is restarted. Possible adverse effects on wildlife should also be considered.

- Coppicing may create a deer problem. Old coppice, especially hazel, is often open and draughty, with neither food nor shelter to attract deer. When coppicing is restarted, deer will be attracted by the food and shelter provided by the young coppice growth, and the deer population will rapidly increase.

- Some stools may have died, or will fail to regrow, leaving gaps in the coppice which are likely to become overgrown with bramble or other growth after cutting. To successfully restart the coppice cycle, the coppice must regrow strongly and evenly, suppressing other growth. Effort will need to be put into restocking, weeding and fencing to get each coupe regrowing strongly. Cutting one or two coupes, without any follow-up management, is likely to have adverse effects for wildlife and amenity.

- Flowering plants, which are such a feature of established coppices in the year after cutting, may be sparse or absent due to the long time which has elapsed since the previous cutting. It may take several cycles for the herb layer to recover.

- Similarly, the invertebrate fauna requiring large areas of active coppice will probably have vanished. For remaining invertebrates, it may be more useful to concentrate on management of rides and other permanent open spaces.

- The neglected coppice may contain large amounts of deadwood, which is valuable for invertebrates, birds, fungi and other organisms. Even if the deadwood is retained during clearance, the change to open, sunny conditions will be detrimental to its wildlife value.

- In small woods of less than 5 hectares (12 acres), the coupes may be too small or the interval between cutting adjacent coupes too long, to see major benefits for wildlife.

- Some neglected coppices have developed their own special fauna and flora, which may be damaged if coppicing is restarted. Those dominated by a single species, notably the northern and western oakwoods, are a particular example. They are probably best left to develop into semi-natural high forest.

- Other neglected coppices can be converted to high forest by singling, and then managed commercially under a continuous cover system (p41).

WORK RATES

A work party consisting of a qualified chainsaw operator and volunteers using hand tools may take up to 300 person-days to clear and sort material from one hectare (120 person-days for an acre) of derelict coppice. Work may be two or three times faster on 15-20-year-old coppice. Professional workers with chainsaws can do the equivalent work in possibly a third of the time or less.

CLEARING UNDERGROWTH

The amount of undergrowth such as bramble, elder or other shrubby growth will vary depending on the age of the coppice, the amount of shading and other factors. Any growth which impedes coppicing operations should be cleared before felling starts.

- Use billhooks, brushing hooks or slashers on brambles and other light growth, keeping a safe working distance from other workers.

- Use forks to gather up brambles and other material for burning.

- Try to retain any small flowering and berrying trees such as hawthorn and crabapple, as these are valuable for wildlife.

Cutting a neglected coppice will normally produce a large amount of regrowth of unwanted species such as brambles, bindweed and thistles, which can easily swamp the young growth from the coppice stools. In-cycle coppices, in contrast, have a smaller bank of weed species and the problem will not be so severe. Thorough hand weeding will be necessary in the first, second and possibly third year after cutting, until the coppice canopy is sufficiently dense to shade out unwanted growth.

WOOD BOUNDARIES

It is best not to coppice wood boundaries at the same time as the adjacent interior coupes, to avoid loss of shelter. However, boundary coppicing at some stage is important to maintain the woodbank flora and to reduce shading of neighbours' land. Where the woodland is surrounded by a hedge, this should be restored by laying. See *Hedging* (BTCV, 1998) for full details.

Coppice woods have had boundary earthworks since the Anglo-Saxon period, and nearly all woods more than 100 years old have some kind of earthwork around the edge. The usual arrangement was a bank and ditch, with the bank next to the wood, and together the bank and ditch could be as wide as 7.5m (25'). To quote Oliver Rackham (*Trees and Woodland in the British Landscape*, 1990), 'Woodbanks are a more eloquent record than any document of the value of woods in the middle ages. Woodland was precious, and people spent thousands of man-hours on defining and defending it.' Existing woodbanks and ditches should not be altered because of their historical value. Where none exist, or for new coppices or other woods, a ditch and bank topped by a laid hedge are valuable additional habitats, as well as making a stockproof boundary.

STOCKING

Where coppice stools are sparse, new plants will be needed to fill the gaps, to leave a maximum spacing of about 3.5m between stools. New plants can be produced as follows:

- Layering involves laying a stem to the ground and pegging it down until it roots. The resulting plant can be left to grow on in situ, or can be dug up after two growing seasons and transplanted. Layering from stools within the coppice has to be timed to fit in with the coppice cycle (see below). Alternatively, stools in a nursery area or alongside a ride can be set aside for layering purposes. This has the advantages that supply of young plants is easier to organise, and as young stems root more easily propagation rates from layering will be improved. The frequently cut stools also form a useful wildlife habitat, which combines well with management work to keep rides and glades open and sunny. A possible disadvantage is that plants are produced from fewer stools, so reducing genetic diversity.

- Stooling involves burying the cut stool and then digging up and replanting the new shoots that develop after one growing season. This should be done on stools set aside for the purpose, as this interferes with the regrowth of the stool and does not fit in well with the coppice cycle.

- Plants can be grown in a nursery from locally gathered seed. See *Tree Planting and Aftercare* (BTCV, 2000) for full details.

Careful planning is needed so that there are sufficient plants available to replant at the time of coppicing. New plants must be planted at the same time as the coppice is cut, so that they can get established during the period when light levels are high. To restore neglected coppice, it's normally necessary to cut all the coppice again after three years, to allow the new plants to produce more stems and grow up strongly with the older coppice stools.

If layering from stools within the coppice (first option above) layering can be done at any of the following three stages in the coppice cycle. Where possible, layers should be pegged down into the gaps which you want to fill, so that the new plants can be left in situ to grow on, without the need for transplanting, which delays establishment. Layers are not always successful, so do at least two layers for every plant you want, to allow for failure.

- **Layer before coppicing**. Where there is sufficient light and space, for example at the edge of the coppice or in a gap, stems can be layered two or three winters before the coppice is cut. Use sun shoots, which are the thin, vertical shoots found growing from older stems, or whatever younger stems are available. The resulting plants will be ready for replanting as necessary at the time of coppicing.

- **Layer at coppicing**. At the time of coppicing, a few stems can be left uncut and layered. Try and layer these into the gaps so they can grow on undisturbed for three seasons before being cut with the rest of the coppice in the second cut.

- **Layer after coppicing**. Where the coppice is very neglected and there are no suitable stems for layering, you will have to wait until the cut stools produce new growth, and then layer first year stems in the winter after coppicing. This is the least efficient option, because these plants, even if grown on in situ, will only be two years old at the time of the second cut, and may struggle to compete. It may be necessary to leave them longer, and do the second cut five years after the first cut.

When transplanting, try to minimise the distance from the mother plants, to retain the original pattern of genotypes within the woodland. Avoid using purchased plants, or plants from another woodland, as these may be of a different genotype to the existing coppice.

Never try and 'thin out' a neglected coppice by cutting stools here and there through the wood. This tends to promote the growth of brambles at the expense of other woodland plants, and is not a solution to the problems of shading. Some cut stools die, whilst others expand the fill the space available. The wood remains as shady as before, with fewer but larger trees.

Mark the site of any layering, stooling or transplanting so that the plants can be easily found again. The young plants will need to be weeded and protected against browsing for the first few years, as growth will not be as vigorous as regrowth from older, larger stools. See advice above (p102).

Stooling

Stooling involves coppicing the stool in the normal way. Then pile earth over the stool, and new shoots will grow with roots formed in the loose soil, making them easy to detach and transplant the following winter.

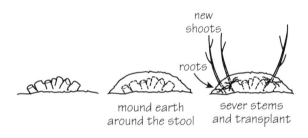

new
shoots

roots

mound earth
around the stool

sever stems
and transplant

Layering

Hazel and sweet chestnut respond particularly well to layering, but other species can also be layered successfully. Layering should be done in late winter, and within a few months plenty of new shoots should appear on the layer.

Thin young coppice stems can be layered simply as described below. Larger, less flexible stems need to be partly cut through. Alternatively, use the 'sun shoots' on old coppice, which are the thin straight shoots arising from mature coppice stems.

Where possible, use thin, young stems at least 2.7m (9') tall.

1. Dig a short trench where you want the plant to root.

2. Carefully bend the stem over, and where it meets the trench, remove a strip of bark and underlying wood about 100mm (4") long.

3. Peg the stem into the trench using wooden pegs (see below), and cover with earth.

4. Cut back the top of the stem to about 150mm (6") beyond the furthest peg, as this helps stimulate root production.

5. The following autumn, cut the stem to create an independent plant. Transplant as necessary.

Where only older stems are available, use the following procedure:

1. Coppice the stool in the normal way, but leave one or two stems for layering.

2. Using a sharp billhook or bowsaw, cut through the stem at a downward angle away from the stool. Cut in the direction in which you want to lay the stem, making the cut as shown.

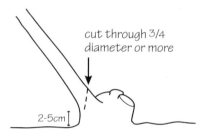

cut through 3/4
diameter or more

2-5cm

3. If you cut too far, the stem may break off as it is lowered to the ground, or it may die after layering. If you don't cut far enough, the stem will split downward into the base as you lower it. When you near the point where you want the cut to stop, gently pull the stem down and to the left top open up the mouth of the cut. Then continue cutting and pulling at the same time until the stem can be eased down to the ground. This may be easier with someone else to guide the stem as you cut.

4. Trim the protruding stub, using a small bowsaw. Begin the cut as low as possible, and slope it upward toward the first cut, so that rain drains away.

5. Mark out the line of the stem along the ground using a spade or mattock. Follow any bends in the stems.

6. Move the stem aside and dig out a trench along the marked line. Dig it deep enough to ensure that bent or whippy stems don't spring out.

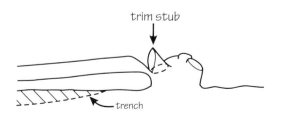

trim stub

trench

7. Some people recommend cutting off or fraying the stem on the underside where you want it to root, but others ignore this step. In either case, position the stem along the trench and peg it down with two pegs facing opposite ways, choosing an 'elbow' if possible. Knock in the pegs with a lump hammer.

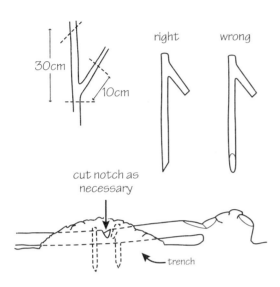

8. Cover the stem with earth (not leaf mould) in the area where you want it to root. Cover it to a depth of 75-150mm (3-6"), and tread the earth firmly around the stem.

9. If you can't get the stem to lie along the ground, cut a notch in the upperside where it's closest to the ground, and then heap earth over the notched section.

10. If the layered stem 'takes', you can either leave it untouched to grow in place, or you wait 7-12 months and then cut if off from the parent stool for transplanting.

To make pegs to secure layered stems:

1. Select hazel or other stems which have a strong side branch emerging at an acute angle. Cut these off with a saw or billhook, to form rough pegs at least 300mm (1') long, with crooks about 100mm (4") long.

2. Trim the pegs on a stump or chopping block. Cut the points in line with the crook, as this makes them less likely to twist when you knock them in.

Establishing a new coppice

PLANTING AND EARLY CARE

Try and obtain planting stock of local provenance (p49). Many of the coppice species, notably sycamore, ash, birch and oak are easy to grow from seed and it is quite possible to gather your own seed and produce planting stock within two years. Willow is easy to propagate from cuttings, simply stuck in the ground in their final planting position. See *Tree Planting and Aftercare* (BTCV, 2000) for further details.

Follow normal planting procedure (p53), planting in autumn and paying particular attention to weed control in the following few years. It's essential to get the plants established quickly so they grow up together and suppress weed growth. Replace immediately any plants that fail, so that even coverage is obtained.

Protection against rabbits and deer will be needed both for a few years after planting, and for the year following each coppice cut. Tree shelters can be used for the establishment of all species listed above except for hazel, because of its multi-stemmed growth. However, as shelters cannot be used to protect new regrowth, a fence which encloses the coppice plot or coupe, and protects both initial growth and regrowth, is preferable. For further details on treeshelters and other tree protection, see chapter 6. For further details on protecting coppice regrowth, see pages 106-109.

STARTING THE COPPICE CYCLE

The first coppice cut should be made as soon as the trees are established, at 5 to 8 years, or when the crop reaches marketable size. Coppices for firewood should be first cut when there is material suitable for the fire, which would normally be between 7 and 10 years. An earlier cut, at 2-3 years, will encourage a better yield in the first crop, but will delay it by a few years.

The first coppicing should be done in March or April, so that the new shoots emerge in June, after any risk of frost.

Coppicing with hand tools

This section covers coppicing procedures and techniques.

COPPICING PROCEDURE

Depending on the size, age and condition of the coppice stems, you can use a billhook, bowsaw or axe. Loppers and a pruning saw may also be useful. Trained and competent operators can use a chainsaw.

Billhooks are neatest and fastest on hazel or other young regrowth up to about 75mm (3") diameter, but on older coppice, saws are normally best. The 530mm (21") bowsaw is useful on multiple-stemmed trees, provided the stems are not too large. A pruning saw is useful for cutting small, closely spaced stems where a bowsaw is too big. Poles larger than 75mm (3") diameter will require an undercut first to prevent splitting (p80).

Follow basic felling techniques (pp79-81), keeping in mind these additional points:

- Take a close look before you begin cutting. Stones, glass or cans wedged amongst the stems can ruin saws and edged tools.

- Using loppers or a billhook, cut away all small, whippy growth from around the base of the stool, to avoid interference when cutting.

- Remove the stems one by one. Where the stems are all about the same size, cut from the outside of the coppice stool around and inwards, in a spiral pattern.

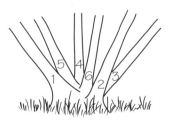

- Where stems are of varying sizes, it is usually easiest to clear the smaller stems first to give access to the larger ones.

- Cut each stem upward towards the centre, to promote runoff of rainwater and help prevent rot.

- In neglected coppice, where the stems lean outward and are heavy, the saw will jam unless a second worker helps by pushing the stem back off the saw while it is being cut. Even where you can cut from the back of the stem downwards, it helps to have someone support the stem to keep it from splitting.

- Cut stems as low as possible. Normally this should be to the previous level, leaving the existing stool without reducing it. Don't try to remove the stems all at once by cutting below the top of the stool, as the saw will jam. If you cut too high, the regrowth will be curved at the base and more like branches than stems, and consequently of less value.

right   wrong

- Where this does not reduce the value of the cut pole, it may be quicker and tidier to cut twice: a high cut to fell the stem and a second cut to remove the stub.

- Hazel should always be cut as close to the ground as possible. This encourages stems to shoot from the ground, rather than from the old stool, which with hazel, can become brittle. Hazel, and to some extent birch and other species, can produce coppice shoots from root buds which are close to the stump.

- In some coppice woodlands, ash and occasionally elm, are traditionally coppiced at 300-900mm (1-3') high. Unless there are other reasons against this, follow the evidence of past practice.

- If the coppice tree is very large, treat each stem as an individual tree and use the appropriate felling techniques (p81).

- Clean up the stool after coppicing. Cut off any splinters or split wood, and brush dirt and sawdust off the cut surfaces. This reduces the chance of water collecting on the stool and causing rot. If water is lodging in the centre of the stool, cut the stool so it will drain.

- During rest periods, don't strike or 'mask' the billhook or axe into a living stump, as this allows damp to get into the stool.

Protecting coppice regrowth

Deer are the main threat to coppice regrowth. Where browsing is very severe, the coppice will fail to regrow, and the coupe may become dominated with rough grasses and sedges. Successful regrowth can also create a deer problem where none existed before, as young coppice is an attractive habitat for deer, and populations may rise in a woodland where coppicing is restarted.

When browsing, deer select leading shoots and upper leaves because they are actively growing, and therefore the most nutritious. Coppice regrowth is most vulnerable to attack in the spring and early summer after coppicing. By late summer the shoots should have grown above the browsing level. However protection for two seasons' growth after coppicing is preferable.

Large populations of deer, and especially muntjac, also damage the woodland flora, including bluebells, wood anemones and other flowering plants, by grazing and trampling. The situation is complex however. Complete absence of browsing may lead to such dense and rapid coppice growth that the flowering plants, together with the butterflies that feed on them, are shaded out too quickly. Limited grazing by sustainable numbers of deer may give the best balance for coppice production and for biodiversity. See Savill, P S, Wright, H L, Miller, H G and Kerr, G (2001).

Techniques of control include:

- Fencing

- Disturbance

- Culling

FENCING

Full-height deer fencing with rabbit netting on the lower section is an expensive option, but forms a secure and durable fence. The Forestry Commission design for deer and rabbit fencing is shown on page 61.

An alternative for species other than hazel, is to use treeshelters against rabbits and deer for the initial planting, and then to use temporary electric fencing or temporary plastic netting for two seasons after the first and each following coppice cut. In older coppices, which will produce a large amount of cut material, dead hedging can be constructed using the cut material.

The choice will depend on the type of protection required, and the availability of labour and other resources.

Temporary plastic netting

High tensile black plastic netting is available from several suppliers (p188) for temporary fencing against deer. The netting is proof against roe, fallow and sika deer, but not against muntjac deer or rabbits, which push and burrow underneath the fence. The netting is available in 1.5m and 1.8m heights, in 100m rolls. It is lightweight, with a 1.8m x 100m roll weighing 22kg. Temporary fencing can be removed after two growing seasons and re-used to protect another coupe. As noted above, this may improve the habitat for flowering plants and invertebrates by allowing grazing and browsing, provided that deer populations are not excessive.

The following specifications (Table 9e) are recommended by the Forestry Commission (*Practice Note FCPN9*, 1999).

The netting should be attached with netting rings to two lines of 2mm high tensile wire, strained between straining posts. A suitable design of straining post is shown below. For the intermediate stakes, ideally use non-preserved locally-cut coppice poles, as the stakes are only required for two to three years.

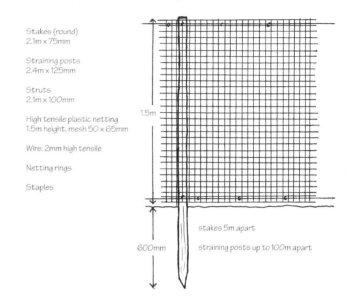

DEER FENCING – high tensile plastic netting

Stakes (round)
2.1m x 75mm

Straining posts
2.4m x 125mm

Struts
2.1m x 100mm

High tensile plastic netting
1.5m height, mesh 50 x 65mm

Wire: 2mm high tensile

Netting rings

Staples

1.5m

600mm

stakes 5m apart

straining posts up to 100m apart

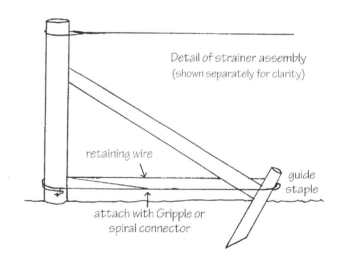

Detail of strainer assembly
(shown separately for clarity)

retaining wire

guide staple

attach with Gripple or spiral connector

Table 9e: TEMPORARY FENCING AGAINST DEER

DEER SPECIES	HEIGHT	MINIMUM MESH SIZE
Fallow	1.5m	220 x 200mm
Roe	1.2m (for areas less than 2.5 ha, which deer will tend to walk around)	200 x 150mm
	1.5m (for areas more than 2.5 ha)	
Muntjac	1.5m, plus 150mm lap at base	75 x 75mm

It's not recommended to attach the netting to standing trees, as without two strained line wires it's not possible to get the fence sufficiently taut.

Measures to make the fence proof against muntjac will add considerably to the cost of the fence, as this will require adding hexagonal wire mesh (1050mm height, 31 mm mesh, 18 gauge) to the base of the fence, with the bottom 150mm lapped and pegged in the direction of attack. A third high tensile line wire is needed for attachment of the netting. This also makes the fence proof against rabbits, which may be useful in some situations.

Temporary electric fencing

Electric fencing can be moved from one coupe to another with the coppicing rotation. Systems using electric wire or tape are available from several manufacturers and suppliers of electric fencing (p188), who should be contacted for further details.

Two examples are shown below. The three-line fence of high visibility electric tape is a deterrent to roe deer. The five-line wire fence is a deterrent to muntjac. The effectiveness of electric fencing will depend on deer population numbers, disturbance and other factors, and success is not guaranteed.

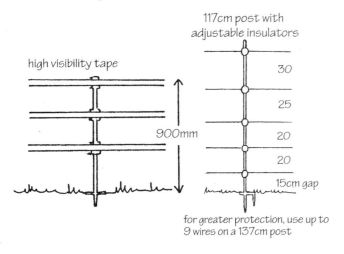

high visibility tape

900mm

117cm post with adjustable insulators

30
25
20
20
15cm gap

for greater protection, use up to 9 wires on a 137cm post

Dead Hedging

Dead hedging involves using some of the coppice material for making a barrier around the cut coupe. This technique has the advantage of using material from within the wood, much of which would otherwise have to be burnt. It is fairly labour intensive, so is very suitable for volunteer projects. Various different techniques are used, according to the labour and material available, and personal preference. The branching tops left after the coppice poles have been trimmed can be used, as well as unwanted scrub, brashings, rhododendron and other bushy material. Dead hedging is vulnerable to fire and vandalism, and the wider hedges may provide unwanted cover for rabbits.

- The simplest technique is to lay the material on the ground, with the butts towards the cut coppice, and the bushy tops outwards, towards the point of attack. A large amount of material is needed, as the barrier should be at least 1.8m (6') high and will spread to at least 2.3m (8') width. The barrier is quick to build, as it only involves carrying or dragging the material to the boundary and piling it up. The barrier must be continuous, and will need regular checking and repairing as necessary. A disadvantage is that, being wide, it provides perfect cover for rabbits.

- A second method, shown below, is to pile up the material lengthwise along the boundary, held in place by two rows of stakes, cut from the coppice. Knock the stakes in firmly using a post-driver, and then fill the area between with lop and top. Trample the lower layers to compact the material. Keep piling it up until the barrier is about 1.8m (6') high. This type of dead hedge takes longer to erect than the method described above, but is more resistant to casual damage, and provides less cover for rabbits.

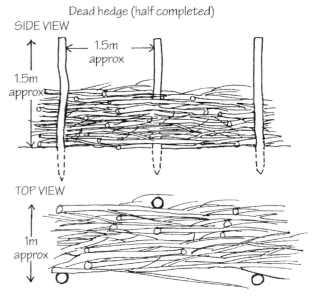

Dead hedge (half completed)

SIDE VIEW

1.5m approx

1.5m approx

TOP VIEW

1m approx

- A third method is to build a woven dead hedge, with the cut material woven through a single line of closely spaced stakes. This provides no cover for rabbits. Space the stakes about 1m (3') apart, and pack the material closely so that it forms a hedge only about 300mm (1') wide and 1.8m (6') high. This uses a lot of stakes, but supply of stakes is not usually a problem when a coupe is cut.

All types of dead hedge can be made more difficult to penetrate by encouraging bramble to grow over it. This works especially well with the thin woven hedge. Dig up any newly rooted bramble shoots from the coppice, where they are unwanted weeds, and replant along the dead hedge. Young bramble plants are also easy to find in overgrown gardens, allotments and waste ground.

White or other easily visible tape stretched along the top of the dead hedge may also act as a deterrent by discouraging deer from jumping. Dead hedges are difficult to make proof against muntjac deer, which can get through by pushing and burrowing at the base. A tightly-packed dense base to the hedge will help deter them.

DISTURBANCE

Make the newly-cut coupe as inhospitable to deer as possible.

- Cut as large coupes as possible within the planned rotation, and keep the shape of coupes fairly square, avoiding long or sinuous shapes which have a poor edge to area ratio.

- Clear the site of all cut growth so there are no places for the deer to lie up near the stools. Clear any adjacent rides.

- People working in the coupe for the following summer, making hurdles or other greenwood products, will discourage deer, as will any dogs which run around and mark the area. Alternatively, encourage public access where appropriate. During the spring and early summer, when the growth is most vulnerable to damage, it may be possible to arrange a rota of volunteers, preferably with dogs, to walk the coupe in the early morning and early evening.

CULLING

As deer range over a wide area, culling is only effective if managed on an area basis. Culling is only permissible by licensed operators. Contact your local Forestry Commission office to see if there is a Deer Management Group in your area.

Coppice products

This section describes materials which are cut from the coppice and generally require no further working apart from cutting to length and tying in bundles. Some cleaning of side shoots or twiggy growth with a billhook may be necessary. Green woodworking, which is the craft of working freshly cut wood into a range of products, is described in the following chapter.

For voluntary groups, there is potential to use these simple coppice materials within the wood for fencing, footpath work, bank revetment, hedgelaying and other uses. There is also the possibility of using material for stakes, bean poles, pergolas and other garden uses, amongst group members and friends in the local community. Transport is often the major issue, so always ask around and advertise

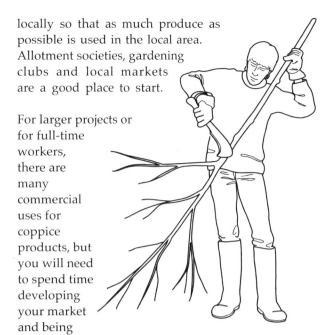

locally so that as much produce as possible is used in the local area. Allotment societies, gardening clubs and local markets are a good place to start.

For larger projects or for full-time workers, there are many commercial uses for coppice products, but you will need to spend time developing your market and being innovative in developing and selling your products. There may be a local coppice association who can provide help, or you may be able to group together with other coppice workers for marketing purposes.

You may also be able to sell coppice material to other craftsmen, such as thatchers, woodturners, hurdle makers and others. Advertise locally, and through networks such as 'Ecolots' (p184).

COPPICE PRODUCTS

Bean rods

Ash or hazel are best, but other species are also suitable. Minimum length 2m (7') with 25-40mm (1-1^1/$_2$") butt diameter, cleaned. Bundle in 10s or 20s.

Pea sticks

Fan-shaped branches of hazel, birch, elm or lime, 1.2-1.5m (4-5') long with 300mm (1') of clear stem, with the butt cut at an angle. Stack off the ground with poles on top to flatten them. Bundle together in 20s.

Flower stakes

Cleaned straight rods of any species, about 1.2m (4') long and 25mm (1") top diameter. The butt is sharpened and the top is cut as shown, as this prevents the stake splitting when hammered in. Bundle in 10s or 20s.

Hedging stakes

Cleaned poles of any species, 1.5m (5'6") long, with a butt diameter of 40-65mm (1^1/$_2$"-2^1/$_2$"), bundled in 10s.

Heathering (ethering, binding) rods

Cleaned rods of hazel, birch, willow or sweet chestnut, 2.1-3.6m (7-12') long, with a butt diameter of 25mm (1"), bundled in 20s. Preferably use fresh, or can be stored for up to 6 weeks if kept damp under a tarpaulin.

Fence stakes

Cleaned round or cleft poles of sweet chestnut, oak or elm, 1.7m (5'6") long, with a 65-75mm (2½-3") butt diameter, sharpened.

Tree stakes

Cleaned poles of any species, 1.2m (4') long, with 40-65mm (1½ -2½") butt diameter, sharpened. For larger trees, use shorter poles in pairs as shown.

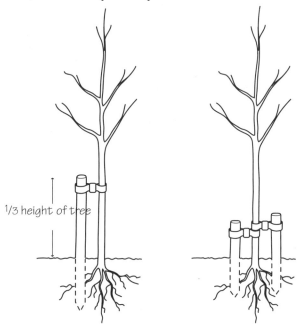

1/3 height of tree

Walking sticks

Straight stems of about 1.4m (4') length and about 40mm (1½") diameter, with minimum taper. Hazel, ash and sweet chestnut are easy to find and popular for stick making, with blackthorn, hawthorn and holly prized for their density and strength, and because they are more difficult to find in suitable lengths. Unusual curves where the length, called a 'shank' joins the main branch or root, and which could be used for the handle, will add value. 'Twisted' shanks, caused by being entwined with honeysuckle are also sought after.

After cutting, bundle the sticks together, about 10 to a bundle, and tie near the top, middle and bottom with soft twine, which will not dig into the bark. Store them upright or laid flat in a shed, unheated spare room or similar. Don't lie them across rafters or cross-pieces on the floor, as the shanks will bow. Season for 9-12 months before sanding, carving, staining, polishing or waxing

as desired. There is an active craft in stick making, with local associations, competitions and so on. See Gowan (1997) for further details on the craft.

Morris sticks

As used by Morris dancers. Requirements vary, but hazel is preferred, with 1m (3'3") length and 40mm (1½") butt diameter a typical size. Sticks must be straight and knot-free, peeled and dried slowly so they do not split. Season for a winter before use, and treat with linseed oil. Ash is sometimes recommended, but is liable to split under heavy use!

Rustic poles

Poles for garden use including fencing, pergolas, arches, gazebos and other uses, according to the customers' requirements. Value can be added by designing such features, and supplying the materials in kit form or assembled on site.

Crotch sticks

Straight poles with a strong fork can be used for clothes-line props, and as props for the branches of fruit trees. Any species is suitable, of a size to suit the use.

Thatching wood

Split hazel rods are used to secure the thatch on roofs. The liggers or runners lie across the thatch, and are secured by hairpin-like spars or broches, pushed down into the thatch. Some thatchers split and point their own spars and liggers from round wood, while others buy from spar makers who convert the round wood. Hazel is the usual material, but willow is also used.

Specifications will vary with the individual thatcher or spar maker, but the general requirement is for straight rods no shorter than 1.3m (4'6"), and between 12mm (½") and 50mm (2") in diameter. The rods should be cleaned of knots, but not debarked, and then tied into bundles. Liggers are best split as soon as possible after cutting, but wood for spars is normally stored for a month or so in a shady place to toughen up before splitting. The unsplit rods are called 'spar gads', and are usually 540-660mm (21-26") long, and 12-25mm (½-2") diameter, bundled in 20s or 30s.

A typical requirement for liggers are rods 1-1.5m (3-5') long and 40mm (1½") diameter, split into four clefts. These are then shaved to remove the pith and make a flat surface to lie against the thatch, with both ends pointed to a long taper. They are bundled in 25s.

Depending on their thickness, spar gads are split into four, six or sixteen clefts, 12mm (½") diameter, and pointed at each end. They are bundled in 200s.

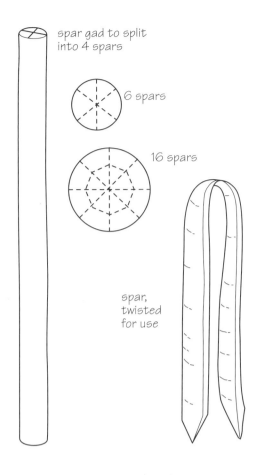

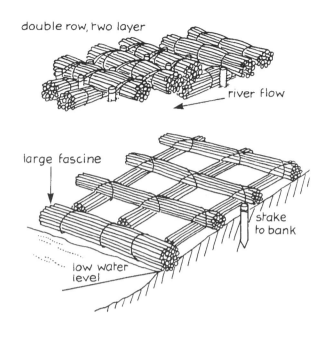

Fascines and faggots

Fascines or faggots are a traditional product made from the tops or brash from coppicing operations, tied tightly in bundles. Long bundles are used for riverbank revetment and stabilisation. With changing attitudes to riverbank management, there has been a growth of demand in recent years from the Environment Agency and other authorities. Volumes needed are usually large, with a minimum of 200 a typical requirement, so commercial production is only worth considering if there is good vehicle access into the wood. Each bundle is normally 2m (7') long and 300-400mm (12-16") diameter, tied tightly in three places with baler twine or similar. Chestnut brash is particularly suitable as it is more durable in water than other hardwoods.

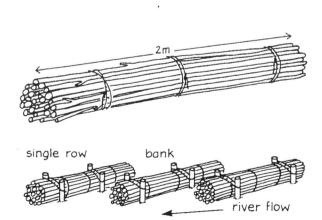

Traditionally, 'faggots' were bundles about 900mm (3') long and 200mm (8") circumference, used for fuelling bread ovens and other heating purposes, with 'fascines' the larger bundles as above. Nowadays either term is used.

Fascines or faggots are useful in smaller quantities for bank revetment work and other purposes by voluntary groups and others. For details see *Waterways and Wetlands* (BTCV, 1997).

Footpath construction

Faggots or other coppice material can be used as the base for paths through damp ground, especially in woodland locations. This base is then topped with a thick layer of woodchips to make a dry and comfortable walking surface.

Use a double layer of faggots, made as described above, laid across the path. Other suitable materials are roundwood poles at least 1.5m (5') long and up to about 75mm (3") diameter, laid across the path at least two layers thick. These are overlaid with edging poles shown, which help secure the base and also prevent the woodchips from spreading. Topping up will be necessary according to use and prevailing weather conditions. See page 171.

Horse jumps

Birch tops 1.5-2m (5-6') long, bundled in 20s, are used by race courses and hunts.

Straight poles, at least 2.4m (8') long and 75-100mm (3-4") diameter are suitable for jumps and trotting poles at riding schools and arenas.

Cordwood

Any wood over 50mm (2″) diameter which cannot be used for any other purpose should be cut into 1.2m (4′) lengths and stacked in cords to dry (p90), and then used for firewood.

BUNDLING, TYING AND STORING

Many coppice products are made up into bundles before being stored or sold. As with all woodland produce, try to plan the work to minimise handling, storage and transport, which add greatly to the cost of utilising wood products. At the commercial level, this means careful planning of handling, storage and marketing, to maximise profits. At the volunteer level, it means never leaving a site with vehicles that don't contain at least a few items of woodland produce or a bundle of bean poles on the roof rack!

Using a grip and cradle

To make up large bundles, such as faggots:

1. Make a 'woodman's grip' of two poles 0.9-1.2m (3′-4′) long and 40-50mm (1¹/₂″-2″) in diameter. Connect the poles with a strong rope, the length of which is about twice the circumference of the bundle to be tied. Attach one end to each pole about 300mm (1′) from the end of the pole.

2. Bolt a hook, made from strap iron, to a post driven into the ground, so the hook is about 300mm (1′) off the ground, and of a size to hold the pole.

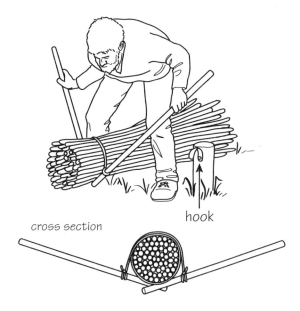

cross section

hook

3. To use, place the grip on the ground with the poles apart and the rope pulled straight, positioned within reach of the hook and post. Lay the tying twine or bond alongside the rope.

4. Lay the bundle neatly on the rope, with the butt ends together.

5. Straddling the bundle as shown, lift the left-hand pole over to your right, and then lift the right-hand pole over to your left.

6. Put your foot on the right-hand pole, and push the left-hand pole down and under the hook to tighten the bundle. This leaves both hands free to tie the twine or bond.

7. Alternatively, another person can hold the right-hand pole, while you tie the twine.

To make up smaller bundles, such as cleft chestnut stakes:

1. Make up a cradle from two pairs of posts driven into the ground, and join each pair with a discarded bucket handle, webbing strap or similar, to form a curved support.

2. Use a woodman's grip with a length of rope slightly shorter than the circumference of the bundle.

3. Place the bundle on the cradle, then put the grip over the bundle and push down on both poles to tighten. Hold in position with the knees while you tie the bond.

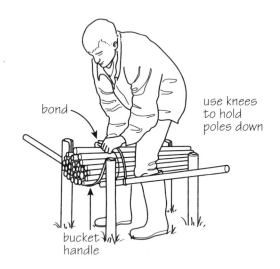

bond

use knees to hold poles down

bucket handle

Tying bonds

Bundled material is held with a bond, tie or rose, traditionally of natural material including hazel, willow or bramble. These are not only available in the wood, but unlike wire or twine, do not damage the rods. Use thin hazel or willow rods, which are made more flexible by twisting to open up the fibres. To use bramble, 'shry' off the thorns by pulling the stems through a thickly-gloved hand.

To make a bond of natural material:

1. Pass the thicker end of the stem which you are using for the bond around the bundle, and then cross the thinner end over it.

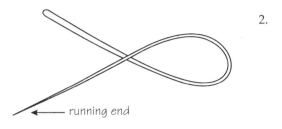

2.

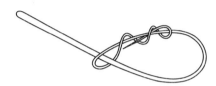

Loop the thin end (known as the running end) over the thick end. Pull the running end up tight and secure it by twisting it round itself a few times and tucking it in.

Alternatively, if the stems used are sufficiently flexible, you can make a more secure bond by first looping the thick end of the stem around itself to make a noose. Pass the running end through the noose, tighten and secure as above.

Storage

Traditionally, the coppice worker cuts material during the winter, for the reasons given above (p98). Bean poles, pea sticks and similar products are sold in the following spring, and the worker spends the summer using the stored material to make hurdles and other products. Wood is easier to split and bend when freshly cut or green, so that the material becomes progressively more difficult to work as the season progresses. Generally then, coppiced material is best used as soon as possible after cutting.

In contrast, wood destined to be used as firewood or charcoal must be stored and dried for six months or so before it is used. Timber from standard trees must be carefully seasoned according to its species and planned end-use.

Coppiced material should be stored in a shady, cool, ventilated place, where it will not dry out too quickly. If possible store it off the ground.

- Bundles of bean poles and stakes of various types are best stored upright in a shady place. In the wood they are normally stored around the trunks of standard trees in a convenient location for removal and sale in late spring. Pea sticks are stored off the ground (p109).

- Binders or ethers for hedging are best used fresh, but if not can be kept damp and pliable for up to six weeks under a tarpaulin.

- Wood for green woodworking is best kept in as long lengths as convenient, as the wood dries out from the cut ends. The lengths can then be cut up as required. Leave the bark on, to reduce drying.

- Split wood dries much more quickly than wood in the round, so generally once wood is cleft into small pieces it should be used immediately, or stored in water.

- Larger cleft material, such as fencing stakes, can be stored as necessary. Stack in a similar way to cordwood.

- Firewood is easier to split when green, which will also speed drying (p131).

- Wood for charcoal or smaller round wood for firewood should be stored in a cord (p90)

Chapter 9 continued.
Please see overleaf for Table 9f.

Table 9f: PERIODS OF COPPICE ROTATION BY SPECIES

Coppice rotations vary according to the site, rate of growth and other factors. General ranges are as follows: A = up to 12 years B = 12-15 years C = 15-30+ years		
SPECIES	ROTATION	USES
Alder	A B	River protection work Brush heads, clog soles, tool handles, charcoal
Ash	B C	Hurdles, walking sticks, yurts, cues Horse jumps, tent pegs, baskets, barrel hoops and rims, scythe and tool handles, hay rakes, furniture, charcoal, oars, hockey sticks, floorboards
Birch	A B	Besoms, garden rustic work, horse jumps, bobbins, spools, reels, darning mushrooms Brush heads, furniture, charcoal
Chestnut, sweet	A B C	Walking sticks, hop poles Chestnut paling, rails, hurdles, ladder rungs Hop ' king' poles, stakes, furniture, shingles, charcoal, floorboards
Elm	C	Beetle heads, turnery, furniture, firewood
Hazel	A B	Wattle hurdles, thatching spars, sheep cribs, hedging stakes and binders, garden rustic work, pottery crate rods, walking sticks, pea sticks Firewood, charcoal
Hornbeam	C	Cogs, firewood, pulpwood
Maple, field	B, C	Turnery, musical instruments, carving, furniture, firewood
Oak	B, C	Fence posts, building, furniture, barrels, shingles, swill baskets, tanbark, trugs, charcoal
Spindle	A	Spindles, skewers, artists' charcoal
Sycamore	B, C	Turnery, clogs, kitchen utensils, veneer
Willow, osier	A	Wattle hurdles, river protection works. Cultivars for basketry
Willow, various	A	Gate hurdles, river protection, trug baskets, artists' charcoal, living sculptures
Mixed	A B, C	Pea sticks, bean poles, stakes Firewood, pulpwood

10 Green woodworking

Wood which is worked when freshly cut or 'green' is easier to split, turn and carve than wood that is dry or seasoned.

Green woodworking has been practised for thousands of years in the making of baskets, hurdles, simple furniture, buildings, tools and other products. Although many of these uses have been partially replaced by other materials, there is an active craft industry and many hobby woodworkers use green wood, both for traditional and new products and uses. Their skills and the ability to find markets for their produce are vital for the maintenance of coppices, which produce their raw material.

As well as the traditional hurdle makers and other craftsmen, in recent years a new generation of coppice and green wood workers has emerged, who are actively extending the craft. The interest in garden design has increased the demand for all sorts of garden products, sculptures and other items. Together with the increase in demand for home-grown barbecue fuel (chapter 10), and the development of ways of using wood 'in the round' for building , this combines to make the future somewhat brighter for traditionally managed woodlands.

Some green woodworking, such as the making of hurdles, is usually done in the woodland itself, with the raw material at hand. Most other products can also be made in the wood, with the aid of simple tools and gripping devices which act like an extra pair of hands. The full time worker will erect a simple shelter in which to work. Turnery, carving and other crafts which require smaller amounts of raw material can easily be done at home or in a workshop.

One of the great attractions to green woodworking is that, with a few simple cutting tools, you can make wooden tools, blocks, grips, brakes, lathes and other devices from the raw material of the coppice. With these tools and devices, you can then make a wide range of products. A skilled green woodworker can walk into the wood carrying a few simple hand tools, and emerge carrying a hurdle, a chair or some other beautiful and useful object!

In addition to the tools described in chapter 4, more specialist tools including drawknives, spokeshaves, twybils and tools for turning are used. For details, see Tabor (2000) or Abbott (1989).

Skills

SAWING

Sawing horse

A simple, fixed sawing horse can be made of round wood as shown below. This holds the wood at a convenient height for safe and easy sawing. The off-centre legs allow different lengths to be easily cut. The legs are driven a short way into the ground to hold the horse steady. This is suitable for sawing wood up to about 130mm (5") diameter.

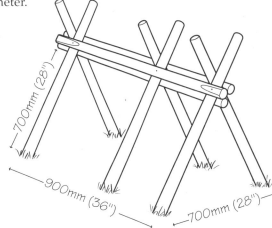

Alternatively, by adding diagonal braces, a moveable sawing horse can be made, of similar dimensions.

PEELING

Note the following:

- Where wood is converted into products with the bark off, peeling is usually best done immediately after felling, before stacking or extraction and conversion. Once the sap dries, the bark holds more tightly and peeling becomes difficult. Wood with bark on is more likely to be damaged by insects.

- Do not peel wood on steep slopes, but extract to level ground first.

- Occasionally, as when round ash poles are to be made into hay-rake handles, only some of the bark is peeled off to begin with. This slows down the rate of seasoning and reduces the chance of splitting.

- Waste bark left at the peeling site may enrich the soil as it decays. Take care to site peeling operations where they will not harm interesting woodland flora, or remove the bark for disposal elsewhere. Composted bark makes a useful mulch for use around newly-planted trees.

Large logs and poles

Specialist de-barking spades or peelers are available from suppliers of forestry tools (p188). As a substitute, you can use a worn spade with a well sharpened edge. To peel a log:

1. Trim off larger branches cleanly, with a light axe. You can cut through small knots with the peeler.

2. If the pole has a kink or curve, peel the bark with the pole in its unstable position first. It is much easier to steady the pole in this position before the bark on the other side has been removed.

3. Stand facing the pole about 1.8m (6') from its butt end. Hold the peeler in both hands with your knuckles on top.

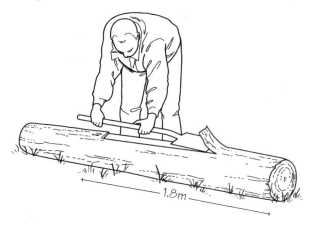

4. Make long, sweeping push strokes with the peeler, running the blade off the end of the pole at each stroke to remove the bark. Peel three quarters of the way around the circumference of the pole.

5. Turn and peel the stem in the other direction. If you have trouble using the tool ambidextrously, step over the pole to use it in a more comfortable position from the other side.

6. Continue peeling until you reach the tip of the pole. Turn the pole, and work back toward the butt, taking off the remaining strip of bark.

Small poles and rods

The shaving brake holds small round wood at an angle of about 30°, which is comfortable for working. Approximate dimensions are given for an average height adult, but the brake should be made to fit the individual user.

Stand as shown, pulling the draw-knife towards you. Longer poles can be reversed in the brake to shave the other end.

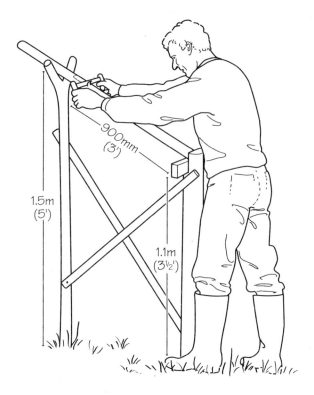

CLEAVING

Cleaving, also called riving or splitting, is one of the oldest woodcraft skills, and has several advantages over sawing:

- Cleaving is the quickest way of dividing a pole lengthways.

- Unlike sawing, cleaving does not cut through the wood cells, and so the face of the split pole or 'cleft' is more durable than a sawn pole. There is also less wastage, as sawing removes a groove of wood, or 'kerf'.

- Cleaving exposes any weaknesses in a piece of wood, so the best pieces can be selected for particular uses.

Note the following:

- To learn the skill of cleaving, start with a clean straight pole of about 130mm (5") diameter and 1m (3') long, which should split evenly. Longer, thinner poles, or those with knots and bends are more difficult to split straight. Freshly cut ash, hazel, willow and chestnut are the easiest woods for cleaving. Any dried wood will be difficult, but elm, hornbeam, box and apple are particularly tough.

- Always start with the thin end of the pole, as the thick end is the tougher to split.

- Split between any knots, rather than through them.

- Make the split through the pith, which on an evenly grown pole will be in the centre. The pith of an uneven pole will be off-centre, and splitting will be more difficult. Uneven stresses in the wood will also result in warping.

-

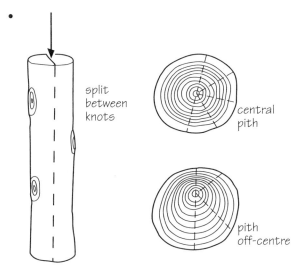

split between knots

central pith

pith off-centre

The general rule is always to split the wood in half, and then in half again until you get the size you want. If you try to split unequally, the split tends to run off in the direction of the smaller part.

Cleaving large poles or logs

Cleaving large poles should be done with a sledgehammer and wedges. Wear goggles to protect your eyes in case a wedge gets chipped. Avoid trying to split logs with many knots, as these will not split easily or cleanly. Inspect large logs carefully for cracks, as you can use these when inserting the wedges.

1. Lay the pole on a hard surface. Two other poles placed side by side make a good support and hold the pole steady.

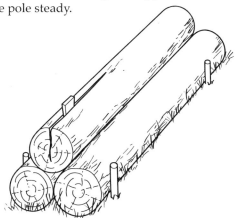

2. Tap in a wedge lightly, so that it stays in position, about 30cm (12") from the end of the pole. Use a sledge or lump hammer. Then hammer the wedge in farther with the sledge to open up a split part way along the pole.

3. Hammer a second wedge in further along the split.

4. Continue to add wedges in line as necessary until the split extends to the far end of the pole.

5. Hammer in the wedges in sequence to cleave the pole.

Cleaving short logs

This method is suitable for logs up to about 13cm (5") diameter and 60cm (2') long, or for larger logs which have first been split by the method given above.

1. Stand the log upright on a block or other flat surface.

2. Position a cleaving axe or hatchet exactly across the pith, to split the log into two even halves.

3. Using a wooden mallet, hit the back of the axe to start the split.

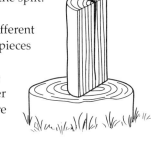

By cleaving a pole in different ways you can produce pieces of different sections. In the diagrams below the numbers show the order in which the sections are cleft.

chestnut pales for

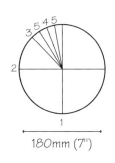

180mm (7")

chestnut palings

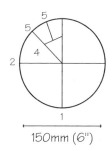

150mm (6")

ash or beech,

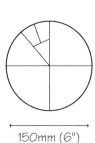

150mm (6")

ash, for

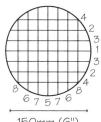

150mm (6")

When cleaving a 17cm (6½″) length of pole into 12mm (½″) squares for hay-rake tines, wrap twine around near the base to keep them from falling apart as they are split.

For further details on making pales, paling fence, tent pegs, rake tines and many other products see Tabor (2000).

Cleaving medium-sized poles

The cleaving or riving brake is used for applying leverage in order to split medium-sized round poles. It has two horizontal bars with space between them to allow a piece of wood to be put under tension. The horizontal bars are not parallel, to allow a range of sizes to be held, from about 25mm (1″) at one end, to about 150mm (6″) at the other.

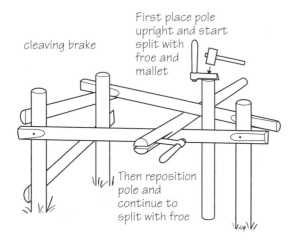

cleaving brake

First place pole upright and start split with froe and mallet

Then reposition pole and continue to split with froe

To use the brake:

1. Place the pole to be cleft upright in the brake so that it is held by the angle of the brake. Place the pole small-end up.

2. Place the froe exactly across the pith of the pole, and strike the back of the froe blade with the mallet to open up a split.

3. Once the split is well started, position the pole into the gap between the horizontal bars, as shown. Continue the split by pressing down on the froe handle, levering the pole open. For larger poles, insert a piece of wood in the crack to keep it open, then remove the froe and put it in further down the crack.

4. As it splits, pull the pole towards you. Try to keep the pole in a position so that the point at which the split is just starting is directly over the point of leverage.

5. If the split starts to move off-centre, turn the pole so that the larger section is underneath. Push down on this section with your left hand and push downwards

with the froe to bring the split back to centre. The split tends to travel towards those wood fibres which are under tension – in this case, those which are curved downwards by the pressure of your hand.

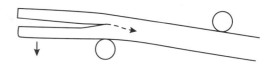

Hazel rods for hurdles and other products are split in a different way. See page 126.

Turning

Another ancient skill is that of turning wood on a lathe, so that the waste wood can be cut evenly away to produce cylindrical objects such as chair legs and backs, candlesticks, utensils, bowls and other items. All lathes have two points between which the piece of wood is tightly gripped. A foot treadle or other mechanism is used to turn the piece of wood, while a cutting tool is held steady against a rest to cut long shavings of wood as the piece turns.

The pole lathe is an ancient tool, in use over 2,000 years ago. It is still popular today, because it can be simply made from a coppice pole and a few other pieces of wood. The piece to be worked is held by two fixed or 'dead' points, and is rotated by a cord that passes around it. The cord is fixed at one end to a treadle, and at the other to a flexible coppice pole. As the treadle is depressed, the cord rotates the piece of wood to make the cutting stroke, at the same time bending the pole. As the treadle is released, the pole straightens, rotating the piece of wood away to make the return, non-cutting stroke.

The pole lathe is safe to use, because the piece of wood will stop turning the moment the treadle is stopped. The speed can be adjusted by the speed at which the treadle is operated. A pole lathe requires no electricity, and can easily be set up in the woodland or in a workshop. Turning green wood does not produce dust or splinters, so goggles are not necessary.

The following section gives basic information on building a pole lathe. For full details see Abbott (1989). There are variations to the basic pattern, and dimensions can be altered to suit the individual worker, or for other particular requirements.

- Traditionally, the bed of the lathe was attached to the stumps of two trees, about 1.2m (4′) high. This is suitable if you only want to work in the woodland, but most people prefer to make a set of portable A-frames to support the bed so that the lathe can be erected wherever you want it.

- The bed should be 1.2m (4′) long to turn items up to 750mm (30″) in length, or 1.5m (5′) to turn longer items.

- The bed supports two 'poppets', through which are threaded two lengths of studding or similar, ground to a point, which hold the piece of wood to be turned. A sliding rest is used to support the tool while working. Various designs can be used.

- Select a suitable pole about 4.5-5m (15-20′) long and 60mm (2½″) at the base, tapering to about 3mm (1¼″) at the top. A coppiced ash pole is probably the best, but alder, willow, birch or beech are also suitable.

- Anchor the base of the pole very firmly by lashing it to a stake, well driven into the ground.

- Erect a support at about the middle point of the pole. The support can be made from two forked poles as shown. In soft ground these may need to be supported on a log or similar.

- The treadle can be made from a strong forked branch, hinged with strips of leather to a base board.

- Attach a length of 3mm nylon cord from the treadle to the top end of the pole.

For indoor working, the pole can be substituted with a length of shock cord, attached to two upright poles about 2.5m (8′) high, lashed to the two A-frames. The length of unstretched shock cord between the two poles should equal the length of the bed. For full details see Abbott (1989).

Structures

Greenwood can be used to make all sorts of structures, including plant supports, pergolas, trellis, indoor and outdoor furniture, playhouses, yurts and permanent buildings. The most flexible species, notably willow, can be used for sculptures, baskets and many other items. For voluntary groups, selling material from local woodlands for garden and other uses can help provide a source of funds, as well as being environmentally sound. There have been some very successful community schemes set up linking woodland management groups with allotment owners and green woodworkers. For the full-time coppice worker, being able to add value by making a range of products is vital for the viability of the enterprise.

There is always a market for simple plant supports, and during the current gardening boom, a very good market for all kinds of garden structures such as arches, gazebos, sculptures and so on. Yurts have also become popular, and have proved a lucrative market for some coppice workers. With the aid of a steamer, all sorts of bentwood furniture and other items can be made. Details of simple DIY steamers are given in Tabor (2000).

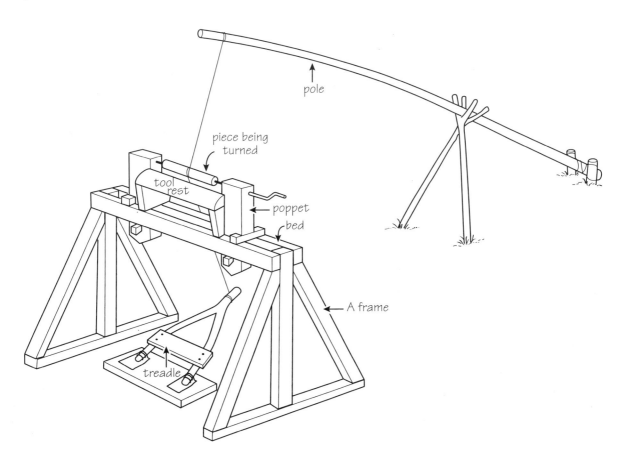

There are several organisations involved with traditional building techniques using green oak and other timbers, and some beautiful buildings have been constructed over the last decade or so. Others are looking at the use of small roundwood for building construction, by developing innovative building techniques. This may provide new outlets for the future which will help sustain broadleaved woodlands.

This section gives basic details on a selection of greenwood structures. Many ideas can be gained from Wood Fairs and other events where greenwood workers and other craftsmen gather.

PLANT SUPPORTS

Details for pea sticks, bean poles and plant stakes are given on page 109. A range of plant supports can be made, from temporary wigwams and frames for annual climbers such as sweet peas, to pergolas and arches for perennial climbing plants.

Small wigwams, trellis and other items can be made by the coppice worker, and sold 'ready for use'. Larger items are difficult to transport, and are best either supplied in kit form, or made up on site by the coppice worker.

Wigwams

Straight, slender coppice poles are needed for the uprights, and long flexible rods for the weavers. With hazel or willow uprights and willow weavers a strong, durable wigwam can be made that will last several years, and can be moved as necessary. For wigwams made up in situ or for temporary structures, other flexible material can be used for the weavers, including dogwood, bramble, old man's beard or various garden plants such as clematis or Virginia creeper.

The general pattern is to use an odd number of uprights, with thin bands of weavers sufficient to keep the structure rigid. Spiral or diagonal bands of weaving can also be used.

For a wigwam 400mm (16") diameter at the base, and 1.6m (5'6") high, use 7 uprights, each about 12mm (^{1}/$_2$") diameter, sharpened at the base. Make a mould from a piece of plywood or similar, and drill holes 180mm (7") apart in a circle to take the base of the uprights.

1. Insert the uprights into the mould.

2. Start with two long rods, woven as shown in a locking weave. Add in new rods as necessary, making sure the ends are hidden on the inside. Build up a band about 100mm (4") high. Various other patterns of weaving can be used as desired.

3. Tie the rods neatly at the top with strong twine.

4. Start a second band of weaving about half way up the uprights, using willow or other flexible material. A simple weave, made by threading a single rod at a time, is easiest. Tuck the ends in to keep it neat.

5. Remove the wigwam from the mould.

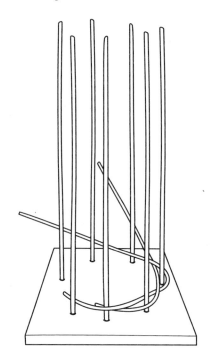

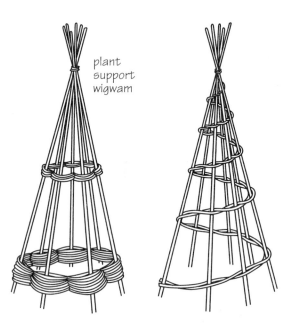

plant support wigwam

From this basic pattern, variations can be made. By leaving the top untied until the end, stronger or more decorative weaves can be used for the middle band. Instead of twine, the top can be bound with willow. Structures larger than the dimension given above are best made in situ, as they are awkward to transport, and need to be strongly made to survive the journey! Space the uprights about 150-200mm (6-8") apart around the base, with thicker uprights required for bigger structures. The mould is not needed. The materials can be supplied in 'kit form' with instructions for people to make up in their own gardens.

Trellis and other plant supports

Various patterns of trellis can be made for supporting climbing plants or as a screen. Trellis can be fixed to a wall or fence, or fastened to posts to make a screen. To reduce rotting at the base, attach the trellis out of ground contact. Use hazel and willow for perennial climbers, and other material for shorter-term use.

Arch

Hazel, willow or other pliable material can be used for arches and other structures. Binding with a soft, workable wire is the easiest method of fastening the rods into the required shape. Black wire (16 gauge) is suggested. Bright nails 1¼" to 1½" (30-40mm) are also useful. The lack of galvanising is not important, as rusting makes no difference to the life of the structure, and rusted nails are almost invisible. Some smaller nails may also be handy, as they are easy to drive, and the tips can be bent over as necessary to fasten.

These structures will be durable for a few years, and can be used for annual climbing plants, or perennials that are pruned low each year, for which the arch can be replaced as necessary.

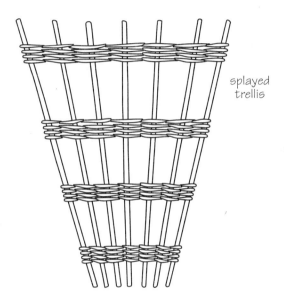

splayed trellis

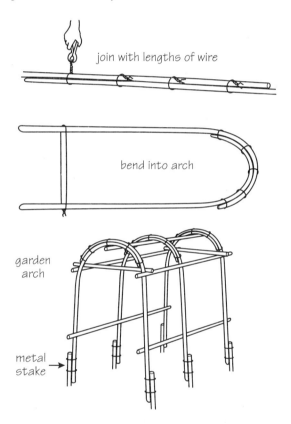

join with lengths of wire

bend into arch

garden arch

metal stake

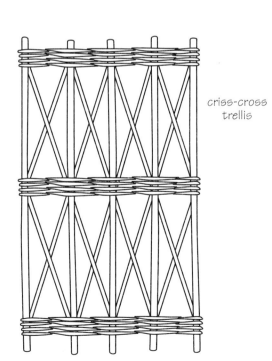

criss-cross trellis

Uprights: 6 x 16' by 1½" diameter

Selection of other wood about 1" diameter, 4 x 4', 10 x 3', 8 x 2'6"

Metal stakes: 0.9-1m (3-4') for securing in the ground

1. Lay two of the uprights in a line, thin ends together and overlapping by about 600mm (2'). Join them together about every 200mm (8") with a length of wire, twisted tightly as shown.

2. With another person helping, bend the length into an arch, and temporarily secure it with wire into an arch. Make a second or more arches as required.

3. Drive the metal stakes into position, and attach the arches to the inside of the stakes, as shown, with the bottom of the upright 25mm (1") clear of the ground to reduce rot.

4. Wire the remaining pieces in place.

Pergola

Larger structures such as pergolas or arbours are best made out of oak or chestnut, as other woods will not be sufficiently durable without preservative treatment. Use the straightest poles you can find, squared off to produce uprights at least 100 x 100mm (4") section, and secure with bolts or dowels to cross pieces of cleft timber (p117). Smaller round or cleft poles can be used for the rafters. The weight of the timber, and the plants it may support can be considerable, so construct all joints with care. Wire can be used, running the opposite way to the rafters, for additional plant support. Set the uprights in concrete, or use additional side bracing as necessary if the structure is in an exposed position. Vines, wisteria, roses and other plants can be trained over the structure.

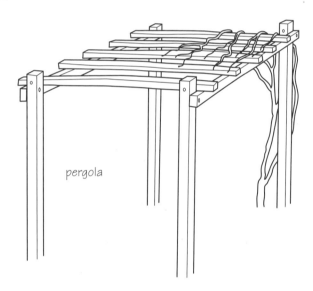

pergola

A temporary structure, for shade or for growing annual climbers, can be made out of hazel, willow or other suitably straight material. Fasten the main joints by wiring tightly. The structure should be replaced after about two or three years, as it will become unsafe as the wood rots.

DWELLINGS

Yurt

Yurts have been the traditional dwellings of the nomads of Central Asia for the last 2,000 years. A yurt is a round, domed tent, made of a light but very strong wooden frame, covered with woollen felt or other material.

Coppiced willow poles are the best wood to use for the roof ribs and wall trellis, with hazel also suitable. Ash is recommended for the roof wheel and door frame. For a 4.8m (16') diameter yurt, the following are needed:

Roof ribs: 40 green poles, 2.6m (8'6") long, 40-50mm (1½-2") at the butt end and 25mm (1") minimum at the tip.

Wall trellis: 80 green poles, 2m (6'6") long and 20mm (³/4") at the tip.

Roof wheel: Knot-free straight ash pole, 2.1m (7') long and 100-200mm (4-8") diameter.

Door frame: 2 straight ash poles, 1.7m (5'6") long and 40mm (1½") diameter, one ash pole 1m (3') long by 100mm (4").

The roof ribs are steamed in a simple DIY steamer and then curved to the required shape. The various parts of the frame are laced together with cord, allowing it to be partly disassembled and folded up for storage or transport. For full details see *How to Build a Yurt* (Centre for Alternative Technology Factsheet, 1997).

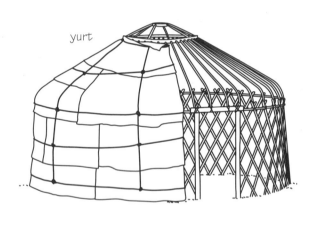

yurt

Tipi

The traditional tipi, lodge or wigwam of North America is built of very long, straight poles, from the Lodgepole pine and other pine species, chosen for their slender form and light weight. For a full-size tipi, at least 14 poles are needed, each about 6m (19'6") long and preferably no thicker than 100mm (4") diameter at the butt, tapering to 50mm (2") diameter measured 1m (3') from the tip.

Thinnings from conifer plantations, either pine, fir or spruce, are the best material to use to build a replica. Choose the straightest and thinnest poles available, and sned off all the side branches. Carefully remove the bark without damaging the wood, and leave the poles to season in a cool, shady place for about three weeks.

Using a surform and then sandpaper, sand the poles carefully to give as smooth a finish as possible. Take care to smooth out any notches or scratches. This is important to avoid snagging the canvas, and to allow rain water to run down the poles without dripping off into the interior. The tipi is erected by lying three poles on the ground and tying at the top with one end of a 10m length of stout rope, using a clove hitch followed by a reef knot. The poles are then hoisted up to make a tripod, and the remaining poles leant up against the tripod, evenly spaced. The ground plan of the poles is not a circle, but egg-shaped, with the door at the narrow end. The rope is wound around the poles four times and anchored to a peg in the ground. The canvas is then attached to the 'lift pole', raised up and unfolded into position. Lengths of hazel, 50mm (2") in diameter, can be cut and shaped to make the tent pegs. 300mm (1') lengths of thinner hazel, 10mm ($^1/_2$") in diameter, can be used for pins to lace the canvas. The pins should be pointed and peeled of bark, apart from a band at the top, in which patterns were traditionally cut. For full details, see *How to make a Tipi* (Centre for Alternative Technology Tipsheet).

For smaller tipis or wigwams, long straight coppice poles can be used, such as ash, hazel, willow or sycamore, although these will be heavier than similar size conifer poles.

BASKETS AND WOVEN STRUCTURES

The weaving of flexible rods of willow or hazel is a basic technique which has been used for centuries for making baskets and containers of all sorts, screens, walls, and many other structures. Willow is the main group of species, both because of its flexibility and because of its prolific growth, but other species can be used.

Baskets and other containers can also be made out of cleft wood, of oak, chestnut, ash and other species. The garden trug is the best known type, but oak swill baskets and other traditional patterns are also found. Tabor (2000) gives details on making trugs, swill baskets and other cleft baskets, as well as pottery crates which include cleft and round material in their construction.

Woodland plants for weaving

Willow or osier is the best material for weaving, and is grown in osier beds or as a commercial field crop. However, there are many woodland plants which can also be used for weaving, as listed below.

Generally choose straight, one-year-old growth, with as few side shoots as possible. Cut between November and March, and tie loosely into bundles. The bundles can then be stored in a dark, cool place outside for a few weeks, such as under a hedge or bush, where they will slowly dry out without becoming brittle, and so remain pliable. If they become too dry, the bundles can be soaked in water for a day or two, and then wrapped in damp sacking to keep them flexible.

Bramble (*Rubus* spp): Remove the prickles by rubbing the stems with a handful of rags. Stems have a uniform thickness, and are commonly found in lengths of 3m (10') or more.

Broom (*Cytisus scoparius*): Shrub of heaths and open woods on acid soils. Green shoots which darken with age.

Dog rose (*Rosa canina*): Remove the thorns in the same way as for bramble.

Dogwood (*Cornus sanguinea*): Common in woods on chalk and limestone. Coppiced plants will produce long purplish-red rods.

Hazel (*Corylus avellana*): One year shoots are pliable. Older stems can be split (p126).

Honeysuckle (*Lonicera periclymenum*): Climbing plant, common in woods and hedgerows. The bark tends to crack and peel away, so is best removed before use.

Ivy (*Hedera helix*): Evergreen climber, abundant in many woods and gardens. Long trailing and climbing stems of uniform thickness.

Traveller's joy or Old Man's Beard (*Clematis vitalba*): A climbing plant found mainly on chalk soils, and which can become a rampant weed in neglected woods, on railway embankments and elsewhere. The thinner stems can be used for weaving, with the joints giving a pleasant texture to basketwork. The thicker stems may find a market with floral artists.

Willow

Willow for basket-making is grown commercially as a field crop in Britain and elsewhere, with different species and varieties grown for their colours and other qualities. *Salix triandra* (almond-leaved willow) is the main commercial species, grown as short-rotation coppice, and harvested every one or two years to produce tall, slender rods. *Salix viminalis* (osier) and *Salix purpurea* (purple osier) are also good for basket making.

For conservation groups, a small area of willow or 'withies' not only provides a valuable wildlife habitat, but provides a crop of rods which will extend the range of products which they can produce from their woodland.

Willow rods can be cut between January and March, tied into bundles and stored in a cool, dark place such as a shed. Before use, the rods must be soaked in cold water for a few days to regain suppleness.

The bark can be left on, which produces 'brown willow', of varying colour according to variety. 'White willow' is produced by cutting in mid spring when the sap is rising, which makes it easier to remove the bark. 'Buff willow' is produced commercially by boiling the willow with the bark on, which releases the tannin and stains the stems a rich rusty brown. The soggy bark is easy to remove.

Willow basket-making and other willow weaving are described in detail in several publications, a few of which are listed in the bibliography. The growing of willow for basketry and other uses is concentrated in the Somerset Levels, where there are several companies which can supply materials and information on willow.

Living willow

Building structures and sculptures with living willow has become popular in recent years. The rods are simply inserted into the ground where they take root and produce vigorous side shoots. It's best to use freshly cut rods, cut when not in leaf. One, two or three year growth, up to about 50mm (2") diameter will sprout, so there is plenty of scope for creating different types of structures, including fences, arches, bowers, wigwams, tunnels and playhouses. Rods which are set diagonally will produce side shoots all along the stem. The structure will need pruning every year, or the new shoots training or tying in as desired. For further details see Warnes (2001).

Hurdles

There are two basic types of hurdle, the gate hurdle and the wattle hurdle, with various regional patterns of each.

The making of hurdles requires various techniques which can also be used to make a range of other products. Wattle hurdles are one of the main hazel products, and a skilled worker with access to good quality hazel coppice can make a living from hurdle making.

THE GATE HURDLE

The gate hurdle, which is like a lightweight farm gate, was traditionally used to pen sheep, pigs or bullocks, but its main use is now in gardens. Sweet chestnut is the best wood, but ash, oak, elm, hazel and willow may also be used. Typical dimensions are shown, but vary with area and use. Some patterns have six rails for better stock control. Kent hurdles have a metal ring or ferrule around the top of each upright, to protect it from damage whilst being driven into the ground.

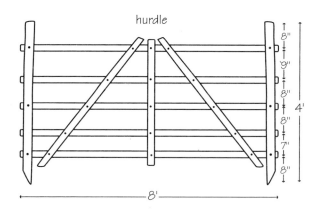

1. Start with some straight coppice poles about 50-100mm (2-4") diameter, and at least 2.4m (8') long. Cleave these using a froe and cleaving brake to produce half-round clefts for the cross-bars and braces.

2. For the uprights cleave a 75-100mm (3-4") diameter pole, at least 1.2m (4') long, into two clefts. Use them as they were cut, with the two cleft faces towards each other, so that any curves are the same at both ends. Point the lower end of each upright.

3. For the cross-bars, cut the required number of 50-100mm (2-3") clefts to length, normally 1.4m (8'). Shave the ends to make tenons, making sure these are in the same plane and do not 'wind' with the wood, otherwise the hurdle will be crooked.

4. Lay one upright cleft face up, and using each cross-bar in turn held upright, mark the positions for the mortises. Mark each cross-bar so you know which mortise it matches.

5. Holding the upright horizontally in the cleaving brake, drill out the top and bottom of the mortise with a brace and bit, and preferably clean out the waste with a twybil (p115). Otherwise, drill out three or four holes, and then clean out the waste with a chisel.

drill, then clean out to
make mortise 50 x 15mm

6. Assemble the uprights and cross bars, by fitting the tenons into the appropriate mortise. Using cut nails, or ordinary nails slightly blunted on the tip with a hammer, nail the joints. The nails should be long enough to protrude, so the ends can be bent over to stop them loosening; a technique called clench-nailing.

7. Finally shape the three braces and nail them in position.

Hurdle – general structure

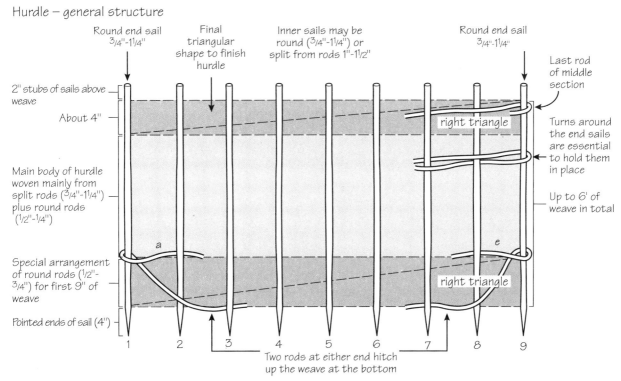

Round end sail 3/4"-1¼"

Final triangular shape to finish hurdle

Inner sails may be round (3/4"-1¼") or split from rods 1"-1½"

Round end sail 3/4"-1¼"

Last rod of middle section

2" stubs of sails above weave

About 4"

right triangle

Turns around the end sails are essential to hold them in place

Main body of hurdle woven mainly from split rods (3/4"-1¼") plus round rods (½"-¼")

Up to 6' of weave in total

Special arrangement of round rods (½"-3/4") for first 9" of weave

a

e

right triangle

Pointed ends of sail (4")

1 2 3 4 5 6 7 8 9

Two rods at either end hitch up the weave at the bottom

WATTLE HURDLES

The wattle hurdle has a dense weave, to make a windproof barrier for sheep pens and garden uses. Hazel is the best material to use, being pliable, strong and long-lasting. Willow can also be used, but is not nearly so durable.

You should be experienced in using a single-handed billhook and in keeping it sharp, and you will need strong wrists and fingers to bend the material to shape.

Hurdles for enclosing sheep are normally 6' (1.8m) long by 3'6" (1m) high, with 10 uprights or sails (also called zales). Garden hurdles are usually the same length, but various heights are made. Because they are moved

HURDLE MOULD

Top View

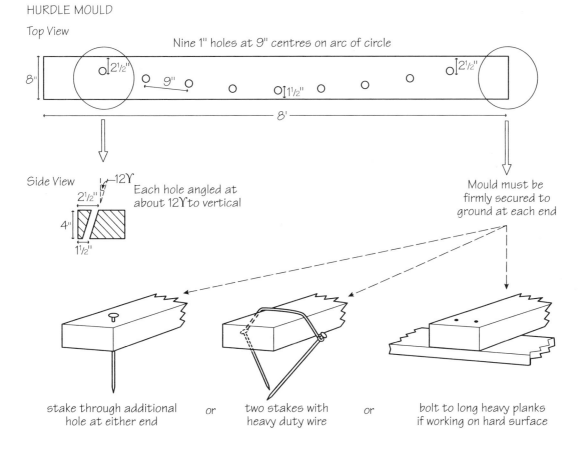

Nine 1" holes at 9" centres on arc of circle

8"

2½"

9"

1½"

2½"

8'

Side View

12Υ

2½"

Each hole angled at about 12Υ to vertical

4"

1½"

Mould must be firmly secured to ground at each end

stake through additional hole at either end

or

two stakes with heavy duty wire

or

bolt to long heavy planks if working on hard surface

less than sheep hurdles and therefore don't have to be quite so robust, only 9 sails are used. The section below describes one method of constructing a garden hurdle, but variations in style and technique will be found. Hurdles are a traditional product, made to imperial measurements, which are therefore used in the diagrams on page 125.

Tools and materials

- Billhook and saw to cut the stems from the stool.

- Spar-hook or light billhook, plus whetstone, for splitting stems.

- An upright post or chopping block to support the stems as you cut them.

- A steel rule or measuring stick for lengths up to 6' (1.8m).

- Billet of wood for compacting the weave.

- Loppers, for trimming the rod ends.

- A mould, made to the dimensions shown below.

A hazel hurdle requires a quantity of straight coppiced rods, from $^1/2''$ (12mm) to $1^1/4''$ (30mm) diameter. Some are used in the round, but most are split. Techniques for splitting thin rods are described below.

Hurdle mould

The mould should be prepared in a workshop from a piece of timber 8' (2.45m) long x 4" (10mm) x 8" (20mm). Angle the holes, as shown, to take the sails. The mould must be firmly secured to the ground at each end, by one of the methods shown on page 125.

Preparing the sails

The end sails should be $^3/4''$-$1^1/4''$ (20-30mm) diameter, used in the round. The remaining sails can be round, but are usually split from stems 1-$1^1/2''$ (25-40mm) diameter. The sails should be straight, and must be stiff enough to ensure that the horizontal rods bend in and out of them without forcing them out of position.

To split a stem, prop it against the post and position the spar-hook across the end, and then tap the back of the blade with a billet to start the split. Then proceed as for split rods (see below).

Sharpen the thicker end to fit into the hole of the mould to a depth of at least 5" (125mm). The safest way is to hold the sail upright on a block or post, and then trim downwards with the spar-hook. Cut to the required length.

The split surfaces of the sails can face either direction. A consistent pattern will help identify your work!

Splitting a rod

Use a thatcher's spar hook or a light curved billhook. The easiest rods on which to practise are those with a 'Y' shaped fork at the upper end of the rod, where the rod is about $^3/4''$ (18mm) diameter.

1. First hold the rod at the butt end and trim off any side shoots with the spar-hook.

2. Then rest the butt end on the ground and, for right-handed cutting, hold the left branch of the Y with your left hand, well away from where you will cut. Snick the spar-hook into the crotch to start the split.

3. Move the handle of the spar-hook from side to side so that the tip of the blade levers the rod apart and extends the split. Run the blade down, keeping your left hand safely out of harm's way behind it to support the rod, and using your thumb and fingers to help prise the halves apart, until the rod is split in two.

That's the theory! In practice, note the following:

- Beginners will find that the blade soon deviates from the centre, 'running out' to one side or the other. If the blade is running out to the right, bend the left-hand half-rod away from the split, and vice versa.

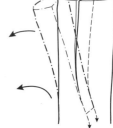

If cut tends to run out to the right...

bend left half rod away from cut

- You can apply a small amount of bending with the spar-hook itself, as moving the haft to the right tends to bend the left half-rod and vice versa.

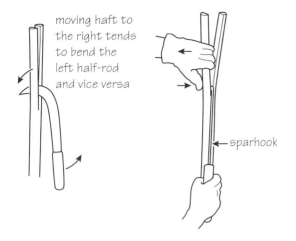

moving haft to the right tends to bend the left half-rod and vice versa

sparhook

- Where there is no convenient fork to start the split, snick the spar-hook into the side of the rod, where it is about $^3/4''$ (18mm) diameter, and apply the above principles to guide the blade into the middle.

- To start a split at the cut end of a rod, rest it over a post or chopping block, position the tip of the blade correctly, and pull gently and carefully towards you, using the post or block to protect yourself from accident.

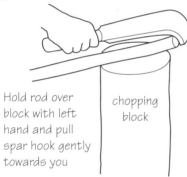

Hold rod over block with left hand and pull spar hook gently towards you

chopping block

Doubling

This is the technique of bending and twisting a round or split rod around the end sails and back on itself. If you merely bend it, the rod will break.

- Ensure the rod is free of knots at the point where you will be bending it.

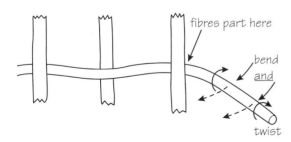

fibres part here

bend and twist

- As you bend the rod it will be nipped tight by the sails, providing resistance so that you can simultaneously twist it. You will feel the rod 'give' as the longitudinal fibres in the wood part from each other.

- Continue to bend and twist together as the rod goes around the end sail.

- Split rods twist through 180° in the course of doubling back. Thus all the split faces appear on the same side of the hurdle, facing away from you as you build it.

- Twisting round rods turns them into a coarse flexible rope. The final rod of the hurdle is wound round the end sail for a complete turn-and-a-half.

- Unless you are very skilled some broken fibres may spring out at the turns, but you will soon be able to feel whether you have turned a rod successfully or nearly broken it.

Starting off

In the following descriptions, sails are numbered 1-9, and rods are a, b, c,

Of the three basic weaving patterns required, the one you need first is the most difficult to master, with numerous different styles adopted by different craftsmen. Round rods are used for this bottom section.

The essentials of the starting weave are that a pair of rods cross at the bottom between 2 and 3, and between 7 and 8. The inner ends of these four rods (a, b, e, f) are woven into the body of the hurdle immediately; the other ends are left protruding until about 8" (200mm) of weave has built up. They are then curved upwards to turn round the end-sails, so 'hitching up the skirts' of the hurdle, so the weave cannot fall down at the bottom (see diagram page 125 top).

No rod has its end in contact with the mould; all ends are supported on other rods. The weave is built up to the right with a succession of rods to create a long triangle, and then levelled out again with an equivalent process to the left, creating another triangle. The first rods are lifted and woven over the later rods, locking the section together.

As you do steps 3-7 below, use your loppers to trim back the ends of each rod as it is woven into its final position, so the ends don't interfere with the next rod.

Rods a and b are preferably at least 9' (2.7m) long. They will hitch up the left end of the hurdle, so choose the best quality material for them, to avoid breakage at a late stage of construction!

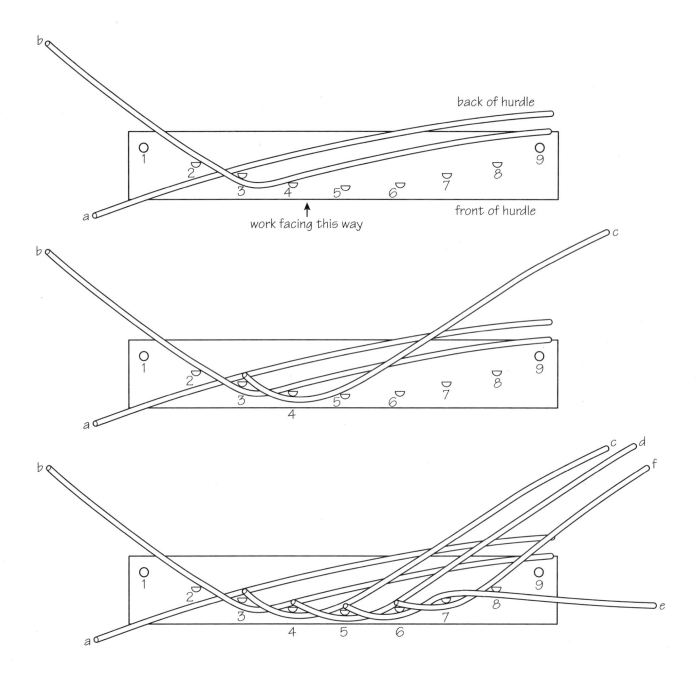

1. Lay rods a and b as shown, with the butts protruding about 3' (1m) to the left of 1, and enough length to the right to later weave slanting up and along to 9, over the rods to the right (top illustration).

2. Rods c, d, e and f must be over 6' (1.8m) long. Choose the longest rods for e and f, as they are used to hitch up the right-hand end. With the tips to the left and starting with c, fit each into position in front of 4, 5, 6 and 7 respectively.

3. Lift e over f so they cross between 7 and 8 (bottom illustration).

4. Lift d over e between 6 and 7 and weave along to 9, turn and weave back to finish behind 7.

5. Lift c over d between 5 and 6, weave along to 9, turn and finish behind 6.

6. Weave the right-hand part of b in front of 5 and along to finish at 9. Rod b will thus end higher than c, d, e and f.

7. Weave the right-hand part of rod a in front of 4 and along to 9, so it finishes at the top of the right-hand triangle. There should be a neat row of rod-ends on the back side of the hurdle.

Level this out with a left-hand triangle as follows:

1. The first rod starts behind 8 and weaves left, round 1 and back to finish behind 3.

2. The second rod starts behind 4 and weaves left, round 1 and back to finish behind 7.

3. The third rod starts behind 6 and weaves left, round 1 and back to finish behind 5. (*Note the resulting pattern, with each rod starting and finishing one sail closer to the middle than the previous one. This technique is used again to build a triangle at the top of the hurdle.)

4. Then add two more rods woven opposite ways from 1 to 9.

5. 'Hitch up' rods a, b, e and f in that order, by curving them up to pass inside the end sail and turning them to continue on top of the weave. Rods a and e should finish behind 4, with b and f behind 5. See main diagram on page 125.

Weaving the main body

As before, stand on the convex side or front of the hurdle, with the cut ends of the bottom section to the back. The split rods are woven so that their flat surfaces face away from you. The simplest form of weaving is used, with each rod going alternately in front and behind the sails. You must keep the sails reasonably in line. A strong rod which tends to push them out of position can be counteracted by a similar weight rod woven in immediately above. Compact the weave by periodically tapping down with the billet.

The only problems are joining in new rods, and maintaining the rectangular shape of this middle section.

To make a simple join, let in the next rod by poking it into the weave, so that it takes over from the old rod and continues in the same direction.

letting in a new rod

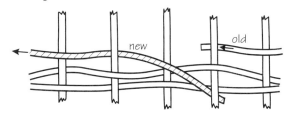

Where the rod runs out at the end, you can use two or three 6' (1.8m) rods in succession without turns, but you must ensure there are enough turned rods to hold the hurdle together.

If one end of the weave gets higher than the other, take advantage of irregularities in your material to even it out. Or when you add a new rod at an inner sail, reverse the direction of weave as shown below.

Measure the dimensions of the developing hurdle at intervals. If an end sail splays outwards, bend it in with

reversing the weave to build up more to the right

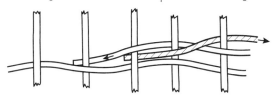

your shoulder as you turn a rod around it. If the sail tends inwards, make the turn and then tug the sail out before continuing the weave. If the inner sails deviate sideways, tap them back into position with your billet. The last rod of the main body should go behind 1 and 9.

The tops of the sails should all finish along the same gentle curve as the bottom ends. You will probably need to strain the half-completed hurdle or individual sails from time to time to keep the hurdle in shape. Some warp in the completed hurdle will flatten out as it dries, but if any sail gets badly out of position you will be in trouble, as the rods will not bend round it without breaking.

Finishing the hurdle

First you must build the final right triangle. Use three 7' (2.1m) rods, each doubling round 9, the technique 1-3* above, reversed.

Thus:

1. Start behind 2 and finish behind 7

2. Start behind 6 and finish behind 3

3. Start behind 4 and finish behind 5

To form a locking weave for the final left triangle, you have to insert both ends of each rod under an existing rod. The trick for the second end of the rod is to bend it into a bow past three sails, push the end into place, and then lift the rod over the 'missed' sail to complete the weave.

1. Use a long split rod for rod a. Sharpen the butt if necessary and tuck it through the weave between 8 and 9, about 9" (230mm) from the top. Turn it round 9 and weave down to 1.

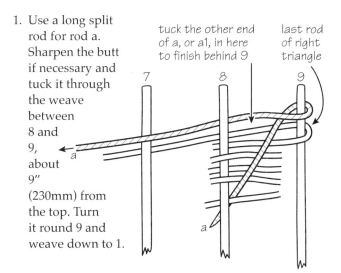

tuck the other end of a, or a1, in here to finish behind 9

last rod of right triangle

2. If rod a is long enough, turn it round 1 and weave it back. Bring it in front of 6, 7 and 8 and tuck the tip in behind 9. Then lift it over 7 to complete the weave.

3. If rod a is too short for this, turn it round 1 and finish behind 3. Reverse the weave with a second rod a1, let in behind 4, turn it round 1 and weave back as described in step 2 above.

4. The butt of b is tucked under a (or a1) behind 8. It is woven down to 1 and back, coming in front of 4, 5 and 6 to finish under itself and behind 7. Then lift it over 5.

5. Rod c is a stiff round rod about 4' (1.2m) long. Tuck its tip under b behind 6 and weave to the left, leaving it hanging out behind both 2 and 1.

6. Rod d is a good round rod over 6' (1.8m) long. Tuck it under c behind 5, weave to 1, do a double turn round 1, tuck it under itself behind 4 and then lift it over 2. Finally lift the butt of c over 1 to pin down d.

Trimming and stacking

Lift the completed hurdle from the mould. Cut off any protruding ends of rods and stack the hurdles on top of one another with their convex sides uppermost to dry out for a week or so.

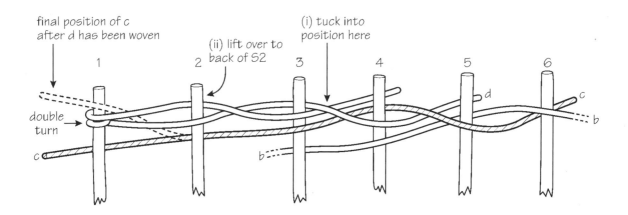

11   Firewood and charcoal

Wood is a renewable fuel, the use of which combines well with the management and maintenance of copses, small woods and hedgerows. When burnt in an efficient stove or furnace, wood produces little smoke and does not contribute to acid rain. Chemically, burning wood is the same process as the natural decay of wood, but at a much faster speed. Burning wood produces no different environmental effect than does the natural decay process, provided the level of fuel use does not outpace regeneration. Wood is a viable fuel for contributing to the heating of rural homes and businesses in Britain, and can support new planting schemes, as well as the management of existing woodlands.

Charcoal is partly-burnt wood which is used for fuel and other purposes. By producing charcoal for local barbecue and other uses, the woodland owner is helping to conserve local woodland through management, reducing transport requirements, and reducing the import of charcoal from places where this trade may contribute to forest destruction.

Wood can also be converted to woodchips and burnt for direct heating or the generation of electricity. Short rotation coppice crops are being grown for this purpose in the UK and elsewhere. Cultivation and harvesting is highly mechanised, with more similarities to arable farming than woodland management.

Firewood

WOOD AS A FUEL

Note the following:

- There is an old rule of thumb that an acre of woodland can produce a cord of wood per year indefinitely (a cord = 3.6m^3 ; see below). However, taking a cord by cutting scattered trees is difficult and can cause ground damage. A better way is to cut a group or stand of trees each year. These can be left to regrow as coppice, or singled (p36) to leave one stem which will grow on to a standard tree.

- Freshly cut or green wood of nearly all species (see below) is useless as a fuel, as it is difficult to light, yields less heat than dry wood, and causes tar deposits in stoves and chimneys.

- Firewood should be dried in the open air until the moisture content is 20-25%. This takes at least six months for most species, and at least a year for elm and beech. Some species produce naturally much drier wood than other species. Freshly felled ash has only about 33% water, and can be burnt without seasoning, whereas fresh poplar is about 65% water. Firewood seasoned for two years is generally best. Wood stored for more than about 3 years may deteriorate due to fungal growth, woodworm or other agents.

- Firewood loses weight as it dries, and as a general rule two tonnes of green wood will produce one tonne of air-dried wood. The table below gives a general guideline for most species.

- A freshly felled cord of wood, which is about 3.6 cubic metres (128 ft^3), weighs about 1.5 tonnes.

- Wood is a poor conductor of heat, and burns less efficiently the larger the piece of wood. For stoves, open fires and for conversion to charcoal (p134), the optimum size of log is about 100mm (4") diameter.

- Wood dries more quickly from cut ends and cleft faces than if left in the round. Larger logs need to be split, both to encourage drying, and to give the optimum size for efficient burning. As splitting involves extra work, cutting the wood when it is no bigger than 10cm (4") diameter, as produced by coppicing, is the most efficient way of producing firewood.

Table 11a: WEIGHT AND MOISTURE CONTENT OF 1M^3 OF WOOD

1 cubic metre	Weight	% water	Use as firewood
Freshly felled	550kg	50%	Not suitable (except ash and holly)
Seasoned 1 year	410kg	33%	Burns adequately
Seasoned 2 years	355kg	25%	Burns well

- All types of wood burn more efficiently in wood burning stoves, than on an open fire. On average, air-dried wood burns at 70% efficiency in a free-standing stove, 60% in a built-in stove, and 35% efficiency in open fires. The problem of some woods creating sparks is less significant in stoves.

- Wood needs to be burnt at a fairly high temperature of around 700°C, which ignites the gases given off by the wood and converts these to carbon dioxide and steam. Filling a stove with wood and then damping it down by reducing the air supply prevent these 'volatiles' from burning, and generates smoke and tar. It's best instead to let the logs burn freely until they almost turn to charcoal, and then damp the stove down. The glowing charcoal will continue to give off heat for some hours.

- Conifer wood is generally less suitable than hardwood for heating. Its resinous nature means it flares up and burns quickly, rather than giving off heat over a longer time. Attempting to burn it slowly means that the resinous sap is not burnt completely, but leaves creosote deposits on the stove and chimney, which can lead to chimney fires.

- Wood ash is a useful garden fertiliser, containing 5-10% K_2O (potash), and should be applied in early spring at 125-270g/m² for improved growth of fruit, flowers and potatoes. It's particularly useful on acid, sandy soils, but should not be applied to chalky soils. Store the ash in a dry place before use.

SPECIES

Two logs of different species but with the same weight and moisture content will have the same value as fuel.

Table 11b:PROPERTIES OF WOOD AS FUEL

	EASE OF SPLITTING			BURNING SPEED			SPARKS	
	Easy	Medium	Hard	Good	Too slow	Too fast	No	Yes
Ash		●		●			●	
Beech	●			●			●	
Hazel	●			●				●
Oak			●	●			●	
Elm			●	●			●	
Field maple		●		●			●	
Hornbeam		●		●			●	
Hawthorn			●	●				●
Birch	●					●		●
Holly			●		●		●	
Rowan			●		●		●	
Sycamore		●				●	●	
Wild cherry		●				●		●
Poplar	●					●		●
Alder		●			●			●
Willow		●				●		●
Sweet chestnut	●					●		●
Horse chestnut			●		●			●
Lime			●		●			●
Conifers		●				●		●
Rhododendron			●	●			●	

However, species differ in their density, so that a larger volume of a light wood such as willow or pine would be required to give the same fuel value as a dense, heavy wood such as oak. Freshly felled oak, beech and hornbeam occupy about 1.5m³ per tonne, whereas freshly felled poplar, willow and most conifers occupy about 2.5m³ per tonne.

The most efficient species for planting new firewood coppices are fast growing species such as willow and poplar. Although their calorific value is lower per unit weight than other species, this is outweighed by their speed of growth. Where yield per unit area is not so important, a mix of the better firewood species at the top of Table 11b is likely to give the best value for wildlife, amenity and fuel value.

In addition to coppicing, firewood can also be produced during thinning, felling, hedging, pruning and other operations.

As well as their initial moisture content (see above) species differ in their ease of splitting, their speed of burning, and whether or not they spark. The above table gives some guide to the various properties, with the species listed approximately in order of usefulness.

FIREWOOD COPPICES

When cutting an existing coppice mainly for firewood purposes, it's important to remember that all the stools in the coupe must be cut, whatever the suitability of the different species for firewood. If you try and select only the best firewood species and leave others uncut, those that you cut may be too shaded by the remaining trees to regrow vigorously. When cutting a mixed block, you can either use all that you cut for firewood purposes, or you can select out wood of particular value for other purposes, and use the remainder for firewood. For commercial operators the profit from firewood is generally low, and the waste left after higher value species and pieces have been selected may be sold as firewood.

The coupe or cant size and the rotation should be chosen to yield material which is easy to cut and handle, and which is not large enough to require splitting. Poles 6-7m (20-23') height and 70-100mm (3-4") diameter are the most efficient size for handling and burning.

Coppices planted mainly for firewood can be designed and planted accordingly with ash, beech, hazel, hornbeam and other species which are best for the purpose, with stools spaced about 3.3m (10') apart. For information on planting coppices, see page 105.

A well managed coppice wood containing a full stocking of mixed broadleaved species should be able to produce about 3 tonnes of air dried wood per hectare per year

(the old rule of one cord per acre per year is roughly equivalent). Output can be doubled by planting fast-growing species such as willow, poplar or alder. The average figure quoted for heating a three-bedroomed house using wood only is 7-9 tonnes of air dried wood per year, though this figure will vary greatly with location, type of house, insulation and other factors. For most householders, an option of using wood in addition to other fuels is more realistic.

For a three-bedroomed household to be fully self-sufficient in wood fuel would therefore require about three hectares (7.5 acres) of coppice. This could be worked on a ten year rotation, in ten cants, each 0.3 hectare (0.7 acre). Each cant should produce between 7-9 tonnes of air dried wood when cut.

Producing smaller volumes of firewood, or other coppice products, from an area less than about a hectare becomes more difficult. This is because coppice regrowth is affected by the shading of surrounding trees. Larger coupes have a better area to edge ratio than smaller coupes, and are also more efficient to protect against browsing by deer or rabbits. For a coppice of one hectare or less, it's probably best to divide it into coupes no smaller than 0.25 hectare (0.6 acre), and to cut one coupe every two or three years, depending on the species and rate of growth. In the intervening years firewood may need to be cut from elsewhere, or bought in. Dividing a hectare into ten small coupes for example will reduce the overall yield, as growth in each coupe will be reduced.

CONVERSION AND STORAGE

There is an old saying that firewood warms you three times – when you cut it, when you carry it, and when you burn it. For the wood-stove owner with plenty of time to spare, the cutting, splitting, carrying and stacking of firewood in sunny winter weather is one of life's pleasures. For larger-scale projects, it's important to make operations as efficient as possible to reduce conversion and handling. Efficiency is all-important for commercial operations, as profits on firewood are low. Power equipment will be essential for splitting and handling.

There are two basic options: either to cut the wood to length to fit the fire immediately on felling, or to cut to 1.2m (4') lengths and stack to make a cord (p90). Cutting to length will speed drying, which may be useful if the firewood can only be seasoned for one year before it is needed. Security for storage may be an issue. Where theft or arson is unlikely, cordwood can be stacked in the wood for a year or so, before it is cut up for use.

Splitting wood by hand

The most efficient method of producing firewood is by growing and harvesting coppice at no more than 100mm (4") diameter. However, splitting larger material from thinning, restoration of neglected coppice and other woodland operations is frequently needed. General information on splitting green wood is given on page 116, with further details given below. Hardwoods are easier to split when freshly cut. Some conifers are easier to split when dry and brittle.

- For any given diameter and type of wood, it is easier to split shorter logs rather than longer. Beginners should start with logs no longer than 200mm (8"), proceeding to 300mm (12") logs as their skills develop.

- Use a wedge axe or log splitting maul, which has a thick blade with shoulders to split the wood, rather than a narrow headed axe and wedge.

- The speed of striking the log is more important than the weight of the maul. A 6lb maul can be swung much faster than a heavier tool, and is therefore more effective.

- Place the log on a firm surface or on a low cut stump, positioned so that you can stand comfortably slightly uphill of the log, in order to maximise the length, and therefore the speed of the strike.

- Aim to split along any existing line of weakness.

- Start at the edge of the log, not the centre, as the edge is easier to split.

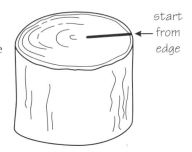

start from edge

- Use one or more blows to get the first split well started, and then aim at the line beyond the centre of the log.

- Put your effort into making fewer, stronger strikes, resting as necessary. Repeated half-speed attempts will only tire you out and have little effect.

- Standing with feet apart, measure the distance from the log by placing the maul on the log with arms extended, and then take a third of a step back.

- Hold the tool with one hand at the base of the handle, and the other just below the head. As you swing the tool up, let the upper hand slide down to the lower hand. At the top of the swing, the tool should be just behind the vertical line from your body.

- Focusing on the point where you intend to strike, bring the axe down as forcefully as you can, bending the knees and waist.

STORAGE

Wood does not have to be stored under cover to dry out, and logs stacked or in a pile will dry out over the summer following cutting. Logs can then be transported to be stacked close to the point of use. Minimise handling and restacking. If possible, stack close to the point of use immediately after cutting and splitting. Don't stack newly-cut wood in a closed shed, as it will rot rather than dry out. Preferably stack in an open-sided shed, barn or lean-to, or in the open, covered with corrugated iron or similar, weighted down. Logs dried for six months or more can be stacked in a dry shed, but ensure there is some ventilation.

If possible, stack small logs and larger logs separately, with kindling in a large box, so that you can easily find what you need. Keep several days' supplies of kindling and logs in the house, near but not touching the woodstove or range, so it dries to give the best fuel value when burnt.

Charcoal

Charcoal is formed when wood or other organic materials are heated out of contact with air. Charcoal has a high carbon content, and burns at a higher temperature than wood. Charcoal making is an ancient process, used in Europe for at least 5,000 years, and has been of huge importance in the development of civilisation. Charcoal was the smelting fuel of the bronze and iron ages. The liquor produced during charcoal making was used by the Ancient Egyptians in the embalming process, and it's likely that glass making, which requires the high temperatures possible with charcoal, was also developed during this period.

Charcoal is still used in industrial processes, for barbecue fuel and for other uses (p141). The popularity of barbecues in Britain and elsewhere has meant a great increase in demand for charcoal. From being virtually a dying craft, there are now many portable kilns in operation in the UK. This not only helps keep woodland management viable, but also reduces imports of foreign charcoal, which is not always produced from properly managed forest resources. Charcoal from British hardwood is lighter in weight than imported charcoal from tropical hardwood, and is easier to light and faster to reach cooking temperature.

Charcoal making is hard and dirty work, and the profits for the small-scale operator are low. However, it is a useful process for adding value to the management of derelict coppices or other neglected woodland, as it uses waste wood which would otherwise have no value. In-cycle coppices (p98) produce very little waste wood, and are managed for higher value products.

Charcoal burning operations can be categorised as follows:

Large scale

Large commercial operators may use four or more kilns on a static site, with machinery for loading and unloading. Collection of tarry residues, recycling of gases, use of retort kilns and other processes are designed to increase efficiency and profitability. Marketing is likely to be on a national scale, for various uses.

Commercial viability is dependent on efficient processes, good marketing and the relative cost of imported charcoal. Various organisations including the Forestry Commission and the Forestry Contracting Association (p183) have studied the commercial viability of charcoal production in Britain in recent years.

Retort kilns are more efficient than ring kilns, as they use a separate heat source to bring the wood to a sufficiently high temperature for carbonization to take place. At the time of writing, one kiln manufacturer in Britain is producing a small retort kiln for charcoal production (p189). Continuous carbonizing retorts, which are very efficient but have a high capital cost, are in use in other countries (Hollingdale, Krishnan and Robinson, 1999).

Medium scale

A small operator or voluntary group with one or two portable ring kilns should be able to produce a few tons of charcoal a year, for which they could find a local market for barbecue fuel, with additional other uses possible. This scale of charcoal production is only likely to be commercially viable if it's tied in with other woodland management enterprises, or if it has a significant voluntary input.

Small scale

Small amounts of wood can be converted into charcoal in a kiln made from an old oil drum, for home use or resale locally for barbecues.

The details that follow relate to medium scale operations. Use of old oil drums is described on page 142.

RING KILNS

The traditional earth kilns are now used only for demonstration purposes, and most charcoal burners use portable metal ring kilns.

Design

Ring kilns comprise a bottomless steel cylinder, with a removable lid, chimneys and air inlet/outlet channels. The air inlets and chimneys can be adjusted to steer the hot gases around the kiln to result in even and thorough carbonization. A 6' kiln, for example, will normally have six inlet/outlet points, with three chimneys that can be moved from one point to another. Various sizes of kiln are available from kiln makers, or can be made by light engineering firms. The optimum size will depend on the scale of the operation, the number of operators, the requirement for portability and other factors. The sizes listed below give a guide to suitable dimensions.

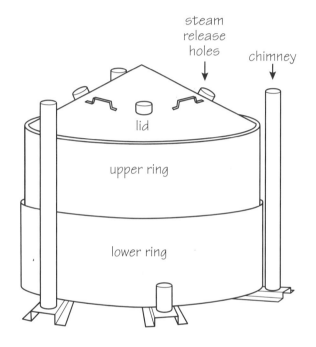

inlet/outlet channel

The larger diameter kilns are made in two stacking rings, to give sufficient height while still making the kiln portable and easy to load/unload. Some stacking kilns have a tapering top ring, but this is more difficult to move around on site as it cannot be rolled along the ground. The diameter/height ratio is important, as for example an 8' (2.4m) diameter kiln with a height of less than about 6' (1.8m) will not burn efficiently. Using only one ring from a double kiln will not produce an efficient yield. Note that at least two people are needed to lift the upper ring and lid into position.

Tall, narrow kilns, for example 5' (1.5m) diameter by 2'6" (0.8m) height also work efficiently. An old oil drum (see p142) makes a useful small kiln of similar proportion.

As they are subject to heat stress and physical damage, ring kilns must be made of a good quality steel, to give an 8-10 year working life. The lower ring should be made of 3mm steel, and the upper ring and lid of 2mm

Table 11c: CHARCOAL KILNS

Diameter	Height	Capacity	Approx. charcoal yield per burn
5' (1.5m)	2'6" (0.8m)	1.4m^3	70kg
6' (1.8m)	3'6" (1.1m)	2.8m^3	150kg
7' (2.1m)	4' (1.2m)	4.1m^3	300kg
7'6" (2.3m)	5'6" (1.7m) in two rings	7.0m^3	500kg
8' (2.4m)	6' (1.8m) in two rings	8.2m^3	600kg

steel. Construction must be simple and robust, to avoid problems with tar accumulation. Design details for a 7'6" (2.3m) diameter double ring kiln are given in Hollingdale, Krishnan and Robinson (1999).

Details of loading, igniting and operating will vary with the type of kiln and the operator, but the general principles for operating a double ring kiln are described below (p139).

The air dried wood is packed tightly into the kiln and then ignited, and burning is controlled by restricting the air supply. Too much air results in the wood burning to ash, which not only wastes the wood and the preparation time, but is also likely to damage the kiln. Too little air results in only partial conversion to charcoal.

Output

The dryness of the wood is important to the efficiency of the operation. If wood is dried to 20% moisture content or less, one tonne of charcoal can be produced from four tonnes of wood, giving a charcoal yield of 25%. Under normal woodland conditions in Britain, wood air-dried for a year or more is seldom this dry, and one tonne of charcoal from six tonnes of wood, or a charcoal yield of 16%, is the more normal conversion rate. In drier climates, charcoal yields of 25-30% are easier to achieve.

The wood or 'charge' not only loses weight during conversion to charcoal, but also loses volume. Typically it will shrink by 25-30%, so for efficient use, the kiln must be packed tightly and to the top, finishing with a shallow cone to leave the minimum of space under the lid. Charcoal yield is also affected by the dimensions of the ring kiln and other design details, and by the skill of the operator in controlling the burn.

The capacity and yield figures are for guidance only. The capacity given is total capacity; the amount of wood a kiln will hold will depend on the uniformity of the wood and how closely it is packed. Charcoal yield will depend on the factors given above.

In British woodland conditions, the rule of thumb is that about half a tonne (500kg) of charcoal will be produced

from 3 tonnes of wood in a double ring kiln (7'6"-8' diameter), equivalent to a 16% yield. Note that 2.5m^3 of air dried wood weighs about 1 tonne.

Operating programme

In Britain, most charcoal burning in ring kilns is carried out during the summer months. This is because most operators will be doing felling, coppicing and other woodland management work in the winter, and also because conversion to charcoal is quicker and more efficient in dry weather. Long hours of daylight, dry ground conditions and the chance of warm, dry weather are important practical considerations.

For efficient commercial operation, at least two kilns are needed, running in overlapping cycles. While one kiln is burning, another can be cooling and so on. Hollingdale, Krishnan and Robinson (1999) give a detailed operating programme for two double ring kilns over a 5 day week, each used twice in the 5 days and producing in total 2-3 tonnes of charcoal a week. This relates to tropical climates, and is not directly applicable to British conditions.

For voluntary groups with one kiln, it may be necessary to load and burn over a day and a night, and then return a few days later to empty the kiln. At least one person must stay on site until the kiln is cool, and the security of the site should also be considered. A kiln full of charcoal is an obvious target for arsonists.

By increasing the draught a quicker burn can be achieved, but less charcoal will be produced than by a slower burn. This may however be the best way for voluntary groups to operate, where supervision over 30 hours or more is difficult. Smaller kilns have faster turnaround times than larger kilns. A 6ft (1.8m) single ring kiln can be filled, burned and shut down in 12 hours for example. It's important to get the kiln well lit at the start of the burn, or burning time will be extended. Dry wood, dry ground and dry weather also speed up the burning time.

Some operators only burn at night, to reduce the nuisance caused by smoke and other emissions.

MATERIALS

Species of wood

Most charcoal making uses thinnings or poor quality waste that is too small or awkwardly shaped for other uses, so a mixture of species is normally available. Species vary in the quality and quantity of charcoal produced, as indicated below. It's best to fill the kiln with one species at a time, as this will make the burning process easier to manage and give more consistent results. The charcoal can be mixed before bagging as required.

- Ash, sycamore, beech, hornbeam and elm make good quality charcoal for barbecue use. Sycamore is quick and easy to convert to charcoal, because of the thin bark and ease of burning, even when 'green' or in wet weather conditions.

- Oak gives the best return by weight, but it's generally a waste to use it for charcoal, when higher value may be gained from other uses. Oak is slow to convert to charcoal, because of the thick bark.

- Birch and hazel are less productive by weight, but make reasonable charcoal. Birch is rather friable and tends to break up in transit.

- Alder charcoal breaks down very fine and is used for gunpowder.

- Chestnut charcoal tends to break up, but it burns very hot so is valuable in forging metal, and may find a market with blacksmiths.

- Charcoal made from willow tends to spit in use and doesn't burn as long as other hardwoods, but has the advantage of lighting easily. Mix it 50/50 with other species before bagging for barbecue use.

- Softwood charcoal burns well, but it breaks up easily in transit and is very dusty.

Size, seasoning and stacking

Lengths of 600-900mm (2'6"-3'), with a minimum top diameter of 50mm (2") and maximum butt diameter of 150m (6") are best, in straight lengths without forks. For efficient conversion rates, the kiln must be packed tightly with the minimum of air space. Because of the extra work involved, it's not usually worth splitting larger diameter wood for charcoal making. A more profitable use for waste wood of this size is to split it and sell it for firewood.

The wood should be cut in winter when the sap is down, and air dried in a stack for at least a year before it is converted to charcoal. Wood cut in the growing season, when the sap is up, will take longer to dry than wood cut in the winter. Chestnut should be dried for two years. Dried wood is much easier to light and cleaner to burn and produces more charcoal per weight of wood.

Where operators are using bought-in supplies of wood, the price paid must reflect whether or not the wood is dried. Trying to keep up production by burning insufficiently dried wood will lead to production problems.

Correct stacking is important for efficient working. Species should be kept separate. Stacking should include sorting by thickness of material, as thicker wood is required for the centre and top of the kiln, and thinnest around the edges. A layer of sheeting under the top layer of the stack, but not enclosing the sides, will help speed drying.

Sand

Sand is required for sealing around the lid and base of the kiln. A cubic metre of sand, sufficient for about four burns, costs £20-30, so try to source from within the wood if possible. Alternatively, dry stone-free soil can be used.

SITING THE KILN

Always check with your local planning authority before starting any charcoal burning operation as planning permission may be needed. Small, temporary operations are likely to be exempt from regulations relating to the change in use of land, but the planning authority should always be consulted.

It is cheaper to transport charcoal than to transport the wood required to make it. This is because the raw material weighs about 5 times the finished product. The wood must be stacked and air dried for at least a year before burning, and for commercial efficiency, the wood should only be handled and stacked once before it is burnt. There are two options:

- Stack the felled wood at the nearest suitable site for burning, and move the kiln to this site when the wood is dry and ready for conversion.

- Keep the kiln on a semi-permanent site, and transport the raw material to this site for stacking, drying and conversion.

The choice will depend on the size of the operation, the availability of suitable kiln sites, the type of transport available and other factors. In practice, a semi-permanent site to which the raw material is moved is normally best. Suitable sites for burning (see below) may be in short supply, and the extra cost and time of transporting the raw material may be outweighed by the benefits of working from one site. In addition to the kiln, other equipment and facilities are needed which are easier to set up efficiently on a semi-permanent site. The efficiency of the system is crucial for commercial operators, but less important for voluntary groups.

Within the wood, the kiln should be sited with care. Note the following:

- The kiln must be sited on flat, dry ground. Water must not be able to run into the kiln, so a ridge or raised area with sufficient level ground is the best choice. Broadleaved woodlands tend to be in wet areas or on sloping ground which were not suitable for cultivation, so finding the perfect site may not be easy! Don't site the kiln on peaty ground, as there is a high risk of setting fire to the peat resulting in an 'earth burn', which will be difficult to put out. Light sandy soils give better results than heavy clays or other wet ground, because a light, well-drained soil more readily absorbs the moisture given off during carbonisation.

- The kiln must be sited near a track or road for easy transport. In coppice woodlands, a location which is fairly central to the coupes to be cut over the following few years will reduce haulage distance for the raw material. Sufficient space to stack wood nearby for air-drying is needed, to minimise handling.

- Charcoal burning produces a significant amount of smoke, so consider the effect on neighbours, roads, airports and other land users. Burning at night may be the best option to lessen adverse effects on neighbours. A site sheltered from the prevailing winds will be best in windy areas. However, bear in mind that charcoal burning usually takes place during the summer months, and trying to burn during an anticyclone, when there is little movement of air to disperse the smoke, can also cause problems.

- A nearby water supply is useful, as water is required for safety precautions, as well as for the domestic needs of the charcoal burners.

- Plan for several burns on a site, even for portable kilns. The first burn on new ground is not efficient, because of the moisture in the ground. Burn some brash on it first to dry it out a bit. With use the site will get baked and burn efficiency will increase.

TOOLS AND OTHER EQUIPMENT

Tools

Pick or mattock
– for levelling the ground to site the kiln

Saws, billhooks
– for preparing the wood

Shovels
– for shovelling sand and charcoal

Wheelbarrow
– for transporting materials

Buckets, stirrup pumps, fire beaters
– for fire precautions

Grading/bagging devices

It's worth making up a device that grades the charcoal, and makes it easier to bag it up. Shovelling the loose material into bags is slow and inefficient, and it is difficult to keep the outside of the bags clean. Clean bags are essential for marketing. See page 141 for further details.

Transport

Transport of raw materials and product within the wood and to the point of sale is likely to be crucial to the success of all but the smallest of operations. Dumper trucks, old tractors and trailers and other old and easy-to-maintain machinery tend to be used within the wood by small operators, especially as they are unattractive to thieves and vandals. A trailer, pick-up truck or other vehicle will normally be needed for transport to point of sale. Vehicles must be properly maintained and used only by competent operators.

Storage and accommodation

A lockable caravan or shed is useful for storing tools, sacks and other equipment, and as shelter for the operators.

SAFETY PRECAUTIONS

General

- The ground for at least 2 metres around the kiln must be clear of leaves, sticks, empty charcoal bags and other flammable material. Most charcoal burning takes place in summer, when there is a risk of fire spreading through the woodland.

- Keep a similar area clear of any hazards so that operators can move quickly and safely away from a flare or other danger. Don't leave tools where they may be tripped over by an operator moving out of the smoke.

- Inform the fire brigade in advance of the site and time of the burn.

- A supply of water and firebeaters should be immediately to hand. If a piped supply is not available, ensure at least 20 litres is to hand in a jerrican or similar container.

- There should always be at least two people on the site, in case of accident or emergency.

- The kiln must be closely supervised throughout the burn, and during the cooling down period (see below).

- Where the public have access, the site must be cordoned off and clearly signed.

- Empty and full bags must be stored in a secure place where they do not constitute a fire risk.

- Insurance through the Forestry Contracting Association is available for coppice workers and charcoal burners. Insurance for voluntary groups is available through The Conservation Volunteers.

Personal protective equipment

Appropriate personal protective equipment should be worn, as listed below.

- Close-fitting, flame-resistant clothing should be worn.

- Leather gloves with gauntlets should be worn for loading and unloading, to give protection to the hands and wrists.

- Wear safety boots to protect the feet from dropped timber or other hazards.

- Face masks should be worn by operators working near the kiln during the burning process, to avoid inhalation of fumes.

- Face masks should be worn during emptying and bagging up, because of the dust produced.

Operating precautions

- Take great care when handling kiln sections, lids, chimneys and other parts of the kiln to avoid trapped fingers.

- Check to see if animals have created burrows under the kiln, as this can allow excess air into the kiln making the burn difficult to control.

- Wood gas is produced during the burning process, which burns with a very hot and almost invisible flame. The pressure in the kiln will drive gas out of vents, chimneys and any gaps left in the kiln joints.

- Opening the lid or breaking any seals during the burn is dangerous as the entry of air can result in an explosion and the expulsion of burning gas. Even when cold, opening the kiln should be done with great care. Insufficiently burnt charcoal, which still has a high volatile content, will re-ignite when air is admitted.

Further safety points are included below, in the description of the burning process.

OPERATING PROCEDURE

This describes the operating procedure for an 8' diameter double ring kiln, with eight outlet/inlet channels and four chimneys.

Loading

Select long, straight logs about 150mm (6") diameter to use as 'stringers', which are placed as shown in the base of the kiln. Between every other pair of stringers, place kindling of paper, leaves and dry twigs, to provide four lighting points for a kiln with eight inlets. Across the stringers lay partly charred pieces of wood ('brown ends' or 'brands') from the previous burn, to form ducts which will draw the air into the centre of the kiln. The centre can also be filled with kindling and brown ends.

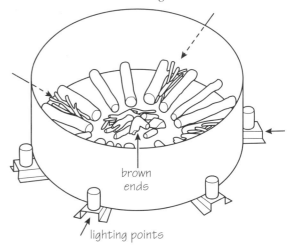

brown ends

lighting points

Load the kiln with layers of wood, packing the pieces as tightly as possible with the larger pieces towards the centre. For double kilns, lift the upper ring into position, and fill that to the top.

Finish with a conical shape to match the shape of the lid, so maximising the load. Fit the lid in position, and open the steam release valves.

Alternative methods of loading and lighting can be used according to the design of the kiln and personal preference. Some prefer to start with the kindling and brown ends in the bottom centre of the kiln, build ducts as described above, and then push a lighted rag, soaked in paraffin, through a duct into the centre of the load.

On smaller kilns, you can place a chimney temporarily in the centre of the kiln on top of some kindling, and then build up the load of wood around it. You then remove the chimney to leave a vent down which some lighted charcoal is dropped to start the fire.

Lighting

With inlets at the base and the vents in the lid open, light the kindling. On kilns with more than one lighting point, it's best to start at a point away from the wind, to make sure that this part of the load is well alight before you light the windward side, which will burn more quickly.

Allow the kiln to heat up for about 30-60 minutes until the kiln is very hot. The traditional test for temperature is when spit bounces off the surface of the kiln! During this time, fill the joint between the two rings, and depending on the design of the kiln, between the lid and the ring. During this period, large amounts of steam will emit from the steam release holes, caused by the moisture being driven out of the wood. Place the chimneys in position on alternate inlet/outlet channels.

Reducing the draught

1. As each part of the kiln reaches the required temperature, cover the base of the kiln with sand or soil, but leave the ends of the eight air inlet/outlet channels open.

2. Using sand or soil, cover the ends of the four air inlet/outlet channels which are supporting the chimneys.

3. Close the steam release holes.

Air should now enter the kiln only through the four air inlet channels at the base, from where it rises up through the kiln, with combustion gases drawn down and out through the chimneys. This is known as reverse draught.

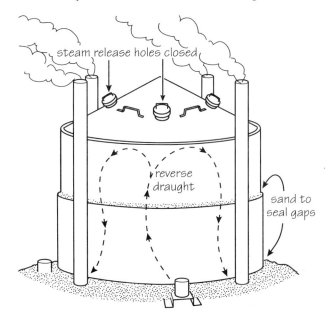

steam release holes closed

reverse draught

sand to seal gaps

Control of charring

After 15-30 minutes, thick white smoke should rise from each chimney. If smoke production slows from any chimney, temporarily remove the sand from the air inlet below to increase the air flow. Seal it off again as soon as sufficient smoke is being produced.

During charring tar is produced, which is deposited in the outlet channels and chimneys. If smoke emission from any of the chimneys reduces noticeably, remove the chimney using heat-proof gloves or thick sacking to protect the hands, and clean out the tar with a long stick. Also clean the outlet channel, and push a long stick into the centre of the kiln to make sure the gas flow is not restricted.

After about eight hours, move the chimneys onto the adjacent air channels. This converts inlets to outlets and vice versa, and encourages an even burn. Take great care as all the metalwork will be extremely hot.

Cooling

Charring is complete when the colour of the smoke from all the chimneys turn bluish and slightly transparent. This should occur 16-24 hours after lighting, for an 8' diameter double ring kiln. A test for moisture can be made by removing one of the chimneys and holding a spade over the outlet. If no moisture condenses on the spade, then charring is complete.

Remove all chimneys and seal outlets with sand. Add more sand to the seal around the rim and steam release ports to ensure that the whole kiln is absolutely airtight. Leave the kiln to cool for 16-24 hours before opening.

Unloading

During unloading, buckets of water, sand or soil should be ready in case of any fires breaking out in the charcoal.

Wait until the outside of the kiln is cold before you open it. If you open it too soon, while part of the charcoal is still alight, you are likely to lose the whole load as it re-ignites, as well as damaging the kiln. If a part is still seen to be alight, cover and re-seal the kiln immediately and leave it for a further cooling period.

The volume of wood will have greatly reduced during charring, allowing the upper ring to be removed from double ring kilns. Lever up the side of the lower ring, to remove the inlet/outlet channels. Then tip up the bottom ring to leave the pile of charcoal easily accessible for bagging. The alternative, of getting down inside the kiln, is dirty and unpleasant work. Depending on the system used, roll the ring to the alternative burning site, where it can be loaded by another team while the first load is bagged up.

GRADING AND MARKETING

Grading is required to ensure the charcoal is suitable for its end use. Barbecue charcoal must be sieved to remove the dust or fines, which can also be marketed. Effective marketing of barbecue charcoal and other charcoal products is essential for the success of any charcoal-making project.

Grading for barbecue charcoal

The British Standard and European Norm for barbecue charcoal (EN 1860-2) is currently under discussion. The following points give a guide to standards.

Charcoal must be uniformly black. EN 1860 states that 85% of the charcoal should pass through a 120mm mesh, and rest on a 20mm mesh. The generally accepted size range for barbecue charcoal across Europe is from 80mm to 20mm.

Chemical tests can also be carried out to check fixed carbon content, volatile matter, ash content and moisture content. Most charcoal makers rely on experience to judge the quality of their product. A simple test of burning the product will check that it ignites easily and burns clear, leaving only ash. Any smoke will indicate excessive volatile matter.

Well made hardwood charcoal has a high fixed carbon content, and a calorific value of about 7200 kcal/kg.

Bagging up

Charcoal can absorb moisture from the atmosphere up to about 5% by weight, but this does not affect quality, and it can be safely packaged. However, if rain gets onto the unpackaged charcoal, it will absorb more moisture which will then seep out when it is packaged. Two-ply paper bags are recommended for packaging. Plastic bags are not recommended as they will cause condensation of the moisture in the charcoal, resulting in unsightly moisture on the inside of the bag.

Most charcoal is sold by weight when packed, with '3kg when packed' being typical. Selling by volume is not recommended as the material settles in transit.

For sales appeal, you must keep the bags clean while bagging up. Have water and soap available so that you can wash your hands frequently to avoid getting the bags dirty. To reduce the dust hazard, wear a face mask and set up the sieve/chute to the leeward side of the pile of charcoal, so the dust is blown away from you.

For efficient grading and bagging use a device which incorporates a sieve for removing dust and a chute for filling the sacks. A sieve chute of the type shown (Hollingdale, A.C., Krishnan, R and Robinson A. P., 1999)

is fairly simple to construct, and should allow at least 60 bags an hour to be filled by two people. For stability, the lower end of the chute can be supported on the edge of the kiln ring, with the dust then falling back into the ring for collection as required.

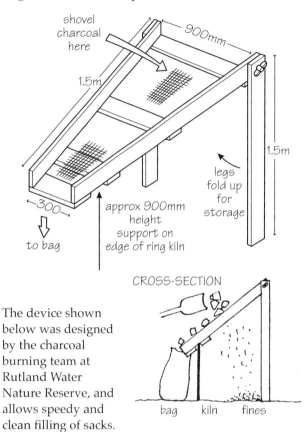

The device shown below was designed by the charcoal burning team at Rutland Water Nature Reserve, and allows speedy and clean filling of sacks. A similar device could be made up by a blacksmith or light engineering firm.

The bags are sealed by stapling or by using a stitching machine which stitches a tape to close the top of the bag.

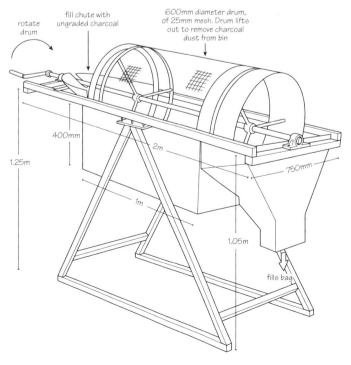

Marketing barbecue charcoal

Timing is important where the main product is barbecue charcoal, as sales are strongly related to season, and affected by weather. Nearly all sales are in the summer, with peaks during school holidays, bank holidays and in fine weather. The main outlets for small operators are petrol stations, caravan and camping parks and garden centres. Most outlets have limited storage space and will not want to hold large stocks. It's therefore important for the producer to be able to maintain regular deliveries throughout the summer, with enough capacity to take advantage of any heat waves. This in turn must be closely linked to the production capacity, bearing in mind the period of up to a year required for drying the wood.

The size of bag or packaging type can vary, and marketing should be directed at particular uses and outlets. Campers and holidaymakers will normally prefer small bags or 'throwaway' barbecues in foil trays. Various forms of packaging are used, including those with bags which are designed to be lit, to avoid the user having to handle the charcoal. Restaurants, cafes, pubs, hotels, activity centres and other regular users will use large sacks, economically packaged.

For sales appeal and to compete with imported charcoal, the importance of local production, reduced transport, links with beneficial woodland management and other values need to be highlighted. Bags may be available through local coppice groups or kiln suppliers. Through personal and community links, local publicity and consistently good production and delivery, a strong local market can be developed.

VAT at the current rate (17.5% in 2001) is chargeable on all fuel charcoal by the charcoal maker to all wholesalers, retail outlets or to other charcoal makers. Charcoal for fuel sold directly by the charcoal maker to the final consumer is charged at the current fuel rate (5% in 2001).

Fines

Charcoal fines are the dust produced from charcoal burning. Fines are used as a soil conditioner and an additive to compost, to raise the pH and keep the compost 'sweet'. A mixture of 10% charcoal to 90% composted wood chips makes a good mulch or compost.

Commercial operators can convert fines to charcoal brickettes, but this can only be done in specialist kilns. Fines are also used in charcoal filters. Small operators would probably need to combine together in order to produce a marketable quantity for these uses.

Fines or dust, particularly of sycamore, may find a lucrative market with herbal apothecaries.

Artists' charcoal

Straight thin stems of spindle, willow, oak, grape vine and other species can be converted to artists' charcoal by placing the stems in a biscuit tin, and then firing it during a normal burn. Spindle makes the best artists' charcoal, but willow is normally used because it is readily available in the required stem form. Provided a market can be found, this can be one of the most profitable charcoal products.

Jewellers

Some jewellers use blocks of charcoal as a heat source for metalworking.

SMALL-SCALE CHARCOAL BURNING

Small amounts of charcoal can easily be made in a DIY kiln made from a 45 gallon or similar size steel drum, in good condition without holes. Drums should be obtainable from farmers or small industrial units, but check for any contents which may be toxic.

Drum kilns are useful for small operations, or for use in woodlands with poor access, or those that lack suitable sites for larger kilns.

Small diameter branches of fast-burning species will give the best results. Large pieces or slow-burning hardwoods will not reach a sufficiently high temperature and will only be partly carbonised. Willow, sycamore, birch or softwoods are suitable.

Wood should be 50-100mm (2-4") diameter, and 300-360mm (12-14") long, air dried for at least six months. Fairly even-sized pieces of the same species will give the best results.

Loading and burning time should be about 3-4 hours, with about 12 hours' cooling required.

Although the volume of wood converted in a drum is much smaller than in a ring kiln, the dangers are similar. Note carefully the safety precautions above (p138). Take great care to avoid injury from sudden flames or 'flare outs' which may occur as the volatiles are driven out during the burning or 'white smoke' phase. Only one person at a time should be required to control the process, with assistants and onlookers keeping at least 2m clear of the drum.

Making a drum kiln

1. Remove the screw cap from the top. Wearing safety goggles, use a cold chisel to make three more holes, 50mm (2") in diameter. These will form the vents.

2. Turn the drum over and cut out the base, about 15mm (¹/₂″) from the rim. Keep the base to form a lid. Knock up the cut edge to form a lip around the rim.

3. Place the drum, open end up, on three bricks. This permits air flow to the vents.

4. Place paper, kindling and brown ends into the base of the drum and light.

5. Once the flames from the kindling have died down and the brown ends are alight, gently drop the prepared wood onto the fire, taking care to avoid any flames. Using the larger pieces first, fill randomly to the top with wood.

6. When the wood is burning well, use a long-handled shovel to pile sand or soil around the base to reduce air entry, leaving a gap of about 100mm (4″). Place the lid on top, propping it on one side to leave a small gap for smoke to escape.

7. Thick, white, damp smoke will be emitted, from the moisture driven out of the wood. When this slows, knock the side of the drum to settle the contents. A further emission of white smoke will result.

8. Depending on the dryness of the wood and other factors, after between 2-4 hours the dense white smoke should change to thin blue smoke. This change indicates that the wood has converted to charcoal and that the charcoal is starting to burn. Block the air gap at the base with sand and close the lid to stop the burn. Add turves, soil or sand to block any gaps around the rim.

9. Leave to cool for about 12 hours. Carefully tip the drum over onto a plastic sheet or similar, and shovel the charcoal into bags or other containers.

Note that other methods can be used to convert charcoal in a drum, which involve either upending the drum or rolling it over during the burning process. There are extra hazards involved in doing this, and these methods are not recommended.

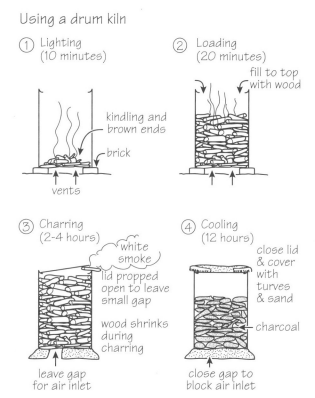

Using a drum kiln

① Lighting (10 minutes)
② Loading (20 minutes)
③ Charring (2-4 hours)
④ Cooling (12 hours)

(Times are approximate and non-cumulative)

12 Woodland habitats

Woodland encompasses a rich and diverse range of habitats for plants and animals, some of which require management for their creation and maintenance.

Woodland is composed of the full range of plant types including trees and shrubs, climbers, perennial herbs, bulbs, grasses, sedges, mosses and lichens. No other habitat contains such a diverse range of plants. Nearly every plant species has its own invertebrate fauna which feeds on it more or less exclusively. Other animals depend on these invertebrates, building the complex web of organisms which make up the woodland community. Deadwood supports a huge range of invertebrates and other organisms.

In its natural state woodland is very varied. Old and dying trees make up a large component of the woodland, with fallen trees creating gaps where regeneration occurs. Glades and other open spaces are maintained by grazing animals, and areas which are too wet, steep or rocky for tree growth create further diverse habitats. From earliest times (p1) domestic animals have been grazed in woodlands, replacing the wild grazing animals and maintaining the wood-pasture habitat. In managed woodlands where animals are excluded, rides, tracks and verges can be mown to mimic the glades created by grazing animals. The importance of grazing animals has been recognised and some areas are now reintroducing cattle or ponies as grazers in old wood-pastures. Deer and rabbits can be important in maintaining open areas, but have a damaging effect on regeneration. In coppice woodland, artificial variety produced by management partly compensates for the loss of structural variation in wildwood, but with a loss of deadwood habitats.

New woodlands can be designed and planted to encourage diversity of habitats and diversity of plant and animal species. Plantations, or woodlands suffering from neglect can be improved by increasing their range of habitats, by widening rides, creating and clearing glades, creating ponds and other management work.

Any changes though to existing woodland must be done with caution, as diversification nearly always requires clearance of woody growth, which itself will have wildlife value. Clearance should only be done if the habitat created is likely to be of higher value, or will have significant advantages for amenity or recreation. Site surveys should be undertaken to ensure that valuable habitats are not lost. Recording of invertebrates is difficult and specialised, but a single visit on a sunny day when the hawthorn is in flower should give a good indication of the wood's value (Kirby, 1992).

Invertebrates in particular move slowly and are very site specific. Woods with a long history are often isolated, and if the invertebrate habitat is lost, for example by the loss of deadwood or old trees, the chances of recolonisation are small. Management of old woodland should be done only with great caution.

Glades, rides and woodland edges

Grassy clearings, glades and woodland edges are amongst the most important habitats for invertebrates and birds associated with woodland. Many of these 'woodland' species cannot survive the shade of a closed canopy, but require the sunlight, warmth and nectar-bearing plants of sunny woodland edges. Many invertebrates, whose larvae develop in leaf litter, soil and dead wood, in their adult stage require nectar from sun-loving plants.

With the exception of the shade-loving green-veined white and speckled wood, nearly all butterflies breed only in sunny, sheltered rides and glades. These habitats provide the specific plants for egg-laying and larval development, as well as nectar sources for the adult butterflies. Many moth species breed on tree and shrub species, notably sallow and aspen, so the shrubby borders of rides are very important.

Many bird species are adapted to the woodland edge habitat, and to the type of growth provided by young plantations and young to middle age coppice. Managing the margins of rides and open spaces to increase this type of habitat will benefit birds.

The fauna and flora of woodland rides and spaces has in some places survived better in woodlands converted to commercial forestry than in unmanaged woods, because of the importance of maintaining rides for management purposes. Neglected coppices have too much shade to be of value for most invertebrates or birds. The creation and maintenance of open space are often the most important management operations to benefit invertebrates and other fauna in former coppice woodland.

Permanent open space in woodland includes grassy clearings, rides or tracks, some of which may be very ancient. Temporary open space is created in coppiced woodlands when a coupe is newly cut, or along rides or other open spaces where areas are cleared in rotation. Permanent and temporary open space support a different assemblage of flora and fauna.

Permanent open space supports plant and animal species adapted to open, sunny conditions, some of which may also occur in habitats other than woodland glades. Other plant and animal species rely on the interface between grassland and woodland, and are mainly confined to woods and wood edges. The flora of woodland glades and rides depends on periodic cutting and grazing, both to control the more competitive species of grasses, herbs and shrubs, and to provide ground disturbance which encourages the germination of seeds.

Temporary open space, as in newly cut coppice coupes, supports plants and animals adapted to take advantage of the sudden increase in light and space after cutting.

When planning new woodlands, sufficient area must be left unplanted and then managed to maintain open space. Rides and tracks are essential for management and must be planned from the outset. It is much more difficult to create rides or glades by clearance of trees at some future date, both because of the work of removing the trees, but also because the removal of trees will cause instability in adjacent trees which are suddenly exposed to the wind. Ground flora will also be more difficult to establish.

To maintain sunny conditions, rides and glades need to be at least 1.5 times as wide as the height of the surrounding trees. This width can include margins of broadleaved shrubs and scrub which do not shade the rest of the ride. Rides and open spaces which appear generously proportioned in newly planted woodlands will shrink as they become shaded as the woodland matures. In general it's easier and more effective to create and maintain fewer larger spaces, rather than a complicated network of smaller open spaces or narrow rides.

The Woodland Grant Scheme (p185) for new woodland planting includes up to 20% open space, which is a minimum at which to aim when planning new woodland. For areas not subject to the grant scheme, up to 50% open space can be left unplanted to create a type of parkland or wood-pasture, attractive for recreation and wildlife. However, management of the open space must be planned from the outset, as this will be a continuing requirement which will be more expensive in time, labour and equipment than the management of the wooded areas.

Open areas must be maintained by regular mowing or grazing. Mowing is expensive, and cuttings must be removed to prevent enrichment and to allow the more interesting flowering herbs to flourish. Mowing can be carefully timed, but it is non-selective, resulting in less interesting plant communities than those created by grazing. Grazing by wild or domestic animals requires protecting the trees by fencing or individual protection. Domestic animals need looking after. Ancient or existing wood-pasture landscapes may be relatively 'low maintenance', but they are costly and difficult to establish. There is always a conflict, as the level of grazing which promotes maximum floristic diversity has adverse effects on woodland regeneration.

GLADES

Existing glades and other open spaces in mature woodland are relatively stable habitats, and should be maintained as such. In some areas the grassy nature of the habitat is kept free of tree seedlings or scrub growth by the grazing of deer, rabbits, cattle or ponies. If the grazing pressure decreases for any reason, mowing may be necessary to prevent shrinkage of the open space. It is not a good idea to plant trees in existing grassy

1.5 x h minimum

clearings, which may have taken decades to develop their specialised flora and fauna.

Where glades have to be mown, cuttings should be removed from the site to prevent them smothering desirable ground flora or causing nutrient enrichment. Various machines are available that are suitable for woodland sites, which may have narrow access, rough or soft ground conditions. These machines include mini-balers, and cut-and-collect machines. Mini-balers are either pedestrian operated machines, or pulled by mini-tractors. Cut-and-collect machines are powered by a tractor and have a hopper for collection of the cut material. For further details see *Practical Solutions Handbook*, English Nature (2001).

Various mowing regimes can be used according to the type of grassy sward, and to encourage flowering at certain times of year, mainly for the benefit of invertebrates (see p75).

RIDES AND TRACKS

A ride is a permanent unsurfaced route within a woodland, which may be used for access, extraction of timber, demarcation and shooting. In commercial

woodlands, rides are normally classified as main rides, 6-9m (20-30') wide, or secondary rides, 3-5m (10-16') wide. Forest roads are surfaced with gravel or tarmac for use by heavy machinery, with wide verges to avoid tree growth overhanging the road and obstructing machinery, giving a total width between the forest trees of 20-30m (65-100').

Old, established rides which have a stable grassy vegetation, maintained by deer or rabbits, should normally be left as they are. Areas of bare ground, including sunny dry areas and damp shady muddy ground can be important for invertebrates.

Old rides which have become overgrown with shrubs or trees will normally benefit from clearance, both to bring them back into use, and to increase their value as a habitat. Where rides remain only as a route on a map or from some indication on the ground, the potential loss of woodland habitat may make clearance inadvisable.

Management of rides

In commercial coniferous woodlands also managed for wildlife and amenity, priority is being given to thinning and felling the zones along roads and other access routes, which 'opens up' the forest for recreation. Oppressive

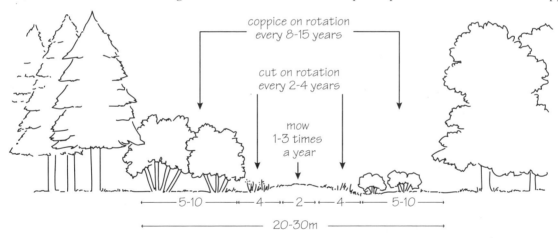

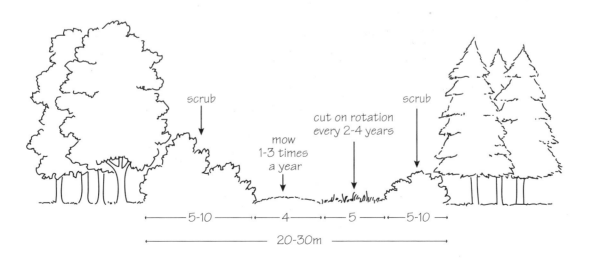

shaded tracks through coniferous woodland are not attractive for recreation in Britain where sunshine is valued, and shade is rarely sought. Invertebrates, birds and other wildlife also seek out the sunny sheltered woodland edges where there is shelter, warmth and food. These felled areas can then either be left unplanted and mown, or planted with the smaller species of native trees and shrubs to create woodland edges attractive for wildlife and amenity.

In woods of mainly broadleaved species, clearance and ride widening may involve losses of mature trees. However, this can be balanced by the introduction of coppicing regimes, where possible from the existing stumps, which will provide valuable alternative habitats, whilst at the same time reducing shading of the ride. Sufficient width needs to be cleared to create an area large enough to support strong coppice growth, which itself will be poor if heavily shaded. A strip 5-10m (16-32') wide is the minimum, with wider strips or blocks of 10-20m (32-65') width preferable. Follow normal coppicing procedure (chapter 9).

Various mowing regimes can be used, according to local conditions and the type of vegetation community which you wish to create. The requirement for management must be planned for at the outset, because in the absence of grazing, at least annual mowing will be required to maintain open, grassy habitats.

The diagrams on the previous page indicate various regimes which can be used for the management of rides. An overall ride width of 20-30m (65-100') is suggested,

including grass, scrub and coppice zones, to retain sunny conditions where surrounded by mature woodland. The lower diagram is a simpler regime, with no coppicing required. Scrub of bramble, shrubs and small trees can be self-maintaining, but any potentially large trees which grow up through the scrub should be cut down to maintain the open conditions. Rides can be wider or narrower as circumstances permit. In Britain (excluding the far north), rides which run east-west receive more summer sunshine than rides which run north-south.

To provide visual variation, and to avoid wind-tunnel effects in long straight rides, the shrubby margins can be varied, or mature trees retained, to create a varied edge. Retain any sheltering growth at entrances to rides, or rises or other points where the wind is funnelled. This growth is important in sheltering the ride and the woodland within. Once removed, it may also be difficult to re-establish woody growth at particular locations exposed to the wind.

In small areas of woodland, the ride edge zone will be limited to 5m width or less. Make the most of sunny, sheltered aspects, points where rides meet or areas where ground conditions prevent tree growth.

Bare ground on sunny, south facing slopes are valuable basking areas for reptiles, and can be created by removing the soil at suitable points, or by frequent cultivation to maintain bare soil. Where natural sites already exist, or where rubble, gravel or other inert material has created suitable conditions, these should be maintained by removing encroaching vegetation as necessary.

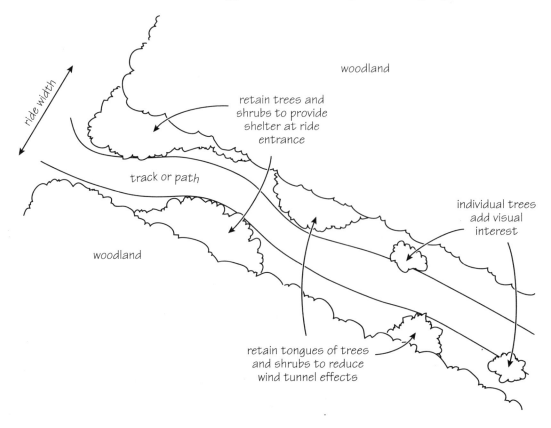

ride width

woodland

retain trees and shrubs to provide shelter at ride entrance

track or path

woodland

individual trees add visual interest

retain tongues of trees and shrubs to reduce wind tunnel effects

For information on mowing regimes for glades and rides see page 75. With time, some stability should develop which makes the system partly or wholly self maintaining. Grazing by rabbits or deer, and frequent trampling by walkers, will keep grass short. Established bramble patches and other shrubby growth can be remarkably consistent in height and width over many years if their spread is checked by grazing.

For further details see *Managing Rides, Roadsides and Edge Habitats in Lowland Forests* (Forestry Commission, 2000).

Veteran trees

Britain, along with Spain and Greece, has one of the highest populations of veteran trees in Europe. Veteran trees are valuable for many reasons:

- They support a rich invertebrate fauna, both of general and specialist species. The nooks and crevices provide nesting sites for birds and small mammals.

- They support a rich flora of lichens and mosses, both of general and specialist species.

- Veteran trees represent a gene pool which may link back to the trees of the wildwood.

- They are living remnants of past land use and management.

- Many veteran trees are remarkable and beautiful.

Veteran trees can be found in many places, and not only in ancient woodlands. Boundary banks, old hedgerows, river banks, churchyards, wooded commons and parkland, including urban parks, are sites where veteran trees can be found. Continuity of ownership is often a significant factor, as new owners tend to want to make changes which may include removal of old trees.

Assessing value and age

A rough rule of thumb can be adopted to assess the value of a tree, for example an oak, in relation to size:

- Trees with a diameter at breast height of more than 1.0m (girth 3.2m) are potentially interesting.

- Trees with a diameter of more than 1.5m (girth 4.7m) are valuable in terms of conservation.

- Trees with a diameter of more than 2.0m (girth 6.25m) are truly ancient.

Absolute age is not necessarily a good indicator of ancient status, as different species have different life spans. Thus willow and birch are short lived and specimens over 100 years old are valuable, whereas beech and oak only start to mature at 200 years. Yew is the most long-lived native tree.

Assessing the age of a veteran tree is not easy. Core samples can be taken, but as many veterans are partly hollow or rotten, this will not tell the whole story. Coring also damages the tree. Counting the rings on major branches, either fallen or being removed as part of essential management work, can give an estimate, although the branch may have been produced at a time after the original growth of the tree.

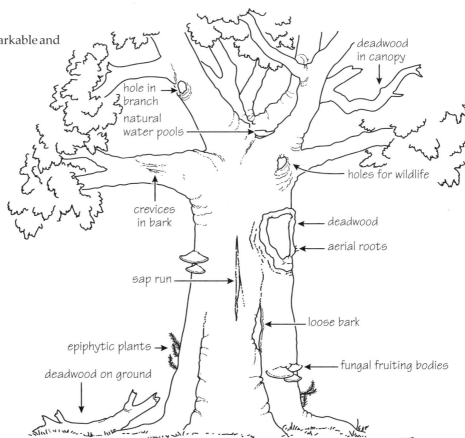

A rule of thumb is that 25mm (1") of girth at breast height is equivalent to one year's growth for a free standing tree, and 13mm ($^1/_2$") of girth at breast height is equivalent to one year's growth for a tree in woodland. This can be applied to uncut trees such as oak in middle age, but is of limited value for older trees. Trees that have been pollarded or undergone natural crown loss are impossible to age by girth, because these factors will have influenced girth increment.

Threats to veteran trees

- Veteran trees may be cut back or removed altogether where there are worries about safety or tidiness. Old hollow trees with reduced crowns are in fact often safer than mature ones with a full crown.

- Compaction from car parking or trampling around the tree can damage the root system.

- Inappropriate management such as filling cavities with concrete, or unskilled tree surgery. Pulling away ivy, removing dead wood and other 'tidying up' is misdirected management.

- Changes in the water table can cause stress to the tree.

- Changes in the surrounding vegetation. Lack of grazing or new planting can cause the veteran to become shaded by other tree growth. Conversely, opening up a previously shaded veteran by removal of surrounding trees can also be damaging.

- Many veteran trees were pollarded in the past, and if this management lapses, the tree is more likely to become unsafe and require felling.

- As the number of veteran trees reduces, the remainder become more isolated, and the ability of organisms to spread to other veterans is therefore lessened.

Management of veteran trees

The general principle is that veteran trees are identified, recorded and checked at regular intervals. Active management should only be carried out if necessary for public safety, or where the threats identified above require action to be taken. Veteran trees are exceptionally hazardous to work on, and pollarding, removal of overhanging branches or other practical work should only be undertaken by trained and experienced operators.

When assessing a veteran tree, both the individual tree and its surroundings need consideration. Trees are individuals, and every tree needs looking at individually. A management plan will be needed which involves assessing the site, deciding on priorities, implementation, monitoring and review.

For full details see *Veteran Trees: A guide to good management* (Read, Helen, 2000).

Deadwood

Rotting wood, both on and off the tree, is a very important habitat for invertebrates. The information below refers to fallen deadwood.

Clearing up and removing or burning rotting timber is an act of vandalism, which in a single act can destroy an important invertebrate habitat. The general rule is that fallen, rotting wood should be left where it is. Large fallen trunks and branches are particularly valuable, and should never be rolled over, chopped up or otherwise disturbed. This can easily happen, either by misguided 'tidying up', or as thoughtless destruction by children for example.

Large dead or dying branches on trees should not be removed unless they are a danger to the public.

Old, rotting wood should always be left where it is, unless you have to move it, for example, to clear a path. In that case, move it carefully the smallest distance, and leave it under similar conditions of light and shade, the same way up, and with the same orientation.

Newly cut wood

Thinning, coppicing or clearance work in woodlands produces a large volume of cut material. For commercial operations, much of this material will be removed from the wood. Where management is mainly for conservation or amenity, commercial use of the cut material may not be feasible. In this case, larger cut material is best left where it falls. Sned off the smaller side and top branches.

Scattered, newly cut coppice poles and thinnings look untidy, and the temptation is to stack them in a neat pile. This should only be done if the wood is going to be removed and reused. Cut poles, branches and trunks are of much greater value to invertebrates if scattered through the wood, rather than piled up, although piles do have some value. Scattered wood not only gives more useful habitat per volume of wood, but it is also less likely to be disturbed in the future, as it will not be attractive to vandals or firewood gatherers. A few piles of cut wood at the edge of a sunny ride or glade is acceptable. If the stacks are likely to get disturbed, either by deliberate or thoughtless action, some old stock netting or similar covering the stack and buried around the base should prove a deterrent. Log habitat piles should be no bigger than about 1m (3') high by 2-3m (6-10') long.

Where stacked wood is going to be removed, it's best stacked somewhere where it will not attract invertebrates or other animals, or the habitat will be destroyed when the stack is taken apart and moved. Preferably stack outside the wood, in a barn or open-sided shelter, or partly cover the stack with plastic to reduce the entry of invertebrates.

Brushwood

The smaller branches and twiggy growth produced from felling and clearing takes up a lot of space. The option of burning versus other methods is discussed on page 86. Cut material is useful for dead hedging (p108) access barriers, or it can be bundled or chipped for uses outside the wood (p88). 'Habitat piles' of twiggy material, left in shady conditions in the wood, are of little value for wildlife. Such material further reduces light reaching the woodland floor, so damaging the woodland flora, and is a nuisance for access and management. Piles of brash left in open spaces can be a quick way of producing a scrub or woodland edge type habitat, with bramble and other plants rapidly disguising the brash and providing a habitat for birds, small mammals and other creatures. This can normally only 'use up' a small proportion of the total brushwood produced. For invertebrates,

brushwood is of greater value if bundled tightly, rather than in a loose pile, as well as taking up less space. The close packing provides relatively constant moist conditions in the centre of the bundles. Tie the material as for fascines (p111), and stack the bundles in dappled shade.

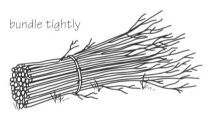

bundle tightly

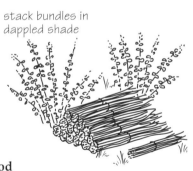

stack bundles in dappled shade

Creating deadwood habitats

In addition to the procedures above for cut material, other measures can be taken to increase the amount of deadwood in a woodland.

In commercial woodlands, thinning operations favour the straightest and healthiest trees, and remove those that are misshapen or damaged. In non-commercial woodlands, it's possible instead to keep trees which have splits, sap runs, fungal growth or other signs which indicate premature rotting. Jagged stumps, splits and holes in the trunks of trees are potentially very useful, and should not be treated or tidied up. One can even go so far as to damage an otherwise healthy tree, although this is best done without publicity!

Newly felled timber can also be brought in from elsewhere, into an area of new woodland. Trunks of trees or large branches from thinning operations, storm damage or other sources can be transported to the wood, and placed on the ground in dappled shade where they are unlikely to be disturbed. Trunks can also be set upright, to provide standing deadwood habitat. This should only be done if you have the skills and equipment to handle and position the timber. Choose a location where the dead tree will not be a danger to the public in following years as it rots. Set it upright in a deep hole, secured by wire guys as necessary.

Ponds, wetlands and streams

With the loss of many ponds and wetlands through drainage and infilling for agriculture and development, those remaining within wooded areas have become increasingly important.

Many lowland broadleaved woods are damp places, with seasonally or permanently waterlogged ground often being the reason that the woodland has survived in that particular location, and not been cleared for agriculture. The sheltering effect of trees keeps woodland soils wetter than similar soils in open conditions. Drainage within woodland may be impeded by fallen trees and branches, creating small temporary pools. The holes left by uprooted trees create small pools. As well as natural ponds, many woods contain artificial ponds such as hammer ponds, flooded mineral workings, old charcoal pits and other man-made features.

PONDS AND WETLANDS

Woodland ponds, temporary pools and damp ground are important for many invertebrates and amphibians, as well as for bats and other creatures. They may also contain a specialised flora.

Some ponds are very stable, changing little over long periods of time. Other ponds tend to silt up with the accumulation of marginal vegetation, decaying organic matter and soil that washes into the pond. As long as they are not polluted, all ponds in all stages have ecological value, and intervention is not necessary. Each stage, from open water, through silted pond, muddy hollow to dry ground will have wildlife interest. It may be better to create several ponds, at different stages in the succession, than to try to intervene and keep one pond at a particular stage in the succession.

Intervention in the natural development of a pond should only take place if the pond will otherwise be lost, and cannot be replaced by creating a new pond nearby. If intervention is necessary, no more than one quarter of the marginal vegetation, sediment or trees should be removed in a five year period.

Ponds which have not been disturbed for 50 years or more will contain sediments which can give important insights into past vegetation and land management. They may also contain interesting artefacts which have been preserved in the anaerobic conditions. Old sluices, artificial linings and other parts of the pond's structure are of archaeological interest, and should not be disturbed. Contact the local authority archaeologist for advice before disturbing an old pond. See *The Pond Book* (1999) for further details on the historical value of ponds.

Note the following:

- Sunny ponds and other wetland areas support a more diverse flora and fauna than similar areas under shade, but this does not mean that shaded ponds are valueless. Shady ponds can support populations of specialised invertebrates and other creatures, which occur nowhere else.

- Ponds which are shaded by mature or veteran trees have been shaded for a century or more, and represent a stable habitat which should not be altered by clearance or felling. Ponds which are shaded by young growth are more likely to benefit from some clearance.

- Branches and other rotting wood in ponds and wet ground are substrates for algae and fungi, and provide egg-laying sites for dragonflies and food for aquatic fly and beetle larvae. Rotting willow exudes tannins into the water which help prevent algal blooms, acting in the same way as barley straw. Tidying-up operations may therefore be misguided.

- Temporary pools which dry out in summer are a valuable habitat for certain invertebrates, and should not be altered in an attempt to make them hold water all year. Ruts created by vehicles and ground trampled or 'poached' by stock can create small pools of stagnant water which are valuable to some invertebrates.

- Shallow pools, less than 1m (3') deep, are much more valuable for wildlife than deeper pools. For invertebrates and amphibians, the important part of any pond is the shallow margins. Deep open water which does not become overgrown with plants by midsummer is the least valuable. Ponds which appear 'choked' with vegetation by mid summer are not necessarily so.

- Muddy pond margins and bare shingle are important habitats for invertebrates, and should not necessarily be vegetated. Bare ground at pond edges can usefully be maintained by trampling of people or animals,

although excessive trampling all around the pond may be destructive.

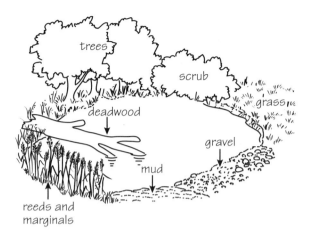

- Where ponds fed by ditches tend to rapidly silt up with runoff from nearby fields or roads, then a silt trap is worth constructing to allow easy removal of the silt before it reaches the pond. This will also reduce nutrient enrichment from agricultural run-off, which is damaging to pond habitats.

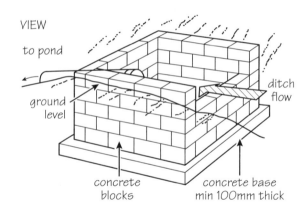

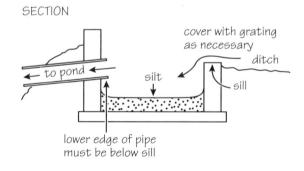

- As an alternative to the silt trap shown above, a simple feeder pond can be dug, in which the water collects before it flows into the pond. This feeder pond can then be cleaned as necessary by hand or digger to remove the trapped silt. Where the runoff is polluted, a balancing pond or reedbed can be constructed and planted with common reed (*Phragmites communis*). This will help absorb and lock up any pollutants, and provide an unpolluted water supply to the wildlife pond. See *Waterways and Wetlands* (BTCV, 1997) for further details.

- Before clearing growth to reduce shading of a pond, assess the value of the species involved. Alder and willow, which thrive around ponds and in other damp locations are especially valuable for the many organisms they support, and should normally not be removed.

- The surrounds of many ponds have been altered in the past by the planting of exotic species such as bamboo and rhododendron. Other exotic species may have spread unintentionally, including the very invasive Japanese knotweed. Clearance of these species is not easy as they all regrow strongly from the stumps or roots. See page 92 for advice on control.

- When planning clearance, consider the effect of the sun and wind. Concentrate any clearance on the south side, where it will have most effect in increasing light to the pond. Don't remove growth which acts as a shelter from prevailing winds.

- Where removal of marginal vegetation and silt is necessary, do the work in September or October to minimise adverse effects on pond wildlife. Marginal vegetation can either be removed in sections on an annual or longer rotation, or by clearing from the 'invading front'. On larger ponds both approaches can be used in different parts of the same pond.

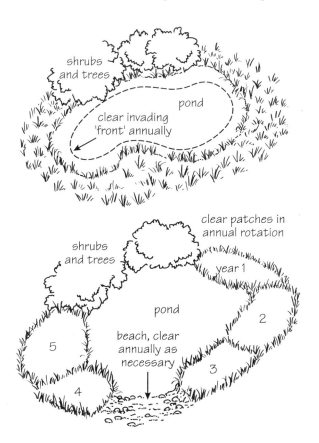

- Deposit the spoil where it can't wash back into the pond, and where it will not smother valuable ground flora. If necessary remove it from the site.

SPRINGS AND STREAMS

Natural springs and seepages occur as a result of geology and landform, and as such may have remained unaltered for thousands of years. Those in woodlands at a distance from habitation or remnants of industrial activity are likely to be the least affected by human activity. The invertebrate fauna associated with these springs and pools may be very specialised, and no attempt should be made to alter the flow by damming or digging.

Streams which run through shady woodland have constant cool conditions, and can support a different fauna from those which run through open ground, where water temperatures will fluctuate. Like ponds, it is therefore not necessary to clear away all shading vegetation, but to leave a variety of streamside habitats. Where new woodland is being created in an area which includes a stream or pond, the margins should be left unplanted, so that conditions in the water and along its margins are changed as little as possible by the new woodland.

Birdboxes and other nest sites

Nestboxes and other artificial homes for birds can be very important for nesting success, especially in habitats where food is plentiful but nesting sites are scarce. Such habitats may include:

- Managed woodlands which have an absence of mature trees, deadwood and undergrowth.

- Newly planted or young woodlands, which have no large or mature trees, or deadwood.

- Gardens, parks and urban areas, where requirements for safety, neatness and other qualities result in a lack of nesting sites.

For comprehensive details on nestboxes and other structures for a wide range of bird species see Du Feu (1993), or for details on structures for birds of prey see Dewar and Shawyer (1996). A wide range of nestboxes for birds, invertebrates and mammals, together with anti-predator devices and other accessories are available from Jacobi Jayne & Company (p189).

Habitat improvement, including retention of old trees for nesting sites and planting new trees and shrubs to form thickets will provide nesting sites. Good woodland edge habitats, ponds and grassy areas provide the insect life on which many birds, bats and other creatures depend.

Boxes, platforms, bundles of brush, artificial cavities and other structures can be used to encourage birds to roost and nest. All sorts of materials and designs can be used, as long as they fulfil the following criteria:

- Nestboxes and other structures must be attractive to nesting birds, and be designed and sited so that a brood of young birds can be successfully raised. Boxes which are flimsy, badly sited or not securely attached may attract birds to nest, only to result in failure. Boxes of thin material such as plastic, thin wood or metal will not provide sufficient insulation.

- Nestboxes must be safe from predators, including other birds, mammals and people. Various design details and devices (p158) can be used to deter magpies, squirrels and other pests. Nestboxes which are hidden and/or difficult to reach are less likely to attract unwanted attention from people. A variety of nestboxes of different types in any one area may help deter predators, which may learn to recognise and raid a 'standard' design.

- Nestboxes and other structures should be simple and cheap to construct, and be easy to inspect and clean.

- Nestboxes must be of durable material, both to repay the effort put into construction and fixing, and because birds may take some years to accept and use them. Boxes may be used for roosting, even if they are not used for nesting.

MATERIALS AND DESIGNS

Wood

Wood for nestboxes should be over 15mm thick to provide sufficient insulation. Other dimensions are not critical, apart from the size of the entrance hole. Recovered materials including pallets, packing cases, floorboards and other scrap wood is suitable provided care is taken in dismantling pallets and removing nails as necessary. Softwood is easier to work, but hardwood will last much longer. Exterior plywood is suitable, but chipboard and other boards for internal use are not.

Basic woodworking tools are sufficient for construction purposes, with a 28mm drill bit useful for making entrance holes.

Note the following:

- Keep the wood grain vertical to help shed water quickly.

- Avoid exposed horizontal end grain.

- Fix the floor just above the lowest point of the side panels, so that water drips off the bottom rather than seeping round into the joint with the floor (see diagram).

- Unless there is a sufficiently wide crack between the floor and the sides, drill drainage holes in the floor to allow any moisture to drain out.

- Construct using galvanised nails or brass screws. Bright wire nails will quickly rust.

- Seal side joints with waterproof glue, to keep the box dry and free of draughts.

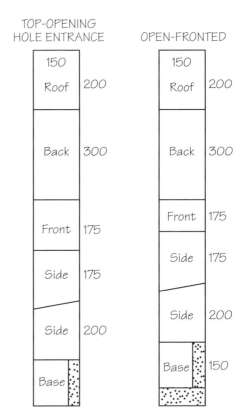

Planks 1200 x 150 x 15mm

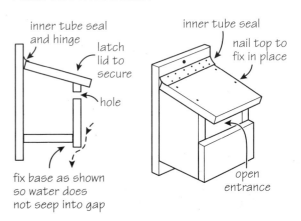

Table 12a: NESTBOXES

Species	Box size	Hole size mm	Filled	Open front	Fixing height	Woodland edge, park, garden	Clear felled or new coppice	Thicket or coppice	High forest	Over mature woodland	Coniferous
Marsh tit	S	25			Low				●	✓	
Willow tit	S	25	●		Low			●		●	✓
Crested tit	S	28	●		Medium					✓	✓
Coal tit	S	25			Low				●		✓
Blue tit	S	25			Medium	✓				●	
Great tit	M	28			Medium	✓		●			
Wren	VS	30		30mm slit	Low	●	●	●	●		
Robin	S			●	Low	●					
Tree sparrow	S/M	28			High	●			●	●	
Treecreeper	#1				Medium					●	
Nuthatch	M	32	●		Medium	●			●	●	
Spotted flycatcher	M			●	Medium	●			●		
Pied flycatcher	S/M	28			Medium	●			●	●	●
Green woodpecker	L	60	●		High	●			●	✓	
Greater spotted woodpecker	M	50	●		High	●			●	✓	
Lesser spotted woodpecker	M	32	●		Medium	●			●	✓	
Tawny owl	Chimney or VL	150 x 150			High				●	✓	
Long eared owl	Basket				High			●		●	✓
Nightjar	Scrape				Ground		●				●
Blackbird	Bundles				Low-high	●		●	●	●	●
Song thrush	Bundles				Low-med	●		●	●	●	

- Perches are not necessary on small or medium size boxes, up to 130 x 150mm base area. Nesting birds do not need perches, which will merely encourage predators.

- Hole entrance boxes must have a hinged or removable lid for inspection and cleaning. A simple hinge made of a piece of inner tube will waterproof the joint as well as allow easy opening. Brass hinges can also be used, but steel hinges will quickly rust solid. The lid should slope sufficiently to shed water, and can be further waterproofed with a layer of vinyl flooring or similar. A hook and eye or nail with piece of soft wire can be used to fasten the lid closed. Fully removable lids should have a lip all round to hold the lid in place.

- The lid or roof should have a generous overhang to prevent rain blowing into the entrance hole, and also to discourage predators.

- The outside of the box can be treated with wood preservative for increased durability, but leave the inside of the box untreated. Preservative is lethal to bats, who may use the box.

Sawdust and cement

Nestboxes of sawdust and cement ('woodcrete') have been commercially available for some years (p189), and make very durable and well insulated boxes which have a high rate of nesting success. As placing and fixing nestboxes can be awkward and time-consuming, investing in these very durable boxes can be worthwhile. Boxes for hanging from branches and other places are also available, and have the advantage of being very difficult for predators to reach.

Du Feu (1993) gives details on DIY methods of using sawdust and cement to make nesting boxes.

Filled boxes

Birds which excavate nesting holes, such as woodpeckers and willow tits, can be attracted with boxes filled with soft, inert material, such as expanded polystyrene, balsa wood, woodshavings or sawdust, which the birds will excavate. Boxes will need refilling after use, so a fresh nest can be excavated the following year.

Chimney boxes

Chimney boxes were originally designed for tawny owls, but may be used by other species. The box is made from 4 x 25mm thick planks, about 750mm long and 250mm wide, with a base of perforated zinc. A hatch near the base can be included for inspection of the nest. Fix the chimney above or underneath a branch as shown, at an angle of about 45°. Cover the floor with bark chippings.

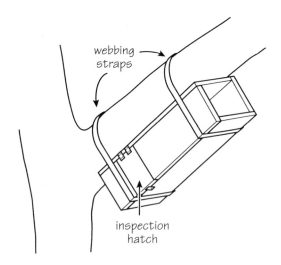

Basket

Long eared owls may nest in baskets fixed to the branches of trees in open woodlands, copses and hedgerows. Use an ordinary 450mm (18") diameter plastic-coated wire hanging flower basket. Weave willow wands or other pliable shoots to thicken the basket and place an upturned turf in the bottom, and then partly fill with twigs and dry leaves. Fix the basket in the cleft of a tree, using plastic cable-clips or tree-ties, loosely fastened to allow for growth.

Scrape

Nightjars nest on bare ground in a scrape, especially in sandy soil in woodland clearings and heathland with isolated trees. Clear a patch of vegetation on the north side of a large shrub to leave a bare patch about 1m in diameter. See page 87 for details of constructing 'doughnuts' of brash to encourage woodcocks.

SITING

- Site boxes so they are sheltered from prevailing wind, rain and strong sunlight, normally from facing north through to south-east. Avoid points where water runs down tree trunks.

- If possible angle tit boxes slightly as shown, to increase the shelter to the entrance.

- Apart from tree creeper boxes, nestboxes must be sited with a clear and convenient flight path into the box.

- See Table 12a for guide to height above ground for different species. Height above ground is generally less important than security from predators.

- The density of boxes depends on the type of habitat and the species involved. Generally start with a selection of boxes at fairly evenly spacing, and keep adding boxes until the occupancy rates indicate that lack of nest sites

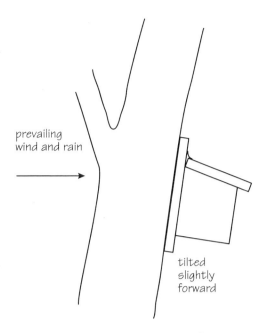

prevailing
wind and rain

tilted
slightly
forward

is no longer limiting population. 100% occupancy is unusual however, with 50% a good success rate. Du Feu (1993) suggests about ten assorted small boxes to the hectare, but denser spacings are possible for some species. Some species nest in colonies.

- Favoured sites are at the edges of woodlands, glades and rides, and other points where two habitats meet. Small copses, hedgerows and isolated trees are also suitable.

- Nestboxes can be put up at any time of year, as birds may use them for roosting as well as nesting, and it may be some time before the box is accepted for nesting. If boxes are not used after three or four years, take them down and re-site them.

FIXING

Boxes must be securely fastened to the support. Where boxes are to be inspected and cleaned annually, location and method of fixing should allow this. Where boxes are to be permanently fixed to living trees, the method must allow the tree to grow. Fixing to man-made structures avoids this problem, and such boxes are often less accessible to predators, but permission must be sought from the owner of the structure.

Safety

- Fixing, inspecting and cleaning nestboxes nearly always involves working from a ladder, which is potentially hazardous. Never work on your own. Preferably use an alloy ladder, with a splayed base for greater stability. If working within 10m of overhead lines, a wooden or non-conducting ladder must be used. Take great care in siting the ladder securely at the base and top, and ensure that a second person holds the ladder steady at all times.

- Take care when using hand tools at a height. Do as much as possible at ground level, for example knocking nails part-way through battens, to avoid any procedures which require using both hands when up a ladder.

- Large or heavy boxes and nesting structures should only be fitted by persons suitably trained to work aloft.

- A 3m long nest box hanging pole is available (p189), which allows nest boxes to be hung or removed without needing a ladder. Similar devices can be improvised. Operators are advised to wear helmets in case the work dislodges anything, or the box itself falls down.

Tying

Various methods of tying can be used to avoid the problems caused by nailing into trees.

- Using screws, securely attach a batten, preferably of hardwood, to the back of the box.

- Use a length of wire, thick polypropylene twine or thin rope, or bands cut from old inner tubes. Wire, twine and rope must be checked annually to make sure they are not strangling the tree. Old inner tubes will stretch, but must be checked annually and replaced if they show signs of perishing.

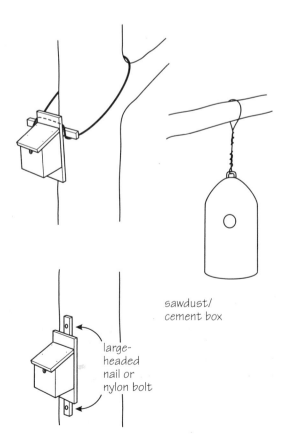

sawdust/
cement box

large-
headed
nail or
nylon bolt

- If the wire or twine is looped around the batten and loosely hung as shown, the box can be simply edged up a little each year to make allowance for expansion of the trunk.

Nailing

- Any nails or screws damage living trees, and should not be used on wood of commercial value.

- Steel screws or nails should never be used as they can cause damage or injury if the timber is cut with a chain saw at some time in the future. Steel screws or nails will quickly rust, making them difficult to remove.

- Screws, nails and pieces of wire can quickly get embedded as the tree grows, and will not be visible from the surface.

- Nails and screws can also be pushed out as the tree grows, causing the nestbox to fall.

- Nylon bolts, or copper, aluminium or brass nails can be used in trees which are not of commercial value, and will not cause damage or injury if the wood is cut with a chain saw at some future date.

- The safest method of securing is to first screw a hardwood batten to the back of the box, fixed either vertically or horizontally. Then attach the batten with large-headed non-steel nails. As the tree grows, the nails should move out with the batten rather than being pulled through.

- Alternatively, use a 100mm long x 15mm nylon bolt which is screwed halfway into the tree. Then using a hacksaw, cut off the head of the bolt. Hang the box on the bolt, and then secure it with a washer and nut. This can then be slackened each year as the tree grows.

- Larger boxes should be fastened to a backing board, which is fixed to the tree with a nylon bolt and a length of webbing. For method see Dewar and Shawyer (1996).

Hanging

Birds are not deterred from using boxes which are hanging freely from branches or other locations. These are also difficult for predators to reach, but may be vulnerable to interference by people as they are more obvious and easy to disturb than boxes which are attached to trunks. Hang the box on a length of galvanised wire securely attached to the box, and looped around a branch or similar and twisted to secure.

DETERRING PREDATORS

Predators of woodland nesting birds may include other birds, squirrels, rats, cats and people. Various methods can be used to deter them.

- Siting the box where it is not easily accessible to people.

- Covering the lid with a flexible overhanging piece of vinyl flooring or similar, so squirrels or other animals slide off if they try and approach from the lid. This also helps waterproof the box.

- Gorse or other thorny material stapled to the lid, and attached around the trunk above and below the box will deter cats, rats and squirrels.

- Hanging boxes (see above). A cone of stiff plastic, open end down, threaded on the wire above the box will be a further deterrent.

- Hexagonal mesh, 40mm mesh size, can be used to cover the front of open boxes to deter crows, jays, cats and squirrels, but not weasels. Alternatively, the smaller 31mm mesh can be used, depending on the species of bird the nestbox is designed for.

- Greater spotted woodpeckers may hammer through wooden boxes to take young birds, but may be deterred by covering the box in rubber sheeting.

CLEANING AND MAINTENANCE

- Boxes should be cleaned annually to remove any parasites which have built up. Don't remove old nests for at least 3 weeks after a brood has fledged, in case a second brood is raised.

- Discard old nesting material at some distance from the nestbox site. Wear a mask to avoid inhalation of fungal spores.

- Use a pyrethrum based insecticide to kill off fleas or other infestations if necessary.

- Place a layer of wood shavings, bark chippings or polystyrene packing chips in the base of large boxes. Do not use sawdust, which sets hard if it gets wet.

OTHER MANAGEMENT WORK

Work can be done to existing trees and shrubs to make them more attractive to nesting birds and bats. Great care must be taken when working from a ladder (p157). Any work which involves tree climbing must only be done by specialists.

Before doing any work, especially to existing holes or cavities, make sure you are not damaging a habitat which is already valuable, for example for invertebrates.

Use natural materials wherever possible, to be less conspicuous to predators. Bark, slabwood with bark attached, and old weathered timber is more suitable than new timber.

- Existing holes which are too open for bird nesting use can be partially boarded up, leaving a small hole at the top.

- In trees with soft wood such as willow or birch, small cavities can be made at points where branches have dropped, at pollards or other pruning cuts.

- Bark or slab wood can be attached at the side of the trunk to make a 'cavity' for treecreepers. Thick barked trees such as oak, alder, poplar and pine are preferred. A deep fork can be converted to a 'cavity' with sides and a roof of bark.

TREECREEPER CAVITY

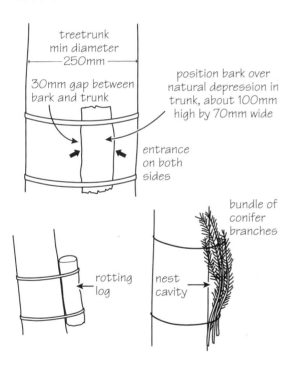

treetrunk min diameter 250mm

30mm gap between bark and trunk

position bark over natural depression in trunk, about 100mm high by 70mm wide

entrance on both sides

rotting log

nest cavity

bundle of conifer branches

- Rotting birch or willow logs can be tied to the trunks of living trees, and may attract willow tits or other birds which excavate cavities in rotting wood.

- Bundles or 'faggots' (p111) of twigs and small branches can be attached to the trunks of trees using twine or similar. Thorny material is particularly good against predators, but handle with care. Bundles of conifer branches, for example from discarded Christmas trees, make a useful early season nest site before shrubs are in full leaf.

- Pruning shrubs to create a mass of dense growth makes useful nest sites, as in a regularly trimmed hawthorn hedge or similar.

Mammals

BATS

All British bat species feed on insects associated with trees, and woodlands, copses and hedgerows are vital for their survival. All bats and their roosts, whether in use or not, are protected by law (p20).

Bats naturally roost in cavities and other sheltered places in mature, old and dying trees, with oak, ash, beech and Scot's pine preferred. Bats also roost in caves, and in buildings of many types. Bats in buildings face problems of disturbance, intolerance, and danger from toxic timber preservatives.

Habitat management for bats follows the general guidelines appropriate to woodland management for biodiversity:

- If planting, use native species, preferably of local provenance. These will support the insects on which bats feed.

- Retain dead, dying and mature trees, and those with holes, splits and broken branches. Do not 'tidy up' trees for appearance sake. If there is danger to the public, consider other measures, such as fencing off the tree, to allow it to be conserved. Legal requirements regarding bats (p20) must be considered.

- Retain or encourage ivy on trees, as this provides bat roosts and insect habitat.

- Provide and manage glades, rides and sheltered open spaces which will encourage insects.

- Encourage a diverse woodland edge habitat.

- Maintain or plant hedgerows, lines of trees and other woodland corridors. These are not only important in supporting the insects on which bats feed, but are also vital features which bats use to find their way around the countryside at night. A gap as short as 10m can deter bats, and cut off routes between roosts and feeding sites.

- Ditches, ponds and marshy ground are important bat feeding areas.

Management work

Woodland management work which may disturb bats

should be done in spring (March, April, May) or autumn (September, October, November), as this avoids the most vulnerable periods when bats are hibernating or non-flying young are present. The legal requirement not to disturb bats or their roosts must be followed (p20).

- Bat roosts are found in holes, cavities and splits in trees. Look out for dark staining on the tree around and below a hole, tiny scratch marks around the hole, or any squeaking or chittering sound from a hole, especially on a hot day or at dusk. Droppings, which crumble to a powder, may be found below holes.

- Watch for bats emerging after sundown, or returning at dawn.

- Retain any trees known to be used by bats, and those trees adjacent. Avoid removing maturing trees which may be suitable for bats in the near future.

- Avoid or minimise tree surgery work which may adversely affect bats.

- Seek specialist advice from your local bat group (contact English Nature or the local Wildlife Trust for details).

Table 12b: A BAT'S YEAR

January	Bats hibernating, individually or in small groups
February	
March	Bats occasionally wake. Hungry and active in fine weather, torpid in bad weather. They may move roost sites.
April	
May	
June	Females in large maternity groups. The young are born, and are suckled for 6 weeks. The mothers leave the roost first, followed by young some days later.
July	
August	
September	Mating takes place, and fat is accumulated in the body for hibernation. Bats look for good winter sites, and gradually become torpid for longer periods.
October	
November	
December	Hibernating

(from *Bats and trees*, The Bat Conservation Trust, 2000)

Bat boxes

Bat boxes cannot replace natural roosts, but they can be an important addition in habitats where suitable roosts are scarce.

- Bat boxes should be made of preservative-free, rough sawn, and preferably weathered timber, at least 25mm thick. Concrete/sawdust boxes are also suitable.

- Site boxes close to a continuous linear woodland feature such as a line of trees, hedgerow or woodland edge, which bats use for feeding and navigation.

- Boxes should be firmly attached (p157) as high as practicable in trees or on buildings or other structures. On buildings, fix the boxes under the eaves to be safe from cats and other predators.

- Site boxes where they are sheltered from wind, and in the sun for part of the day. Ideally put up three or more at each site, facing from south east through to south west, providing a range of temperature conditions.

- It may be several years before bat boxes are used. Never open a box, but look for droppings, urine staining and other signs of occupation. Avoid any disturbance between June and mid-August, when bats are giving birth and lactating.

Use the cutting pattern shown, and fix together with waterproof glue and screws. Secure the lid with screws, so that it can be removed by a licensed bat handler, while deterring others. The box should last at least 10 years, and longer if durable hardwood is used.

For further information contact your local Bat Group, or the Bat Conservation Trust (p182). A selection of 'woodcrete' boxes designed for different species of British bats is available from Jacobi Jayne & Company (p189).

BADGERS AND FOXES

Foxes are common in most areas where there is sufficient food and cover, and will be present in most woodlands and copses, especially near urban areas. Badgers are also associated with woodlands, and will make their setts in sandy or other easily excavated soil in woods, copses, hedgerows and other uncultivated places. When fencing new or existing woodlands against rabbits, deer or stock, take care not to fence across established badger runs, as the badgers will burrow under or break through the fence, making it no longer proof against other animals. If fencing across a run is unavoidable, install a badger gate. See *Fencing* (BTCV, 2001) for details. Badgers and their setts are legally protected (p20).

DEER AND RABBITS

These are often pests of woodland, and measures to prevent them eating young planted trees, natural regeneration and woodland flora are often necessary. See pages 60-62 and 106-109.

BAT BOX

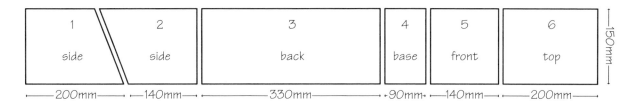

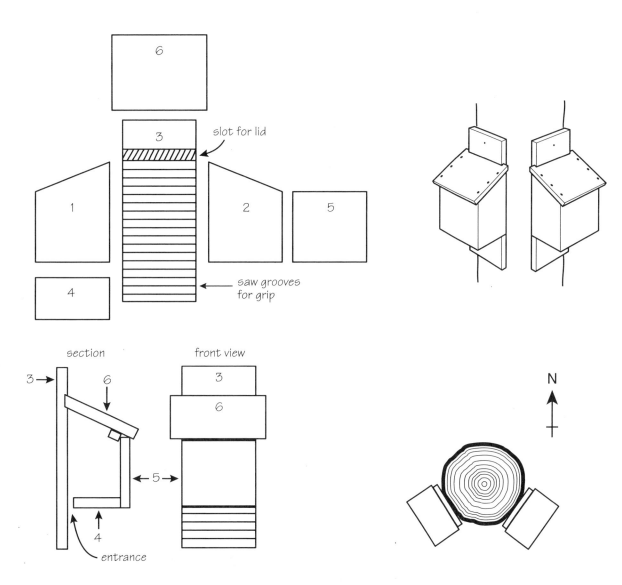

SMALL MAMMALS

Small mammals are encouraged with plantings of native berrying shrubs which provide food, and by plenty of undergrowth and other cover. Hedges, hedgebanks, dry stone walls and piles of logs, stones or rubble provide valuable cover for many small mammals. Provision or retention of such features will provide habitat for a variety of animals.

Voles and squirrels can become pests in woodland, because of the damage they can cause to newly planted and pole stage trees (p69).

Reptiles and amphibians

Reptiles, including adders, slow-worms and lizards are found in open woodlands, especially on sandy soils in southern England. They can be encouraged by providing open basking areas on sunny banks, or by the construction of hibernation sites. Dry stone walls, stone faced banks, piles of stones, compost heaps or piles of bark in sunny, sheltered locations may attract reptiles to hibernate. For details of constructing a hibernacula using hollow concrete blocks, plastic pipes and bark see *Enact* Vol 8 No2 (2000). Ponds in woodland areas will provide habitat for amphibians. See page 151.

13   Access and recreation

Woodlands in Britain have been managed and altered by man for many centuries, and access through woodlands along tracks and paths has been an integral part of this management.

Factors to consider

Good access is important for efficient woodland management and to allow people to enjoy woodlands. Well managed access provision is the best method of ensuring that such recreation takes place in a way which minimises adverse effects on the woodland.

Woodlands can absorb high numbers of visitors without seeming crowded, and zoning can ensure that different recreation requirements can be fulfilled within a single area of woodland.

Most visitors feel safer with clearly-signed routes and defined paths to follow. The fear that many people have of woodlands needs recognising so that steps can be taken to encourage access for all (p177). Most people like wooded landscapes, woodland edges and glades, parklands and views of trees, but do not necessarily like feeling enclosed by trees.

Bridges, steps, handrails and other built features must be properly constructed and maintained in a safe condition (p172). The landowner must take every reasonable precaution to avoid situations which may endanger visitors. This requires regular inspection of trees close to car parks, paths, picnic sites and play areas. Removal of unsafe limbs or other work may be necessary to ensure such trees are not a danger to visitors.

Woodlands are very variable, and provision for access will depend on many factors, including the type of woodland, its location in relation to housing and areas of public access, its size and so on. Woodlands with existing public access within or close to residential areas tend to be heavily used, especially by dog walkers and children. Direct routes and other paths through the woodland are likely to be well worn and no inducement is needed to encourage recreation. Management is likely to be aimed at managing access in a way that lessens damage to the woodland.

Large areas of conifer plantations or dense woodland may have little appeal for recreation, and if the aim is to encourage use, management will have to be directed into construction of car-parks, clearance of paths, waymarking and other provisions. There is a great demand for recreational cycling on traffic-free routes, a demand which can be well met by commercial conifer forests, which tend to be too monotonous and large-scale for interesting walking, but make an ideal landscape for cycling through, where suitably surfaced tracks are provided.

Ground conditions have an important role in access provision. Woodlands on well drained soils with an absence of steep slopes are relatively easy to manage for recreation. Woodlands on damp ground or steep slopes have obvious physical restrictions which will make access provision more difficult.

Before work is undertaken on rights of way, to create new roads or tracks wide enough to take a vehicle, or to make other access provisions it is essential that local authorities are consulted. There may also be implications for water resources, conservation and archaeological interests, which will require consultation with nature conservation and other agencies. The 'winning' of stone from borrow pits (p169) is normally permitted on an agricultural unit, provided it is used only on that unit and is not transported elsewhere. However, the local planning authority must be informed and a 'determination' sought as to whether prior planning permission is required (England and Wales). If access tracks are part of a Woodland Grant Scheme application or similar, consultation with local authorities and other bodies is automatic. Construction of tracks which improve access for management work may be eligible for grant aid. Access work or recreational activities must not disturb badger setts or other protected sites.

The information in this chapter relates to woodlands where management for access and recreation are a priority, and are not general recommendations for all woodlands. Ancient woodlands, those in remote locations or woods of particular nature conservation value may be best left mainly unvisited.

Recreation levels

Many organisations involved with woodland management include public access high on their agenda, aiming at multi-purpose woodlands managed for amenity, recreation, wildlife and timber production. The Forestry Commission owns 37% of the UK woods and forests, and

163

have a policy of freedom of access wherever possible. The Woodland Trust, local authorities and other organisations have similar policies.

Recreation provision can include campsites, visitor centres and other facilities which are a direct way of earning income from woodland access. Sporting and educational facilities in woodland are another way of generating income.

The list below gives a guide to levels of recreational provision, from the simplest to the most complex.

- Rights of way. Many woodlands are crossed by public footpaths, bridleways or byways, which must be maintained in a usable condition, normally by the highway authority. There is no statutory minimum width for a public right of way, although statements accompanying the definitive map of rights of way may give guidance. A working minimum when clearing paths is 2m x 2m high for a footpath, and 3m x 3m for a bridleway. Regular maintenance may be needed to cut back growth, depending on the type of vegetation and levels of use. Access through fences, across streams and so on must not restrict legitimate users of the path, and possible liabilities under the Disability Discrimination Act (1995) must be considered. Stiles are a barrier to many older and disabled people, and simple gaps, pedestrian gates or kissing gates should be the priority. See British Standard 5709:2001 *Gaps, gates and stiles* for further details.

- Car parking. Small areas of car parking are important for encouraging access to woodlands which are not on existing rights of way, and which are not near residential areas. A sign with the name of the wood, and an information board with a map of the paths not only gives useful information for users, but gives the wood a name and an identity which can help to encourage a feeling of security (p177).

- Paths. In addition to rights of way, other paths can be cleared, signed or improved by surfacing or other work. Direct routes which provide an access link through the wood, or circular routes for recreation are the most useful. In residential areas, paths which provide safe routes to school, commuting routes, greenways or off-road links are considered a priority, so funding may be available.

- Nature trails with numbered posts or similar, linked to leaflets, or with information boards, are a popular way of encouraging access. They are also useful for directing use along certain paths, and protecting areas which may be vulnerable to damage.

- Picnic tables near car-parks or in glades or at viewpoints close to access points are often popular.

- Permanent natural or man-made features such as unusual trees, rocks, sculptures, view markers, trig points or other features add variety to a woodland walk, and can be important markers for visitors to orientate themselves in woodland.

- Play areas, play trails, tree-top trails, look-out platforms and other built structures will greatly increase the popularity of woodland areas. The landowner's liability for public safety must be considered before any such features are built. The huge success of woodland parks which include some of these attractions, and the distances that families are prepared to drive to visit them, is in marked contrast to similar woodlands without 'attractions' which are almost unvisited.

- Camp sites, adventure trails, rope courses, mountain bike tracks.

- Some woodland parks, country parks and other tourist enterprises include information centres, cafes, shops, miniature trains, golf, fishing and many other activities within a wooded setting.

There are also various activities which can be organised in woodlands, without necessarily requiring permanent buildings or other structures, most of which will require good access provision:

- Guided walks, fungus forays, seed gathering, bat walks and other activities.

- Children's educational activities, including natural history projects, shelter building and play, crafts, art and creative writing.

- Outdoor activities including orienteering, mountain biking, paintball, survival skills.

Access requirements

VEHICLES

Vehicle access should be considered for most woodlands, apart from those that are very small, steep or isolated. Vehicle access can be provided and managed in a way which is sympathetic to the woodland landscape. Note the following:

- Vehicle access is essential for efficient woodland management operations. Removal of coppice products, thinnings, firewood, charcoal and other woodland products is very much easier if a vehicle can be used.

- Tracks which are wide enough to take a vehicle can also be constructed and managed by vehicle. Track or path construction which requires felling, scrub clearance, cut and fill operations, ditch digging, spreading of surfacing material or other heavy work can be done by machine. Mowing, trimming, flailing or scrub clearance to keep tracks and glades open can be done by a vehicle where access is suitable.

- Vehicle-width tracks are attractive for walkers, horse riders and other users of woodland. Most people much prefer to walk along a track wide enough to walk side by side, or with space to pass other woodland walkers or dogs. Narrow paths can be intimidating, and are more likely to suffer from erosion or muddy conditions than are wider paths.

- Wider tracks with grassy margins are a valuable wildlife habitat (p148).

- Bridges, culverts and other structures must be built to a standard to take vehicles (p168).

- Surfacing material may not be required if vehicle access can be limited to times when the ground conditions are suitable, such as dry summer periods, or when the ground is frozen in winter.

- Providing access for permitted vehicles may cause problems if it allows entry for other vehicles. Locked gates or other barriers at access points from the road will be necessary (p179). Moveable barriers such as heavy logs or boulders can be used to block gateways against most vehicles, and then moved by machine when legitimate access is required. Access along rights of way and for firefighting must not be restricted.

WALKERS

Most visitors to woodlands go there with a purpose, with dog walking top of the list. Children love woodlands for play, so family visits are also popular. Otherwise, walkers tend to have specific reasons for visiting woodlands such as birdwatching, or seasonal features and activities including spring flowers, autumn colours, collecting fungi, gathering sweet chestnuts, holly and so on. Other wooded areas are visited as part of visits to stately homes, parks or other attractions. Woods may also be walked through by rights of way users, but otherwise most people when going for a walk in a rural area in Britain will choose open land such as commons, farmland, downland, heathland, coasts, hills and mountains, with open views being the over-riding attraction. If part of the aim of woodland management is to attract visitors, provision for walkers must be good. This includes:

- Paths or tracks which are easy to follow and which reduce any fears of getting lost.

- Surfacing which is reasonable for walking in most weather conditions. Tracks which remain waterlogged in dry weather conditions will not be well used.

- Steps on steep slopes.

- Bridges over streams, and boardwalks over permanently waterlogged ground which cannot be avoided.

HORSE RIDERS, CYCLISTS

- Horse riders prefer wide tracks without overhanging vegetation, and with reasonable surfaces. Where tracks can be provided for horse riding only, this is the safest and best solution for all users.

- Family cyclists require fairly level tracks with reasonable surfacing. Infrequently used vehicle access tracks with surfacing are ideal.

- Mountain bikers will ride on any permitted tracks, with steep slopes and rough ground an attraction rather than a problem.

ACCESS WITHOUT PATHS

Some wooded areas are suitable for access without paths. These fall into two main categories:

- Wood-pastures, parks and wooded commons which are grazed, and have open grassy areas with scatterings of trees and small woods. Where unrestricted access is permitted, walkers and other users can walk freely, without having to keep to paths or particular routes.

- Mature woodlands with little undergrowth or shrub layer. Beech woods are the most notable type, with their heavy shade preventing undergrowth. Most other types of woodland have some undergrowth which restricts access, or ground flora which does not tolerate frequent trampling.

GLADES AND OPEN SPACES

These tend to be the most popular locations within woodland for recreation, and may be used for picnicking or children's play. The bright green of a grassy glade within woodland is visually very appealing. Points where paths meet are an obvious place for making a new glade. Use of existing glades will be increased if made easily accessible by good paths.

Glades need to be at least 40m in diameter to retain their open nature as trees mature. Glades will tend to shrink if grazing pressure or recreational use is low. New glades are best created in areas of poor tree growth, perhaps which are too dry or where disease or windblow has caused loss of trees. Areas of scrub and brambles can be converted to glades by clearance and regular cutting. Glades must be regularly mown to create grassy conditions, until grazing or recreational use is sufficient to keep down growth of rough grasses and scrub.

Some woodlands or plantations have derelict industrial remains, old dumps, hard standings or similar. These can be converted to glades by removal or burying of unwanted metal or other material, levelling, and as necessary covering with a thin layer of topsoil. This can then be seeded with a grass/wildflower mixture, or left to regenerate naturally.

VIEWS

Views both within the woodland and to the land beyond will enhance the woodland for most users, and will make it easier for visitors to orientate themselves. Management work could include:

- Clearing undergrowth to give views through the wood. Some visitors will feel safer if the undergrowth is mainly cleared from the margins of paths, to leave a clear view into the woods on either side. Concentrate on the margins of tracks leading from car-parks, and the most popular routes. Complete clearance is not necessary, and will result in a loss of valuable habitat, as well as making the woodland draughty. Clear away clumps of undergrowth which are overshadowed and of little wildlife value, and prune lower branches of some trees. Conifers can be brashed (removal of lower dead branches) to leave clear stems. Thin trees as necessary (p71), to create a more open woodland. This will also benefit tree growth where trees are getting crowded.

- Consider clearing views to particular features in the middle or far distance beyond the wood, so that they can be seen from one or more locations within the wood. Features do not have to be 'attractive' to be of interest, with power stations, wind turbines and radio masts the most notable features in some landscapes. Visitors who are worried about losing their way will be reassured if they can see familiar buildings, roads or other features beyond the wood, from which they can orientate themselves.

- Make the most of any high ground within the wood. Most high points have some sort of path leading to them, but it may be worth upgrading the path so that the viewpoint is made more easily accessible.

- Keep views clear by keeping vegetation low at particular viewpoints. This may require mowing or flailing of grassy banks at intervals through the year, or clearance of scrub growth every few years.

- Views of water are usually valued, although this may lead to problems of unwanted access to ponds or streams.

- Platforms or lookouts can be constructed to make the most of views. If visible from the car-park or from a main track within the wood, these create a feature to aim for and to walk to.

- Raised walkways or tree top trails. These have been constructed in some woodlands as a visitor attraction, and to give the visitor the experience of being amongst the tree tops.

Construction

Construction of vehicle width surfaced tracks normally requires the hire of a suitable machine and operator. The simplest tracks, for example made by clearing and grading a track on well drained ground, can cost as little as 20p per metre. Where suitable material can be obtained from a borrow pit, and working conditions are fairly straightforward for a suitable machine, costs may be about £2-3 per metre. Costs rise sharply where stone has to be purchased or where geotextile is needed, up to about £9 per metre (Forestry Commission 1999). Grants may be available towards the cost of track construction where this improves recreation access, or makes possible the management of neglected woodland.

When planning new woodlands, the site survey should include possible sources of surfacing material from within the woodland area. Any gravel deposits for example could provide useful surfacing material, at the same time as creating a wildlife pond. Soil reorganisation (p169) is a cheap method of track construction, which is very much easier to do before the woodland is planted.

Where tracks for management purposes cannot be provided, or will be too damaging to the woodland environment, other options include:

- Converting the woodland crop on site to a product which is easier to extract. This could include conversion to charcoal, drying the wood for a season or more until it is lighter and easier to extract, or converting it with a mobile bandsaw.

- Extraction by horse, or by pedestrian controlled harvesting machine may be possible even where there are no tracks.

DRAINAGE

Many lowland woods are on poorly drained land. The shady sheltered conditions in woodlands reduces evaporation from the soil surface, and fallen branches and leaves impede surface drainage. Unlike pastures and cultivated land, which may have underdrainage systems installed, woodlands generally have no artificial drainage systems.

Paths in lowland woods or those on heavy soils are therefore likely to be on poorly drained ground, and trampling in wet weather can rapidly reduce the surface to mud. Paths which are intended to attract regular use are likely to need some sort of drainage and surfacing work.

Waterlogged ground without any discernible flow is best dealt with by raising the path level. Any water that flows across a path should be drained away by grading the profile of the path, by installing cross-drains or culverts, or crossed by bridges.

Paths in upland woods or on sloping ground are likely to suffer from surface erosion, as rainfall runs across and down paths, washing away thin soils and exposing subsoil and rock. Path grading, cross-drains and cut-offs to take the water off the path without damaging it are the basic requirements. For full details see *Footpaths* (BTCV, 1996).

Grading

Grading involves altering the profile of a path or track to encourage water to drain off the surface. Grading either requires making a camber, which sheds water both ways, or a cross-fall, to shed water one way. Cambers are generally used on flatter ground, and cross-falls on slopes. For small projects this work can be done by hand, but most work will require an excavator and skilled operator. The camber or cross-fall can be formed by the base material, or by surfacing material which is imported to the site from borrow pits or commercial quarries. A suitable camber and cross-fall for walkers, cyclists and wheelchair users is shown in the diagram.

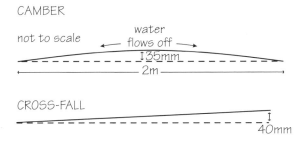

A tracked 3 tonne mini-excavator with a bucket and blade can be used to clean, regrade and widen an existing path. On slopes, the bucket can be used to 'cut and fill'

as necessary, excavating on the uphill side of the path and building up on the lower side. The blade is used to create a free-draining profile. The cross-fall of the track should be no more than 5%. The diagram gives a guide to forming a 2m width track on a 25% slope. To reduce erosion down the track, the slope of the track should not exceed 7%.

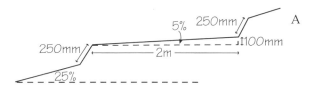

skilled operator can complete 50-100m per hour, depending on conditions. The resulting track, of about 2m width, should be suitable for all-weather walking, and for extracting timber in dry conditions only, using pedestrian controlled harvesting equipment, horses or manual labour. To further improve the track, drainage and surfacing works could be completed. For further details on machine-built tracks, see Forestry Commission Technical Note 27/98 *Access Track Construction in Small Woodlands*.

Cross-drains

These are used mainly on paths to take surface flow which crosses paths after rainfall, but which does not flow all year. Cross-drains are best made of large stones, to be resistant to erosion and trampling. Cross-drains of logs or planks can be constructed, but are not usually robust enough to last long. Cross-drains smaller than about 100mm across tend to block up quickly with stones and debris.

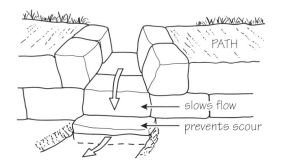

Cut-offs

These can be made of round timber, sawn timber or stone, angled to direct water off the path and prevent it flowing down the path. The timber or stone should be set into the ground as shown, with a small ditch on the upper side to catch the water. Install at frequent intervals on sloping paths which have evidence of erosion. Cut-offs need regular cleaning to remain effective.

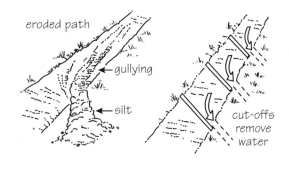

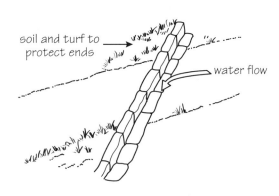

CROSS SECTION

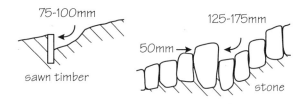

Culverts

These should be installed at points where the track needs to cross small streams or ditches. Depending on the size of the flow, flexible perforated plastic, solid plastic or concrete pipes can be used. It is important that the pipe is installed carefully at the correct level and with supporting headwalls as necessary, so that the drain functions properly over a long period, and does not become exposed from erosion by water or the action of trampling.

Where the construction of a culvert is likely to alter the flow of a watercourse, approval must first be obtained from the Environment Agency. Where the track is used by vehicles, the culvert must be built to a suitable standard as shown below.

Pipes should be a minimum of 225mm (9") diameter, set on a firm bed of aggregate (10 or 14mm nominal size), and set so that the pipe is 25mm (1") below the bed level of the stream or ditch.

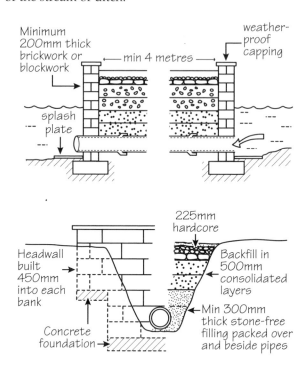

Smaller culverts suitable for pedestrian tracks should be built in a similar way, with headwalls and surfacing to protect the pipe, even if this means raising the level of the path over the culvert. Pipes which are simply set in the stream bed and covered with surfacing, without the protection of a headwall will soon become blocked as material becomes eroded from around the pipe end.

Side drains or ditches

This form of drainage can be used to take surface flow which runs alongside paths, or to provide storage for ground water where the water table is high. The spoil

Table 13a: MATERIALS FOR CULVERTS

PIPES	HEADWALLS	SURFACING
Concrete	Concrete blocks	Consolidated hardcore or aggregate
uPVC, polypropylene or polyethylene	Engineering bricks Local materials	
Vitrified clay	Turf	

from the drains will normally need to be spread away from the ditch. Stony subsoil may be suitable for raising the level of the path.

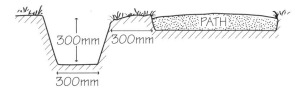

Where stony subsoils are covered with a thin layer of topsoil or peat, it's possible to strip away the topsoil or peat across the width of the path and side ditch, excavate the subsoil from below the line of the ditch and use it to form the path. Topsoil is then used to fill the base of the ditch. The success of this 'soil reorganisation' technique depends on having suitable stony subsoil without too much clay content, which forms a durable walking surface. This can be done by hand on a small scale, but any work which involves moving large volumes of surfacing, soil or other bulk material is best done by a tracked excavator operated by a suitably qualified and experienced person. See *Footpaths* (BTCV, 1996) for further details.

SURFACING

The rule of thumb for stone aggregate and other stone surfacing material is two tonnes per cubic metre. The table gives estimated figures in tonnes per cubic metre for a range of materials. Suppliers of commercial stone should be able to give an accurate figure. These figures can be used to assess the amount required for a particular path, the transport requirements or the amount which will have to be excavated from a borrow pit. Materials from borrow pits will be variable. For example, studies by the Forestry Commission of borrow pits in shale on four different sites yielded 1.5, 2, 3 and 3 tonnes per cubic metre respectively (Forestry Commission Technical Note 27/98).

Table 13b: SURFACING MATERIALS

Material	Tonnes per cubic metre
Concrete	2.30
Sand	1.90
Bricks	1.76
Gravel/aggregate	1.76
Limestone, crushed	1.75
Topsoil	1.60
Shale, from borrow pit	1.5-3.00
Woodchips	0.16-0.50

The diagram below gives a simplified view of a cubic metre of surfacing and how it could be used to make a narrow footpath, or a wider track.

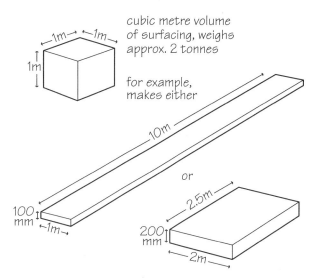

As a rough guideline, narrow footpaths 1m wide need only have about 100mm depth of surfacing to give adequate load bearing ability. Wider tracks, normally for vehicle use, need to have a greater depth of surfacing to take the heavier loads. Allowance must also be made for wastage. Some tracks will not require uniform depth of surfacing along their length, depending on the ground conditions and the desired finish.

Borrow pits

A borrow pit refers to a pit or small quarry which is dug to provide stone for surfacing or other construction work nearby. Many old tracks which climb slopes or hillsides have borrow pits at intervals alongside. Borrow pits provide the nearest, and normally the cheapest source of stone, and being local, should with time blend fairly naturally with the surroundings. Shale, chalk and other types of fairly soft, easily quarried stone may be suitable.

An experienced operator is required to identify and safely excavate suitable stone, using a tracked excavator or similar. The work is destructive, and can be extremely unsightly in the wrong location. However, when working is finished, most borrow pits gradually revegetate so that they become partly disguised, and often form valuable sheltered wildlife habitats.

The excavated material can then be transported by dump truck or tractor and tipping trailer. The same or another excavator then spreads, grades and consolidates the material. This work should only be done in dry conditions.

Bought stone

The choice is normally made from the nearest suitable stone, to reduce transport costs. Visit local suppliers to check on what is available and to gain their advice on the most suitable material for the location and job in question. Various different types are available:

- Crushed limestone, dolerite or other type of rock, to the specification 'Type 1 sub-base' is the highest grade material, as used for road building. This comprises material from 75mm diameter down to dust, with the dust making up about 25% of the total. This can be laid in a single layer, or topped with a layer of finer surfacing material, of 6mm down to dust, to give a smoother finish. 'Type 2 sub-base' consists of natural sands, gravel, crushed aggregate and subsoil. Type 2 is cheaper and has a lower load-bearing capability than Type 1, and should only be laid in dry weather.

- Quarry bottoms. This is the waste material from the quarry bottom, and is very variable, but should contain plenty of dust so will bind well. Inspect before purchase.

- Stone as dug. This usually contains clay or subsoil, and is very variable.

- Hoggin and self-setting gravels. These are gravels with a high clay content which bind when rolled to form a durable surface.

Recycled materials

Recycled materials can look very unattractive in a natural setting such as a woodland, and are not generally recommended. However, where they are available cheaply or for free, the benefits to access may outweigh the disadvantages. Recycled material can be fairly safely used as a base course in locations where it is unlikely to get exposed, typically on flat or gently sloping ground.

Preferably top with a surfacing material of crushed stone or woodchips. Where sunlight levels are sufficient for grass growth, top with a free draining soil and either seed or allow to grass over naturally. Avoid using recycled materials as surfacing on sloping tracks, where there is a high chance of erosion exposing the material.

Recycled materials include:

- crushed concrete from demolished buildings.

- hardcore, including bricks, concrete and rubble from demolished buildings

- tarmac 'planings', which is the worn tarmac scraped off roads prior to re-surfacings.

- Industrial waste products such as fuel ash are not recommended, because of potential pollution problems.

Recycled surfacing materials may be available from suppliers of aggregates, or from demolition companies. Small amounts may be obtainable locally from various sources. As far as possible, check at source that the material does not contain steel reinforcing rods, other waste metal, glass, asbestos or other noxious substances.

Geotextiles

The term 'geotextiles' includes a large range of materials used in road building, landscaping and other construction work. For construction of tracks and paths, a geotextile

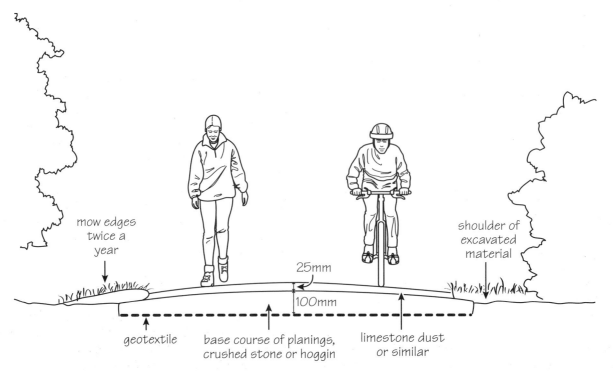

mow edges twice a year

shoulder of excavated material

25mm

100mm

geotextile

base course of planings, crushed stone or hoggin

limestone dust or similar

2m width for walkers/cyclists and light vehicle users

can be used as a bottom layer in fine soils, silts and clays, to retain sub-base and surfacing material and prevent it becoming mixed with the ground beneath. Makes include Terram, Tensar, Lotrak and Wyretex, available in various grades and widths. Further details are given in *Footpaths* (BTCV, 1996), or are available from suppliers (p189).

In woodlands, geotextiles can be used in the construction of tracks and paths across fairly level, badly drained mineral soil or areas of damp peat. Geotextiles are not generally recommended for sloping ground, as it is likely that the geotextile will become exposed as the surfacing erodes away. The finished path surface should be at least 75mm (3") above the existing ground level, to raise it above damp ground. Excavate a level 'formation' for the path, removing any rocks or roots which might puncture the geotextile. Pile up the excavated material neatly so it can be re-used to make the shoulder of the path, and bury the edges of the geotextile.

Brash and woodchips

Woody material from within the wood can be used as surfacing material. At its simplest, brash is often deliberately left on the ground to provide support for machinery being used for extracting timber. For more permanent paths, bundles of brush or roundwood poles can be used to provide a sub-base for woodland paths and tracks through damp ground. Lay the material across the path, and then secure it as shown, with poles and stobs. Top with a layer of woodchips, at least 100mm thick. Periodic maintenance will be needed to top up the woodchips, and to check that the edging poles are securely held and that the wires are not exposed.

Woodchips can be produced from within the wood by chipping thinnings, brash, scrub and other unwanted woody material. A range of woodchippers are available from suppliers of forestry machinery. Woodchippers should only be used by trained and competent persons. Voluntary groups, or owners or managers of small woodlands need to assess whether their requirements for woodchipping justify the purchase or hire of a machine, together with the relevant training.

Some heathland nature reserves and other areas have an excess of woodchips, due to a continuing need to remove saplings and other woody growth to maintain open habitats. Parks departments and other authorities involved with tree management may also produce woodchips in quantity.

The weight of woodchips per cubic metre is very variable, depending on chip size, moisture content, loading procedure and settling. One tonne of newly chipped woodchips at 70% moisture can occupy up to 6 cubic metres. With drying and settling, one tonne at 20% moisture may occupy as little as 2 cubic metres. Preferably stack for a few months before use.

Table 13c: LENGTH OF PATH PER CUBIC METRE OF WOODCHIPS

	Width of path		
	1m	1.5m	2m
Depth of surfacing			
100mm (footpath)	10m	6.66m	5m
250mm (bridleway)	4m	2.66m	2m

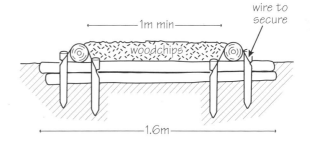

For bridleways, a deeper layer up to 250mm thick may be necessary, depending on the amount of use.

Woodchips and bark are available commercially for path and bridleway surfaces, riding arenas, play areas and for mulching. They are sold loose in bulk by weight, or by the bale. The cost will normally rule out their use for woodland paths or rural rights of way, except in special circumstances.

Grass

Where light levels are sufficient, and trampling pressure is fairly low, grass makes an attractive path surface, which should be durable on free draining soil. Grass on wet ground rapidly gets cut up by trampling. Grass will only thrive in woodland where the canopy is high and fairly sparse, for example in recently thinned or storm-damaged woods. Where there is sufficient light for bramble to thrive, there should be sufficient light for grass. On bare ground, the surface can be prepared by harrowing, and then seeded with a mixture of native shade-tolerant trample-resistant grasses. A mixture including perennial rye-grass, creeping red fescue and creeping bent may be appropriate, but each site should be individually assessed and advice sought from seed suppliers. Grasses and woodland edge flowering plants (p74) can be sown along the edges of the new ride. Where there is already some grass growth, regular cutting and light trampling will encourage a grassy sward to develop.

Once grass is established, regular mowing will encourage the development of a close turf. The path edges can be left to grow longer as desired. The mown width should be at least 1.8m (6'), to spread the trampling pressure and allow mowing by mini-tractor or other vehicle. Grazing by rabbits or deer, together with the trampling of walkers, may be sufficient to maintain a short grass sward. However, this needs regular checking, because once the grass becomes too tall for comfortable walking, trampling will be limited to the centre of the path, which will then be reduced to bare earth and mud.

In some locations, paths or tracks of crushed stone or gravel will eventually vegetate over naturally with a mixture of grasses and herbs, which helps bind the surface together.

Simple bridges and boardwalks

Bridges on public rights of way in England and Wales which cross streams or other natural obstacles are the responsibility of the Highway Authority, who should be consulted over design and construction. Bridges which are not on public rights of way will normally be the responsibility of the landowner.

The site must be carefully checked to choose the best crossing point where banks are stable and unlikely to erode. The likelihood of flooding should be assessed, and the design of abutments to support and secure the bridge should be considered. See *Footpaths* (BTCV, 1996) for further details.

Consider using material from within the woodland for bridge and boardwalk construction. Durable hardwoods and some softwoods (see below) can provide bridge beams. Durable hardwoods can also be used for handrails and posts, and where planking machinery is available, for decking.

The abutments, which support the beams of the bridge, can be made from mortared stone from the stream bed, or gathered from nearby as available. Log cribs can be constructed as shown. Small sleeper bridges can be supported by sleepers, as shown below (p173).

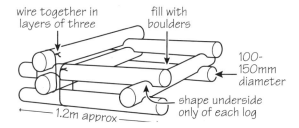

wire together in layers of three

fill with boulders

100-150mm diameter

shape underside only of each log

1.2m approx

Alternatively, concrete abutments will be needed. See *Footpaths* (BTCV, 1996) for further details.

Footbridge with handrail

Where available in the woodland, the main beams of the bridge can be made from straight trunks of Douglas fir,

larch or Scots pine. For short spans, oak or sweet chestnut could also be used, where they are available in sufficiently straight lengths. Mature 'overstood' sweet chestnut coppice may yield suitable material. The table gives a guide to dimensions required for different spans.

Table 13d: BRIDGE BEAMS

Average diameter of log	900mm wide deck	
	No of logs	Span
250mm	2	5.0m
300mm	2	6.7m
350mm	2	8.0m

Average diameter of log	1200mm wide deck	
	No of logs	Span
250mm	3	5.5m
300mm	3	7.0m
350mm	3	8.5m

900mm

 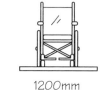

1200mm   1200mm

Logs must be straight, and of the diameter specified for the middle third of the log length. Remove bark and branches, but do not trim flush. For softwood logs, soak all cut areas with at least three coats of water-based wood preservative, as soon as possible after felling. Although this will not soak in far, it eliminates fungal growth on the cut ends, and reduces end cracking by slowing the rate of drying out. Wear protective clothing when applying wood preservative, and take care not to allow any leakage into the soil or stream.

Logs should not be used if they have knots larger than 100mm (4"), signs of fungal decay, or a marked spiral grain slope. Also reject logs that have surface cracks of 0.2mm width at time of felling, or 3mm after seasoning.

The total depth of cracks in any section must not exceed one third the diameter of the log. A working life of no more than 10 years should be expected.

Decking should be of sawn softwood, pressure treated with preservative. Durable hardwoods, such as oak or sweet chestnut could also be used if available in the woodland. These can be converted to planks with a mobile bandsaw operated by a trained operator, and then carefully stacked and dried in the woodland before use.

Decking should overlap the outer edge of the main beam by about 50mm. Pre-drill the decking, and attach using no.12 x 90mm sherardised screws. A strip of bituminous felt 20mm wider than the main beam, laid between decking and beam, will help protect the beam from rot.

In low risk situations, where there is a drop of less than about a metre to the bottom of a narrow stream bed, ditch or gully, handrails are not necessary. Most people will have no problem in crossing a bridge of, for example, 2m length and 1.2m width. Handrails should be provided in situations where there is a drop greater than about 1 metre, where there are likely to be strong cross-winds, or where the pathway is in a popular location which is likely to be used by older or infirm walkers, who may require a handrail. If a handrail is provided, it must be strong enough to withstand people leaning on or falling against it. A weak handrail is more hazardous than no handrail.

The handrail posts are supported by a raker, attached to two deckboards, which are extended to a distance equivalent to half the height of the handrail post. The handrail posts, of treated softwood, should be spaced 1m apart, on one side only in normal situations. A single handrail 100 x 50mm is sufficient for normal situations,

joined by a half-lap joint as necessary at posts. The toeboards are attached on either side as shown, using no. 12 x 90mm sherardised screws. In hazardous situations there should be handrails on both sides of the bridge, 1.4m high, and with three rails on each side.

Materials:

Beams	Logs of suitable length and diameter (see Table 13d)
Decking	150 x 50 x 1125 (4 per metre length of bridge), treated softwood
	150 x 50 x 1650 (2 per metre length of bridge), treated softwood or 100 x 36 for hardwood
Toeboards	75 x 50 x twice length of bridge
Handrail posts	75 x 75 x 1.3m
Handrail	100 x 50mm x length of bridge

A winch and chain block, operated by suitably experienced workers, may be required to lift the beams into position.

Sleeper bridge

Reclaimed railway sleepers and telegraph poles are useful materials for bridge building, on sites where vehicle access to the site is possible. Sleepers are available from reclamation companies in the following sizes:

250 x 125mm x 2.6m

300 x 150mm x 2.4m-6m (crossing sleepers)

Sleepers can be used for simple pedestrian or light traffic bridges up to 2.6m span, where the sleepers are lain as shown across the gap. Alternatively, they can be used as beams for bridges with decking and handrails attached. Note that the attachment for the handrail requires placing the sleepers on edge, to give sufficient depth of timber for attaching the handrail posts. Where handrails are not essential, it is easier and probably cheaper to build a wide bridge even if only for pedestrian use, rather than a narrower bridge where handrails then become necessary.

RAKED HANDRAIL FIXING

12x140mm coach bolt with two 50x30mm washers

raker

h

½h

75mm

75mm

75x75mm raker

toeboard

12x140mm coach screw

12x200mm coach screw

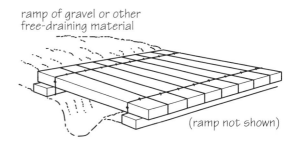

ramp of gravel or other free-draining material

(ramp not shown)

Where flooding is possible, the sleepers should be wired together and attached to the sleeper abutment, to prevent them being dislodged by flood. For ditches and dry gullies which do not flood, attachment is not essential as the weight of the sleepers holds them in position. A minimum 20 year life can be expected from a bridge of good quality sleepers.

For a narrow pedestrian bridge, or for spans over 2.6m using crossing timbers, a structure with handrails and decking becomes necessary. Use a cantilever attachment for the handrail posts as shown, with a 20mm mild steel tie rod through the width of the structure. The main beams should be not less than 150mm deep and strutted apart, with spacers and a bottom strut as shown.

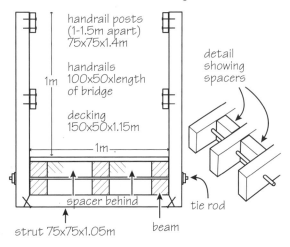

PEDESTRIAN BRIDGE 2-6m length

handrail posts (1-1.5m apart) 75x75x1.4m

handrails 100x50xlength of bridge

1m

decking 150x50x1.15m

1m

detail showing spacers

spacer behind

tie rod

strut 75x75x1.05m

beam

For further details on bridges, see *Footbridges in the Countryside* (CCS, 1988) or *Footpaths* (BTCV, 1996).

Boardwalks

Boardwalks can be useful for crossing ground that would be damaged by uncontrolled trampling. This may include:

- Damp ground, where the vegetation breaks up under trampling, turning soil to mud or damp peat to a morass.

- Dry or sandy ground, with thin soils and sparse vegetation. Some woodlands have a delicate flora of mosses and lichens, which trampling would destroy.

Various designs of boardwalk are given in *Footpaths* (BTCV, 1996). The design must be robust, and create a surface that is more comfortable to walk on than the ground it traverses, otherwise the boardwalk won't be used.

Railway sleepers are used for many boardwalks, as they are durable and simple to use. On soils or peat which are damp but without areas of standing water, it should be sufficient to lay the sleepers on the ground as bearers, with half or full-length sleepers forming the decking. The decking sleepers are held in place by their own weight, but a wire stapled as shown will discourage vandalism.

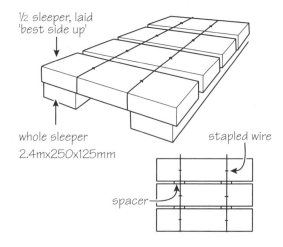

½ sleeper, laid 'best side up'

whole sleeper 2.4mx250x125mm

stapled wire

spacer

For short lengths of boardwalk, those that are 'one way' or only receive limited use, sleepers can be laid lengthways as shown.

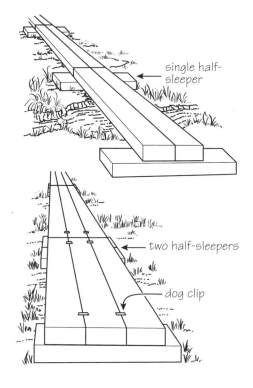

single half-sleeper

two half-sleepers

dog clip

Boardwalks can be constructed from materials available in the wood. These are suitable for crossing damp ground, but are unlikely to be successful on dry ground, because their uneven surface makes them less attractive for walking than the surrounding ground. They are suitable for more remote woodland locations, where an uneven walking surface may be appropriate. Sweet chestnut or oak are the most durable, and can be used for bearers, stringers and decking as shown. The boardwalk should be checked annually and any weak parts replaced.

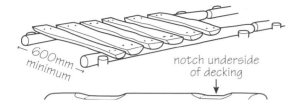

600mm minimum · notch underside of decking

A very ancient design of wooden trackway is shown below. This is the Sweet Track in the Somerset Levels, which is a 6,000-year-old, 2km length of wooden trackway found buried in peat deposits. The crossed poles are made of oak, ash and lime, and the trackway itself is made of oak. Although not a practical proposition for today's needs, a replica section could be an interesting project and a good test of skills in riving oak!

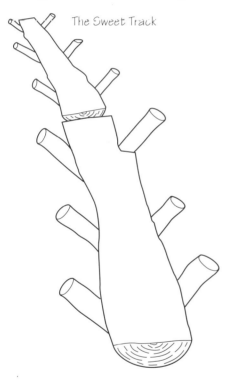

The Sweet Track

Signs and information boards

As detailed further below, many people find woodlands intimidating, and need clearly marked paths to follow, together with maps at car-parks, leaflets and other information to feel confident to walk in woodland. Because of their size and uniformity, conifer plantations can be especially confusing.

People are often rather conservative in their use of local woodlands, tending to walk the same routes that they know, often ones that they learnt from their parents or friends, rather than exploring areas which are new to them. Horse riders often have the best knowledge of routes, along with mountain bikers, joggers, naturalists and others who visit woodlands with a particular purpose in mind. Where the aim of management is to encourage recreational use, effort needs to be put into signing and other information.

Rights of way

Rights of way must by law be signposted at junctions with metalled roads. Signposts must indicate whether the path is a byway, bridleway or footpath. Information on distance and destination is often included, but is not required by law. The local authority must also place signs or waymarks at points along a right of way where the authority considers that a person unfamiliar with the locality would need a sign to find the correct route.

Any waymarking of public rights of way should be done in consultation with the local authority and with the landowner. The recommended colours for arrows are:

Footpath	yellow	(BS 08 E 51)
Bridleway	blue	(BS 20 E 51)
Byway	brick red	(BS 06 E 55)

Arrows can be painted directly onto objects, or plastic, metal or resin arrows can be attached to objects. Most authorities have their own supplies of arrows or waymarkers which can be made available to approved voluntary groups. Arrows are aligned in the same way as road signs, and should normally be placed on vertical surfaces as shown:

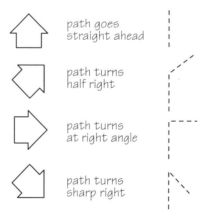

path goes straight ahead

path turns half right

path turns at right angle

path turns sharp right

In farmland, arrows are normally placed on stiles, gates, walls and other objects at boundaries. In woodlands, such objects are usually absent. Painted or attached arrows are not very successful on tree trunks, because surfaces may be rough or liable to get obscured by foliage, and arrows may not be easy for the walker to spot. It is difficult to make arrows obvious, without making them unsightly. Separate waymarking posts, with arrows on them, are one answer, but involve extra cost and the increased likelihood of vandalism. Junctions of several paths can be very confusing to sign on vertical posts, as shown. It may be clearer to use finger posts, or to attach the arrows on a horizontal surface as shown.

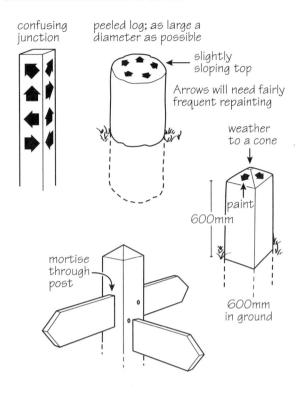

confusing junction

peeled log; as large a diameter as possible

slightly sloping top

Arrows will need fairly frequent repainting

weather to a cone

paint

600mm

600mm in ground

mortise through post

Other routes

Routes to encourage use of woodland areas are normally circular routes, marked by markers on the ground, with an accompanying information board and / or leaflets.

The first priority is that routes must be along paths which are clear and pleasant to walk, or they are unlikely to be used. At the start of the route, there must be a board, finger post or some other sign which gives distance, type of marker to follow and destination as appropriate.

As with waymarking arrows, there is a problem in making markers obvious, robust, but not obtrusive. Markers attached to trees need to be brightly coloured to show up. Attach at a consistent height, just out of reach to avoid vandalism, and use copper nails to reduce damage to the tree. Alternatively, use sturdy posts, cut locally from the woodland, and paint on or attach a marker.

Decide whether the route is going to be marked from both directions, or if a circular route from the entrance point, from one way only. Non-directional marks, such as blobs or bands of colour, only confirm the route and give no idea of direction. Where there is likely to be confusion, for example at junctions, consecutive marks need to be in view of each other.

Numbers or letters which refer to a leaflet may also need arrows nearby to direct to the next marker.

Before making any firm decision on types of marker, their positioning and accompanying leaflets or boards, do a few trial runs with some people who are unfamiliar with the area. When you know an area well it is difficult to put yourself in the position of someone who doesn't. Fix up temporary markers, use a draft leaflet or board as required, and observe what happens. From this you can fine-tune the positioning of arrows, where additional markers are needed, and clear up any ambiguities in the information given.

Routes for cyclists and horse riders should be clearly marked by appropriate signs which can be read without stopping or dismounting.

Information

On supervised or frequently wardened sites, leaflets or route cards can be made available at the visitor centre or car-park, with an honesty box as appropriate. Alternatively, a nearby shop or pub may be willing to stock leaflets.

Decide on the type of information required. Choose from:

- Basic information which enables a walker to find and follow the route.

- Nature trail information, linked to markers along the route.

- Details of woodland wildlife, management, local history and so on, not necessarily linked to the route, and normally better read before or after a walk.

- Information aimed at a particular audience, for example children, bird-watchers and so on.

Basic information which is designed to be read as you walk is best kept as simple as possible. It can be distracting to have to keep unfolding a leaflet. An A5 card with the basic details needed to find your way may be all that is needed, and also leaves you more time to look around and observe for yourself. Alternatively, put the map on the back of a descriptive leaflet, with details inside to be read before or after the walk as desired. Two or more routes can be shown on the same map, to give a selection of routes for different users. However, don't make it complicated or it will become confusing. Concentrate on getting one or two routes in use and regularly walked. The basic map should show:

- The car-park or start point, and the route of the path.

- Average time taken to walk the route.

- Scale and orientation.

- The colour and type of waymarkers, if any.

- Unmistakable features which a walker will find along the path. If there is a lack of such features, then it may be necessary to create them. Logs, boulders, a stone cairn, wooden bollards, sculptures, specimen trees of suitable species or other features may be appropriate.

Leaflets for cycle routes should include similar basic information required to find the start of the route and to follow it. Few cyclists will want to stop in order to read a descriptive leaflet.

Information boards

An information board at a car-park or start of a woodland walk should include:

- A map showing the wood, including its location in relation to the surrounding area. People feel more secure in exploring a woodland if they know how it links with other places that they know.

- Scale and orientation.

- Rights of way and other access routes.

- Who owns and/or manages the wood.

- The location of the nearest phone in case of emergency.

- Information on wildlife, local history and so on as appropriate.

A signboard with the name and ownership of the wood is important in giving the woodland an identity and to encourage use. Responsible visitors will not venture into a woodland if they are not sure of their right to be there. A signboard should be robust and attractive, as its appearance will convey a message about the management of the site. Most organisations involved with owning and managing woodland have their own standard signs.

Various companies specialise in producing information boards for countryside recreation sites (p189), and there are a large number of sign making companies in all areas. Alternatively, you can make your own signboard, with the name of the woodland in painted or routered lettering. Maps and other information can be produced cheaply on paper and encapsulated, and replaced at intervals as necessary. Signs are normally best erected out of direct sunlight, in order to reduce fading. The signboard should be easily visible from the road, and positioned where people reading it are out of the way of traffic turning in. Check with the local authority regarding planning permission.

A robust structure can be built of local oak or sweet chestnut, if possible sourced from the woodland itself,

prepared using green woodworking techniques (p000). Use mortise and tenon joints for the roof support, braces and rails. Roof with shingles, split from a straight butt of oak or chestnut. Purchased plywood will be needed for the information board.

Fear of woodlands

Many people have a fear of walking in woodlands, and need encouragement to explore them.

Woodland edges, broad rides and tracks and wood-pasture or parkland landscapes are very popular for recreation, because they are attractive landscapes in which you are unlikely to get lost, and where you can see and be seen. Venturing into narrow paths under the woodland canopy or through dense woodland with thick undergrowth is generally less appealing.

This fear of woodlands is particularly high amongst women, including mothers with young families, older women and ethnic minorities, and may reduce their ability to take advantage of recreational opportunities in their local woodlands. Fear of woodlands may include the following:

- Fear of getting lost, or parents' fear of children getting lost. Many people have a poor sense of direction, and woodlands can be confusing places. Children normally have little fear, but parents will be uneasy if young children are not within view. There is both a fear of getting lost within the woodland, and of being disorientated so that you emerge from the woodland at an unknown point. Some people are also worried that if they have an accident, there may be no-one nearby to give help.

- Fear of being attacked. This understandable fear is much stronger in places where you are hidden from general public view, and on paths which are little used.

Woodlands are by their nature dense and closed, with few open views. It is impossible to rid a woodland of the features which some people fear, while at the same time retaining the woodland habitat. However, there are actions which can be taken to make woodlands accessible to more people.

Path design

Where new woodlands are being designed and planted, paths should follow a simple layout both to make routes easy to understand, and to improve visibility along them.

A simple layout which follows direct routes or 'desire lines' across a site is easy to follow, as well as encouraging regular use by people wanting access across a site. Meandering routes which add length and variety can be included as necessary. Visibility along paths will be improved by making paths straight or with long gentle curves.

Where access routes are being created in new woodlands, a width sufficient to take a vehicle should be the minimum (p164), except on steep ground.

Glades and open spaces

Wide sunny paths, woodland edges and glades and open spaces within a wooded setting are very appealing for walking and other recreation. In general most people will prefer to walk along the edge of a woodland, rather than venture into it, especially where there is undergrowth and the view is restricted. Mature beechwoods or other open woods with little undergrowth are an exception. For design and management of glades and woodland edges see pages 75 and 146.

Trails, maps and signs

Marked trails, signs and information boards will encourage use of paths. See details above (p175-177).

Encouraging regular use

Most people find 'safety in numbers', and use will be encouraged if people either visit a wood as part of a group, or know that the woodland is regularly used by other people.

- Dog walkers are the most regular users of woodlands, especially near residential areas, and are a reassuring legitimate presence for other woodland users. Dogs also have the useful function of disturbing deer, which are a problem in many woods. Encourage dog walkers by providing good access from nearby housing, or by providing car-parking areas.

- Consider upgrading any paths which provide a 'short cut' or direct access through a woodland. Surfacing of crushed stone or similar (p169) which provides an all-weather surface will encourage regular use throughout the year.

- Cycle paths (p170) are popular both for regular daily use and for recreation. Any cycle paths which link schools and residential areas are especially useful and may attract special funding.

- Circular routes with all-weather surfacing are popular with joggers.

- The needs of mobility vehicle users should be taken into account for all suitable routes.

Activities

Any organised activities which take place within a woodland will increase use, and familiarise visitors with the wood so that they are more likely to return. These can included guided walks, children's activities, woodland crafts, woodland management, green gym activities and many others. Some activities may require temporary closure of particular parts of the wood to other users, which should be publicised in advance, and should not restrict the use of rights of way.

Discouraging mis-use of woodlands

Some woodlands attract unsocial or criminal behaviour, including dumping of household and garden rubbish, cars and other items. Drug taking and other criminal behaviour may occur in certain locations. Many people will have a fear of being attacked. Such problems tend to escalate, as bad behaviour attracts more, and legitimate users are discouraged from using the woodland, so leaving it further open to abuse. Local householders may suffer associated problems such as vandalism or nuisance.

The problems are likely to need tackling by various local agencies and groups working in agreement with the owner of the land.

CLEARANCE OF LITTER AND RUBBISH

Clearing up all signs of neglect and making an area looked cared for is the first step in discouraging further dumping of rubbish and other antisocial behaviour. Enlist support from local groups if possible to help with tidying and clearance, so that they have a stake in preventing further problems and in improving the area.

An 'action day' or similar is a good way of tackling rubbish clearance, as it can bring people together through practical action, generates publicity and may be the starting point for further projects. The Tidy Britain Group can give advice, and the local council may be able to help with rubbish bags, litter-pickers, skips and so on. Volunteers must be capable and suitably equipped for the task. The area should be checked first for material which may pose a health and safety risk, such as chemicals, asbestos or other material. Care must be taken with glass and sharp items, discarded syringes and needles, very heavy objects and other items which may be hazardous.

Abandoned cars and other large and heavy items which are accessible by vehicle can be removed by recovery vehicles or tractors. Large items which have become surrounded by trees may have to be left in situ.

Some woodlands contain remnants of former industrial activity including machinery and buildings which may be of local or archaeological interest. Removal may not be an option, and by limited clearance and tidying they can become of a focus of interest within the wood, rather than an eyesore. Liability from unsafe buildings needs to be considered by the owner of the land.

Concentrate on improving the appearance of the visible margins of the wood, the boundaries with roads and car parking areas and path edges. Remove all litter regularly, and consider regular mowing of grass edges and car-park entrances. Regular mowing may not be best for wildlife, but creates a 'cared-for' appearance, and may lessen the incidence of littering.

Barriers to prevent vehicle access for litter dumping and abandonment of cars may be necessary, but must not infringe legal rights of access for horse riders, mobility vehicle users or other legitimate users, or for emergency vehicles. Several companies (p188) specialise in producing vehicle barriers, anti-vandal padlock boxes and other devices. See *Fencing* (BTCV, 2001).

A simple vehicle barrier can be made out of round timber as shown, with a hinge of chain, and an eyebolt and padlock to secure. Wires are stapled along the bar and down the posts to discourage the use of saws.

To block all vehicle access, barriers can include banks and ditches, large logs, large boulders and wooden bollards.

CLEARANCE OF UNDERGROWTH

Fear of potential attackers hiding in undergrowth is not backed up by statistics of such attacks, but access will be encouraged if walkers have a clear view through woodlands to either side of the path.

Open up views under the canopy by pruning lower branches, and thinning trees as necessary. Removal of shrubs and smaller trees beneath the upper canopy can be considered, and where the canopy is dense, regrowth is likely to be weak. It's not necessary to clear right through the woodland, as this will result in too much loss of habitat, will make the woodland draughty and inhospitable to many creatures, and will appear monotonous. Clear zones near the path, or strips that open up views to other paths or open spaces, and leave other parts uncleared.

When planning clearance, consider the future management requirements. There is no point in cutting undergrowth if it's going to regrow rapidly. Annual clearance with a brush cutter may be needed to maintain open conditions.

LOCAL OWNERSHIP

Mis-use of woodlands is less likely to be tolerated when local residents have an interest in the woodland through time and effort spent in helping manage it. 'Friends of ....' and other local interest groups which may evolve from local action are invaluable in helping by practical work, by informal wardening and generally 'keeping an eye' on local areas and reporting any problems. Criminal or antisocial behaviour is discouraged where wrongdoers feel they are being watched.

Much of the practical work described in this handbook will help to make woodlands accessible, both through the practical improvements made, and by the presence of people working in the wood encouraging others to visit.

chain stapled to secure

bar

stapled wires to discourage vandalism

padlock through eyebolt

TOP VIEW

bar

drill hole large enough to take eyebolt

Appendix A
Conservation and the volunteer worker

The Conservation Volunteers is the largest practical conservation organisation in the UK. It supports more than 85,000 volunteers from all sections of the community in activities to protect and improve the environment. With more than 110 offices around the UK, we are able to work in a range of areas carrying out different activities. The Practical Handbooks series is one of the ways of helping to ensure that work undertaken by volunteers and other conservationists is to the highest standard.

To ensure the success of any conservation project, it is important to establish:

- Whether it is a worthwhile conservation project. Any work to be carried out should respond to a real need which is directly related to a broad framework of development. In terms of conservation, this means that projects should be undertaken as integral parts of site management plans, not as isolated exercises. The prime purpose of the work should also be made clear. For instance is it to improve local wildlife habitats or to improve access to the countryside?

- That the work is suitable for volunteers. Volunteers cannot successfully tackle all types of work and they should not be involved where there is a risk of serious accident or injury, where machines can do the same job more effectively and for a lower cost, or where the skills required are beyond their capabilities. The latter can be overcome if professional training is provided so that a situation can be avoided where volunteers become dispirited or the work is not done to a high standard.

- Where the project will take place and how much time it will take to complete. Once this has been done it is necessary to establish whether there are any hazards and risks associated with the site.

- Whether the work should be done by paid staff. Voluntary service should not replace paid, local labour but complement it. Employers should make sure in advance that the position of volunteers and paid workers is clear with respect to any relevant labour unions.

Volunteers should not be regarded as providing 'free labour'. Someone has to pay for transport, materials, tools, insurance, refreshments and any accommodation charges. Before each party makes a commitment to a project it should be clear who is to pay for what. While volunteers may willingly fund their own work, clients should be prepared to contribute and should not assume that all volunteers, who are already giving their time and effort, will be able to meet other expenses out of their own pockets. Several grant-aiding bodies may help pay the cost of environmental and conservation projects. For details of grants and awards, contact The Conservation Volunteers at the address on page ii. Information is available in publications by the Charities Aid Foundation (see page 114).

It is important that volunteer workers are covered by public liability insurance for any damage or injury they may cause to third party property or to the public. Cover of at least two million pounds is recommended. Additional insurance to compensate the volunteer for injury to him or herself or to other volunteers on a project should also be considered. Specially tailored insurance is available through The Conservation Volunteers community group membership scheme. Contact address on page ii.

The volunteer group organiser should visit the work site well before the project to check that it is suitable and that volunteers will not be exploited, and to plan the best size of working party and the proper tools and equipment. Volunteers should be advised in advance on suitable clothing for the expected conditions, they should be physically fit and come prepared for work. Above all, individuals should genuinely want to volunteer – those 'press-ganged' into volunteering may do more harm than good and will not enjoy the benefits associated with volunteering. Young volunteers need more supervision and are best suited to less strenuous jobs, and it is recommended that where they are involved, the project should emphasise education. Recent legislation, including The Children Act, gives comprehensive guidance on supervisory ratios and other means to safeguard the welfare of young people. The recommendations of the Home Office report *Safe from harm*, should also be followed, and for any activities in remote areas, organisers should also be fully aware of the Adventure Activities Licensing Regulations.

Volunteer group organisers and clients should keep records of the work undertaken: the date of the project, jobs done, techniques used, number of volunteers and details of any notable events including accidents, unusual 'finds', publicity etc. Such information makes it easier to handle problems or queries which may arise after the project. It also provides a background on the project site for future visits, supplies practical data by which the site management plan can be evaluated and allows an assessment to be made of the volunteer effort.

As well as directly managing project work, whether for a day or longer, we support volunteers indirectly through the local group service, run a year round programme of training courses and organises hundreds of conservation holidays in the UK and abroad. To find out more about what opportunities are available please get in touch (address on page ii).

Appendix B
Contacts

This is a list of some of the organisations in the UK which are involved with environmental matters. The web site www.tcv.org.uk provides links to a large number of environmental organisations throughout the world. A selection of relevant websites, that are not included under the addresses below, are listed at the bottom of this section.

Arboricultural Association
Ampfield House,
Ampfield, Hants SO51 9PA
Tel: 01794 368717
www.trees.org.uk

Bat Conservation Trust
15 Cloisters House,
8 Battersea Park Road,
London SW8 4BG
Tel: 020 7627 2629
www.bats.org.uk

British Trust for Ornithology
The Nunnery, Thetford, Norfolk IP24 2PU
Tel: 01842 750 050
www.bto.org

Butterfly Conservation
Manor Yard, East Lulworth,
Near Wareham, Dorset BH20 5QP
Tel: 01929 400209
www.butterfly-conservation.org

Campaign to Protect Rural England (CPRE)
128 Southwark Street, London SE1 0SW
Tel: 020 7981 2800
www.cpre.org.uk

Centre for Alternative Technology
Machynlleth, Powys SY20 9AZ
Tel: 01654 705950
www.cat.org.uk

Common Ground
Gold Hill House, 21 High Street,
Shaftesbury, Dorset SP7 8JE
Tel: 01747 850820
www.commonground.org.uk

Countryside Council for Wales
Maes-y-Ffynnon, Penrhosgarnedd, Bangor,
Gwynedd LL57 2DN
Tel: 0845 1306229
www.ccw.gov.uk

Countryside Management Association
Writtle College, Lordship Road, Writtle,
Chelmsford, Essex CM1 3RR
Tel: 01245 424116
www.countrysidemanagement.org.uk

Dept. for Environment, Food & Rural Affairs (Defra)
Nobel House, 17 Smith Square,
London SW1P 3JR
Tel: 020 7238 6000
Helpline: 08459 335577
www.defra.gov.uk

Dry Stone Walling Association
c/o Westmoreland County Showground,
Lane Farm, Crooklands, Milnthorpe,
Cumbria LA7 7NH
Tel: 01539 567953
www.dswa.org.uk

Environment Agency
General Enquiries: 08708 506506
Emergency Hotline: 0800 807060
www.environment-agency.gov.uk

Environment Council
212 High Holborn, London WC1V 7BF
Tel: 020 7836 2626
www.the-environment-council.org.uk

Environment and Heritage Service
Natural Heritage, Commonwealth House,
35 Castle Street, Belfast BT1 1GU
Tel: 028 9054 6595
www.ehsni.gov.uk

Farming and Wildlife Advisory Group
National Agricultural Centre,
Stoneleigh, Kenilworth,
Warwickshire CV8 2RX
Tel: 02476 696699
www.fwag.org.uk

Flora locale
Denford Manor, Hungerford,
Berkshire RG7 0UN
Tel: 01488 680 457
www.floralocale.org

Forestry Commission
231 Corstorphine Road, Edinburgh EH12 7AT
Tel: 0131 334 0303
www.forestry.gov.uk

Forestry Contracting Association Ltd
Dalfling, Blairdaff, Inverurie,
Aberdeenshire AB51 5LA
Tel: 01467 651368
www.fcauk.com

Game Conservancy
Fordingbridge, Hants SP6 1EF
Tel: 01425 652381
www.gct.org.uk

The Greenwood Trust
Station Road, Coalbrookdale Telford TF8 7DR
Tel: 01952 432769
www.greenwoodtrust.co.uk

Health and Safety Executive
Rose Court, 2 Southwark Bridge,
London SE1 9HS
Tel: 020 7717 6234
Infoline: 0845 345 0055
www.hse.gov.uk

Lantra
Lantra House, Stoneleigh Park, Coventry,
Warwickshire CV8 2LG
Tel: 024 7669 6996
www.lantra.co.uk

Landlife
National Wildflower Centre, Court Hey Park,
Liverpool L16 3NA
Tel: 0151 737 1819
www.landlife.org.uk

National Hedge Laying Society
The Secretary, 88 Manor Road, Toddington,
Bedfordshire LU5 6AJ
www.hedgelaying.org.uk

Natural England
Natural England, 1 East Parade,
Sheffield S1 2ET
Tel: 0114 241 8920
www.naturalengland.org.uk

Northern Ireland Environment Agency
Natural Heritage Protected Landscapes /
AONBs Klondyke Building, Cromac Avenue,
Gasworks Business Park, Lower Ormeau Road,
Belfast BT7 2JA
Tel:0845 302 0008
www.ni-environment.gov.uk

Plantlife
14 Rollestone Street, Salisbury,
Wiltshire SP1 1DX
Tel: 01722 342730
www.plantlife.org.uk

Ponds Conservation Trust
BMS, Oxford Brookes University, Gipsy Lane,
Headington, Oxford OX3 0BP
Tel: 01865 483199
www.pondtrust.org.uk

Ramblers Association
2nd Floor, Camelford House,
87-90 Albert Embankment, London SE1 7TW
Tel: 020 7339 8500
www.ramblers.org.uk

Royal Forestry Society of England, Wales and Northern Ireland
102 High Street, Tring, Herts HP23 4AF
Tel: 01442 822028
www.rfs.org.uk

Royal Society for the Protection of Birds (RSPB)
The Lodge, Sandy, Beds SG19 2DL
Tel: 01767 680551
www.rspb.org.uk

Scottish Environment Protection Agency (SEPA),
SEPA Corporate Office, Erskine Court,
Castle Business Park, Stirling FK9 4TR
Tel: 01786 457700
www.sepa.org.uk

Scottish Natural Heritage
12 Hope Terrace, Edinburgh EH9 2AS
Tel: 0131 447 4784
www.snh.org.uk

Small Woods Association
The Cabins, Malehurst Estate, Minsterley,
Shropshire SY5 0EQ
Tel: 01743 792644
www.smallwoods.org.uk

Sustrans Ltd
National Cycle Network Office, 2 Cathedral
Square, College Green, Bristol BS1 5DD
Tel: 0117 926 8893
www.sustrans.org.uk

Thrive
The Geoffrey Udall Centre, Beech Hill,
Reading RG7 2AT
Tel: 01189 885688
www.thrive.org.uk

The Tree Advice Trust
Arboricultural Advisory and Information
Service, Alice Holt Lodge, Wrecclesham,
Farnham, Surrey GU10 4LH
Tel: 01420 22022
Tree Helpline – *premium rate*: 09065 161147
www.treehelp.info

Tree Council
51 Catherine Place, London SW1E 6DY
Tel: 020 7828 9928
www.treecouncil.org.uk
...continues overleaf

WWF-UK

Panda House, Weyside Park, Godalming,
Surrey, GU7 1XR
Tel: 01483 426444
www.wwf.org.uk

Woodland Trust

Autumn Park, Grantham,
Lincolnshire NG31 6LL
Tel: 01476 581111
www.woodland-trust.org.uk

WEBSITES

The following are a selection of websites for woodland and other environmental information, services, products and networks. Details subject to change.

www.adas.co.uk
(consultancy and research organisation for the land-based industries)

www.aie.org.uk
(Arboricultural Information Exchange)

www.alphasearch.co.uk
(index of woodland suppliers, services, training)

www.cafonline.org
(Charities Aid Foundation)

www.communityforest.org.uk
(The Community Forests)

www.coppice.org.uk
(Wessex Coppice Group)

www.dendrologist.org.uk
(The Dendrologist)

www.dsc.org.uk
(Directory of Social Change)

www.ecnc.nl
(European Centre for Nature Conservation)

www.ecolots.co.uk
(Rural products, equipment and services, for sale and wanted)

www.jncc.gov.uk
(Joint Nature Conservation Committee)

www.naturenet.net
(Nature conservation network)

www.nhbs.com
(Natural History Book Service)

www.nbn.org.uk
(National Biodiversity Network)

www.recycle-it.org
(Timber Recycling Information Centre)

www.tree-register.org
(Tree Register of the British Isles)

www.treesource.co.uk
(tree bookshop and information)

www.treetrader.co.uk
(UK native tree nurseries)

www.ukbap .org.uk
(Biodiversity Action Plans)

www.wildlifetrusts.org
(The Wildlife Trusts)

www.woodlands.co.uk
(woodlands for sale)

www.woodnet.org.uk
(service for wood producers and users),

Appendix C
Grants

Various organisations may give grants towards the cost of tree planting and woodland management work. Eligibility depends on many factors, including the objectives of the work, the area of the country, any special site designations, involvement of the local community, public access, contributions to biodiversity targets and other matters.

Outline information only is given here, with contact details for further information.

SOURCES OF INFORMATION

Local

Contact The Conservation Volunteers, Forestry Commission, local authority woodland or tree officer, or local office of the government nature conservation agency (English Nature, Countryside Council for Wales, Scottish Natural Heritage or Environment and Heritage Service for Northern Ireland) for information about your area.

Royal Forestry Society

The Royal Forestry Society of England and Wales publish the *Grants for Tr££s Booklet*, which gives comprehensive details on grants related to trees and woodlands, and is updated regularly. The information is also available online at www.rfs.org.uk

WOODLAND GRANT SCHEME

The Woodland Grant Scheme (WGS), administered by the Forestry Commission, is the main grant available in Great Britain for creating new woodlands and managing existing woodlands. Within the WGS, various other schemes and supplements may be available. The information below gives a general outline. For current details, contact the local Forestry Commission office or visit www.forestry.gov.uk

Creating new woodlands

To qualify, a new woodland normally has to be at least 0.25 hectare in area, and at least 15 metres wide, but smaller areas may qualify if, for example, it adds to existing woods. To be approved, applications in England must meet the priorities of the England Forestry Strategy, with similar strategies in Wales and Scotland. In awarding grants, a scoring system gives priority to new woodlands which will contribute to economic regeneration, provide access, or contribute to a named national or local BAP, HAP or SAP target. Larger woodlands score higher than smaller woodlands.

Grants for new planting are paid in two instalments: 70% when planting is finished, and 30% after five years. Normally the planting rate is 2250 trees per hectare. For broadleaves this can be reduced to 1100 trees per hectare for small schemes below 3 hectares, where the broadleaves form part of a mainly coniferous scheme, or for new native woodlands on appropriate sites. Grants are also available to create new woodlands through natural regeneration.

Additional payments may be available for planting on former agricultural land, for community woodlands or in Community Forest areas.

New native pinewoods in the Highlands of Scotland attract the same rate of grant as broadleaves, with eligibility restricted to those areas within the former natural distribution of Scots pine-dominated pine-birch forest.

Provided that it is consistent with the environmental requirements of the WGS, grants may be payable on suitable sites for the establishment of new coppices for traditional management.

In some areas, 'challenge funds' are available for which bids can be made, and for which a high rate of grant is payable. These are available for a limited time, and for particular types of planting.

Farm Woodland Premium Scheme

The Farm Woodland Premium Scheme supports the creation of farm woodland by encouraging farmers to convert productive agricultural land to woodlands, through annual payments to compensate for agricultural income forgone. These are normally for schemes already approved under the WGS.

Existing woodland

For existing woodland, grants are available for restocking by planting or natural regeneration. Where natural regeneration is practical and appropriate, the Forestry Commission will not normally agree to proposals for planting.

The Annual Management Grant may be available to help towards the cost of maintaining and improving woodland, where this safeguards or enhances the special environmental value of a woodland, or improves public access. The Woodland Improvement Grant is a single payment made to improve public access, bring undermanaged woods back into management, or encourage woodland biodiversity.

AGRI-ENVIRONMENT SCHEMES

The Environmentally Sensitive Area (ESA) scheme in England protects 22 areas of national environmental significance, totalling 10% of agricultural land, where changes in farming methods may pose a threat, and conservation depends on adopting, maintaining or extending particular farming methods. Farmers receive an annual payment based on income forgone for entering into 10 year management agreements.

Outside ESAs, the Countryside Stewardship Scheme in England is the main government scheme for the wider countryside, and offers annual payments and capital grants to manage particular habitats and features in the interests of conservation. Agreements normally run for 10 years. The Countryside Stewardship Scheme is open to anyone who owns or manages suitable land, including farmers, landowners, local authorities, voluntary bodies and community groups. For further details on ESAs and CSSs contact your local DEFRA office, or visit www. defra.gov.uk/erdp/schemes

In Scotland, the Rural Stewardship Scheme is an agri-environment scheme designed to encourage farmers, crofters and others to adopt environmentally-friendly practices and to maintain and enhance particular habitats and landscape features. This may include management of native or semi-natural woodland, hedges and coppices. For further details visit www.scotland.gov.uk

In Wales, Tir Gofal encourages farmers throughout Wales to maintain and enhance the agricultural landscape and wildlife habitats. Tir Gofal is run by the Countryside Council for Wales. For further details visit www.ccw. gov.uk

England Rural Development Programme

The England Rural Development Programme runs from 2000-06 and supports schemes aimed at protecting the environment and supporting the rural economy and communities. These schemes include Environmentally Sensitive Areas, the Countryside Stewardship Scheme, the Woodland Grant Scheme, the Farm Woodland Premium Scheme, the Energy Crops Scheme and others involved with enterprise and training. For further details visit www.defra.gov.uk/erdp

Separate Rural Development Programmes are being drawn up for Scotland, Wales and Northern Ireland.

WOODLAND INITIATIVES

There are many regional and local woodland initiatives which can give advice on funding and other matters relevant to woodland management. The Woodlands Initiatives Register is compiled by the Small Woodlands Association and is available on their website at www. smallwoods.org.uk

NATURE CONSERVATION

Grants may be available for particular management work which benefits biodiversity or contributes to a local or national HAP, BAP or SAP. Veteran trees and coppice management for butterflies are examples of work which may attract advice and funding. For details of schemes contact the local office of the nature conservation agency (EN, CCW, SNH) or biodiversity officer of the local authority.

Appendix D
Training

The organisations listed below provide training in woodland management skills. There is a wide variety of training available, from short courses in woodland ecology, to training and assessment in the use of chain saws and other power equipment. Outline details of qualifications and assessments are also given.

TRAINING ORGANISATIONS

The Conservation Volunteers

We have over 50 years' experience of practical conservation, and is one of the leading providers of training in practical conservation skills. Training is an important part of every activity, whether run locally or through the national and international conservation holidays programme. Learning whilst doing has always been an important concept for us, and all our activities include a training element.

In the area of woodland management, we run a range of short courses on tree identification, woodland ecology and management, coppicing, coppice crafts, green woodworking, and basic tree felling using hand tools. Training and assessment in basic chainsaw use and maintenance, leading to qualification in the relevant NPTC units (see below) is also available. Similar courses are run in Northern Ireland.

Over 50% of the UK National Vocational Qualifications (NVQs) in Environmental Conservation are gained through The Conservation Volunteers (see below). In Northern Ireland we run a six-month environmental employment programme which includes training and qualifications in the use of chainsaws and pesticides, and the NVQ Level 2 in Environmental Conservation.

Under the guidance of the Tree Council, we are the approved training provider for the Tree Warden Scheme, which is a network of volunteer Tree Wardens who help to protect their local tree heritage.

We run a national training programme on behalf of the Environmental Trainers Network, which is a network of training managers in environmental organisations. The programme includes short courses and workshops designed for staff and volunteers working on environmental issues and activities.

For further information on training and other activities, contact your local office, phone Customer Services on 01302 388883, or visit www.tcv.org.uk/shop.

Small Woods Association

The Small Woods Association runs a programme of short courses designed for the owners of small woods and others interested in woodland management, and covering a range of topics on the practical, financial and legal aspects of owning and managing a small wood. For further details contact the Small Woods Association on 01952 432769 or visit www.smallwoods.org.uk

The Green Wood Trust

The Green Wood Trust runs a range of courses on green wood working skills, coppicing and related crafts. In association with other coppicing organisations, they are developing a programme of accreditation in coppice skills. For further details contact the Green Wood Trust on 01952 432769, or visit www.greenwoodtrust.org.uk

Lantra

Lantra provides a focus for the development of skills, knowledge and enterprise of people in the land based sector, with training and assessment provided through Lantra Awards. Integrated training and assessment courses are available in the use of chainsaws and brushcutters. The Environment and Conservation courses, which are not assessed, include managing woodlands, designing and planting new woodlands, hedgelaying and fencing. For further details contact Lantra Awards on 02476 419 703 or visit www.lantra.co.uk

Competence standards in the forestry industry which were formerly set by FASTCo are part of the responsibility of Lantra, who should be contacted for further details (024 7669 6996 or visit www.lantra.co.uk)

Other organisations

Short courses in aspects of woodland management may also be provided by the Field Studies Council, county wildlife trusts or particular interest groups related to woodland ecology and wildlife.

QUALIFICATIONS AND ASSESSMENT

Chainsaw training and assessment

It is a legal requirement for chainsaw users to be trained. Under the Provision and Use of Work Equipment Regulations 1998, employers are required to provide adequate training and to ensure that chainsaws and related equipment are operated only by employees who have received appropriate training in their safe use. The regulations also apply to the self-employed. Training should be provided by instructors recognised by Lantra. Assessors must be recognised by either the

National Proficiency Testing Council (NPTC), Scottish Skills Testing Service (SSTS) or Lantra.

Regular re-assessment is a requirement in many organisations, with a formal re-assessment by a registered assessor recommended every 3 years. The NPTC assessment comprises separate units. The chainsaw maintenance unit is mandatory, and there are currently 15 other optional units covering all aspects of chainsaw use. Chainsaw users must only carry out operations covered by the units for which they have been trained and assessed as competent. For further details contact the NPTC (01203 696553 or www.nptc.org.uk), SSTS or Lantra.

NVQs/SVQs

The National Vocational Qualifications (NVQs) or Scottish Vocational Qualifications (SVQs) are work-related, competence based qualifications, which are available to anyone at any age or stage of their career. Candidates do not have to follow a course, but need to provide evidence that they have the competence to meet the NVQ/SVQ standards. NVQs/SVQs can be gained at work, college or through training courses. The Conservation Volunteers can provide training and work experience towards NVQs/SVQs in Environmental Conservation, and in some areas, in Forestry or Horticulture.

Appendix E
Suppliers

This is a brief list of suppliers of tree planting products. Other firms may produce similar suitable products. Horticulture Week and Forestry and British Timber (monthly) are useful sources of information. Websites worth checking for products, services and links include www.ecolots.co.uk (sales, wants and events, rural products and services) www.woodnet.org.uk (network of UK producers and users of wood) www.treetrader.co.uk (native trees and flowers) and www.alphasearch.co.uk (forestry products and services).

Alba Trees plc
Gladsmiur, East Lothian,
Scotland EH33 2AI
Tel: 01620 825058
www.albatrees.co.uk
Native trees and shrubs, tools for planting
Rootrainers

Acorn Planting Products Ltd
Little Money Road, Loddon,
Norwich NR14 6JD
Tel: 01508 528763
www.acorn-p-p.co.uk
Treeshelters, shelterguards, gro-cones,
mulching mats

Arien Products
99 Church Street, Highbridge,
Somerset TA9 3HR
Tel: 01278 785268
www.arien.com
Countryside signs

Blackburn Fraser Ltd
6 Choir Street, Salford M7 9ZD
Tel: 0161 8352069
www.blackburnfraser.co.uk
Steel access control products; gates, barriers,
disabled access

Bramley and Wellesley Ltd
PO Box 167, Gloucester GL2 8YS
Tel: 01452 300450
www.bramley.co.uk
Electric netting, permanent electric fencing

Centrewire Limited
PO Box 11, Wymondham, Norfolk
Tel: 01953 602085
www.centrewire.com
Temporary deer fencing, wire, fencing, stiles and
gates, access control

Charterhouse Richmond
Weydown Road, Haslemere,
Surrey GU27 2BR
Tel: 01428 643328 www.charterhouserichmond.
co.uk
Forestry tools, equipment, books, accessories

Farm Forestry Co Ltd
Eaton Farm, Bishop's Castle,
Shropshire SY9 5HX
Tel: 01588 650496
www.farmforestry.co.uk
Temporary deer fencing, tree guards

Jacobi Jayne & Company
Freepost 1155, Herne Bay CT3 4BR
Tel: 0800 072 0130
www.wildbirdnews.com
Bird and bat boxes, protection devices, hanging pole

John Chambers' Wild Flower Seeds
15 Westleigh Road, Barton Seagrave, Kettering,
Northants NN15 5AJ
Tel: 01933 652562
Wildflower and grass seed

Landlife Wildflowers Ltd
National Wildflower Centre, Court Hey Park,
Liverpool L16 3NA
Tel: 0151 7371819
www.landlife.org.uk
Wildflower seeds

Ronaash Limited
Kersquarter, Kelso, Roxburghshire TD5 8HH
Tel: 01573 225757
www.ronaash.co.uk
Rootrainers

Shelley Signs Ltd
Eaton-on-Tern, Market Drayton,
Shropshire TF9 2BX
Tel: 01952 541483
www.shelleysigns.co.uk
Countryside signs

Somerset Levels Basket and Craft Centre Ltd
Lyng Road, Burrowbridge, Bridgwater,
Somerset TA7 0SG
Tel: 01823 689688
www.somersetlevels.co.uk
Live willow and bolts of willow for basketry

Stanton Hope Limited
11 Seax Court, Southfields, Laindon SS15 6LY
Tel: 01268 419141
www.stantonhope.co.uk
Clothing, tools, tree protectors, chainsaws,
safety signs, chemicals, sprayers, measures

Symbio
38 Bookham Industrial Park, Church Road,
Great Bookham, Surrey KT23 3EU
Tel: 01372 456101
www.symbio.co.uk
MycoForce mycorrhizal and microbial products

The Conservation Volunteers
Sedum House, Mallard Way
Doncaster DN4 8DB
Tel: 01302 388883
www.tcv.org.uk/shop
Trees, shrubs, tools, tree planting products

Terram Ltd
Mamhilad, Pontypool, Gwent NP4 0YR
Tel: 01495 757722
www.terram.com
Geotextile for track and path base

Tornado Wire Ltd
Waterloo Road Industrial Estate,
Bidford-on-Avon, Warwickshire B50 4JH
Tel: 0870 759 3610
www.tornadowire.co.uk
High tensile fencing specialists

Traditional Charcoal
10 Manor Crescent, Middlewich,
Cheshire, CW10 0EW
Tel: 01606 835243
Ring and retort charcoal kilns, grader

Woodland Improvement and Conservation Ltd
Cwmbychan Farm, Ferryside,
Carmarthenshire SA17 5YD
Tel: 01267 267 276
www.woodland-improvement.co.uk
Native and introduced trees, tools, tree guards,
accessories, books

Woodland Management
Bridge Farm, Reymerston, Norwich,
Norfolk NR9 4QD
Tel: 01362 821082
www.gengard.net
Genguards

Appendix F
National Vegetation Classification

New native woodland types

The following tables detail the major and minor tree and shrub species suitable for creating new native woodlands, based on National Vegetation Classification (NVC) woodland types. The distribution and soils of the NVC types are shown on pages 193 and 194.

NATIVE TREES

Major and minor species for new native woodland types

● = major species throughout range

■ = major species locally or in part of range

❑ = minor species throughout range

○ = minor species locally or in part of range

KEY TO WOODLAND TYPES

W2   Alder woodland with common reed
W4   Birch woodland with purple moor-grass
W6   Alder woodland with stinging nettle
W7   Alder-ash woodland with yellow pimpernel
W8   Lowland mixed broadleaved woodland with dog's mercury
W9   Upland mixed broadleaved woodland with dog's mercury
W10 Lowland mixed broadleaved woodland with bluebell
W11 Upland oak-birch woodland with bluebell
W12 Beech-ash woodland with dog's mercury
W14 Beech-oak woodland with bramble
W15 Beech-oak woodland with wavy hair-grass
W16 Lowland oak-birch woodland with bilberry
W17 Upland oak-birch woodland with bilberry
W18 Scots pine woodland with heather
W19 Juniper woodland with wood sorrel

NATIVE TREES Major and minor species for new native woodland types														
	W8	W9	W10	W11	W16	W17	W12	W14	W15	W18	W19	W2	W6	W7	W4
Alder		❏										●	●	●	❏
Ash	●	●	○				●	❏				❏	❏	●	
Aspen	○	○	○	○	○										
Beech							●	●	●						
Birch, downy	❏	●	○	●	■	●				○	❏	●	❏	❏	●
Birch, silver	❏		●	○	●	○	❏	❏	❏	○					
Crab apple	❏		❏												
Elm, wych	■	❏	■												
Field maple	■						❏								
Cherry, gean	○		○					❏							
Cherry, bird		❏												○	
Holly	❏	❏	❏	❏	❏	❏	❏	●	●				❏	❏	
Hornbeam	○		○				❏								
Oak, common	●	○	●	○	●	○	❏	●	●			❏	❏	❏	
Oak, sessile	■	❏	■	●	■	●		○	○					❏	
Rowan	○	●	❏	❏	❏	❏		❏	❏	❏	❏			❏	
Scots pine										●	❏				
Whitebeam	○				○		❏								
Willow, crack												❏	●		
Willow, goat	❏							❏					❏	❏	❏
Yew							❏	❏	❏						

NATIVE SHRUBS Major and minor species for new native woodland types														
	W8	W9	W10	W11	W16	W17	W12	W14	W15	W18	W19	W2	W6	W7	W4
Blackthorn	□		□										□	□	
Broom			□												
Buckthorn, alder					○				□			□	○		
Buckthorn, purging	○											□	○		
Dogwood	○						□								
Elder	□	□	□		○		□	□					●	□	
Gorse			□		□										
Guelder rose	□		□				□					□	□	□	
Hawthorn	●	□	●	□		○	●	□				□	□	●	
Hazel	●	●	●	□		○	●	□						●	
Wild privet	□						□	□							
Spindle	○						□								
Wayfaring tree	○		○				□								
Juniper				○		○	□			□	●				
Willow, almond													□		
Willow, bay														○	□
Willow, eared												□			□
Sallow, grey	□	□										●	●	●	●
Willow, osier													□		
Willow, purple													□		

DISTRIBUTION OF NVC WOODLAND TYPES

Map 1: The lowland zone of Britain			
NVC number	W8	W10	W16
NVC name	Lowland mixed broadleaved woodland with dog's mercury	Lowland mixed broadleaved woodland with bluebell	Lowland oak-birch woodland with bilberry
Soil type	Rendzinas and calcareous brown earths	Base-rich brown earths	Podzolic and ironpan soils

Map 2: The upland zone of Britain					
NVC number	W9	W11	W17	W4	W7
NVC name	Upland mixed broadleaved woodland with dog's mercury	Upland oak-birch woodland with bluebell	Upland oak-birch woodland with bilberry	Birch woodland with purple moor-grass	Alder-ash woodland with yellow pimpernel
Soil type	Rendzinas and calcareous brown earth	Base-poor brown earths	Podzolic and ironpan soils	Wet peat	Wet gleys and brown earths

 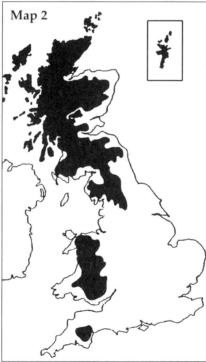 

Map 3: The zone of semi-natural beech woodlands			
NVC number	W12	W14	W15
NVC name	Beech-ash woodland with dog's mercury	Beech-oak woodland with bramble	Beech-oak woodland with wavy hair-grass
Soil type	Rendzinas	Base-poor brown earths	Podzols

Map 4

Map 5

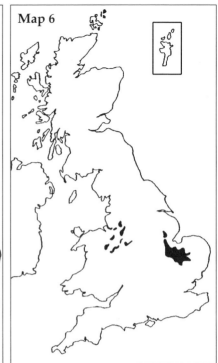

Map 6

Map 4: The zone of semi-natural pine woodland	
NVC number	W18
NVC name	Scots pine woodland with heather
Soil type	Highly acidic podzols

Map 5: The zone of upland juniper woodland	
NVC number	W19
NVC name	Juniper woodland with wild sorrel
Soil type	Neutral brown earths

Map 6: Wet woodland on fen peat	
NVC number	W2
NVC name	Alder woodland with common reed

Map 7: Wet woodland on alluvium	
NVC number	W6
NVC name	Alder woodland with stinging nettle

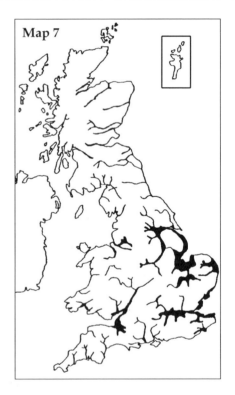

Map 7

Appendix G
Latin Names

NATIVE TREES: LARGE AND MEDIUM SIZE	
COMMON NAME	LATIN NAME
Alder, black	*Alnus glutinosa*
Apple, crab	*Malus sylvestris*
Ash	*Fraxinus excelsior*
Aspen	*Populus tremula*
Beech	*Fagus sylvatica*
Birch, downy	*Betula pubescens*
Birch, silver	*Betula pendula*
Cherry, bird	*Prunus padus*
Cherry, gean	*Prunus avium*
Elm, wych	*Ulmus glabra*
Hornbeam	*Carpinus betulus*
Lime, small-leaved	*Tilia cordata*
Lime, large-leaved	*Tilia platyphyllos*
Maple, field	*Acer campestre*
Oak, common	*Quercus robur*
Oak, sessile	*Quercus petraea*
Pine, Scots	*Pinus sylvestris*
Poplar, black	*Populus nigra*
Poplar, grey	*Populus canescens*
Rowan	*Sorbus aucuparia*
Service tree	*Sorbus torminalis*
Whitebeam	*Sorbus aria*
Willow, crack	*Salix fragilis*
Willow, goat	*Salix caprea*
Willow, white	*Salix alba*
Yew	*Taxus baccata*

NATIVE SHRUBS AND SMALL TREES	
COMMON NAME	LATIN NAME
Blackthorn	*Prunus spinosa*
Box	*Buxus sempervirens*
Broom	*Cytisus scoparius*
Buckthorn, alder	*Frangula alnus*
Buckthorn, purging	*Rhamnus catharticus*
Butcher's broom	*Ruscus aculeatus*
Dogwood	*Cornus sanguinea*
Elder	*Sambucus nigra*
Gorse	*Ulex europaeus*
Guelder rose	*Viburnum opulus*
Hawthorn, common	*Crataegus monogyna*
Hawthorn, Midland	*Crataegus laevigata*
Hazel	*Corylus avellana*
Holly	*Ilex aquifolium*
Juniper	*Juniperus communis*
Privet	*Ligustrum vulgare*
Rose, dog	*Rosa canina*
Rose, field	*Rosa arvensis*
Spindle	*Euonymus europaeus*
Spurge laurel	*Daphne laureola*
Wayfaring tree	*Viburnum lantana*
Willow, almond	*Salix triandra*
Willow, bay	*Salix pentandra*
Willow, eared	*Salix aurita*
Willow, grey	*Salix cinerea*
Willow, osier	*Salix viminalis*
Willow, purple	*Salix purpurea*

Bibliography

Abbott, Mike (1989)
Green Woodwork
Guild of Master Craftsman Publications

BSBI and JNCC (1999)
Code of Conduct for the conservation and enjoyment of wild plants BSBI and JNCC

Bright, P, Morris, P and Mitchell-Jones, T (1996)
The Dormouse Conservation Handbook
English Nature

British Charcoal and Coppice Specialist Group (undated)
Charcoal Production in the UK
Forestry Contracting Association

Broad, Ken (1998)
Caring for Small Woods
Earthscan Publications Ltd

Brown, R and Robinson, R (1997)
Bracken Management Handbook: integrated bracken management
Rhone-Poulenc (from Aventis Crop Science Ltd)

Burgess, J (1995)
Growing in Confidence – understanding people's perceptions of urban fringe woodlands
Countryside Commission

Butcher, Mary
Willow Work
Mickle Print

Child, L and Wade, M (2000)
The Japanese Knotweed Manual
Packard, Chichester

Coulthard, Nonie and Scott, Michael (2001)
Flowers of the Forest
Plantlife

Countryside Commission for Scotland (1989)
Footbridges in the Countryside
CCS (Scottish Natural Heritage)

Dewar, Sue M, and Shawyer, Colin R (1996)
Boxes, Baskets and Platforms – artificial nest sites for owls and other birds of prey
The Hawk and Owl Trust

du Feu, Chris (1993)
Nestboxes
British Trust for Ornithology

Edlin, H L (1949)
Woodland Crafts in Britain
Batsford

English Nature (1999)
Guidelines for Identifying Ancient Woodland
English Nature

FACT (2001)
Practical Solutions Handbook 2nd edition
English Nature

Ferris-Kaan, R (1995)
The Ecology of Woodland Creation
John Wiley and Sons

Francis, Joanna L and Morton, Alan (2001)
Enhancement of Amenity – woodland field layers in Milton Keynes
In British Wildlife Vol 12 No 4, 2001

Gowan, Leo (1997)
Stickmaking
The Crowood Press

Gulliver, Richard and Gulliver, Mavis
Key to Plants Common in Woodlands
Field Studies Council

Hampshire County Council (1995)
Hazel Coppice – past, present and future
Hampshire County Council

Hodgetts, N G (1996)
The Conservation of Lower Plants in Woodland
JNCC

Hollingdale, A C, Krishnan R and Robinson A P (1999)
Charcoal Production – A Handbook
eco-logic books

Humphries, Chris, Press, John and Sutton, David (2000)
The Hamlyn Guide to Trees of Britain and Europe
Hamlyn

Kirby, K J (1992)
Forest Operations and Broadleaf Woodland Conservation
JNCC

Kirby, K J and Drake, M (1993)
Dead Wood Matters
English Nature

Kirby, P (2001)
Habitat Management for Invertebrates
RSPB

Lambert, F (1977)
Tools and Devices for Coppice Crafts
Young Farmers' Club Booklet (available from
Centre for Alternative Technology)

Law, Ben (2001)
The Woodland Way
Permanent Publications

Macpherson, George (1995)
Home-grown Energy from Short-rotation Coppice
Farming Press Books

Miles, Archie (1999)
Silva: The Tree in Britain
Ebury Press

Mitchell, Alan (1974)
*A Field Guide to the Trees of Britain and
Northern Europe*
Collins

Mitchley, J, Burch, F, Buckley, P and Watt, T A (2000)
Habitat Restoration Monitoring Handbook
English Nature Research Report No. 378

Mummery, C, Tabor, R and Homewood, N (1990)
A Guide to the Techniques of Coppice Management
Essex Wildlife Trust

National Urban Forestry Unit
Urban Forestry in Practice – Case Studies
NUFU

National Small Woods Association (1998)
Small Woods Information Pack
National Small Woods Association *
(*now the Small Woods Association)

O'Donnell (2000)
Turning Green Wood
Guild of Master Craftsmen

Parkes, Charlie and Thornley, John (1994)
Law of the Countryside
Countryside Management Association

Parrott, J and Mackenzie, N (2000)
Restoring and Managing Riparian Woodlands
Scottish Native Woods, Aberfeldy

Peterken, George F (1981)
Woodland Conservation and Management
Chapman and Hall

Peterken, George F (1996)
*Natural Woodland – Ecology and Conservation in
Northern Temperate Regions*
Cambridge University Press

Rackham, Oliver (1980)
*Ancient Woodland. Its History, Vegetation and Uses in
England*
Arnold

Rackham, Oliver (1986)
The History of the Countryside
J M Dent

Rackham, Oliver (1990)
Trees and Woodland in the British Landscape
J M Dent

Read, Helen J (2000)
Veteran Trees: A guide to good management
English Nature

Read, Helen J and Frater, Mark (1999)
Woodland Habitats
Routledge

Rodwell, J (editor) (1998)
British Plant Communities Vol 1: Woodlands and Scrub
Cambridge University Press

Savill, P S, Wright, H L, Miller H G and Kerr, G (eds)
(2001)
Forestry Vol 74 No3
Special issue: Ecological impacts of deer in woodland
Oxford University Press

Scottish Natural Heritage (2000)
*The Effects of Mammalian Herbivores on Natural
Regeneration of Upland, Native Woodland*
Information and Advisory Note 115

Smart, N and Andrews, J (1985)
Birds and Broadleaves Handbook
RSPB

Tabor, Ray (2000)
The Encyclopedia of Green Woodworking
eco-logic books

Taylor, Michael Bradley
A Guide to Wildlife Law Enforcement in the UK
www.defra.gov.uk/paw

Thomas, Peter (2000)
Trees: Their Natural History
Cambridge University Press

Vera F W M (2000)
Grazing Ecology and Forest History
Ministry of Agriculture, The Hague, Netherlands
CABI Publishing

Vivian, John (1976)
Wood Heat Rodale Press Ltd, USA

Whitbread, A M and Kirby, K J (1992)
Summary of National Vegetation Classification woodland descriptions JNCC

Warnes, Jon (2001)
Living Willow Sculpture Search Press

Williams, P; Biggs, J; Whitfield, M; Thorne, A; Bryant, S; Fox, G and Nicolet, P (1999)
The Pond Book
The Ponds Conservation Trust

Worrell, Richard (1999)
The Birch Woodland Management Handbook
Highland Birchwoods

Forestry Commission Publications

These are mainly listed by author, and are available by mail order on 0870 1214180.

Davies, R J ((1987)
Trees and Weeds
Forestry Commission Handbook 2

Evans, J (1984)
Silviculture of Broadleaved Woodland
Forestry Commission Bulletin 62

Ferris-Kaan, Richard (1992)
Monitoring Vegetation Change in Conservation Management of Forests
Forestry Commission Bulletin 108

Ferris, Richard and Carter, Clive (2000)
Managing Rides, Roadsides and Edge Habitats in Lowland Forests
Forestry Commission Bulletin 123

Forestry Commission (1985)
Wildlife Rangers Handbook
Forestry Commission

Forestry Commission (1975)
Forest Mensuration
Forestry Commission Booklet 39

Forestry Commission (1985)
Timber Measurement – A Field Guide
Forestry Commission Booklet 49

Forestry Commission (1994)
The Management of Semi-Natural Woodlands
(A series of 8 Forestry Practice Guides on the management of different types of native woodland)
Forestry Commission

Forestry Commission (1995)
Forest Operations and Badger Setts
Forestry Practice Guide 9

Forestry Commission (1999)
Domestic Stock Grazing to Enhance Woodland Biodiversity
Forestry Commission Information Note 28

Harmer, Ralph (1999)
Using Natural Colonisation to Create or Expand New Woodlands
Forestry Commission Information Note

Herbert, R, Samuel G and Patterson, G (1999)
Using Local Stock for Planting Native Trees and Shrubs
Forestry Commission Practice Note

Hibberd, B G (ed.) (1989)
Urban Forestry Practice
Forestry Commission Handbook 5

Hodge, Simon J (1995)
Creating and Managing Woodlands around Towns
Forestry Commission Handbook 11

Hodge, Simon and Pepper, Harry (1998)
The Prevention of Mammal Damage to Trees in Woodland
Forestry Commission Practice Note

Kerr, Gary and Williams, Hugh V (1999)
Woodland Creation – Experience from the National Forest
Forestry Commission Technical Paper 27

MacKenzie, Neil A (1999)
The Native Woodland Resource of Scotland
Forestry Commission Technical Paper 30

Mayle, B (1999)
Managing Deer in the Countryside
Forestry Commission Practice Note 6

Mayle, B (1999)
Domestic Stock Grazing to Enhance Woodland Biodiversity Forestry Commission Information Note

Moffat, A J and McNeill, J D (1994)
Reclaiming disturbed land for forestry
Forestry Commission Bulletin 10

Morgan, John (1999)
Forest Tree Seedlings – Best Practice in Supply, Treatment and Planting
Forestry Commission Bulletin 121

Pepper, H W (1992)
Forest Fencing Forestry Commission Bulletin 102

Pepper, Harry and Currie, Fred (1998)
Controlling Grey Squirrel Damage to Woodlands
Forestry Commission Practice Note

Rodwell, John and Patterson, Gordon (1994)
Creating New Native Woodlands
Forestry Commission Bulletin 112

Rollinson, T J D (1999)
Thinning Control
Forestry Commission Field Book 2

UK Woodland Assurance Scheme (2000)
Certification Standard for UK Woodland Assurance Scheme
The UK Woodland Assurance Scheme Guide to Certification. UKWAS Steering Group

White, John (1998)
Estimating the Age of Large and Veteran Trees in Britain
Forestry Commission Information Note 1998

Willoughby, Ian and Dewar, Jim (1995)
The use of Herbicides in the Forest
Forestry Commission Field Book 8

Willoughby, Ian and Clay, David (1996)
Herbicides for Farm Woodlands and Short Rotation Coppice
Forestry Commission Field Book 14

Journals

Relevant journals on trees and woodlands include the following:

Arboricultural Journal
(Arboricultural Association quarterly journal)

British Wildlife
(independent bi-monthly magazine)

Ecolots
(www.ecolots.co.uk)

Enact
(English Nature quarterly magazine)

Forestry and British Timber
(monthly)

Small Woods
(quarterly magazine of the Small Woods Association)

Tree News
(Tree Council twice-yearly magazine)

Publications

The Practical Handbook series was started in the 1970s, with most of the original titles remaining in print throughout, and new titles being added over the years. There is a rolling programme of revision with most handbooks now in their second or third edition. We welcome feedback on any aspect of the handbooks, whether the comments are general or detailed, practical or academic, complimentary or critical. Please contact:

The Conservation Volunteers,
Sedum House, Mallard Way,
Doncaster DN4 8DB
Tel: 01302 388883
e-mail: information@tcv.org.uk

The Handbook series comprises:

Fencing
Sand Dunes
Woodlands
Toolcare
Tree Planting and Aftercare
Footpaths
Waterways and Wetlands
Hedging
The Urban Handbook
Dry Stone Walling

Other publications relevant to this handbook:

BTCV (2000)
Conservation Volunteering – how and why

BTCV (1998)
Risk assessment – a learning resource pack

BTCV (1999)
Health and Safety overview

To order any of these, or for details of other publications and merchandise, please get in touch at the above address.

Glossary

This is a list of specialist words concerned with woodlands and trees.

Afforestation
The planting of trees on previously unwooded land.

Agroforesty
The growing of trees on land also used for the production of crops or livestock

Ancient woodland
Woodland that has existed continuously on the site since 1600 AD or earlier.

Arboriculture
The cultivation of trees and shrubs to produce specimens mainly for ornamental and landscape value rather than for timber production.

Assart
An historical term for a woodland area cleared for arable cultivation.

Bare-root tree
Tree lifted for transplanting without soil around its roots.

Bark
Outer protective tissue of a woody stem.

Bast
Thin layer of tissue between the bark and the cambium, which carries leaf-sap downwards to the roots.

Beam
A squared section of timber for use in construction, typically with a minimum length of 6m (20') and minimum sides of 200mm (8") and cut from heartwood of a straight oak log with no large side branches.

Beating up
Replacing failures after tree planting, also known as filling up.

Blaze
To mark a tree, usually for felling, by removing a piece of bark from the trunk.

Bole
The stem or trunk of a tree.

Bolling
The permanent trunk of a pollarded tree.

Brash
Small branches trimmed from the sides and top of a main stem. Also known as 'lop and top' or 'slash'. (v) To cut away the side branches of conifers to about 2m (6') height to improve access or to reduce fire risk.

Bryophytes
Mosses and liverworts.

Butt
Bottom (root) end of a log/pole.

Buttress
Reinforcing projection near the base of the tree. Also known as a spur.

Callus
Healing tissue formed by the cambium which grows out over a wound.

Cambium
A layer of growth cells which form bast to the outside and wood on the inside.

Canopy
The uppermost layer of woodland structure.

Carr
Fen scrub.

Chase
A tract of land where wild animals were conserved for hunting, similar to a Forest but not owned by the Crown.

Clearfelling
Felling a whole woodland or compartment at one time.

Clone
A tree or strain of trees propagated vegetatively from a single individual.

Collar
The part of the stem at ground level where shoot meets root. Usually shown by a soil mark.

Compartment
A management area within a woodland that is given an individual name or number.

Coppice
Broadleaved woodland which is cut down to near ground level at regular intervals to produce shoots from each stool. Also a multistemmed underwood tree or shrub created by coppicing. (v) To cut the stems from a stool so that more will grow.

Copse
Another name for a coppice.

Cord
A volume of stacked logs, usually 2.4 x 1.2 x 1.2m (8' x 4' x 4'), but varying in different districts. (v) To cut wood to cord lengths and stack it in a cord.

Coupe
A coppice plot cut on a regular basis, or a clear-felled area in a plantation. Also known as a cant or panel.

Covert
A small wood, usually within farmland, managed primarily for game.

Crown
The spreading branches and foliage of a tree.

Crown lifting
Removal of the lower branches of a tree, leaving the upper crown untouched.

Crown reduction
Pruning back the crown to its main branches whilst maintaining its overall shape.

Cutting
A short length of young shoot or root used to propagate a new plant.

Danger zone
The area within two tree lengths, in any direction, of a tree being felled.

Drift
Cut coppice material or brash laid in rows for sorting or disposal.

Drip line
The ground below the outermost branches of a tree's crown, where most of its feeding roots are concentrated.

Emergent tree
A tree whose crown overtops the standards in the woodland canopy.

Epicormic shoots
Shoots sprouting from dormant or adventitious buds on a tree's main stem.

Epiphyte
A plant growing on another without being parasitic.

Extraction
The removal of felled timber from a woodland.

Extraction track
A track cut for the extraction of timber.

Feathered tree
A young tree well furnished with branches to near ground level.

Felling cut
The cut made from the back of the stem which fells the tree. Also known as the back cut.

Field layer
The part of the woodland structure containing low-growing shrubs, herbaceous plants, grasses, bulbs and ferns.

Flush
An area of ground receiving nutrient-rich runoff. (v) The first spurt of growth after winter dormancy when the buds break.

Forest
Originally, a tract of heath, moor or woodland controlled by the Crown for the purpose of conserving deer and other wild animals, and subject to Forest Law. Now, used to describe a densely wooded area, normally a conifer plantation.

Formative pruning
The pruning of branches, usually within three to ten years of planting, in order to improve timber quality.

Greenwood
Freshly felled wood.

Ground layer
The part of the woodland structure which comprises mosses, liverworts, lichens and fungi.

Group felling
Felling of a group of trees or a subcompartment within a woodland.

Hanger
A wood growing on the side of a hill.

Harden off
The process of acclimatising nursery grown plants to the conditions in which they will be planted.

Hardwood
Any broadleaved (deciduous) tree, irrespective of the actual hardness of the wood.

Heartwood
The inner wood of large branches and trunks, which no longer carries sap. After felling, it becomes the most durable part of the timber. In older living trees, it may decay.

High forest
Woodland dominated by full-grown trees, suitable for timber.

Hinge
A portion of stem which is left uncut during felling, in order to help control the timing and direction of fall. Also known as a hold.

Hoppus foot
Unit of measurement for the cubic contents of round timber.
1 Hoppus foot = 0.036 m^3
$1m^3$ = 27.74 Hoppus feet

Kerf
The cut made by a saw.

Layer
A side shoot which roots to form a new but connected plant where it touches the ground.
(v) To bend over and peg down a shoot so that it will take root.

Laying in
Cutting away the buttresses of a tree before felling. Also known as rounding up.

Leader
The main top shoot of a tree.

Maiden tree
Any tree not grown from a coppice stump.

Mast
The fruit of the oak and beech tree. A mast year is a year in which large quantities of mast are produced.

Natural regeneration
Trees and shrubs which arise from naturally-shed seeds, without help by man.

Node

A swelling on a shoot which marks the position of a resting bud.

Nurse species

Hardy, quick-growing trees grown for the purpose of providing shelter for other young trees which are less hardy, slower growing or more valuable.

Park

Originally, land enclosed for the keeping of deer and other animals. Later, an area enclosed for amenity.

Plantation

Woodland where most of the trees have been planted.

Pole stage

Stage between the thicket stage and maturity in a timber crop. For broadleaves, from first thinning to about 50 years. For conifers, from first thinning to about 40 years.

Pollard

Tree which is cut at 2-4m (6'-12') above ground level, and left to produce a crop of poles or branches. (v) To cut a tree in this way.

Primary woodland

Woodland that has had a continuous cover of native trees throughout its history.

Prog

A stout forked pole used for pushing and levering trees during felling and conversion.

Provenance

The place of origin of a tree stock, which remains the same no matter where later generations of the tree are raised.

Pruning

Cutting branches from a standing tree, to alter its shape, encourage upright growth, remove diseased branches or encourage fruiting.

Recent woodland

Woodland which has grown up since 1600, on land which had previously been cleared, or was previously not wooded.

Respace

To cut out surplus young trees from natural regeneration.

Ring shake

Splitting of timber along the annual rings.

Roundwood

Wood of small diameter used for fencing stakes and other purposes for which splitting or other conversion is not needed.

Rotation

Length of time between successive fellings of a plantation or cuttings of a coppice coupe.

Sapwood

Wood which carries sap. This may be all the wood in a young stem, or the outmost layer in an older, larger trunk or branch. Sapwood resists decay when alive, but is not durable when felled.

Sawlog

Timber of a size and quality acceptable to a sawmill. Typically, straight, clean stems at least 16cm (6") diameter and at least 3m (10') long.

Screefing

Scraping away surface vegetation prior to tree planting, to reduce initial weed competition.

Secondary woodland

Woodland growing on a site that was formerly not woodland. Can be ancient, if it grew up before 1600.

Selective felling

Felling to remove particular trees of commercial value.

Semi-natural woodland

On ancient sites, woods made up of native species growing where their presence is apparently natural rather than planted. On recent sites, woods which have originated mainly by natural regeneration. Both types are subject to man's influence.

Set

A large unrooted cutting, usually of willow or poplar.

Shake

Cracking of timber due to stresses of growth, impact of felling or drying.

Shredding

A method of cropping branches for fodder, by periodically cutting off the side branches of a tree. Obsolete in Britain, but still used on the continent.

Short rotation coppice

Coppice grown on a short rotation, of up to about ten years, and used for hurdle making and other crafts. Also a modern system of coppicing using fast growing species of willow or poplar, which are cut on a three to five year rotation, for the production of woodchips for wood-fuelled electricity generation.

Shrub layer

The part of the woodland structure which includes shrubs and young growth of canopy trees. This layer may be coppiced.

Singling
Retaining one stem on a coppice stool and allowing it to grow into a standard tree.

Sink
A wedge-shaped cut made in the front of a tree, in order to control the direction of fall when felling. Also known as a bird's mouth.

Snedding
The removal of branches from a felled tree.

Softwood
The timber of a coniferous tree, irrespective of the hardness of the timber.

Stag-head
Old tree with crown that has died back, leaving the upper branches dead.

Standard
A tree with a clear stem or trunk. A transplanted tree with 1.8m (6') or more of unbranched stem. In woodland structure, a tree forming the dominant layer of the canopy.

Stem
The living trunk of a shrub or tree.

Stool
The stump or cut base of a shrub or tree, from which new shoots grow.

Stooling
A method of propagating coppice in which cut stools are earthed over to encourage new shoots to produce roots.

Stored coppice
Coppice which has been left to grow beyond its normal rotation.

Structure
Determined by height and density of crowns, presence of layers, glades and types of wood margin.

Succession
The process by which one community of plants gives way to another, normally from coloniser to climax.

Sucker
A young tree arising from the roots of an older tree.

Thicket stage
Stage after planting and before the pole stage, when young trees have grown up to form a dense thicket.

Thinning
Removal of selected trees from a a a crop to give the remainder more growing space. A tree so removed.

Timber
Tree trunk suitable for making beams or sawing into planks; a tree with such a trunk, the use made of such a trunk.

Transplant
Tree moved from one place to another, eg from nursery to growing site.

Undercut
Cut made in the front of a tree to reduce the chance of splitting when felling. Also refers to cutting the roots of tree seedlings in a nursery without removing them from the soil, in order to promote branching roots.

Underplanting
The planting of a new forest crop under an existing one.

Understorey tree
A tree with a crown below those of the dominant trees in the canopy.

Underwood
Coppice growth, shrubs or pollard growth, either growing or cut, and used for fuel and other purposes.

Whip
A young tree for transplanting, 120-180cm (4-6') height.

Windblow
Trees blown down and wholly or partly uprooted. Also known as windthrow.

Wood
The part of the stem, inside the cambium, which supports the tree, carries water to the crown and stores reserves of food over the winter. Also poles and branches of smaller diameter than timber.

Woodbank
A boundary bank surrounding or subdividing a woodland.

Wood-pasture
Wooded land which is regularly grazed, and includes areas of grassland.

Yield class
A system of assessing the productivity of a crop of trees based upon the measurement of tree height and age.

Abbreviations

LAND

The value of particular woodlands for their age, wildlife, landscape and historical value and other criteria are recognised in various designations. Other designations are given below which may affect woodland management plans and grant applications.

Conservation

National Nature Reserve	NNR
Site of Special Scientific Interest	SSSI
Proposed SSSI	PSSSI
Local Authority Conservation Area	LACA
Ancient Semi-Natural Woodland	ASNW
Ancient Woodland Site	AWS
Tree Preservation Order	TPO
Plantation on Ancient Woodland Site	PAWS

Landscape

Area of Outstanding Natural Beauty	AONB
National Park	NP
National Scenic Area	NSA

Recreation and public access

Community Forest	CF
Public Right Of Way	PROW

Archaeology

Scheduled Ancient Monument	SAM

Agriculture

Set Aside	SA
Less Favoured Area	LFA
Environmentally Sensitive Area	ESA

SCHEMES, PLANS AND REGULATIONS

BAP	Biodiversity Action Plan
COSHH	Control of Substances Hazardous to Health
CSS	Countryside Stewardship Scheme
EIA	Environmental Impact Assessment
ERDP	England Rural Development Programme
FWPS	Farm Woodland Premium Scheme
HAP	Habitat Action Plan
LEAP	Livestock Exclusion Annual Premium
SAP	Species Action Plan
UKBAP	UK Biodiversity Action Plan
UKWAS	UK Woodland Assurance Scheme
WCA	Wildlife and Countryside Act
WGS	Woodland Grant Scheme
WIG	Woodland Improvement Grant

Index